WHITNEY F. BOLTON (born 15.10.30, New York City) obtained his PhD at Princeton University and subsequently came to England first as a Fulbright Scholar and then as a Research Fellow at Reading.

In 1959 he returned to America to take up a post at the University of California and then in 1961 he became a lecturer at Reading University. In 1965 he was appointed Professor of English. Professor Bolton is currently Professor of English at Rutgers University, New Jersey.

He is the author of *A Short History of Literary English* (1967), *A History of Anglo-Latin Literature* (1967), *The English Language Vol. 1* (1966) and *Vol. 2* (1969). He has also edited *An Old English Anthology* (1963), the New Mermaid edition of *Sejanus His Fall* (1966) and Vol. 1 of the Sphere History of Literature in the English Language, *The Middle Ages* (1970).

SPHERE LIBRARY

HISTORY OF LITERATURE IN THE ENGLISH LANGUAGE

Volumes marked with an asterisk are in preparation.

HISTORY OF LITERATURE
IN THE ENGLISH LANGUAGE

Vol. 10 The English Language

The English Language

EDITED BY W. F. BOLTON

BARRIE & JENKINS
COMMUNICA · EUROPA

In association with
Sphere Books Ltd

First published in Great Britain in 1975 by Barrie & Jenkins Ltd
24 Highbury Crescent, London N5 1RX

© Sphere Books 1975

A paperback edition of this volume is available from
Sphere Books

PE
1072
E55

ISBN 0 214 65152 5

Printed in Great Britain by
Lowe & Brydone (Printers) Ltd,
Thetford, Norfolk

CONTENTS

INTRODUCTION

'The common tie of society', Locke called language; 'that composite and multiform speech—fitted, like a mirror, to reflect the thoughts of the myriad-minded Shakespeare', De Quincey wrote of English. For the language of the greatest poets is only a particular employment of the faculty which at once distinguishes man from all other creatures and unites man to man. In this volume of nine chapters, ten writers contribute introductory essays on the general nature of language; the forms, grammar, and stylistic varieties of present-day English; the history of the language; and the role of English language study in the study of English literature.

As long ago as 1876, the leading historian of English, Henry Sweet (whose acquaintance George Bernard Shaw took him as the model for Henry Higgins in his play *Pygmalion*, later made even more famous in the musical version *My Fair Lady*) remarked that 'the growth of a language like English can be observed in a series of literary documents extending from the ninth century to the present day. ... But before history must come a knowledge of what now exists. We must learn to observe things as they are without regard to their origin'. Sweet here suggested a division of language study into the historical (or *diachronic*) and descriptive (or *synchronic*), the former tracing the development of the language from age to age and the latter studying it at a single moment in time, usually the present—the only state of the language that the vast majority of its users, including its writers, ever know. But Sweet went further in the passage just quoted: he gave priority to the descriptive approach. Here his words went unheeded for over seventy years, and are only now gaining acceptance in university courses in English. The present book is among the first to adopt them as a basic principle, arranging the material so that the present-day language is fully surveyed before the retrospect of the past is begun.

The scheme has more than theoretical advantages. The student is given in the first instance a firm understanding of his own language, and can compare the former stages of English with this. Moreover, the terminology of language description is best introduced as it relates to modern speech, but it then becomes available as well for characterizing the English of centuries past. The arrangement of the book consequently assumes that the reader will go through it continuously from beginning to end, but the chapters have been planned with a great deal of autonomy and can be read as independent studies in their various fields. To achieve this independence, some material has had to be repeated from chapter to chapter. Readers are in any case urged to read the first chapter, in which the broad outlines of the modern view of language are sketched with reference both to what follows and to what have for long been the most common . . . and the most erroneous . . . ideas about language.

From chapter two onwards, the subject is specifically English. It is convenient to talk about the structure of a language in terms of its sounds, its forms, and its sentences, and of what the structure operates on as its vocabulary. The distinctions that the language makes at the level of sounds receive attention first because the contrasts they embody are basic to the rest of the system. The system extends from individual sounds to formal patterns, like *chose* from *choose*, *houses* from *house*, *ungentlemanlinesses* from *un* + *gentle* + *man* + *li* + *ness* + *es*. Obviously if the sound system did not make regular contrasts, the complicated correct sequence could not be distinguished from the equally complicated but impossible *man* + *gentle* + *un* + *li* + *es* + *ness*[1] (although it contains the quite acceptable *man* + *li* + *ness*, etc.), but equally obviously the selection of the correct sequence is not a matter of sound but of another level of structure entirely: form. And the organization of elementary or complicated words into the strings we call phrases, clauses and sentences is, by the same token, yet another level of structure ('syntax') as well, although it partakes of the distinctions of form so that we accept *The dog bites the man* but not *The man the dog bites* as a sentence (but *The man the dog bites is my brother*); *A house is red*, *Houses are red*, but not *A house are red* (except, for example, in *The guardians of a house are red setters*).

Priority is given to these considerations of organization because many students of a language begin with the assumption that the language is the words in its vocabulary: *Schwester* 'means' *sister* in German, or is the German word 'for' *sister*. Far more important is the fact that English has no sound like the *r* in German, no sequence of sounds like the *Schw-* in German, forms no plurals by adding only *-n* as German does in *Schwestern*, and if the sentence *I wish you could have seen my sister* were 'translated' into German word-for-word, no German would recognize it as his own language. Yet for all the misleading prominence that vocabulary has had, it is still the aspect of language that is the focus of all the other categories: the three levels of organization must organize something in addition to each other, and what they organize or structure are the items in the vocabulary of the language, its words. These, more-

10

over, have long been and will probably to some perhaps reduced extent remain the chief concern of writers looking for 'the right word', and of critics analysing their success or failure in finding it.

This consideration brings us to chapter six, the first of two reviews of the problems and potentialities of language study in the analysis of utterances, including those we call 'literature'. Stylistics proceeds by mapping the specialization in each of the categories of language, that is sound, form, syntax and vocabulary, that distinguish a given utterance from the more general linguistic practice of which it is a part. It is a form of synchronic linguistics applied to literature, among other things, much as physiology can be applied to identify a single member of a species as well as to generalize about the structure and function of the species as a whole.

The second section of the book likewise offers several chapters of description followed by one of application, this time in the historical or diachronic dimension. The two which describe the growth of the language over the centuries begin with its derivation from the parent language and trace it down to the present day; their dividing-line is the death date of the greatest poet of the English Middle Ages, Chaucer, in 1400. In the concluding chapter a brief review of the study of the English language over the last few centuries leads to considerations about its future application, particularly to literary studies. Yet by its very nature such a plan cannot be definitive, any more than the chapters which precede it can be exhaustive. The volume is intended as an introduction to linguistic study that will serve to outline the essentials and at the same time point the way to further investigation.

The bibliographies at the end of each chapter are similarly inceptive. The field of linguistics is so vast that they can be only selective. What is more, it is so active that they rapidly fall out of date. The reader is urged to consult them both as a guide to the sources of the views and information that each chapter puts forward, and as a suggestion for the next stage of further reading. Nothing about man is so properly his study as his language, 'the common tie of society'.

NOTES

1. Here and throughout this book, the asterisk signifies an unrecorded linguistic form; in synchronic description, usually an impossible one; in diachronic, usually a hypothetically reconstructed one.

LANGUAGE AND LANGUAGES

Professor F. R. Palmer, University of Reading

The language we speak is one of, perhaps, 4,000 or more throughout the world. We cannot be sure of the precise number; estimates have varied between 2,000 and 4,000, but it seems probable that even the higher figure is an underestimate. A recent survey of the languages of Africa lists over 700, yet this excludes from its list all the Bantu languages which form the largest single language group, including almost all the languages spoken in the southern half of that continent; and Africa is only a small part of the entire world.

One of the reasons why we cannot give a precise figure to the number of languages in the world is simply lack of information about the languages themselves. Probably less than 10 per cent of them have ever been seriously investigated and perhaps as many as a half are still virtually unknown. Attention has naturally been focused upon the languages of the greatest political or commercial interest, languages such as Hausa, Arabic, Hindi, Chinese. The national languages of most countries have been described, though not always in a satisfactory way, but in many countries the national language is only one of many. In Ethiopia, for instance, the official language, Amharic, has been described in a number of grammars dating back to the seventeenth century, but only one of them is really adequate and the phonology (the sound system) of Amharic has hardly been considered at all. There are, moreover, between 30 and 50 other languages in Ethiopia but only about 10 of these have been investigated, and the only complete grammars of most of this small number were written by a single scholar as long ago as the end of the nineteenth century.

It is difficult in principle to decide how many languages there are in the world, because it is often not clear whether we are dealing with different languages or different dialects of the same language. We must be careful, however, to use the terms *language* and *dialect* in a systematic way. In ordinary conversation people often make the distinction between dialect and language in terms of spoken and written languages, so that in this sense English, Arabic and Chinese are 'languages', but most of the speech-forms of Africa are 'dialects', perhaps even 'mere dialects'. This would, of course, reduce the numbers of languages to a few hundred and largely solve the problem of deciding how many languages there are, but it is a quite unsatisfactory viewpoint. Many of these 'dialects' are by any reasonable standard languages in their own right (the notion that they are in some way inferior, primitive or exotic is, as we shall see shortly, untenable), and in any case, they always *can* be written down, and in some cases *will* probably be written down, either in the Roman alphabet that we ourselves use or in the national script of the country in which they are spoken (Ethiopia, for instance, has its own writing system).

There is a further problem. The Chinese system of writing carries little or no indication of the way in which the language is spoken—there is almost no systematic correspondence between the written symbols and the sounds of the language. As a result, a speaker of Mandarin Chinese and a speaker of Cantonese can both read the written form though their speech is quite different. Neither can understand the other, and if they read a text aloud, they will read it quite differently. It is rather as if there was in Europe a system of writing such that the same symbols could be read as 'I see a dog' or 'Je vois un chien'. In fact we find something like this in our numerals; 1, 2, 3 can be read as 'One, two, three', 'Un, deux, trois', 'Ein, zwei, drei', etc. Chinese is an extreme case, but English spelling too does not provide a very clear indication of the pronunciation. It turns out moreover that, precisely because of the much maligned vagaries of English spelling, the same written text can be used by people with very different kinds of English. Natives of London, Edinburgh, New York or Sydney will read the same texts with complete ease, but if they read them aloud, they will read them quite differently, and this is in part possible simply because we do not expect the English spelling to be a faithful representation of the way we speak. Paradoxically perhaps, one of the greatest assets of the English language is that there is no one-to-one relation between sound and symbol.

It is obvious, moreover, that in these days of mass communication we all succeed in understanding the speech of people whose words would have been quite unintelligible to our grandparents. We have learnt familiarity with the speech of Liverpool, of Glasgow, of Texas (often perhaps in an inaccurate or caricatured form) and it could be argued that some of these 'dialects' are so different that they ought really to be thought of as different languages and that with the help of radio, films and television we have, in effect, learnt new languages. It is an open question, then, whether English really is just one language—whether the English of Bombay is the same language as that of Manchester. But this is an academic point—it depends on the definition of language.

Let us assume that we know what is meant by *the* English language and turn to another question—whether this language is in any sense better or more important than other languages in the world. From the purely linguistic point of view the answer to this question is a simple 'No'.

This is not to say that English is not a very important language, but only from two other points of view. First, it is probably the language with the largest number of native speakers (people for whom it is the first language)—though this estimate depends on whether or not we regard Chinese as one language; if we do, English comes second. But it is quite certain that English is the language that is spoken or understood by the largest number of people in the world, either as a second or as a foreign language; it is certainly *the* modern international language.

Secondly, English is important, as this collection clearly shows, for its literature. Yet there seems to be no clear evidence that the quality of English literature (or its quantity) is in any way dependent upon the nature of the language itself. This is not to deny the close links between literature and language, but it is to say that they are, perhaps, incidental. Of course, the language is the vehicle for the literature, and as translators know well, English literature is and will always remain essentially English. In other arts there is no such restriction. Painting and music are obviously more international because they can more easily cross national boundaries; the instruments of the symphony orchestra produce the same basic sounds in Germany as in England, but Shakespeare can never sound like Goethe. (Literature does, in one sense, cross these national and 'linguistic' boundaries—the literature of one country may profoundly influence that of another—but this observation even further weakens any belief that the literature derives from any intrinsic excellence of the language itself.) More importantly, there are 'literary' languages, languages which have a long tradition of literature and which have thereby acquired not only the 'producers'—the authors whose very existence obviously depends upon the tradition (even when they try to be non-traditional), but also the 'tools'—the linguistic forms and their meanings; we need only consider the number of words in the English language as evidenced by the Oxford English Dictionary —and sheer quantity of words is a relatively unimportant characteristic of a language. But, however possible it may be to link literature with the social, political,or economic features of the society in which it is produced we cannot be at all sure that it is in any way linked with any characteristic of the language. In other words, we cannot disprove the thesis that if the inhabitants of Britain had been the same in all other respects but had spoken a Bantu language, they would not have produced an equally fine body of literature.

We are, of course, all inclined to feel that our own language is in some ways better or more natural than that of other people. The grammarian Jespersen tells of the little girl who made the wonderful discovery that pigs are called pigs 'because they are such swine'. A similar story appears also in Aldous Huxley's *Crome Yellow* where, looking at pigs wallowing in the mud, a character remarks, 'Rightly is they called pigs'. A little sophistication, indeed the mere recognition of the fact that there are other languages, teaches us to expect that languages other than ours will have different words for the same things, but it takes much more sophistication to realize that many of the other characteristics of the language may be different too. Many learners of a foreign language never accept, in their practice at least, the idea that the sound system of the language is different; they are willing to change the words, but still pronounce them in their own familiar way. Even those who are more sophisticated find great difficulty in accommodating themselves to the intonation of the new language; deep down perhaps they feel that the patterns they use must be the correct ones—the ones that most naturally carry the intended meaning. But there are more subtle points than this. Few speakers of English realize that the order of words in English is arbitrary and conventional—there is no 'natural', 'logical' or other reason why the subject should come before the verb and the object after it (though, admittedly, the exact reverse of the English order does not seem to occur in other known languages). In Welsh the verb (or at least part of it) comes first, before the subject; my own son at the age of 10 had to learn Welsh and complained that it was a stupid language because 'every time they want to say something, they ask a question'! Even at that age he had come to accept a purely English device—the use of word order for questions—as a necessary characteristic of language.

Professionals, too, sometimes fail to see that what is strange about another language is on closer inspection no stranger than what happens in their own. M. Bréal, who at the very end of the nineteenth century wrote a book entitled (in its translated form) *Semantics* and thereby invented this term, commented on the superiority of the Indo-European languages over the other languages of the world. His chief evidence is the ambiguity found in other languages; in Chinese, for instance, the same sentence may mean 'The saint aspires to Heaven', 'He is a saint to aspire to Heaven' and 'He is a saint who aspires to Heaven'. But we can easily match this in English with a sentence that is now a notorious example in linguistics classes: *It's too hot to eat.* This has three obvious different interpretations—and others are possible with sentences of the same structure; sentences of this grammatical type are 'multiply ambiguous'. More recently a writer suggested that one characteristic of the Bantu languages is 'syncretism of the grammatical elements', i.e. that one grammatical form may have a number of different functions and he quotes Swahili *na*: 1. to have; 2. with; 3. and; etc. A moment's reflection will reveal that these three functions have much in common ('to be with' is 'to have' especially in a society where private property is unknown), and again we may look for a parallel in English—the verb 'to be' is used, for being in a place, for existing (*There are people who* . . .), for class membership (*He is a teacher*), for identity (*This is John*), to mark duration (*He is reading*) or intention (*They are to be married*), and for the passive. It has at least eight functions.

In spite of this it is still thought sometimes that English and the other European languages are civilized languages whereas many of the languages of the world remain primitive. From a linguistic point of view this is a fallacy. Of course a language reflects in some respects the society in which it is spoken, but this is almost entirely confined to the vocabulary—the vocabulary required for the artifacts, institutions, etc. peculiar to that society. English has the words to talk about art and about science, words for 'sonnet', 'surrealism', 'hydrogen', 'nuclear reactor', 'industrial dispute', for which a language of Africa might have no parallel. But that language would almost certainly have many words that have no translation in English. Well-known examples are the three words that Eskimo has for snow—depending on whether it is falling, on the ground, or the hard-packed material for making igloos, and the vast number of words that the Bedouin has for his camel, depending on size, age, sex, colour and use. This does not imply that there are primitive languages, except solely in this one fact that they have a vocabulary adapted to primitive societies. It does not even seem to be true that such languages have a smaller vocabulary; there have been tales of languages with only a few hundred words (and the same has been said of the language of the Wiltshire ploughman), but on investigation these tales have proved to be false. Moreover, all the other characteristics of a language—its sound system, its grammar, even the structure of its semantics—seem to be utterly unrelated to the society in which it is spoken. Surely this must be so; otherwise the language of Shakespeare could not have been used as it has been used, with only slight modifications, for the purposes of modern science. If we go even further back, it is probable that the language of our remote ancestors was much more like the English we speak today, than, say, a North American Indian language, though the societies of these ancestors and of Indians may have been equally primitive and equally distant culturally from our own.

If there are no primitive languages, are there exotic languages and difficult languages? Perhaps there are, provided it is understood that these are relative terms—exotic and difficult for the speaker of English or of a European language. In absolute terms there are certainly no difficult languages—the reply to a complaint that a certain language is difficult is simply 'Why, even the little children can speak it'. Judgments about languages are often made on purely superficial grounds. A language is often thought to be strange or difficult simply because it does not use the Roman script. This is, no doubt, why many people are scared by Russian. Yet a new script, provided it is alphabetic and not like Chinese which has virtually a different symbol for thousands of different words or parts of words, can be learnt in a few days, a tiny fraction of the time it takes to learn a useful portion of the vocabulary. A slightly more justifiable complaint can be made against the sounds of the language, but here too the exotic nature or difficulty of the sounds can easily be over-rated by the non-specialist. Most English people would have difficulty with the Swahili word for 'cow', *ngombe*, but the difficulty lies only in the fact that the sound indicated by the *ng*, which is exactly the same as in English *sing* (a 'velar nasal') comes at the beginning of the word in Swahili, but in English can occur only in the middle or at the end; a familiar sound in an unusual position causes difficulty. A slightly more complex example is the initial consonant of the name of the language Twi spoken in Ghana (phonetically [tʃᵘ]). This consonant does not appear as such in any European language and therefore sounds very strange to European ears, but its component parts do occur—it involves no more, in effect, than a combination of the first consonants of the English word *church* and of the French word *huit*, produced simultaneously. It is true, nevertheless, that some languages have sounds that are quite unfamiliar to European ears. English makes no systematic use of the back part of the mouth, the 'uvular' and 'pharyngeal' areas, yet Arabic has no less than four different consonants in that area (and even French has one!). But, on the other hand, English makes a distinction between vowel sounds that would sound alike to speakers of many other languages. In an area of articulation in which many languages have only one vowel, English distinguishes between the vowels of *cat, cut, cot, caught, cart*, and *curt*.

Moreover, we are inclined to fail to realize how limited is the use made by European languages of the total capabilities of the vocal mechanisms. Almost without exception the whole of the articulation of sounds in European languages is powered by air expelled from the lungs (it is 'pulmonic egressive'). Yet there is no natural or physical reason for this. In some languages air for articulation is drawn in, instead of being expelled—this produces the implosive consonants of West Africa (and even in one form of American English). In other languages sounds are produced by suction—the clicks of South Africa (we use clicks in English but only, it has been said, for addressing horses, babies and attractive young ladies!). Pressure can be created by moving the larynx (the 'voice-box') itself and this produces the ejective or glottalized consonants that are to be found in such widely-separated places as North America, Korea and Ethiopia. Perhaps if we must talk about exotic languages it is English that is exotic in its restriction upon the use it makes of its phonetic potential.

The way in which languages use the phonetic 'tools' they have varies and a language that uses them in an apparently non-European way will be thought difficult and exotic. Many of the languages of Africa have two or three tones; the tones distinguish different words, different entries in the dictionary. In Agau, for instance, a 'Cushitic' language of Ethiopia, *sǝr* on a low tone means 'boy', but on a high tone it means 'vein'. But these are simple compared with the languages of South-East Asia. Chinese has no less than five tones, though not all of them are level tones—that is to say, it does not just distinguish between five different pitches, but has, in addition to level tones, falling and rising ones. Yet it is by no means certain that this is in absolute terms any more difficult than what happens in English. It is usually said that English is not a tone language but that it makes a great deal of use of intonation. That is to say, it makes use of the pitch of the voice, but not to distinguish words as such. This is not strictly true. The difference between *export* the verb and *export* the noun is largely carried by pitch features. Although the usual explanation is that the verb has stress on the second syllable and the noun stress on the first, experiments have shown that what the speaker of English actually listens to is almost entirely a matter of pitch. In any case, is this use of intonation any easier or more natural? If we say *She's very pretty* with one intonation tone (a fall or a low rise) it is a compliment; if we say it with another (a rise-fall) it is far from complimentary—it means something like 'She's very pretty but ...'. This is, of course, a wholly English feature—a linguistic convention of the English language that is, surely, quite as strange as the use of tone by the tone language.

It would be easy to give countless further examples of 'exotic' features in languages, but they usually turn out on reflection not to be very strange. The Celtic languages, for instance, are characterized by 'initial mutation'—by, in naive terms, the practice of changing the first 'letter' or words as in Welsh *pen* 'head', but *ei ben* 'his head', *eu phen* 'her head', *fy mhen* 'my head'. But why should it be any more strange to change the beginning of a word rather than the end (cf. English *wife* but *wives*) or the middle (English *foot* but *feet*)? Moreover, to talk about changing 'letters' distorts the facts. In speech (and speech must be regarded as primary—see below p. 26) the difference between the forms is simply one of the phonetic features of voice, friction and nasality. It is not a matter of replacing one consonant by another but simply of voicing (vibrating the vocal cords), of friction (partially instead of completely obstructing the passage of air) or of nasalization (lowering the soft palate to allow the air to escape through the nose); b = p + voice, ph = p + friction, mh = p + nasality. The change from one consonant to another in mutation involves the minimum of effort. An even stranger feature is to be found in the report that in some North American Indian languages the words for 'river' and 'mountain' are verbs. At least this sounds a strange feature until we think of English *It is raining*. There does not seem to be any more compulsive reason why we are permitted to say this instead of 'There is rain', than 'It is rivering' instead of 'There is a river'. Of course, the two are different—rain is temporary and rivers permanent, but that is not what would usually be thought to be the essential distinction between noun and verb.

There is one clear moral to be drawn. The linguist must never be surprised at anything he finds in language. We have no means of judging what limits there are upon the patterns of phonology, grammar or semantics in languages. A new language will always bring surprises, though on reflection we often find that the novelty is basically no stranger than what we find in more familiar languages.

If there are no primitive, difficult or exotic languages in any strict sense of these terms, can the languages of the world be characterized or classified in any other way? One classification was that suggested by the early nineteenth-century scholar W. von Humboldt—into 'isolating', 'agglutinative' and 'inflectional' languages. In the 'isolating' languages each word is a single grammatical form that is unchanged in all its occurrences—in technical linguistic terms it is a morpheme with but only one allomorph; Chinese and some other languages of South-East Asia are examples of this type. In the 'agglutinative' languages words are made up of a string of grammatical forms (morphemes) in a fixed order, but again the forms are unchanged in their various occurrences. Examples are Turkish and, to a large extent, Swahili. In Swahili, for instance, *nilikuona* consists of *ni* 'I', *li* past tense, *ku* 'you' and *ona* 'see'. Each of these elements is separable and replaceable by another so that we can have *alikuona* 'he saw you', *aliniona* 'he saw me', *nitakuona* 'I will see you' etc. The 'inflectional' languages are represented by Latin and Greek and many of the modern European languages. In these the various grammatical elements cannot be separately identified. It has been pointed out for instance that in Greek the *o:* of *luo:* 'I loose' identifies number, person, tense, mood and voice and it is rarely in this language that we can separate the elements (though this is possible perhaps with *lusaontai* 'they will loose for themselves'—*s* future, *o* indicative, *n* plural, *t* third person, *ai* middle or passive). It has been thought by some that languages have progressed through these stages—first of all being isolating, then by grouping the elements into clusters and becoming agglutinative, and finally by 'fusing' the elements and becoming inflectional. The last stage is then thought of as the classical ideal, followed in more recent time by a breakdown into isolating types—for not only did Chinese once have inflection, but English is surely very largely an 'isolating language', since it has lost most of its 'endings'. But this view is not supported by any real evidence, and, in fact, most languages have characteristics of all three types. In English there are many words of the isolating type (all the prepositions, for example), the formation *take/taken/taking* is agglutinative, while *take/took* is an example of inflection. But a more important criticism of this classification is that it is in terms of one feature only of a language—the morphology of the word. Studies of this kind, 'typological' studies as they are called, are valuable, but they are essentially studies of parts of a language rather than of a language as a whole, and ought not therefore to be used for classification of languages.

The best-known type of classification of languages is into language families; and the language family that has been most thoroughly investigated is Indo-European, which includes almost all the languages from India to Ireland (Turkish, Hungarian and Basque are the notable exceptions). The Indo-European family can be sub-divided into groups; in Europe the four most important are Romance: Spanish, French, Italian and Rumanian; Germanic: English, German, Danish, Norwegian, Swedish; Celtic: Welsh, Breton, Gaelic; Slavic: Serbo-Croat, Czech, Slovak, Bulgarian, Russian, Polish. But this classification into families and into groups is very largely a purely linguistic exercise and does not provide much information beyond the classification itself. Indeed there are two conclusions that must *not* be drawn, though they often are. First, it must not be assumed that the linguistic divisions represents racial or ethnic divisions. There is no such thing as the Indo-European race. The notion of the 'Aryans', which formed such a basic part of Nazi policy, was largely a result of this mistaken view—the term 'Aryan' having been used by philologists for 'Indo-European'. A moment's reflection shows clearly the fallacy of this assumption. American Negroes now speak, as their native tongue, an Indo-European language, but are clearly not the same race, if 'race' means anything at all, as their white fellow countrymen. Equally we may reflect whether it is sensible to consider the millions of Hindi and Bengali speakers in India (these are Indo-European languages) as racially closer to Europeans than the Hungarians or the Basque-speaking peoples of Bilbao. Secondly, and perhaps a little more surprisingly, linguistic relationship is no clear guide to the history of the people who speak or spoke the languages. Some measure of what is called 'linguistic palaeontology' is possible—it can be argued that, because the relevant words are to be found throughout many of the Indo-European languages, the ancient 'Indo-Europeans' had domesticated cattle and used wagons and that they lived in a European-type country where there were pigs, wolves, bears and many other familiar animals. But it is by no means certain that the spread of a language always meant the migration of a population or conquest by an invading master-race. Certainly we know how the Romance languages came into being—a result of the spread of Latin by the Roman Empire. Often, however, there seem to be no cultural changes accompanying the arrival of a new language form. Archaeologists have searched in vain for evidence of the coming of the Celts. It seems fairly certain that Celtic languages were spoken in much of Western Europe at the time of the Roman conquests but there is no break in the cultural features evidenced by archaeology for us to speak of a Celtic invasion at any time.

It does not make much sense, therefore, to talk about a Welshman as being a 'pure Celt' (though I have seen this as a description of a Welsh actor). It is true that the language he speaks is Celtic and true that there is a distinctive culture that is associated with that language, but that does not imply that he himself is Celtic. Indeed the popular misconception about a Celtic race is belied by the equally popular image of the short, dark Welsh, the tall, fair Scots, not to mention the dark-haired, blue-eyed Irish. Equally it makes no sense to talk about the Rumanians as 'of Latin stock', because Rumanian is a Romance language. Not only is it doubtful whether they differ physically from their 'Slavonic' neighbours (not to mention the 'non Indo-European' Hungarians), but it is doubtful whether even their ancestors were 'Latin' —the Romans brought their language but did not replace the original inhabitants of their Empire with their own people.

The language family is often illustrated by a family tree as in Figure 1. But it is a mistake to take this idea of a linguistic family tree at all seriously: there is no direct descent, and this genealogical model can be most misleading. For every language is a complete hybrid deriving from a variety of sources—even more perhaps than are the nations of the world. If we look at modern dialects rather than languages we find that any one dialect at one time may have derived from several dialects of a previous age—it may have a multiplicity of 'parents', some of whom it may share with other dialects, and this is almost certainly true of the 'Indo-European dialects' from which the language groups are purported to have descended.

Indo-European is not, of course, the only language family, though it is the one that has been most studied, studied continuously since a famous address in 1786 by Sir William Jones in which he argued for a common source for Latin, Greek and Sanskrit. Other well-known

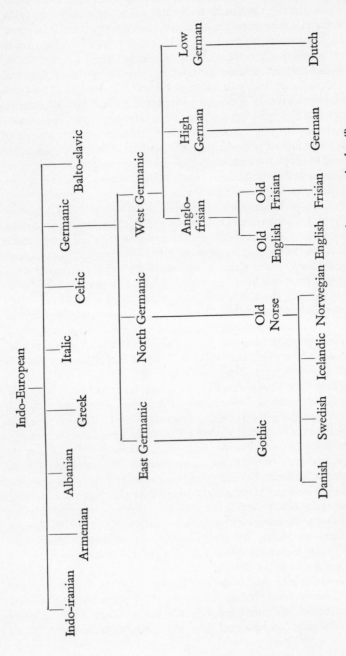

Fig. 1. The Indo-European family tree (with Germanic only set out in detail)

families are Semitic (chief members: Arabic, Hebrew and some languages of Ethiopia), Bantu and Malayo-Polynesian. The languages of the North American Indians are to be placed in a large number of different families, and there are, perhaps, a dozen or more families in Africa. Territorially, and in numbers of speakers, Indo-European is the largest, but this is not evidence of any special quality of the speakers of the Indo-European languages or of their ancestors, except in one respect—that they had writing. For our ability to establish this huge Indo-European family as compared with the numerous much smaller families of Africa or North America depends largely upon the existence of the classical languages. For all we know, languages in other areas may be as closely related as the languages of the Indo-European family, but without the 'key'—written records of much older languages—the relationships cannot be established. This point is quite clearly shown by just a few examples. We know that English words *cow* and *beef* are the same words if viewed historically, both derived from a single Indo-European 'root', the former having come through Germanic, the latter through Latin (and even then not directly, but probably first through a non-Latin dialect of the early languages of Italy). If we had no written records we could never have guessed the relationship. An equally striking example is provided by English *wheel* and Hindi *cakka*, again with a common origin; the Greek word *kuklos* (from which we have English *cycle*) and the Latin word *circus* are also from the same root as these.

Further examples can be found in the numerals which in spite of being derived from common roots now look and sound so different in the various languages, especially those for '4' and '5'—English *four*, French *quatre*, Welsh *pedwar*; English *five*, French *cinq*, Welsh *pump*.

Looking for language families tells us nothing more, then, than that linguists have succeeded in certain areas in establishing certain kinds of linguistic relationships between languages. These relationships are essentially of a formulaic kind for they are expressed by setting up formulae for IE (Indo-European), formulae which sometimes look (as they are perhaps intended to look) like an ancient language but which at other times can hardly be thought to have existed as linguistic forms. We find initial consonant clusters of the type $*^w$ðh and $*k^w$Φh; we obviously cannot read much 'reality' into these.

It is easy to be fascinated by some of the discoveries of comparative philology—to realize, for instance, that the same root appears in *feather*, *pin*, *pen* and the *-pter-* part of *pterodactyl*, and *helicopter*, or to resurrect the Latin of the Roman soldiers from the Romance languages—a Latin in which the word for a horse was *caballus* and not *equus* (French *cheval*, Italian *caballo*, etc.) and the word for head was *testa*, literally a 'tile', not *caput* (French *tête*, etc.). Most dictionaries are, for this reason, 'on historical principles'. Yet it is a mistake to be so fascinated by the history of a language or languages to fail to see that languages, as they now are, can and indeed should be studied in their own right. The Swiss linguist Ferdinand de Saussure was the first scholar to state in a clear directive the need to distinguish between the 'synchronic' and the 'diachronic' aspects of language—between the study of a language at a particular point in time (perhaps, but not necessarily, the present), and the study of a language through time. A moment's reflection will show that synchronic studies are logically prior to diachronic ones—we cannot trace linguistic change from period A to period B unless we know the facts about the langugage at each period. Yet many scholars have failed to see the need to keep these two aspects of language apart and often have heaped confusion upon confusion in that they not only have tried to describe present-day language in terms of its history, but have also combined this with the natural human propensity to think that what has gone before is always better than what we have now and have, therefore, made statements that give preference to the older form. When for instance, someone says of a word that it 'really means . . .' (that, for instance, *nice* really means 'precise'), he is not merely tracing the history of the word, but also claiming that the older meaning is the correct one. But why? Surely *nice* today means 'nice'!

The confusion of synchronic and diachronic studies of language takes at least four forms. First, there is, as we have seen, the belief that the older forms are the 'correct' ones. An extreme form of this point of view sees languages as in a state of decay—the Romance languages as being a degenerate form of Latin—having lost, for instance, all the case inflections of the noun and even many of the endings of the verbs. By such a standard, English is in an advanced stage of decomposition. This kind of approach to a language is nonsense. There is no way by which we can judge one state of a language to be better than another, and the judgments that have been made have simply assumed that highly inflectional languages are somehow in the most perfect condition, presumably because the classical languages Latin and Greek were of this kind. The real difficulty in looking backward for a 'better' or 'more correct form of a language' is that we cannot, in principle, decide how far back to go. Should English just go back to Anglo-Saxon or to Proto-Germanic or to Indo-European? The example quoted in the previous paragraph, the meaning of *nice*, provides a good illustration of this point. The modern meaning 'agreeable' etc. appears only at the end of the eighteenth century. The other meanings are all of the kind 'delicate', 'precise' etc. and we may be led to think that this is the 'real' meaning of the word. The earliest meaning is usually given as 'foolish' —closely connected with the Latin from which it is derived, *nescius*, 'ignorant'. Is not this then *really* its real meaning? Perhaps not, for *nescius* is derived from a negative root plus a root meaning 'to cut' (found also in *schism, scissors*). The 'real' meaning of *nice* might then be 'blunt' since we cannot go back any further.

Secondly, it is easy to confuse historical and non-historical explanations. We are often asked, especially by foreigners, why English has a particular form. Why, for instance, do we say *feet* and not *⋆foots*? The most likely answer that a question of this kind will elicit (though naturally, this will mean consulting books or an English scholar) is that English once had a plural ending in -*i* and that there was in 'pre-English' a plural form of the word *fōt* which was *fōti* and that the final *i* influenced the preceding vowel and was then lost: the process known as mutation. Now this may be very interesting and the foreign student may well remember the form simply because he has heard the explanation. But an explanation can be non-historical, an explanation, that is to say, in the sense of placing a form in its regular pattern. If, for instance, we are asked why we say *He ought to go* instead of *⋆He oughts to go* (cf. *He wants to go*) a historical explanation is that ought is the past tense of *owe* and that past tense forms do not have -*s* endings. But a non-historical explanation is much more illuminating: *ought* is one of a group of a special class of verbs in English which have a particular place in English syntax and of which none has an -*s* ending in the 'third person form'—*will, shall, can, may, must, ought* and (in the negative and question forms at least) *dare* and *need*.

Ought leads on to our third point—the confusion of synchronic and diachronic features in the grammatical description of the language. '*Ought* is the past tense of *owe*' is a false statement. It may be true that '*Ought* WAS the past tense of *owe*' but the past tense of *owe* IS *owed*. Similarly, some school texts still ask for the singular of *dice* and the answer expected is *die*. But *die* is NOT the singular of *dice*—it has its own plural *dies*. I am not sure whether *dice* has a singular at all though for many people the singular is the same as the plural, *dice*. (What do we say—'There is a .... on the floor'?) Perhaps we prefer to avoid the problem altogether and talk about 'one of the dice'.

Fourthly,—and this is a rather more subtle point—it is all too easy to use words in describing a language that carry with them by implication, if we are not careful, the notion of a historical process. Words of this type are 'assimilation', 'palatalization' and the word 'change' itself which appear in many descriptions of languages without any clear indication whether or not a historical process is being implied. Let us consider 'palatalization' in Italian. We have in Latin *centum* and Italian *cento* an example of the change of an initial velar [k] to a palatal [tʃ] consonant. In Italian *amico* 'friend' and *amici* 'friends' we also find a change from a velar to a palatal (indicated, in the writing, by the letter *c* which is 'hard' before *o* and 'soft' before *i*). But there are obviously two different kinds of change, two different types of palatalization: the one is the development of Italian from Latin, the other is Italian as it is today—one diachronic, the other synchronic. Of course, it can be pointed out that Italian *amici* with a palatal has come from Latin *amici* with a velar and that the synchronic palatalization results from the diachronic palatalization; but this important observation can be made *only if* we keep the two aspects distinct. Some linguists have been so afraid of this confusion that they have banned all 'process' words from the vocabulary of linguistic description. They have argued that in a language no one form ever actually changes into another—*foot* does not literally change into *feet* on paper or in our brains, and that therefore 'change' can only imply historical change and should be avoided. But if it turns out to be convenient to talk about one form changing into another or at least to write one's description of a language in symbols that imply such change, there seems to be no valid reason for not using such language or such symbols—provided that we are sufficiently sophisticated never to confuse diachronic and synchronic.

It is important also to realize that language is to a very large extent spoken language. There are very few people who write more than they speak and the sum total of written texts in the English language would be insignificant in volume if compared with the amount of spoken language produced at the same time. Moreover, our initial training in language is the spoken rather than the written word. The child has mastered all the essential parts of his language, almost the whole of its sound system and its grammar as well as most of the basic vocabulary before he begins to write.

However much, therefore, we may be impressed by the literature of our language, we ought not to forget the importance of speech. It is a mistake to attempt to establish norms for speech that are based upon the writing. Because English spelling is so notoriously non-representative of the sounds of the language (but this defect can be exaggerated—see the next section) we are used to the idea that English may not be pronounced as it is spelled. Nevertheless many people feel that the written language somehow indicates the 'correct' form. As with comments in terms of history we sometimes hear 'We pronounce it that way but it's *really* .. .' and a spelling pronunciation follows—that, for instance, we say [bɑːskɪt] but it is 'really' [bɑːskɛt]. If two words are spelled differently but pronounced the same, a statement that they are pronounced in the same way will often meet with incredulity or contradiction. Many people would insist that *mince* and *mints*, for instance, are pronounced differently because the second 'has a t' in it; but this is an inference drawn from the spelling that seems to have no validity at all for the spoken form.

The written form has in fact sometimes influenced the pronunciation —thought not of really odd words like the notorious - *ough* set. The days in which *waistcoat* was pronounced [weskɪt] have gone and the pronunciation favoured by the spelling has prevailed, and the days of the pronunciation [fɔrɪd] for *forehead* seen to be numbered. Yet this completely spoils the nursery rhyme about 'the little girl who had a little curl right in the middle of her forehead' who 'when she was good was very, very good, but when she was bad she was . . . . . .'! There has not been a similar general change for *breakfast* or *cupboard*, though in certain types of 'polite society' 'spelling' forms of even these have been heard.

Nevertheless, it would be foolish to ignore the fact that we are a literate society and that spelling pronunciations can be used to clear up ambiguities: 'I said compl*i*ment, not compl*e*ment' or 'v*o*cation not v*a*cation' are perfectly possible utterances in English. The danger is in assuming that these special pronunciations are 'normal' or 'more correct'.

There is an opposite way of looking at the relation of speech and writing. Instead of requiring speech to conform to writing we may demand that our writing conforms to speech. English, we are sometimes told, is 'not a phonetic language' though Spanish is—and presumably is superior for that reason. But to talk about 'phonetic languages' is to talk nonsense. All languages are phonetic—except perhaps the 'dead' ones, since 'phonetic' means, according to the O.E.D., consisting of vocal sounds. What is usually meant is that the writing, the orthography, is *phonemic*, that there is a one-to-one relation between distinctive sound and symbol.

Most proposals for spelling reform aim at producing such a writing system for English (though not all of them: some aim at a 'narrow' phonetic orthography showing all varieties of sound, not a phonemic one showing only those that are distinctive in the language). But few stop to ask if it is necessarily a virtue of a language that its orthography should faithfully represent speech. We have already noted the nature of the Chinese script which allows people speaking quite different languages to communicate, and that it is perhaps to our advantage that English spelling is in a small way similar, since this easily permits people with different kinds of spoken English to use the same writing system (or almost the same, since there are a few differences across the Atlantic).

In fact, for the native speaker at least, there seems to be very little advantage in having a script that faithfully represents the writing. All that is needed is that the written form can be identified and then read aloud. For this purpose much less than a complete phonemic transcription is needed—as is made clear by the use of shorthand by secretaries. This quite deliberately implements the fact that for the purpose of identification as speech much of our writing is redundant, and can be left out. Indeed, some alternative forms of writing quickly, or of writing in a condensed form for advertising, have shown we can leave out most or all of the vowels and still produce something that is intelligible, e.g. *Dtd mdn hse 3 brms.* . . . Arabic has been described as a natural shorthand script for this very reason. The vowels are all indicated by marks above or below the actual writing itself and though they are always to be found in print, they are usually left in out handwriting. This is particularly remarkable when it is remembered that almost the whole of the morphology (the inflection) of Arabic is carried by vowel change—as in English *take/took* or *goose/geese.* Thus we have *kataba* 'he wrote' but *kutiba* 'it was written'. Even so, with all the vowels omitted the writing can be read with ease by a native speaker. It is true that it will be difficult for a foreigner. But orthographies are surely not to be designed for the foreign language learner; if they require a written form, phonetic transcriptions can always be provided.

There is a much more important reason why the spelling should not faithfully represent the sound. If we had a phonemic spelling for English we should no longer form the plural of *cat, dog* and *horse* by merely adding *s.* Phonemically the added endings are /s/, /z/ and /ɪz/ respectively. These three are distinct in terms of the sounds of the language but grammatically ('morphemically') they are identical. Surely a spelling which uses one symbol here, and so ignores the fact that differences between the endings of *cats,* and *dogs* are phonetically similar to those between *loose* and *lose* [luːs] and [luːz] is to be preferred to one that distinguishes them. Worse, if we had a phonemic spelling we should have to provide quite different representations for *photograph, photography* and *photographic* since these are [fəʊtəgraːf], [fətɑgrəfiː] and [fəʊtəgræfɪk]; the first two of these have no vowels at all in common. Yet the pattern found in these three is shared by all words of a similar type e.g., *telegraph, telegraphy* and *telegraphic* and even if someone invented say, a 'domograph' no English speaker, would have difficulty in pronouncing its name or the related words *domography and *domographic.* Spelling then is not, or should not be, phonemic; it might perhaps be argued that it should be 'morphophonemic' (halfway between phonemic and morphological), but that is another question.

Finally in this section, let us glance at the main difference between spoken and written language. Some of the differences are obvious. Clearly they are in different media. Also, as we have seen, English spelling does not correspond to the speech sounds so that (to take obvious points) *x* represents two sounds /ks/ but *th* only one (though it may be either /ð/ or /θ/). The writing has only five vowels, but however we analyse the English spoken vowel system we cannot reduce it to less than six (and some scholars would argue that there are over twenty). The need for at least six is shown by the contrast of the six 'short' vowels, a contrast that appears totally in only two sets of words in

English: *pit, pet, pat, pot, putt* and *put*; *rick, wreck, rack, rock, ruck* and *rook* (note the devices used to account for the 'extra' vowel). But there are more serious problems. It is by no means clear that there ARE words or sentences in speech as there are in writing. Both words and sentences belong to the conventions of writing and they are not marked in speech as they are in the written form. That is to say, there are no spaces between words in the spoken language—not even 'slight' pauses as one grammarian thought, though there are some devices (known as 'juncture features') that SOMETIMES mark some word divisions. This can be proved by showing that we can distinguish in quite normal speech between *keeps ticking* and *keep sticking* between *a nice cake* and *an ice cake*. Yet we do not distinguish in normal speech between *a pier* and *appear*. The device is not always available. Sentences too are not always marked by intonation, though one might have expected this. Two sentences such as *I'm not going, I'm tired*, can be said with a single intonation (a single 'tone group') whereas *That one's mine* can be uttered with a double intonation tune. Further, of course, as we have already seen, intonation can do a great deal that cannot be done in the writing. In this respect the written form is a vehicle far inferior to speech.

On close inspection we find that even the grammar of the spoken language is different from that of the written. In the written form, for example, there are three main kinds of plural formation of the noun as exemplified by *cat/cats, sheep/sheep* and *foot/feet*. There are three similar types in speech, but the members of each class are not the same. For in writing *postman/postmen* is like *foot/feet*, but in speech it is like *sheep/sheep*—the single and plural forms are identical. If someone says 'the [pəʊstmən] came up the street' we cannot tell if there was one or more than one of them. Moreover, the plural *houses* is perfectly regular in writing but utterly irregular in speech, for the plural of [haʊs] is not *[haʊsɪz] but *[haʊzɪz]. There are plenty of other examples—the reader need only consider *does* which is as regular as *goes* in the written language, but quite idiosyncratic in speech. One may expect irregularity with verbs like *do* since they are auxiliaries and perform a semi-grammatical function, but English has just one 'full' verb with an irregular *-s* ('third person') form. I have for some years asked audiences of students and others to tell me which one it is, usually without a reply—so unaware are we of the characteristics of our speech. The answer is *say* with the form [sez] not *[seɪz]. Oddly enough, and without justification, the written form *sez* is sometimes used in humorous writing as an indication of sub-standard speech—but it is in fact a faithful indication of the speech of most of us.

Just as we ought not to confuse synchronic and diachronic aspects of a language or speech and writing, so we must keep clear the distinction between *form* and *meaning*. Some linguists, especially 'structural linguists', have been accused of neglecting meaning. This is probably fair, but it happened only because they succeeded in some degree in making useful observations about the form or structure (if we use 'structure' in that sense) of a language, but found meaning too difficult to handle. But the simple point is that the two can and must be kept distinct wherever possible and one lesson that has been learnt is that grammatical categories cannot, without confusion, be defined in 'notional' terms. It is valueless, for instance, to define *noun* as 'the name of a person or thing'. For is fire a 'thing'? Is peace? Is suffering? If the answer to these questions is 'Yes', since they are not physical objects, the only reason is presumably that they are indicated by nouns—and so the definition is circular. The point can be made by trying to prove that *suffering* is a noun in *His sufferings were intense* but *suffered* is not in *He suffered intensely*. But why not? Are we taking about 'things' in the first sentence but not in the second? Similarly, singular and plural cannot be defined in terms of 'one' and 'more than one' since this does not account for the difference between *wheat* which is singular and *oats* which is plural. (Do we really think of wheat as a single object and oats as a collection of objects?) More striking examples are provided by gender in French and German. If masculine, feminine and neuter are defined in terms of male, female and sex-less creatures we have no explanation at all for the use of the feminine *la sentinelle* in French to refer to the very male guardsman, while a young lady in German is referred to by the most inappropriate neuter nouns *Fräulein* and *Mädchen*. Clearly, then, the categories of number and gender are formal categories—based upon the form and in particular, the syntax of the language—*The oats are, The wheat is*; *la table, le livre*; *der Kopf, die Stadt, das Haus* (in French and German the choice of the article is one of the relevant formal features).

There are more subtle points than this. Tense has, or should have, no direct connection with time. Indeed it is related that in one North American Indian language the tense distinctions do not refer to temporal features at all, but to spatial relations. This ought not to be surprising. There is no 'logical' or 'natural' reason why a language should always refer to time relations on each occurrence of a verb. It would seem that the division into past, present and future, however natural it may appear in terms of chronological time, is, in so far as it relates to the meaning of forms of the verb, largely a feature of certain western Indo-European languages. The Latin trio *amo*, *amabo*, and *amabam* is by no means typical of languages in general. Indeed it is very doubtful whether even English has this three-term category of tense. Basically the English system distinguishes only two tenses as exemplified by *take* and *took*. Of course, English has ways of referring to future time, but this is in itself of no more relevance than that it has ways of referring to greater and lesser distances. The only question of relevance is whether it has *special* forms to future time and the answer to this question is in all honesty 'No'. The traditional grammars refer to *will* and *shall* as the auxiliaries used to provide the future tense. (This is usually accompanied by the wholly fictitious paradigm *I shall*, *you will* etc. with the alternation of *shall* and *will*.) But these two verbs pattern exactly as do *can* and *may*, and there is no reason therefore to isolate them as tense makers, unless we treat all the 'basic' forms of the verb as tenses and so end up with about 200 tenses for English. Moreover, if we insist on looking for a future tense why should we select *will* and *shall*? In colloquial English at least, *going to* is equally common or perhaps even more common, and it has the added advantage that unlike *will* it always refers simply to future time. *Will*, unfortunately, can be used to express willingness or habit (*He'll not be there for hours*) or even probability (*That'll be John*), so that we have either to distinguish two verbs, one used as the future auxiliary, the other not, or else say that the English future tense is often used not to refer to future time!

There are even stronger paradoxes if we turn to past tense. For though there is every reason for distinguishing a present and a past tense as exemplified by *takes* and *took*, it turns out that the past tense is often used where there is no reference at all to past time as in *I wish I knew* or *If I knew*. .... The past tense is used simply for 'unreality', for non-existent or improbable contingencies. A way out of this is to treat these as the English subjunctive or one of the forms of the subjunctive; but it is a strange subjunctive that in almost every case is identical with the past tense. There is really no problem. Just as French gender does not refer directly to sex (though there is indirect reference—hence *l'homme* is masculine and *la femme* is feminine), so tense does not always refer to time relations.

The formal categories of the language must be defined not only without direct reference to notions of non-linguistic features such as time or sex, but must as far as possible be defined in terms of the characteristics of the language itself and not in terms of any other language. It is because we are inclined to think in terms of our own language that we find it difficult sometimes to learn new languages. I have already commented on our natural 'ethnocentric' attitude towards language—we never *really* believe in the patterns of another language. But there is another influence perhaps even more dangerous—that of the classical language, and in the case of Europe, of Latin. We may smile when we hear of the missionary who reported that Japanese was 'defective in the gerund' but Latin Grammar is, perhaps, still with us. When teachers have maintained, as some have, that the teaching of Latin was essential for the teaching of English grammar, they have been right, for the English grammar they taught was essentially Latin grammar clothed in English words and it is not surprising that the pupils failed to understand it until they were introduced to the original model. No longer, perhaps, do our children learn the paradigm 'Table, O table, table, of a table, to or for a table, from or by a table,' but some English grammars will have a place for the genitive and the dative in English and I strongly suspect that the chief motivation for the insistence on the retention of a future tense is the feeling that Latin had one, that Latin is grammatically the best model, and that English must have one too.

We have not yet asked 'What is language?' It is easy enough to provide a definition that merely identifies—something like 'The communication system based upon the vocal organs used by human beings'. It is also possible to characterize languages in terms of the kind of statements that can be made about it. Such a characterization is to be found in the later chapters of this book where various aspects of language are discussed—sound systems, morphology, syntax, semantics, varieties of language and the history of English.

There are, of course, communication systems other than human language, but are these to be regarded as language, and, if not, why not? Many animals communicate by the use of sound; some of the apes make use of a system of a considerable number of different calls. Not all animal communication is by sound; one of the most remarkable systems is that of the dances of the bees, by which one bee can inform the others of the direction and distance of nectar-producing flowers. Human communication, as we have already seen, is fundamentally based upon the noises we make. Writing is derived from this and other systems such as semaphore and Morse are, in turn, derived from the writing system. But there are communication systems used by human beings that are not based primarily upon the language system—though they can always be 'verbalized', since we can always talk about anything that we understand. An example is the system used by traffic lights. This is not derived from any one language though the Red, Green and Amber can be interpreted as 'Stop', 'Go' and 'Get Ready'. There are other natural systems too, such as those of facial expression and gestures; strangely enough, these are not always easily translated into speech.

Clearly language is much more complex than any of these and there is no difficulty in practice in distinguishing between language and non-language systems, no greater difficulty perhaps than in distinguishing between men and apes. But it is not at all clear where we should, in principle, draw the border-line. It is difficult if not impossible, that is to say, to establish what are the theoretical restrictions and limitations on language. We find it almost impossible to establish what features a language must have in order to be a language. Some linguists have tried to establish 'universals' of language but such attempts are unlikely to succeed for three reasons. First, the investigator himself is always, so to speak, encaged in language. He is quite incapable of standing aside, as perhaps a visitor from Mars might, and looking completely objectively at language. His observations are necessarily influenced largely by his own pre-conceptions. Let us take a rather trivial but obvious example. Is the distinction between nouns and verbs, for actions, a necessary distinction in language? Must all languages make this distinction? Investigation shows that *most* languages, in fact, have two distinct word classes that can without any hesitation be labelled 'noun' and 'verb' respectively. But this is not true of *all* languages. There are some which have instead word stems which by the addition of suffixes 'become' nouns or verbs; in these languages the distinction is not between different words in the sense of different lexical stems in the way in which *cat* is different from *penetrate*, but between different forms of the same lexical stem—there are examples in English, e.g. the noun with the forms *man* and *men* and the verb with *man*, *mans*, *manning* and *manned*. Could we have a language without any distinction of this kind? Almost certainly if there were such a language we should be quite unable to understand it and equally unable to describe it. Secondly, we cannot establish what are the universal features of language, in the sense of NECESSARILY universal features, by examining all the languages of the world. For even if we find a given feature to be universally present, this is no proof that it is a necessary universal—it is possible that for some language this is a result of a common origin and for others that it has been borrowed. We simply cannot tell whether its universality is merely accidental. Thirdly, no kind of serious experimentation is possible. We cannot for obvious moral reasons take a large number of infants and use them as 'guinea pigs' to establish what is, and what is not, possible in human language. There is a famous story of the Egyptian King Psammetichus II who attempted an experiment with two new-born infants. He wished to decide whether the Egyptian race was older than the Phrygian, and for this purpose arranged for two new-born babies to be reared apart from all contact with human speech. After two years the children were heard to cry 'Bekos' when asking for food; since this was the Phrygian word for bread, Psammetichus reluctantly concluded that Phrygian was the older race. Modern experiments would, no doubt, be more sophisticated, but are unthinkable.

The American linguist C. F. Hockett suggested that there are seven characteristics that are not *all* shared by other communication systems. The first feature is that of *duality*—that a language has a phonological system and a grammatical system—that it is as some linguists have said 'double-structured'. This is not now accepted by many linguists; one modern theory sees no clear distinction between such levels, while another recognizes not two 'strata', but six. But basically the point Hockett is making is that there is no direct correlation between the element of sound in language and what it 'stands for'. With traffic lights the sign 'Red' means 'Stop', but the sounds of a language do not mean anything at all—the smallest units of language that can be correlated with meaning are far more complex than single sounds. Secondly language is *productive*—every speaker can understand and produce sentences that he has never heard before. This point was not always fully appreciated by some linguists, but today it is considered to be of fundamental importance. It is quite clear that the number of potentially possible sentences in any language is, like the system of numbers in mathematics, infinite. This can be proved in mathematics by pointing out that however large a number is mentioned we can always add one to it; similarly, in language, however long a sentence may be, another word can always be added. The structure of language involves 'recursion' of the kind illustrated by 'This is the house that Jack built', 'This is the mouse that lived in the house that Jack built' and so on—if necessary *ad infinitum*. It is clear from this that we do not learn sentences by mere repetition (as the parrot does)—we create and understand new ones all the time. Thirdly, language is *arbitrary*; there is no necessary connection between a sound and what it means—*chien* is as good as *dog* for the name of the animal. Some communication systems use symbols that are iconic, that in some way directly represent their meaning: the hieroglyphs were drawings of objects, the bees' dance shows in a direct form the direction of the nectar. There are, of course some words of this kind in all languages—the onomatopoeic words like 'cuckoo', but these form only a tiny section of the vocabulary.

A fourth feature is *interchangeability*. Speakers can become hearers and vice versa, but traffic lights do not relay information to other traffic lights. Fifthly, language is *highly specialized*—there is a close relationship between linguistic behaviour and the results it achieves. I am not sure that this is true. It probably derives from a behaviourist approach to linguistics (stemming from the great American linguist Bloomfield) in which meaning is thought of in terms of stimulus and response. Unfortunately the same words will produce quite different reactions, and a physical stimulus quite different linguistic responses. It has been pointed out that in accordance with a behaviourist theory, the response to a painting might be 'Dutch' but in actual fact someone might well react with 'Clashes with the wall-paper' or 'Hanging too low'. There is not much specialization here. Sixthly, language can be, and often is, *displaced*, dealing with events removed in time and space. One linguist once commented that language was invented for the purpose of telling lies. As long as primitive man merely made noises in response to his immediate sensations—for instance to indicate to his fellows that he could see food—he had not acquired language; but as soon as he made the same noises when the food was not there he had learnt to speak. Finally *cultural transmission* is an important characteristic—a language is handed down from generation to generation. The forms of language (though not, perhaps, the ability to speak) are not known instinctively, but have to be learnt. This, of course, is the reason why languages differ in the different parts of the world and even within small areas where there is little cultural contact.

These characteristics of human language may largely, perhaps, be summarized by saying that it is far more complex than other communication systems. The complexity of language is, of course, related to Man's greater intelligence, though equally his greater intelligence must have developed as a result of his acquisition of language. It might well be argued that the definition of Man should be in terms of 'Man the speaking animal' rather than 'Man the tool maker', especially now that it is known that the apes use primitive tools.

We do not know when Man began to use language (even if we knew exactly how to define language). At some time in his evolutionary history he developed his organs of speech, for these organs are in origin the organs for eating and breathing and have become highly specialized for the purpose of speech. These organs are, however, entirely made of flesh and do not affect the bone structure. They do not, therefore, survive as fossils and we cannot learn anything about the origin or development of speech from archaeology. There can be little doubt that the origin of speech must be traced to noises similar to those made by apes and gibbons, but precisely how and when Man significantly advanced beyond them we shall never know. There have been many theories of the origin of language. Most of them are fanciful, and in any case, seem to ask only how the particular sounds of language were selected. The naivest theory, perhaps, is that primitive man had a natural feeling for the right name for objects; this is surely belied by the arbitrary nature and variety of sound-meaning relations in language throughout the world. Another view is that he imitated the natural sounds—that language, therefore, originated with onomatopoeia, with words like 'cuckoo'; but this would not have taken language far—the number of onomatopoeic words in language is very small. Others have suggested that language developed from the natural noises we ourselves make— our sighs, our groans, etc.; there may, perhaps, be a little truth in this— danger signs may well have developed from cries of fear, but this does not take us even as far as the present ape 'language', and tells us nothing at all about human language. A further theory sees the origin of language in the imitation by the tongue of natural gestures. None of these theories can ever be proved, or disproved, and they are all largely uninformative.

Language is essentially a human characteristic—this is well known. Though it is related to greater human intelligence, however, there is reason to believe that it is not dependent solely upon greater intelligence, or at least not solely upon the fact that Man has a much larger brain than all other creatures. There is evidence that the human brain is in some way specialized and that speech is, therefore, restricted to humans for neuro-physiological reasons. This is proved by the fact that there are some sub-normal humans with brain sizes smaller than those of the apes. These sub-normal humans can, nevertheless, be taught to speak (though their speech is limited), whereas the apes cannot, no matter what training they receive. It does not need a larger brain to make speech possible—it needs a human brain.

The precise way in which the human brain differs from that of other creatures is not fully understood. One suggestion, which has been backed by investigation, is that in other creatures there is no direct link between the various regions of the brain that deal with sensation, but that these are independently linked to the areas that are concerned with the emotions, appetites, etc. In Man, by contrast, there are direct connections and, in particular, links between the regions of sight and hearing. In human language, it is argued, the naming of objects, the association of sound with 'things', is a necessary first step and this is possible only with a brain that can directly link sight and hearing. Since Man alone has a brain that can do this, he alone can speak.

These last few paragraphs demonstrate once again what was said in the opening sections of this chapter—how little we know about language and languages. All too much of our knowledge, moreover, is distorted by prejudice and misconception. In the twentieth century we are becoming more curious about ourselves and our behaviour, and ever more determined to make only precise and objective statements about it. But the field of scientific investigation of language is still vast and largely unexplored.

BIBLIOGRAPHY

The scientific study of language—linguistics—begins, in a sense, in this century with F. de Saussure's *Cours de linguistique générale* (Paris, 1916)—translated into English by Wade Barkin as *Course in General Linguistics* (New York, 1959). In America the great names are those of Edward Sapir and Leonard Bloomfield, both of whom wrote a book entitled *Language*—E. Sapir, *Language: an introduction to the study of speech* (New York, 1921—reprinted in Harvard Books, 1955), L. Bloomfield, *Language* (New York, 1933, and London, 1935). The great Danish scholar Otto Jespersen wrote many books on language and on English, but these are in more traditional terms and deeply concerned with a historical approach. Two of the best known are *The Philosophy of Grammar* (London, 1924) and *Language: its nature, development and origin* (London, 1922).

More recent works by American linguists are *A Course in Modern Linguistics* (New York, 1958) by C. F. Hockett, Professor of Linguistics at Cornell University, and *An Introduction to Descriptive Linguistics* (New York, revised edition, 1961) by H. A. Gleason, Professor of Linguistics, Hartford Seminary Foundation. From Britain the best introduction is that of R. H. Robins, Professor of General Linguistics at the University of London—*General Linguistics: an introductory survey* (London, 1964).

A book in a much more popular style than any of these is that of R. A. Hall, Professor of Linguistics at Cornell University—*Linguistics and your Language* (New York, 1960). A really basic introduction is *What is Linguistics?* (London, 1968) by David Crystal of Reading University, who is a contributor to this volume.

2

PHONOLOGY—THE SOUNDS OF ENGLISH

P. F. R. Barnes

This chapter deals with the sound-system of English. It does not how-ever attempt a detailed survey of the whole subject, because authoritative studies of this kind are already available (see bibliography at the end of the chapter—though even the works cited there cannot hope to have said all there is to say on such a vast topic); and also because of limitations on space—this is not a book on English pronunciation alone but on various different aspects of the language. In what follows, therefore, the aim has simply been, first, to explain something of the ideas we need to handle 'the sounds of English', then to show, by selected examples, how these ideas might work out in practice.

The subject-matter of Chapter 1 was language in general and illustrations were taken from a number of different languages. It is now being presumed, however, as can be seen from the titles of this and succeeding chapters, that each of a number of aspects of English can be examined more or less separately, without doing undue violence to the facts. For instance, we can take an utterance—say 'Where's that big atlas got to, Mary?'—out of a conversation, and while of course we are quite ready to admit that such an utterance represents a great deal more than two seconds or so of sound, nevertheless we can consider it as if it were little more than that. We can ignore (which in an ordinary situa-tion we would not) the fact that the sentence is a question, that the word 'atlas' is a noun, that 'big' means 'large', and so on. By ignoring all this, we are not necessarily falsifying the data, we are merely doing one job of description at a time; describing a language, or even a rela-tively small part of one, is such a herculean task that we may easily be forgiven if we attempt to take it bit by bit. Furthermore, as has been pointed out in the preceding chapter, since there is no necessary cor-respondence between sounds and what they 'stand for', there are strong grounds for claiming that the sound-system of a language can be studied separately, because that separation reflects a basic fact about language in general.

To talk clearly, at any length, about the 'sounds of English' (or of any other language) unfortunately involves terms of an unfamiliar kind, and we must spend a fair amount of time, first of all, clarifying what we mean by 'sounds' (and indeed, in a later paragraph, by 'English'). We will have to adopt a minimum of theory, with its accompanying technical terms, to describe, classify and label these sounds; such terms are lacking in the everyday vocabulary. These labels will first of all refer to the human vocal mechanism, and not particularly to any one language; for there is no sense in which a sound is 'English' by nature—only the use to which it is put is unique to one language. And there is of course no sense either in which particular sounds are characteristic of a particular racial group—human beings find it difficult or easy to make this or that vocal noise because of their linguistic environment since birth, and not for genetic reasons. The children of West Indian immigrants in London, for example (frequently in spite of their parents' West Indian accents), find no difficulty in speaking perfect Cockney; the American English of the fully assimilated Negro, Chinese or Puerto Rican is potentially the same as that of his Mayflower-descended neighbour, and any differences are ascribable rather to social class or regional factors than to 'race'. In view of this then, we can begin our discussion of the English sound-system by asking how a human being produces the vocal noises he does.

Basically, a noise is a disturbance in the medium which separates the source of the noise from the hearer. This medium is of course usually air. The disturbance originates in changes of air-pressure (generally known as SOUND WAVES) emanating from the nose and/or the mouth. The air in the VOCAL TRACT (the wind-pipe, pharynx or throat, mouth and nose—see Fig. 1, page 40) can be made to move either outwards or inwards by various kinds of AIR-STREAM MECHANISM. For our purposes, this will almost always be of the type known as PULMONIC EGRESSIVE—lung air being pushed upwards and outwards by the contraction of the space available for it in the lungs. Other air-stream mechanisms rarely occur in English, or occur only on the fringe of the linguistic system, as in the 'clicks' (often spelt 'tut tut', 'tsk tsk', etc.) used by English speakers to express sympathy or disapproval, for instance, or to encourage beasts of burden. As the air moves through the vocal tract, up into the cavities of the pharynx, mouth and nose, we can interfere with its passage in a variety of ways; this interference, as we shall see, may merely involve altering the size and shape of the cavities (by moving the tongue or the lower jaw, for example) or it may involve blocking off the air-stream altogether. The shape and

NC.—Nasal Cavity.
OC.—Oral Cavity.
Ph.—Pharynx.
Ep.—Epiglottis.
Wp.—Windpipe, 'Trachea'.
Fp.—Food-passage, 'Oesophagus.'
L.—Lips.
T.—Teeth.
TR.—Tooth-ridge.
HP.—Hard Palate.

SP.—Soft Palate, 'Velum'.
Uv.—Uvala.
Tt.—Tongue-tip.
Bl.—Blade of tongue.
Fr.—Front of tongue.
B.—Back of tongue.
VC.—Vocal Cords.
La.—Larynx.
The dotted line represents the soft palate in its *raised* position.

Fig. I. The organs of speech

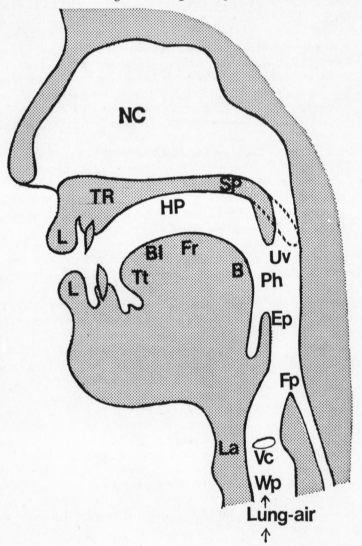

position of the speech-organs is called ARTICULATION; and as the articulation changes, so of course does the sound-wave it gives rise to. Since that sound-wave is perceived by the listener as a 'sound' (or 'sounds'), there seems to be justification for describing sounds in articulatory terms. The study of how our speech-organs can be moved and positioned to produce one sound-type or another is the subject-matter of ARTICULATORY PHONETICS, and its categories are by far the most common way of describing speech-sounds. Perhaps, however, we ought to remind ourselves here that the title ARTICULATORY/AUDITORY PHONETICS would be more appropriate; for it must be remembered that our hearing-sense 'monitors' the sounds we ourselves are articulating. There is a feedback to the brain via the ear, whereby we can check, as it were, that the instructions sent to the muscles of the articulating organs have produced, in auditory terms, the intended result. There is thus a close, built-in link between what we hear and what noises we speak.

It is possible, then, to describe sounds by detailing the salient characteristics of the speech-apparatus at the time of production; but there are at least two good reasons why our description can never be more than approximate. The first is that no two human beings have identical versions of that apparatus. Individual difference will inevitably mean that our description is a generalization; that is, we will have to take 'sound' as meaning 'type of sound', however precise the descriptive labels may appear. The second reason lies in the complexity of the speech-organs and of their simultaneous activity in the act of speaking; the difficulty of measuring this activity is such that an exact statement of *all* the articulatory variables involved in the production of one sound by one set of speech-organs, is probably impossible (if only because the measuring devices themselves would tend to interfere with articulation to such an extent that it would no longer resemble natural speech). We must therefore be prepared to accept that our phonetic description will appear, in absolute terms, rather rough and ready; but it will be a great deal more precise than the vague and impressionistic labels and the loose metaphors we often find applied to the sounds of speech. The approximateness of the description, however, should be seen in the light of our purpose in carrying it out—which is to be able to identify all those differences of sound which are capable of being perceived, consistently, by the human ear. Any differences below this threshold, after all, could not be used in anything other than a sub-conscious, non-meaningful, and therefore non-linguistic way. Such differences are thus not the concern of the linguistic analyst, and our phonetic description will be *over*-precise if it takes note of them.

Up to now we have used the word 'sound', in both its singular and its plural form, rather indiscriminately—we have for instance allowed it to suggest (one of) a number of separate, or at least separable, units put together in sequence to form an utterance. Yet when we examine graphic displays of speech (which are produced by instruments giving us in effect partial pictures of the sound-wave), then we see immediately that what we think of as a series of units, of separate events, is in fact not a series at all but, from the physical point of view, one continuous noise. On this purely acoustic level, sound is not treated as representing an utterance of a language but as a complex sound-wave, defined in the physicist's terms of frequency, time and amplitude, and varying more or less continuously from any one fraction of a second to the next. Must we then abandon, on evidence of this kind, the idea of segmenting the utterance, of cutting it up into its component 'sounds', the better to examine it? The answer to this has almost always been 'no': it is still open to us to segment speech in this way provided we accept that each unit, each 'sound', in the sequence merges into its neighbours (or into silence if at the beginning or end of the utterance), and that therefore there will be no point of time at which sound A 'becomes' sound B. An analogy sometimes used in cases like this is that of two hills with a valley between them—although we cannot point to two lines on the ground where the valley stops and the hills begin, nevertheless it is still meaningful to talk of two hills and a valley (perhaps because the notions of 'hill' and 'valley' do not depend on boundary-features so much as on the characteristics of their central parts). No doubt it is a gross over-simplification of the physical facts to conceive of the phonetics of an utterance as a series of units, even if we add the idea of TRANSITION-FEATURES joining them together; but there is also no doubt that there will always be oversimplification in talking of phenomena as complex as articulation. In fact, we will see below that once we look at either the sound-wave or the articulatory continuum from the point of view of the *linguistic* units it represents, there will be stronger reasons for accepting the imposition of a 'segmental' framework of analysis. (Indeed, the examination of the physical properties of the sound-wave from this point of view has led to much new thinking in phonetics over the past twenty years. The question has been asked, 'What acoustic features in this mass of noise are crucial for the perception of this or that linguistic unit?' and answers to it have proved most reveal-ing. We shall not, however, have much further to say on this topic, since it requires specialized knowledge which is here rather outside our scope.)

We have decided, then, to consider a 'sound' as an articulation, that is as a typical set of movements and/or positions of the speech-organs. 'Typical' means typical of the infinite number of possibilities which would produce the same auditory effect; and 'same' in this last phrase means for any practical linguistic purpose the same. Having arrived at this definition, if such it can be called, the next task is to set up articulatory categories for describing the various sounds, and this we must now proceed to do.

The first line is traditionally drawn between VOWELS and CONSONANTS, terms which (in spite of their long pedigree) are notoriously difficult to define. For our purposes at the moment, the distinction can be made by specifying that if the air-passage is constricted (either partially or wholly blocked) above the larynx, then this 'stricture' marks the articulation as that of a consonant. Vowels will simply be sounds produced without this stricture. Thus a sound-sequence like (that which represents) the word 'sat' in English has a consonant-vowel-consonant type of arrangement. Now, this definition appears to be fairly arbitrary, and so indeed it is. The reason for this arbitrariness is that there are no classes into which sounds *naturally* fall. We may think we see such classes in the way our own native language arranges its phonetic material, but this would be a mistake (and a mistake of a type to which generalizations about language are rather prone), because it takes for granted that our language is 'natural' to all human beings, rather than merely seeming natural to those who happen to speak it. If there are thus no natural classes on the articulatory phonetic level, then our classification system will have to invent its own. As far as our knowledge of actual languages goes (which is probably not very far), our classification will tend to reflect the kinds of phonetic differences which languages have been found to make use of; but the arbitrary factor must remain, turning up throughout our categories at this level of analysis and certainly not only in the case of the first two, vowel and consonant. (However, our categorization will also reflect the fact that our concern here is to describe a variety of contemporary English.)

To take consonants first, we have so far specified the presence of a stricture in the air-passage. If we can now state *where*, in the cavities above the larynx, the passage is constricted, and then *how* (i.e. by what organs and to what extent) this constriction occurs, then we will have provided ourselves with at least two methods of description. For example, if we ask where a stricture is located, we can label a fair number of positions without difficulty (see Fig. 2, page 47): between the two lips (sounds so produced are said to be BI-LABIAL), e.g. the *p*-sound of 'pan'; between the lower lip and the upper teeth (LABIO-DENTAL), e.g. the *f*-sound of 'fix'; between the tongue and the back of the upper teeth (DENTAL), e.g. the *th*-sound of 'thick'; between the tongue and the tooth-ridge (ALVEOLAR), e.g. the *s*-sound of 'some'; and so on. The roof of the mouth, from tooth-ridge to uvula, we can divide up (again more or less arbitrarily, our main guide being the kinds of distinction we have found languages making in this area) into hard palate and soft palate (or velum); the hard palate in turn can then be sub-divided into as many parts as are thought necessary. In *particular* cases, whether we need to catalogue certain finer distinctions and ignore others can depend on what use the language concerned makes of the total phonetic possibilities. And since this chapter is concerned with the phonetics of one variety of English, the distinctions to be drawn will in general be based on what seems most convenient for our examples of the ways in which the English sound-system operates; we will be able to adjust our general classes of sound in the foreknowledge of the ways in which English uses the resources of the human speech-mechanism.

A so-called 'consonant-chart' (see Fig. 4, page 56) is one widely-used type of general classification. As we have seen, the terms on the horizontal axis, from bi-labial to glottal, form a set of labels for positions in the vocal tract where consonantal stricture may occur, i.e. for PLACE OF ARTICULATION. On the other, vertical axis, the labels refer to the MANNER OF ARTICULATION—*how* the passage is constricted—and we shall now look at this second set of terms.

First, the STOP (or PLOSIVE) consonants. These involve the pressurization of air pushed up from the lungs into the vocal tract: if this pressurization is to take place there, the outlets (nose and mouth) must be closed against it. The nasal cavity is shut off by raising the soft palate against the back wall of the pharynx, thus sealing the passage. The mouth, however, may be sealed in a variety of ways, as we have seen— bi-labial as in 'bee', alveolar as in 'tea', velar as in 'key'—and when this CLOSURE in the mouth is released, the resultant explosion of pressurized air will sound different according to the position of the speech-organs at that moment. According to the place of articulation, in other words, the shape of the oral cavities will differ, as between for example a dental and a velar stop; so the air which is contained there and which resonates there on its release, will produce a different impact on the air outside, i.e. a different sound-wave (and hence, in auditory terms, a different sound). And this will of course be true also of articulations other than stops.

Second, the NASAL consonants. These are like the stops in that there is a complete closure at some point in the mouth, but different from them in that the soft palate is lowered, allowing air to escape freely, and only, through the nose. Examples are the sounds at the end of the words 'ram' (bi-labial nasal), 'ran' (alveolar) and 'rang' (velar).

Third, the LATERAL consonants. These are formed by a closure between the middle (i.e. not the side) part of the tongue, and a point along the front or top of the mouth. The closure is not complete, however, since the sides of the tongue are kept lowered (sometimes one more than the other, exceptionally only one side) and air is allowed to escape over them. The *l*-sounds in the words 'fly', 'lily' and 'fool' are examples.

44

Fourth, the FRICATIVES. Here the air is forced out, with a 'hissing' noise, through a narrowed passage formed between, for example, the tongue-tip and the tooth-ridge, as in the *s*-sound of 'see', or between the tongue-tip and the upper teeth, as in the *th*-sound of 'these'. The noise so produced is often referred to as AUDIBLE FRICTION.

The remaining categories needed for the English consonants are less easy to handle within the set of terms we have outlined so far. For instance, the *r*-sound of 'red' or 'very' usually has no audible friction and will therefore not fit into the fricative category. Indeed, one is scarcely aware of any stricture at all. However, the label FRICTIONLESS CONTINUANT has been used elsewhere, and we will accept it here rather than be forced either to treat such sounds as 'non-consonants'—i.e. as vowels—or to redefine 'consonants'. That is, we will take the *r*-sound as having a stricture of a very weak kind.

Another difficulty is caused by the nature of the 'aitch', the sound which begins words like 'hit' and 'hot'. This is produced simply by breathing out, the vocal organs being in the position of the following vowel-sound. There is no stricture as for the other consonants; this sound is therefore a sort of 'breathed vowel'. But we will probably wish to treat it like a consonant, for reasons which, as in the similar case of *r*, will be more concerned with how the language uses the sound than with how it is articulated; such reasons should become clearer later on. And if we do wish to treat it along with the other consonants, we can refer to it as a fricative, since we can claim that most of the noise is made by the air passing over the irregular surfaces of the pharyngeal and oral cavities, and there is thus audible friction.

A further difficulty is found with the so-called SEMI-VOWELS, the initial sounds in words like 'yet' and 'wet'. Here we plainly have a vowel-like articulation: no stricture at all, and the vocal organs in very much the same sort of positions as for the vowels in e.g. 'pit' and 'put'. However, we have not yet gone far enough with our analysis to see why such sounds have so often been treated as consonants, and further discussion of the semi-vowels must therefore be left till later in this chapter (see page 57).

We have now established, or rather borrowed, a rough framework within which the place and manner of the articulations involved in English consonants can be described. There is however a further dimension to be considered—that of the modification which the larynx may impose on the stream of egressive lung-air. The larynx is the so-called 'voice-box' or 'Adam's apple' at the top of the wind-pipe (see Fig. 1, page 40), and within it are two lips, or folds, running from front to back. These are the VOCAL CORDS. They may open and close (VIBRATE) very rapidly as the air passes upwards between them, and if they do then the articulation is said to be voiced—i.e. it is accompanied by VOICE (or VOICING), the name given to this vibration. If on the contrary the vocal cords are not vibrated but held open for the air to pass freely through the space between them, then the sound will be referred to as VOICELESS. Thus the consonant-articulations can be voiced or voiceless; that is, each type of articulation will produce not one but two sounds. For example, compare the middle consonant-sounds in 'fuzzy' and 'fussy' (voiced and voiceless alveolar fricatives), 'stable' and 'staple' (bi-labial stops), 'saver' and 'safer' (labio-dental fricatives), etc. Most of the consonant-articulations we have detailed above occur in English in both voiced and voiceless forms; this is not the case, however, with the nasal consonants or with the *h*-sound—for practical purposes, the former are always voiced, and the latter always voiceless.

Traditionally, consonant-sounds are labelled in the order (i) voiced/voiceless, (ii) place of articulation, and (iii) manner of articulation. Thus for instance the *g*-sound in 'foggy' is usually called a 'voiced velar stop'; and so on. Labels of this kind are, as we have seen earlier, no more than rough and ready; each of the three terms in 'voiced velar stop' could be expanded further—in the case of 'voiced', does the vocal cord vibration continue throughout the different phases of the stop-articulation, and at the same intensity? exactly where on the velum is the 'velar' closure made? for how long is the closure of the 'stop' held, and how much pressure is built up before the explosion? In addition, we could ask what the lip-position is, to what extent the jaw is opened, what the front part of the tongue is doing, and so on. However, our three-term consonantal labels will probably be adequate for our present purpose; we can refine them later if we find the language using sound-differences with which our terminology cannot cope.

Let us now turn to the vowel-sounds, and attempt to set up a general classification-system which we can use to describe, economically, the vowels of English. We have already defined vowels negatively, by saying that their articulation is not like that we held to be typically consonantal. To this we can now add the assertion that vowel-sounds are voiced—for us, therefore a 'voiceless vowel' is a contradiction in terms. Vowel-sounds, unlike consonants, cannot be described according to the location and type of structure, since the negative definition specifically excluded stricture. The principal factor to be described here is the size and shape of the oral cavity; and this can be done in terms of where the highest point of the tongue is, relative to four extreme positions. The notion of 'extreme' is the following (see Fig. 2, page 47): when the (highest point of the) tongue is in position (a), any further movement upwards or forwards, all else being equal, would produce a stricture, hence by definition a consonantal type of sound; in position b), any movement upwards or backwards would similarly produce a

46

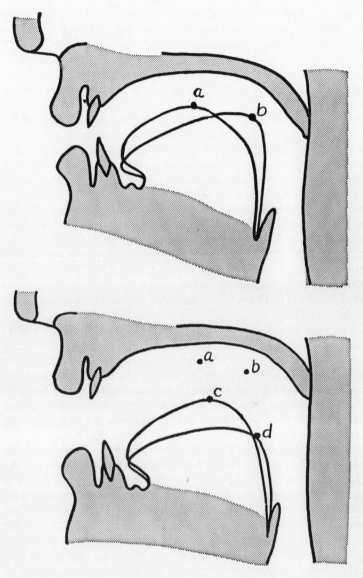

Cardinal Vowel no. 1 is produced when the highest point of the tongue
is at position (a); no. 8 at position (b); no. 4 at position (c); and no. 5 at
position (d). (See Fig. 3 on page 49).

Fig. 2. Tongue-positions at extreme-points of the 'vowel-area'

47

consonant; in position (c), the jaw is at its maximum degree of opening, and the body of the tongue is pushed forward as far as possible; and in position (d), the jaw is again wide open, with the tongue this time pulled back as far as possible without, once again, causing a stricture. If we connect up these four points in a drawing we shall have a rough picture of the so-called 'vowel-area', within which the highest point of the tongue must be if a vowel-sound is being articulated. This shape can be formalized into the 'Cardinal Vowel' diagram first proposed many years ago by Daniel Jones, and now in widespread use (see Fig. 3, page 49). In this diagram, the area is divided up into, on the vertical axis, CLOSE, HALF-CLOSE, HALF-OPEN and OPEN; and on the horizontal axis, into FRONT, CENTRAL and BACK. For our purposes, we may assume that the eight numbered reference-points represent vowel-sounds that are more or less fixed from the auditory point of view—i.e. that any speaker of any language will produce the same sound as any other speaker if they both put their tongue in the position described above for e.g. 'Cardinal Vowel no. 1'. Therefore any other vowel may be plotted on the diagram relative to these Cardinal points. For instance, the vowel in the English word 'kit' may be described as a very centralized version of C.V. no. 1; that in 'cot' as half-way between nos. 5 and 6; and so on.

However, our descriptive apparatus for vowel-sounds will need to take account of (at least) two additional factors. The first of these is lip position; if the lips are ROUNDED (and protruded), as for instance in the word 'caught', then the overall shape of the oral cavity is changed, and so therefore is the sound produced. Lip-rounding, more or less noticeable according to the individual speaker, his regional accent, etc., is characteristic of several of the English vowels, and this additional modification will thus be necessary to our description.

Secondly, we will need to take account of those vowels which are not PURE, i.e. in which there is a clearly distinguishable movement of the tongue from one vowel-position to another, rather than a relatively steady state. Vowel-sounds of this type are known as DIPHTHONGS; examples are to be found in words like 'boy', 'bay', 'bough', etc. (The answer to the question 'why are these not to be treated as *two* vowel-sounds in sequence, merging into one another as adjacent sounds in any case will always tend to do?' should emerge from discussion below.)

So far we have been largely concerned with setting up categories within which we can describe and classify speech-sounds (and in particular those of English) from an articulatory point of view. To some extent, however, we have found our choice of descriptive categories dictated, or conditioned, by *non*-articulatòry criteria, by considerations of 'how English uses' the various resources of the sound-producing mechanism. We ought now to move on to this more abstract, more linguistic level; to move from the phonetic to the specifically PHONO-LOGICAL. The questions to be asked at this point are no longer of the type 'how is this noise produced, and how can its production be concisely described?', but rather of the type 'what part does such and such a phonetic feature, or set of features, play in the transmission

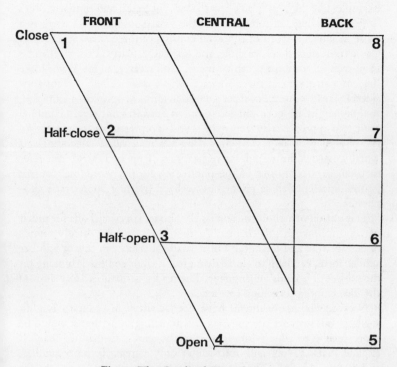

Fig. 3. The Cardinal Vowel Diagram.

and reception of various kinds of meaning?'. We shall confine our examples to English, just as we outlined only those phonetic categories which we need for English sounds, but most of the ideas and methods to be used may of course be equally applicable to any other language. That is, there are theories and techniques of GENERAL PHONOLOGY just as there are of GENERAL PHONETICS.

Let us begin looking at the sound-differences which can be used 'distinctively' in English—i.e. to distinguish meanings—by taking a MINIMAL PAIR of words (so-called because the two words differ as regards only one of their sounds), such as 'bit' and 'bet'. These two are consistently recognized by an English speaker as 'different words', with different meanings. The phonetic difference between the two vowel-sounds is therefore distinctive—a change in tongue-position from one sound to the other will produce a change of meaning. If we then go on to make other changes at the same place—the vowel in the middle—we will find e.g. 'beat', 'boot', 'bat', 'Bert', and so on. If we change, on the same principle, the consonant at the beginning, we will produce examples like 'bit', 'pit', 'sit', 'mitt', 'kit', 'lit', etc.; and similarly, 'bit', 'biff', 'bin', 'big', etc. by altering the final consonant. So there is a sense in which a word of this kind consists of three *units* or PLACES IN STRUCTURE, since there are three, and *only* three, places at which changes in vowels or consonants can be made. And clearly, to see a word like 'big' as a structure of three abstract units is very different from con-sidering it as a sequence of three sounds, in terms of vocal cord vibration, tongue-height, lip-position, and so on. We can to some extent combine these two approaches by seeing the sound as representing, or REALIZING, the phonological unit. The unit itself we may call a PHONEME; and when we view the sounds as realizations of phonemes, we can refer to them as ALLOPHONES of the phonemes. So the word 'big' consists phonologically of three phonemes, realized by their appropriate allo-phones.

This notion of a phoneme and its allophones is a crucial one for much of what follows in this chapter. At first blush, it undoubtedly sounds rather abstruse and technical, but it is a tool which, in this or another similar form, can help to elucidate a great deal of confused thinking on the subject of 'sounds' in language. The reader is thus urged to assimilate the idea before proceeding further.

Now so far our examples have been written in ordinary English spelling, but such are the vagaries of this orthography that it would be more precise to allot symbols to our phonemes, so that we make it explicit that e.g. 'pit' and 'mitt' differ only as regards the beginning, and not at the end. The tradition has grown up (and not just for English) of using the Roman alphabet for many of these symbols, with additions and modifications where necessary, and of enclosing them in slant lines to indicate that they represent phonemes and not ordinary letters. Thus 'pit' and 'mitt' will be transcribed phonemically as /pɪt/ and /mɪt/.[1] The following is a list of the phonemes of English, with a symbolization and a 'key-word' for each.

Symbol	Key-words			Symbol	Key-words	
/iː/	bead	peat	bee	/p/	pie	
/ɪ/	bid	pit	—	/b/	by	
/e/	bed	pet	—	/t/	tie	
/æ/	bad	pat	—	/d/	die	
/ɑː/	barred	part	bar	/k/	—	⎧ core
/ʌ/	bud	putt	—	/g/	guy	⎩ gore
/ɔː/	board	port	bore	/f/	—	⎧ fear
/ɒ/	'bod'	pot	—	/v/	vie	⎩ veer
/uː/	booed	—	boo	/θ/	thigh	
/ʊ/	—	put	—	/ð/	thy	
/ɜː/	bird	pert	burr	/s/	sigh	⎧ sink
/ə/	—	—	—	/z/	—	⎩ zinc ⎧ ruse
/eɪ/	bade	pate	bay	/ʃ/	shy	⎨ ruche
/aɪ/	bide	—	buy	/ʒ/	—	⎩ rouge
/ɔɪ/	buoyed	—	boy	/h/	high	
/aʊ/	bowed	pout	bough	/m/	my	⎧ ram
/əʊ/	bode	—	bow (and arrow)	/n/	nigh	⎨ ran
/ɪə/	beard	—	beer	/ŋ/	—	⎩ rang
/ɛə/	bared	—	bare	/l/	lie	
/ʊə/	—	—	boor	/r/	wry	
				/j/	—	⎧ year
				/w/	Wye	⎩ weir

(One vowel, /ə/, is not exemplified in this list, because monosyllables like those used above as key-words are always stressed when quoted in isolation, and /ə/ does not occur except in *unstressed* syllables. Minimal pairs can be found, however: compare unstressed 'but', as in 'But *really* I didn't!', with unstressed 'butt'—an opposition between /ə/ and /ʌ/; or 'An *orange*' with 'In *orange*'—/ə/ and /ɪ/. In fact, /ə/ occurs a good deal more often than any other vowel in conversational English; and furthermore its use currently seems to be spreading to many words hitherto pronounced with /ə/).

Notice first of all that there are gaps in the lists of key-words; there are no words to fit in these places for one of two reasons: either (a) because the words are possible English ones which the language does not happen to use—examples are ⋆/bʊd/ or ⋆/paɪt/; or (b) because the phoneme concerned is not allowed to (=does not in practice) occur in that position in a word—for instance, ⋆/ŋeɪ/ or ⋆/be/ are not possible

51

English words. We shall be mentioning below at greater length the idea that a language allows the speaker to combine its phonemes together only in specific ways.

Secondly, we should notice that the symbols themselves are chosen with their traditional values very much in mind. For example, the letter *t* is chosen to symbolize a phoneme which is usually realized as a voiceless alveolar stop, and phonemes with similar allophones in other (European) languages are very often written with the same *t*-letter. This practice has the advantage of reminding us, by our experience of ordinary writing in these languages, how the symbol should be realized; but it also has the disadvantage of inviting confusion between orthography and phonemic transcription—hence the importance of the slant lines enclosing phoneme-symbols.

Thirdly, we could reduce the total number of phonemes from 42 to 34 at a stroke, by treating the eight diphthongs as sequences of two vowels we have already catered for. E.g., /eɪ/ as in 'pate' would be the /e/ of 'pet' plus the /ɪ/ of 'pit'. This we shall not in fact do, for reasons discussed later, but it is an example of the ways in which other analyses of the same material might treat the phonemic contrasts differently. However, these relatively minor differences of approach to the phonology need not concern us here.

Fourthly, and perhaps most important, we should now make it clear that the variety of English we are describing is only one among many; many, indeed most, speakers of English would find that our list of phonemes did not correspond exactly to their own speech. For instance, a Scotsman would be unlikely to distinguish between /uː/ and /ʊ/ (e.g. between 'fool' and 'full'); nor would a speaker of 'general' American have a contrast between /ʌ/ and /ə/; and a Cockney would not have an /h/ at all.

Up to now we have been using the term 'English' in rather a loose fashion, and it would be as well if we were to explain the limitations to be placed upon it. The accent of English which we are (have been and will be) talking about is that known as RECEIVED PRONUNCIATION, or R.P. for short. It is the accent regarded (at least up to quite recently) as 'standard' in the United Kingdom, though the number of speakers who use it is relatively small. Other labels applied to it are 'Queen's English', 'the Oxford accent', 'correct', 'educated', 'upper-class', 'B.B.C.', 'high-falutin'', 'affected', 'high-class', and a large number of others, all equally misleading in that they do not identify or describe the accent, so much as approve of or condemn it, for reasons which are usually socio-cultural rather than linguistic. R.P. is the accent generally used in nationally or internationally broadcast news-bulletins by the B.B.C., and it is the norm in the 'straight' theatre—i.e. departures from it are normally motivated by the playwright or the director (one would not be altogether surprised to hear a Macbeth with a Scottish accent, but Lear will speak R.P.). Furthermore, it is spoken all over the United Kingdom, and to that extent is non-regional; it is not the local accent of Londoners, for instance, as is often assumed. The subject of R.P. is bedevilled with prejudice and mis-information, no less among the highly-educated than among those with very little formal education. Current attitudes to R.P. and to the other accents of the English are part of our 'culture', in the anthropologist's sense, and we will find it difficult if not impossible to react to these accents in a totally rational way; but this does not of course prevent us from recognizing our own linguistic prejudices as such, rather than attempting to rationalize and justify them. Be that as it may, for our purposes here the most important point to bear in mind is that the linguist's own view of English accents is largely irrelevant to the description of one of them, whether he speaks it or not. We may regard R.P., for instance, as a bastion of traditional moral and social values; or as the last iniquitous vestige of bourgeois class-consciousness; or (perhaps more sensibly) as the mark of a large social group, defined in other ways by the socio-economic status and the educational background of its members. In whatever way we look at it, we should not allow such non-linguistic judgments to intrude on our description of linguistic features. We may strongly disapprove, for instance, of the habit which R.P. speakers (among many others) have of 'dropping the *r*' before consonants, e.g. of pronouncing 'hard' as /hɑːd/ rather than /hɑːrd/, but our feelings on the matter are or should be entirely divorced from our descriptive statement, that 'in R.P., /r/ does not occur before consonants'.

The choice of R.P. to represent 'the sounds of English' in this chapter is dictated by a variety of factors; its wide intelligibility among speakers from other parts of the English-speaking world, and the thoroughness of the descriptions of it available in print, are two of the principal ones. 'English' as applied to a form of pronunciation, therefore, means here 'a type of accent coming under the general heading of R.P.', unless otherwise stated.

We now have before us, then, a list of the 42 English phonemes, consisting of 20 vowels and 22 consonants. We have referred to them as abstract 'phonological units'; from the point of view of describing the articulatory, physical facts of utterances, we talk about each phoneme being 'realized' by a sound—the 'allophone'. We must now take account of the fact that recognizably *different* sounds represent the *same* phoneme, depending on the context in which it occurs. That is, a given phoneme (say the English /t/) will have *more than one* allophone: /t/ is realized as a *dental* stop (tongue-tip against the upper teeth rather than against the tooth-ridge) before /θ/ or /ð/, the dental fricatives, as in 'eighth' or 'write this'; before a vowel in a stressed syllable, it will be

ASPIRATED (i.e. the explosion will be followed by a breathy release of air, often involving audible friction, before the vocal cords start vibrating for the vowel-sound)—compare the aspirated sound in 'tore' with the unaspirated /d/-allophone in 'door'; before a pause, it will very often be UNEXPLODED (i.e. the oral air-pressure is not released, as else-where, by pulling the tongue sharply back from the tooth-ridge, but reduced to normal by drawing air back down into the lungs), as in 'There's a cat'; and so on. The phonetic detail need not detain us for the moment; the important point is that the /t/-phoneme is realized by several quite different sounds, depending on its position. One some-times hears it said that 'there are 42 sounds in English'; but statements like this seem to confuse phonemes with allophones, to ignore what we have seen as a crucial distinction between the level of phonetics and that of phonology.

Sometimes the rules for the selection of an allophone in a given context appear rather arbitrary—why aspirate the /t/-allophone before a stressed vowel, after all?—and the answer to the question 'why?', as so often in language-analysis, is simply 'because the language is like that' or 'because that is what speakers of the language say'. Sometimes the rules appear to result from a pressure towards economy of articu-latory movements, as when /t/ is a dental stop before a dental fricative. And sometimes, as in the case of the unexploded final stop before a pause, it is not clear whether its occurrence in that position is governed by arbitrary linguistic pressures, by phonetic economy, or by both.

To take a few further examples of allophonic variation: /r/ in a word like 'try' has a voiceless allophone, but in 'dry' a voiced one; the sound representing /iː/ in 'sea' is slightly shorter (all things being equal) than that in 'seed', but slightly longer than that in 'seat'; the /l/ at the begin-ning of 'lull' sounds different from that at the end; and so on. Thus, in a phonological description of English, we have not only an inventory of phonemes, but also a list of allophones for each, with an accompany-ing statement of the contexts in which the different sounds occur. And we have not yet finished, for there is still another facet of how the phonemic side of a language works.

This next stage concerns the question of which sequences, or combina-tions, of phonemes are permitted, and which are not: in what ways can we combine the phonemes to make up English words and syllables? As we saw earlier, for instance, /ŋ/ cannot occur at the beginning of a word, and neither can /ʒ/, whereas /h, j, w/ cannot occur at the end. The group /str/ is allowed at the beginning, but not /stl/ or /ʃtr/. We can end a word with a vowel, provided it is one of /iː, ɑː, ɔː, ɜː, uː/ or the diphthongs; but none of those vowels occurs before /ŋ/. /r/, as we have mentioned, is found only before vowels; and so on. Prohibitions of this kind are known as PHONOTACTIC RULES; they are 'rules', of course, only in the sense that they reflect what invariably happens in the language, or what never does. These were the considerations which led us earlier to claim that */bʊd/ and */peɪt/ were 'possible English words', which the language did not happen to make use of; i.e. they are permitted by the phonotactic rules. On the other hand, */ŋeɪ/ and */be/ are not so permitted, and are therefore not 'unused' so much as *impossible* words for the English speaker. Nôn-occurring words of the first type need a moment's reflection (and often a look in a dictionary) before they are ruled out; words of the second type sound un-English to a degree, and are frequently quite difficult for us to pronounce. Commercial concerns (or their advertising agencies) very often make use of the first type of word to provide a name for a new product; but they would usually avoid un-English phoneme-combinations. We would be likely to believe an English-speaking engineer who told us that 'pite' (/paɪt/) was the technical name for a special component of a jet-engine; but we would be more sceptical about a /ŋeɪ/.

If we now go on to examine further the phonotactic rules of English, we ought to find that, as predicted earlier, the notions of 'vowel' and 'consonant' become clearer. The rules will produce a vast number of possible English words, and we will notice that the possibilities in one position in one type of word will tend to resemble those in another position elsewhere. For instance, if we look at what phonemes can occur between /b/ and /t/ in monosyllables, or between /sw/ and /m/, or after /fl/ and before a pause, we will find only phonemes drawn from our list of vowels. If we ask what can replace the /b/, the /t/, etc., the answer will be a consonant. In other words, we divide the phonemes into these two groups because broadly speaking they seem to 'pattern' in either one way or the other. Further support for this is provided by a case we have already mentioned—the non-use of /r/ before consonants; that is, the statement of where /r/ occurs corroborates our finding that vowels and consonants pattern differently. Going outside the phonotactic rules, we may notice that before vowels the definite article 'the' is pronounced /ðiː/ and the indefinite article /ən/; before consonants, on the other hand, the former is /ðə/ and the latter /ə/. In short, the language seems to force us to recognize these two large groups of phonemes.[2]

We can now see that our vowel/consonant division on the phonetic level, the apparent arbitrariness of which we noted at the time, is one which derives in fact from the phonological level. We divided the articulation-types into two groups, using the convenient criterion of 'stricture', because we knew in advance that this would more or less reflect the distinction we would be forced to make in the phonology. We would then have been able to claim that consonant-phonemes have consonantal allophones, and vowel-phonemes vowel-allophones. We

PLACE OF ARTICULATION

MANNER OF ARTICULATION	Bi-Labial	Labio-Dental	Dental	Alv-eolar	Post Alv.	Palatal	Velar	– –
STOP	p,b			t,d			k,g	
NASAL	m		n				ŋ	
LATERAL			l					
FRICATIVE		f,v	θ,ð	s,z	ʃ,ʒ	(ç)		h
FRICTIONLESS CONTINUANT					r			
SEMI-VOWEL	w					j		

Fig. 4. Chart of English Consonants.

Each of the above symbols represents a sound which commonly, but by no means always, realizes one of the English consonant phonemes. Where there are two symbols in a box, the first represents a voiceless sound, the second a voiced. The symbol (ç) stands for one realization of the intial cluster /hj/—see page 60. The 'semi-vowels' /j/ and /w/ are included here by virtue of their occasional consonant-sound allophones—see below. The allophones of /w/ are always accompanied by lip-rounding; those ôf /ʃ, ʒ/ and /r/ often so.

---

can see that this apparent symmetry is in fact an artifice, and rather a misleading one at that, since it obscures the important difference between (a) sounds and (b) the way they function.

This is also perhaps the place to tie up another loose end. On page 45, mention was briefly made of the 'semi-vowels' /j/ and /w/. We can now explain the term more fully by noting that these two phonemes, belonging structurally to the *consonant*-group, have some *vowel-sound* allophones. That is, the two levels do not 'match' at this point, hence the use (now traditional) of the catch-all term 'semi-vowel'.

Thus the terms 'vowel' and 'consonant', in most discussions of English pronunciation, are used in two very different ways. Up to now we have not consistently observed the distinction, but from now on we will use VOWEL-SOUND and CONSONANT-SOUND for the phonetic articulation-types, reserving VOWEL and CONSONANT for the structural categories into which phonemes seem to fit in English. The first phoneme in 'yet' or 'wet', therefore, will be a consonant realized by a vowel-sound allophone; and we can thus dispense with the vague 'semi-vowel' label.

We may now at last feel that we have equipped ourselves with enough theoretical and terminological apparatus to handle a partial, outline description of the 'sounds of English'. Unfortunately there appears to have been little alternative to such a long preamble, for phonetics and phonology comprise a highly technical subject. Attempts to understand something of the workings of a sound-system, enormously complex as it will inevitably turn out to be, involve us in technicalities which we cannot very well do without.

Let us look first, then, at the consonant-phonemes of R.P., at where and how they are realized in the current of speech. The consonants are often divided into two large groups, the 'voiced' and the 'voiceless', and as we have found with other terminology, these two labels occur in descriptions of both the phonetics and the phonology of English. We have seen earlier what they mean in articulatory terms—vocal cords vibrating, or held open; but they have also been commonly used to identify the two classes of consonant-*phonemes*. That is, we risk once again a confusion of the phonetic with the phonological. We should perhaps ask ourselves what exactly are the main criteria on which we would divide the consonants into these two large groups: for instance, when one phoneme from the group /p, t, k, f, θ, s, ʃ, h/ occurs at the end of a word, then the vowel preceding it is relatively *short*; but when that final consonant is other than one of these—i.e. drawn from the group /b, d, g, v, ð, z, ʒ, m, n, ŋ, l, r, j, w/—then the vowel is relatively *long* (particularly in stressed syllables); all this provided the vowel concerned is one of the group /iː, aː, ɔː, ɜː, uː/ or one of the eight diphthongs. Compare 'moot'-'mood', 'leak'-'league', 'mouth'-'mouthe', 'race'-'raze', etc. (see page 62 for a further look at this pattern). So in the way in which they seem to affect the choice of allophone in the preceding vowel, these two groups of consonants indeed appear to differ one from the other. (Note that we have included /h, j, w/ in the pattern, although as we have said earlier they do not occur at the ends of words; for other reasons [see below] we will wish to include them here.)

A second criterion for this grouping of the consonants is that all the phonemes in the first group are invariably realized by *voiceless* allophones; while those in the second group are in some contexts (e.g. between vowels) realized by *voiced* sounds, and in others (e.g. immediately before or after a pause) by sounds which are partially or wholly *voiceless*. And a third criterion is that allophones of the first group are very often, all things being equal, articulated with greater energy, more breath-force, than their counterparts from the second group.

From this we see that though there certainly is evidence for dividing the consonants in this way, the division does not always 'match' the phonetic division of the allophones into voiced and voiceless articulation types.

Let us now look at another pattern, or set of patterns, within the consonants, this time a less general one—the group of six 'stop-consonants' (so-called, though really of course it is their allophones which are stops, not the phonemic units themselves). These six are /p, t, k, b, d, g/, and they form a sub-group within the consonants, not only because their allophones share a common phonetic feature of stop-articulation, but also and perhaps more important, because they function in similar places in structure. Where one of them can occur, the others are at least likely to be permitted also. Consider the following formula (really an extract from our phonotactic rules): (/s/+) stop-consonant (+/r, l, j, w/). This is a quick way of writing down what appears to be a major pattern among those groups (or CLUSTERS), of either two or three consonants, which can begin English words. The pattern will produce two-consonant clusters of /s/ + stop-consonant, as in 'spy', 'sty', 'sky'; or of stop-consonant + /r, l, j, w/ as in 'cry', 'play', 'dune', 'twice'; or it will produce three-consonant clusters like those in 'spray', 'street', 'scream'. There are other initial two-consonant clusters, such as /sm, sn, θr, fj, tʃ/ etc., but none of these may be preceded by /s/ or followed by /r, l, j, w/ to form three-consonant clusters. There are gaps and restrictions[3] in the pattern, though one notices that these irregularities themselves seem to show a degree of 'sub-patterning', e.g. the non-occurrence of /pw, bw, dw, gw/ or of /tl, dl/; or the fact that if /j/ is the last of the consonants in the cluster, then only /uː/, or sometimes /ʊə/ or /ʊ/, can follow.

We might note several other sub-patterns which have emerged from the discussion above. For instance, /p, t, k/ versus /b, d, g/; /p, b/ versus /t, d/ versus /k, g/; /r, l, j, w/ 'go together' in much the same way as the stop-consonants went together.

The above brief look at one small area of the phonemic structure of English has already served to illustrate the complexity we referred to earlier, a characteristic we must expect to find, indeed, whenever we look closely at any aspect of a language. At all events, it seems indisputable that there is more than a simply phonetic, articulatory connection between these six stop-consonants; and further consideration of other patterns into which they enter (e.g. clusters at the ends of words) would certainly tend to support the contention.

If we now go on to look at the phonetics—i.e. at the allophones—of some of the oppositions derived from our pattern-formula, then we may find sub-systems operating here, too. For instance, in the pairs /pl-bl/ as in 'plead'-'bleed', /tr-dr/ as in 'try'-'dry', /kl-gl/ as in 'clue'-'glue', or /tj-dj/ as in 'tune'-'dune', in these oppositions the allophones of /r, l, j, w/ are *voiceless* after /p, t, k/, but *voiced* after /b, d, g/. So we can say that part of the opposition at least is carried by the allophone of the neighbouring phoneme, rather than only by the allophone of the phoneme we have changed; and experiments have shown, for instance, that the perception of the voiceless allophone of the *second* phoneme is crucial for the identification of the first. Thus in /pliːd-bliːd/, we seem to 'hear' one word rather than the other more on the basis of the /l/ than on that of the /p/ or /b/.

If we accept this, then we can no longer view an English word as, on the phonological level, simply a row of phonemes in a permitted order, each with its allophone on the phonetic level; for we are obliged to recognize that the relationship between the phoneme-sequence and the corresponding sound-sequence may be, from the perception point of view, much more subtle than simply a case of phoneme no. 3 being represented and identified by allophone no. 3c, and so on. So we must be prepared to complicate our phoneme-idea, in practice, still further (another case where we need to do this is mentioned on page 63).

Let us now continue our examples with a less general one—the phoneme /h/. This is rather different as regards the phonetics of its allophones, as we saw, from the other consonants, since there is not normally a stricture. Secondly, whereas the other fricatives seem to be 'paired'—/f-v, θ-ð, s-z, ʃ-ʒ/—/h/ is not. Thirdly, it can occur only before a vowel (though note that /ʒ/ is also restricted, this time by non-occurrence at the beginning of a wᴜrd). Fourthly, there is the question of the initial clusters /hj, hw/, and we will now go on to examine these two briefly.

The first of them, /hj/, patterns like the other clusters which end in /j/ in that it too must be followed by /uː/ (as in 'Hugh', 'huge', 'humour', etc.). But in many people's speech, what we actually hear for the cluster is a single sound, similar to the so-called 'ich-Laut' in (some) German (e.g. in 'mich', 'dich', 'sich', etc.); this is the voiceless palatal fricative. Thus we have a situation in which *two* phonemes are realized by *one* sound; so again we must allow a further complication into our picture of the relationship between phonemes and sound-sequence. (We could conceivably claim, in fact, that English has another phoneme —let us write it '/ç/'—which is realized by this voiceless palatal fricative. This would allow us to retain the one-to-one relationship of phoneme and sound, but we would have to set up another phoneme for the sake of a very few words, all with /uː/. It seems preferable by comparison to treat it as /hj/, because the cluster fits relatively neatly into the pattern of consonant + /j/ + /uː/ that we have already discerned. Furthermore, some speakers do consistently say /hj/ as a sequence of two sounds—the first sound of 'who' plus the first of 'you', more or less; other speakers, more significantly, sometimes say it as one sound, sometimes as two— for these people, therefore, we could not allow a phonemic opposition between '/ç/' and /hj/).

The second cluster we are considering, /hw/, is similar to the first, in that there is often a single sound—this time a voiceless fricative, made with the rounded lips as the point of stricture, and also with tongue-raising at the back—functioning as the allophone simultaneously of the two phonemes. However, only a very restricted number of R.P. speakers use /hw/ consistently; most do not have it in their phonotactic rules, except occasionally in very studied or carefully 'correct' speech. Where it does occur in R.P., we would probably want to regard it as a 'spelling-pronunciation'—i.e. a pronunciation which supposedly follows the orthography rather than the other way round. Compare 'whales' with 'Wales', 'which' with 'witch', 'whiled' with 'wild', etc. The reduction of /hw/ to /w/, incidentally, does not appear to be a modern tendency—an example of the 'lazy', 'corrupt' speech of to-day—but to have a long pedigree in the history of the language. Note also that speakers of e.g. Irish and Scottish English do consistently maintain the

/hw-w/ difference reflected in the 'wh-w' spellings, and this is one of the ways in which those accents are definably different from most forms of R.P.

Let us now turn to the /r/, noticing first that in many other accents of English—e.g. 'West Country', Scottish, Irish and most forms of American—the occurrence of (their) /r/ is much less restricted than /r/ is in R.P. In these accents, /r/ occurs before both pauses and consonants, as well as before vowels, whereas R.P. (as we have seen) permits it only when a vowel follows immediately. The device which many English pop-singers adopt, of using an American type of r-sound in all these positions, succeeds in giving their pronunciation a characteristically 'mid-Atlantic' flavour—envied and copied by some, deplored as almost unpatriotic by others.

In R.P., we cannot say that /r/ 'does not occur at the end of a word', as we can in the case of /h/, for if a word (e.g. when said on its own) ends in one of the vowels /ə, ɜː, ɪə, ɛə, ʊə, ɔː, ɑː/, then we find a /r/ added when another word beginning in a vowel follows immediately. For example, the words 'porter', 'fur', 'beer', 'care', 'tour', 'core', 'star' are pronounced /pɔːtər, fɜːr/ etc. in phrases like 'the porter isn't here', 'fur on the back', 'beer all the time', 'care about it', 'tour England', 'core an apple', 'Star and Garter'. Notice that in these examples there is an r-letter in the spelling; but in addition there are a fair number of words which end with one of these vowels, but do *not* have an r-letter to represent the /r/-phoneme; e.g. 'China' /tʃaɪnə/ (and many other names of countries), 'idea' /aɪdɪə/, 'Shah' /ʃaː/, 'draw' /drɔː/, etc. It should not surprise us that there are commonly-heard pronunciations like 'China-r and America', 'the very idea-r of it', 'Shah-r of Persia' 'draw-r a picture', and so on. These are often condemned by purists as containing an 'intrusive r', which the word 'does not really have'. Apart from the confusion here about the nature of written letters (which are after all a representation of the spoken form, not the other way about), we should remember that the vast majority of R.P. speakers use this 'linking r' both when the spelling includes the letter and when it does not—a fact publicly deplored in many a 'letter to the Editor', but nonetheless probably widespread in the speech of the writers of such letters. There is clearly a rule in R.P. (a phonological rule, of course, not a spelling one) of the kind formulated at the beginning of this paragraph. Young children learning R.P., along with the rest of the language, do not of course have the process complicated by the orthography, and their speech consistently reflects the rule in words new to them, e.g. proper names like 'Anna' ('Anna-r isn't coming'), 'Shaw' ('Johnny Shaw-r and his brother'), and so on. However, children later learn that some of these forms are disapproved of by the adult world, in particular by parents and school-teachers; they earn furthermore that some instances of 'intrusive *r*' are regarded as more objectionable than others—e.g. in our examples above, 'China-r and America' is much more often to be heard than 'draw-r a picture' among those who are careful that their pronunciation in public should sound 'correct'.

The result of all this is that many speakers of R.P. are inconsistent in their use of this /r/-feature; and the work of describing their usage is made more difficult by the operation of this type of non-linguistic factor.

We have seen something of the descriptive problems that arise in attempting statements about various parts of the English consonant-system. We shall now go on to consider some examples from the vowels, and perhaps we should bear in mind that there is some disagreement among linguists here (more at any rate than with the consonants). It is not so much a disagreement on the facts, of course, as on the analytical framework which should be used to describe them. A digression on the merits and salient features of various descriptions would be out of place in this context, and we shall therefore not attempt to argue the case for the schema adopted in the following paragraphs. However, it should be recognized that there is no one 'correct' way of handling the data.

The broadest division we can draw in the vowel-system is between 'long' and 'short' vowel-phonemes, that is between /iː, ɑː, ɔː, uː, ɜː, eɪ, aɪ, ɔɪ, ɑʊ, əʊ, ɪə, ɛə, ʊə/ on the one hand, and /i, e, æ, ʌ, ɒ, ʊ, ə/ on the other (see list on p. 51). This division is made on the basis, once again, of both the phonetics and the phonology. To take the latter first, we have already seen that the 'long' vowels occur at the ends of words— 'do', 'die', 'dare', for example—whereas the 'short' vowels normally do not (with the exception of /ə/, which is a special case in other ways, too). We have also seen that only the 'short' vowels can occur before /ŋ/; here the exception is /ʊ/ (which is again exceptional in that it cannot begin a word). Secondly, as regards the phonetics (i.e. the *allophones*) of the vowels, the main descriptive point to be made is that the 'long' vowels are pronounced relatively *long* in syllables (particularly accented syllables) which have a 'voiced' consonant at the end; and relatively *short* in those with a 'voiceless' consonant at the end—compare 'feed' with 'feet', 'maze' with 'mace', for instance. Length-variation is much less marked among the allophones of a 'short' vowel, for the nature of the following consonant does not appear to affect it to any very noticeable extent—compare 'bid'-'bit', 'as'-'ass', where the vowel-sounds may well be of equal length. (The list of 'key-words' on page 51 gives further examples.) Earlier, we used vowel-length as one of the criteria for separating out 'voiced' and 'voiceless' consonant-phonemes; and, conversely, we have now used this division of the consonants to help us separate out 'long' and 'short' vowel-phonemes. The systems thus interlock and, in part, define each other.

We are again faced with a terminological difficulty here, in that we are using a pair of adjectives on two levels: (a) the phonological, where 'long' and 'short' refer to different classes of vowel-phonemes; and (b) the phonetic, where allophones are long or short in the everyday sense of 'relative time'. English has no other suitable pair of adjectives, and we have therefore had to make do with the typographical device of enclosing the words in inverted commas where they refer to the phonology. Thus the 'long' vowels have both long and short allophones, the 'short' vowels only short; again the two levels do not 'match'. Similarly, 'voiced' and 'voiceless' consonant-phonemes, as we saw earlier, do not always fit with the phonetic classes of voiced and voiceless sounds; nor indeed did vowels and consonants fit with vowel-sounds and consonant-sounds, though there at least we could use two sets of terms.

Looking again at the length-differences in the vowel-sounds, we can see another case in which a change from one phoneme to another is perceived mainly through the allophone of the neighbouring phoneme. In minimal pairs like 'leaf'—'leave' (/li:f-li:v/), where the vowel-sound may be twice as long in the second word as in the first, this length-difference seems to be very important to the perception of the /f/, rather than the /v/; and thus the difference between the two words may well be carried rather by the length of the /i:/-allophone than by the /f/- or /v/-allophone. Again, therefore, our theory of phonemes will need to take account of the (frequent) cases of this kind.

The 'long' vowels divide up further, as we have already indicated, into two sub-groups: the SIMPLE vowels /i:, ɑ:, ɔ:, u:, ɜ:/, and the COMPOUND vowels /eɪ, aɪ, ɔɪ, aʊ, əʊ, ɪə, ɛə, ʊə/. By using these two new terms, we can reserve 'diphthong' for vowel-sounds which have an audible glide from one tongue-position (and/or lip-position) to another, and 'pure' for those vowel-sounds where the articulation is relatively stable. There is a tendency among some R.P. speakers, particularly perhaps those with a London background, to diphthongize /i:/- and /u:/-allophones (especially those used at the ends of words, e.g. 'tea', 'two'). These diphthongs are very short, gliding from a centralized Cardinal Vowel no. 1 (in the case of /i:/) or no. 8 (in that of /u:/) to a less centralized position—i.e. towards the Cardinal point (see Fig. 4 on page 49). These variants can be described as *diphthongs* which are allophones of *simple* vowels. Conversely, we also find pure vowel-sounds realizing the compound vowel-phonemes (again in some people's speech only): e.g. /ɪə, ʊə/ ɛə, as in 'bearded', 'cure anything' (with 'linking *r*'), 'daring', etc.; in these cases we often hear a *pure* vowel-sound realizing a *compound* vowel-phoneme.

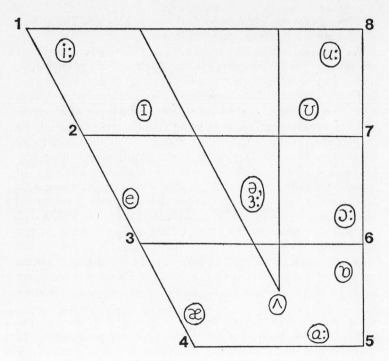

Fig. 5. Cardinal Vowel Diagram, with English Vowels ('short' and 'long' simple only). Each of the circles on the diagram represents the articulation of a typical allophone of the phoneme symbolized. The allophones of /ɔː/ and /uː/ are almost always accompanied by lip-rounding; those of /ɒ/ and /ʊ/ usually by only slight rounding, and sometimes by none at all. (A similar diagram for the 'long' compound vowel-phonemes will be found on page 65, Fig. 6).

The compound vowels can be sub-divided into three kinds (see Fig. 6 on p. 65): those gliding towards an /ɪ/-type (/eɪ, aɪ, ɔɪ/), towards an /ʊ/-type (/aʊ, əʊ/), and towards an /ə/-type (/ɪə, ɛə, ʊə/). The last kind, along with /aː, ɔː, ɜː/ of the simple 'long' vowels, are of course subject to the rule concerning 'linking r' which was mentioned above.

Another pattern which has sometimes been discerned in the English vowels is the pairing of 'long' and 'short' phonemes, so that /iː/ goes with /ɪ/, /ɑː/ with /æ/, /ɔː/ with /ɒ/, /uː/ with /ʊ/ and /ɜː/ with /ə/ (the other two 'short' vowels, /e/ and /æ/, are left without a 'partner'). The reasons for doing this are partly phonetic resemblances—e.g. the articulatory differences between /iː/ and /ɪ/ are similar to those between /uː/ and /ʊ/ (see Fig. 5 on this page). Partly they involve the different

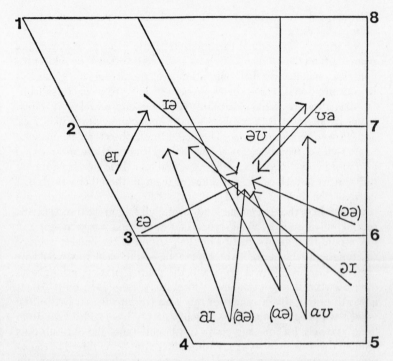

Fig. 6. Cardinal Vowel Diagram, with English vowels ('long' compound only). Each arrow represents the 'gliding' articulation of a typical allophone of the phoneme symbolized. The allophones of /ɔɪ/ and /ʊə/ (and /ɔə/) usually have slight lip-rounding at the start, those of /aʊ/ and /əʊ/ towards the end of the glide.

phonemic forms a work may take when unstressed—e.g. 'sir' when stressed is /sɜː/ but its 'weak' form is usually /sə/; stressed 'been' /biːn/ may similarly become unstressed /bɪn/; etc. And partly the reasons are MORPHOPHONEMIC—i.e. concerned with those phoneme-differences which are correlatable with grammatical (or specifically 'morphological') changes: for instance, to produce the negative form of 'can' /kæn/ and 'shall' /ʃæl/, one of the phoneme-changes in R.P. is that from /æ/ to /ɑː/—thus 'can't' /kɑːnt/ and 'shan't' /ʃɑːnt/. In spite of all this, we might hesitate before going on to say that for instance /iː/ and /ɪ/ belonged to the same phonological unit—the same 'super-phoneme'—since the link between them is by no means *consistently* evident. There are relatively few examples in English (though probably they occur with some frequency) of these linked forms, whether the link is a matter of accentuation or of morphological change. However, there certainly are patterns to be discerned of this type, even if they are only partial ones.

We have so far ignored the question of the relation of vowel and consonant, on the one hand, with *syllables* on the other. The subject is a complex one, and we shall only note here, and accept, the generally-held assumption that each vowel-phoneme belongs to a separate syllable, i.e. that a monosyllabic word will only have one vowel in it. Now, many if not most R.P. speakers usually pronounce words like 'flier' and 'flower' as *monosyllables*. They could not, therefore, be analysed as two-vowel sequences, /aɪ-ə/ and /aʊ-ə/; it appears we must set up two more vowel-phonemes where we find that these two are not only different from each other, but different from all the other vowels. Let us transcribe them as /aə/ and /ɑə/, since their allophones would begin roughly where those of /aɪ/ and /aʊ/ begin, gliding in the direction of a central vowel-sound—an /ə/-type. The opposition between /aə/ and /ɑə/ would therefore be carried by the position of the highest point of the tongue at the start of the diphthong—with /aə/, this would be between Cardinal Vowel no. 4 and the central open position; with /ɑə/, between that position and Vowel no. 5, (see Fig. 6 on p. 65). It is worth noting that a system of this kind fits into the analysis of the vowels we proposed above—we would simply have added two more 'long' vowels (of the sub-class 'compound' and the sub-sub-class 'gliding towards an /ə/-type'), without therefore being forced to elaborate new categories; in a sense, these two new phonemes would fill 'gaps' in the system we have already outlined.

Two-syllable pronunciations of /aɪ-ə/ and /aʊ-ə/ do exist, but they are characteristic of a very careful, deliberate style which is recognized as a departure from that of ordinary conversation. Usage also varies here, in that not all speakers will reduce the two syllables to one in the same situations; and the grammar may be a factor in which words a speaker reduces first—'higher' is perhaps less likely to be reduced to a monosyllable (/haə/) than is 'hire', because it has two grammatical 'bits'—'high' and the comparative suffix '-er'. However, there are certainly many people who distinguish reduced /ai-ə/ from reduced /aʊ-ə/, and both of these from /ɑː/; these speakers have sets of three (minimally different) monosyllabic words, such as the triplet 'tire', 'tower' and 'tar'. Other speakers use a different pattern: they have another 'long' simple vowel—we could write it as /aː/ for /aɪ-ə/ words like 'flier' and 'tire', and use /ɑː/ for /aʊ-ə/ words like 'flower' and 'tower' (thus no longer distinguishing between e.g. 'tower' and 'tar', 'cowered' and 'card', etc.). Others again use /ɑː/ for all these words, and 'tire', 'tower' and 'tar' become homophones. The language appears to be particularly fluid in this area; and there are other cases too where a reduction in the number of syllables, in ordinary, rapid, colloquial speech, produces forms which it is difficult to fit into a 'static' descriptive framework.

The syllable-reduced forms we have been discussing are also examples of another descriptive problem: how to account for changes taking place at the moment in the system being described. We saw in Chapter 1 of this book that the linguist is usually concerned with 'synchronic' description—that is, with the language as it is (or was) at one point in time. However, the truism that 'spoken languages are permanently in a state of change' applies to the sound-system as much as to the grammar or the vocabulary. In most of our discussion so far, we have assumed relative stability in the systems we have chosen to exemplify but this cannot always be done, as we saw with the /aɪ-ə/ and /aʊ-ə/ reductions. Before leaving the subject of the vowel-phonemes, we shall look at two further cases where the phonology seems to be changing.

First, the vowel /æ/. This has a *long* allophone (most often heard in monosyllables with /b, d, g, ʒ, m, n/ at the end), whereas the regular 'short' vowel pattern is for very little length variation to take place; examples are 'cab', 'stand', 'rag', 'badge', 'Sam', 'pan'. The allophones of other 'short' vowels differ very little in this respect—the similarity in the length of the vowel-sounds in 'pot'-'pod' or 'sit'-'Sid' contrasts with the short-long difference in those of 'sat'-'sad' or 'pat'-'pad'. One speaker's habits may differ from another's, and differ again from one situation to the next, so that any single comprehensive statement about the pattern of long and short /æ/-allophones in R.P. would almost certainly be over-generalized. The most we can say here is that there clearly exists a tendency to lengthen the vowel-sound of /æ/ before some 'voiced' consonants, particularly in monosyllables. (One explanation that has been proposed for this contemporary tendency is that since the distinction between /æ/ and /e/ (in e.g. 'sad' and 'said'), is carried simply by a small difference in tongue-height, it is being 'reinforced' by the addition of a further phonetic feature—length, already used elsewhere in the vowel-system and thus 'ready to hand' as it were.)

Another change taking place within present-day R.P. is the loss of the compound vowel /ɔə/. This phoneme has not been included in our earlier discussion because its disappearance seems already well under way: most speakers of R.P. (particularly younger people) probably do not use it at all, at least in ordinary colloquial speech. Words hitherto pronounced with /ɔə/ now have /ɔː/; thus the distinction between e.g. 'pour' and 'paw' (/ɔə/ and /ɔː/), 'bored' and 'board', 'lore' and 'law', etc. has been lost, and these are now pairs of homophones. There is a related tendency, though perhaps less far advanced as yet, for /ʊə/ also to be replaced by /ɔː/. Thus many speakers of R.P. nowadays say e.g. 'sure' and 'poor' as /ʃɔː/ and /pɔː/ (i.e. the same as 'Shaw' and 'paw'), though the number who have no /ʊə/ left at all is probably still quite small—pronunciations of e.g. 'cure' and 'tour' as /kjɔː/ and /tɔː/ (rather than with /ʊə/) tend still to be regarded as 'affected'. We might feel less wary about making a firm statement here than in the cases of the syllable-reduced forms or of the long /æ/-allophone; in a fairly general variety of colloquial R.P., there is no /ɔə/ phoneme, and occurrences of /ʊə/ are relatively infrequent.

We shall now leave the subject of phonemics, and move on to a different but related area of English phonology. This is the area of so-called NON-SEGMENTAL features—i.e. features which extend over one *or more than one* phoneme, over phoneme-*structures* like syllables, words, and even longer stretches of the utterance.

The first of these features is STRESS. This is roughly defined here as relatively greater energy of articulation expended on a syllable (said to be STRESSED) as compared with other, less-energetically articulated syllables (said to be UNSTRESSED) in the immediate environment. This stressed syllable will be *heard* as louder and more sonorous. This is a rough and ready categorization of syllables (e.g. how much greater is 'greater', and how is it to be measured in ordinary speech-situations?); but we can sometimes supplement it, or help to confirm a decision as to whether a syllable is stressed or not, in at least two ways. First, we can examine the allophones of the phonemes in that syllable—e.g., if a 'long' vowel allophone is not as long as it might be in this phonemic context, or if the initial /p, t, k/-allophone is unaspirated, then the syllable is probably to be judged 'unstressed', since the features of (maximum) vowel-sound lengthening and of aspiration are particularly associated with stress. Secondly, in many cases we can also check on the choice of the phonemes themselves. A number of common words in English have more than one phonemic 'shape', a STRONG FORM and one or more WEAK FORMS: for instance, 'can' in 'You *can* tell' is the strong form /kæn/, but in '*You* can tell' it is weak—/kən/; 'does' is strong, /dʌz/, in '*Does* he like it?' but a weak /dəz/ in 'Does *he* like it?'; similarly 'will' is strong /wɪl/ or weak /(ə)l/, 'been' is /biːn/ or /bɪn/, 'an' is /æn/ or /(ə)n/, and so on. In most cases, the use of a strong form, where there is a choice, correlates with the syllable concerned being stressed.

However, it is comparatively rare to find stress being used on its own to carry a major contrast in meaning, without the help of other non-segmental features. When syllables make use of stress alone, its function is usually no more than to impart a rhythmic 'beat' to the utterance. Stress is significant much more often when working together with a second non-segmental feature, PITCH. Pitch is the name given to the auditory effect of changes in the rate at which the vocal cords vibrate. That is, during a *voiced* sound (for practical purposes the voiceless sounds do not have pitch at all) the vocal cords allow air through in short bursts between the closures, and this gives to the sound-wave a

FUNDAMENTAL FREQUENCY (to use the physical term), measured in cycles per second. We do not perceive a sound-wave as a series of vibrations with a certain frequency, however, but as a musical note—a pitch—which we perceive as (a) 'high' or 'low' relative to what we know, or expect, of the speaker's pitch-range; women and children will have 'higher voices' than men, and some individuals differ from the average within these groups, e.g. 'he's got a very deep voice, for a child'. We also perceive pitch relatively in another sense, as (b) 'higher than', 'lower than', or 'the same level as' neighbouring pitches.

The pitch of a syllable may be LEVEL; or it may glide up or down from one level to another (a RISE or a FALL), or quite often up and then down (a RISE-FALL), or the reverse (a FALL-RISE); and occasionally it may even go in three directions—up, then down, then up again, though this 'rise-fall-rise' seems to be sufficiently rare in English for us to disregard it here. An utterance may contain anything from one to many syllables, and each syllable will have either a level pitch or one of the above gliding pitches. These pitches are not of course random, but organized into a systematic sequence, *patterned*, and it is these patterns which are known in phonology as INTONATION.

The difference in intonation between (rising) '*Really*, Mr. Jones?'[4] and (falling) '*Really*, Mr. Jones!' is a matter of a choice which the language offers the speaker, a choice from among several permitted possibilities, each with a different meaning in the particular context. Such a contrast in meaning is brought out by a more specific example, such as the following: a wife's request for an opinion—'Do you like my new dress?'—might be answered by her husband with the monosyllabic 'Yes'. If he said this with a rise-fall, it would imply 'It's *very* nice'; if with a fall-rise, it would imply 'Yes . . ., but . . .'; and there would of course be a number of other possibilities. The wife's reaction to the first 'yes' will be considerably more favourable than to the second, yet the vocabulary, the grammar, the stress and of course the phonemes are the same in each case. In this example, pitch alone (working within the intonation-system) has distinguished sharply between two very different types of meaning; and the wife is quite justified in reacting with pleasure (or annoyance) to the response, for the husband has deliberately (if unconsciously) chosen an intonation-pattern from the range of possibilities which English allows him, to fit the meaning he wishes to convey.

Though the non-segmental features of stress and intonation can, as we have seen above, be considered separately, they seem to work very much together in English. Once we know what the intonation-pattern is, and how it is distributed over the syllables, then we can to a large extent predict which of them will be stressed. For instance, in the sentence 'But you said *John* did it!' the information that there is a fall in pitch on 'John' means automatically that that syllable is stressed; but the reverse is not true—knowing a syllable is stressed does not tell us anything about its pitch.

Now within an intonation-pattern, it will be noticed that changes—jumps or glides—in pitch occur, on at least one of the syllables. (If the utterance contains only one syllable, as in the husband's 'Yes' above, a pitch-change will necessarily occur on that syllable, since one such change is obligatory in every utterance.) It will also be noticed that such syllables are, obligatorily again, stressed. In our last example above, 'John' was of course the syllable treated in this way. This concentration of pitch-features and stress is called ACCENT; its function appears to be to 'emphasize' a particular word (or the only word) in the utterance, to make it stand out as important. To put it another way, a word is made PROMINENT by accenting one of its syllables, or prominence is *realized* by accent; and accent is a combination of phonetic features—(a) stress (with its associated vowel-sound length, aspiration, etc.), and (b) pitch. So not only can a speaker choose which intonation-pattern to use, but also which words he is going to make prominent; not only which pitches will make up the pattern, but how they will be distributed over the words and syllables.

However, there is one area where a choice cannot normally be made at all, namely the way multi-syllabic (or 'polysyllabic') words are made prominent. Each English polysyllable is made prominent by accenting *one* of its syllables, and there is no choice as to which one; the ACCENTUAL PATTERN of such words is fixed, and learnt along with their phonemic structure, grammatical status, lexical meaning, etc., when they are first assimilated into the learner's vocabulary. Thus '*ac*cident' is made prominent by accenting the first syllable, '*enor*mous' by accenting the second, 'abso*lute*ly' by accenting the third, 'responsi*bi*lity' by accenting the fourth, etc. Often, the morphological structure of the word will determine, or help to determine, its accentual pattern; e.g. 'responsibility' is like other words with that type of suffixation ('-ibility', '-ability') in being accented on the '-bil-'; and there are a large number of cases like this. However, most English speakers are familiar with the dilemma of knowing a word (in the sense of knowing its place in the grammar, its meaning, and its spelling), but of being uncertain how to pronounce it. This uncertainty is very often about where the accent should go in the word (hence the controversy over the pronunciation '*con*troversy' as opposed to 'con*tro*versy'); and as a result, the uncertainty is also about the phonemes—compare those of /ˈkɒntrəvɜːsi/ and /kənˈtrɒvəsi/ (the mark ' being used here before an accented syllable). Apart from marginal cases like this, our statement above that the accentual pattern of English polysyllables is 'fixed' holds good; dictionaries can indicate it, by various typographical devices, and teachers of the language can prescribe it, without much fear of contradiction. So if we say, for instance, 'That's his *signature*', we have chosen to use (apart from the grammar and the vocabulary) a certain intonation-pattern, and also to make 'signature' (rather than 'that's' or 'his') the (only) prominent word; but the placement of the accent on the first syllable of 'signature' is as it were done for us, in advance.

We can see from this that intonation in English, working together with stress, functions *meaningfully* in allowing the speaker to single out a particular word for emphasis; to prove the point with a minimal pair, contrast 'It's *his* book' (i.e. 'not *hers*') with 'It's his *book*' (i.e. 'not his *newspaper*'). But this is not the only way these non-segmental features can convey a difference of meaning. As we saw in our earlier husband-wife example, the two 'Yes' responses differed substantially in meaning, yet their accentual pattern was of course identical (since there was only one syllable concerned, it was automatically accented). So the change was the result not of siting the accent on a different word, but of changing the pitch which helped to make up that accent, i.e. of changing the intonation-pattern. This type of meaning is often called ATTITUDI-NAL, because it is concerned with the attitude of the speaker towards the overall situation in which he is speaking. This 'situation' will include the nature of what has preceded in the conversation (or the fact that this utterance is the first), what grammar and vocabulary is being used, what words are made prominent, and so on, together with non-linguistic factors like the personal relationships between the partici-pants in the conversation (whether as speakers or listeners), their age, sex, status, frame of mind, etc.; in addition, the utterance may be accompanied by effects like gesture and facial expression, which seem to function on the fringes of the linguistic system, without actually taking part in it. All these factors—linguistic, non-linguistic, and 'fringe'—may play a part in the choice, and interpretation, of the speaker's intonation, and hence in the meaning of the utterance.

We assume that a change of intonation in a given situation will change the attitudinal meaning; we also assume, of course, that the same utterance in two different situations will imply different attitudes. For instance a 'Good morning' may be interpreted between equals as merely friendly; the same greeting, with the same intonation, might very well seem over-familiar to a superior, or rather patronizing to a junior.

The conclusion we must come to is that here is an area of meaning that is almost impossible to cope with in its totality—there are too many variables, and too many of these are non-linguistic, and unamen-able to systematization and labelling. The best we can do, probably, is to show that a change in intonation-pattern is capable, all other variables remaining constant, of differentiating between one general type of meaning and another; but we shall not be able to state at all clearly either the nature of each type or the degree of difference between them. Furthermore, it is only in a specific situation, real or imagined, that we can show even this to be true; the notion that a certain intonation is associated with a certain range of meanings in English, without reference to the situation in which it occurs, seems a doubtful one. For instance, if it is claimed that 'a fall tends to sound definite' we can easily find a counter-example in which the meaning seems to incline rather to a wondering, or questioning, or puzzled kind of attitude. Similarly, it seems likely that *any* English intonation may occur with *any* grammatical structure, provided only that the situation and the speaker's attitude to it make that particular combination of syntax and intonation appropriate. There is after all an infinite range of situations and attitudes; and we should not rule out any combination at all until we find a sentence which it is *impossible* to imagine being said with a certain intonation-pattern.

We have seen that English intonation functions in two main ways: in emphasizing particular words in the utterance, and in conveying attitudinal meaning. We shall now move on to consider, briefly and in general, the nature of the intonation-patterns which carry out these functions; that is, how the patterns are made up of their component parts—syllables, each with its gliding or level pitch.

If we start with utterances consisting of a single monosyllable, as being the shortest and easiest to handle, we find of course that the word concerned—e.g. 'Yes', 'No', 'Now', 'Ten', 'Up', 'Thanks'—is prominent (by definition, since every utterance has at least one prominent word), and that its single syllable is therefore accented; and this means the syllable will display both stress and pitch-features. The gliding pitches we have mentioned are all allowed to occur here: fall, rise, rise-fall and fall-rise. There are probably sub-divisions to be made also, into e.g. a fall which starts about the middle of the pitch-range and falls to the bottom ('low' fall), as against another which starts towards the top and falls similarly to a low pitch ('high' fall), as against a third which starts high but only fails as far as a middle pitch ('mid' fall); thus:

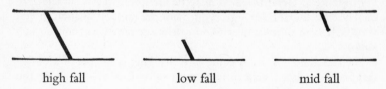

| high fall | low fall | mid fall |

If we could show that the potential meaning-difference between any two of these three is of the same order of importance as that between e.g. a fall and a rise, then we should have to increase our number of basic possibilities. Of course, the kind of judgment we will have to make is more or less subjective and arbitrary; there is no easy way of measuring this 'importance'. We may feel confident in claiming that a rise is sufficiently different from a fall, in their potential effect on the attitudinal meaning, for us to place these two unequivocally in separate phonological units (here, intonation-patterns); but there will always be cases where our intuition does not provide a clear answer—for instance, if two rises both start at the same pitch, but the first finishes slightly higher than the second, do these belong to *two* patterns, or varieties of the same one? and how much difference must there be between the finishing pitches to make a 'significant' opposition? This is markedly different from the minimal pairs we found in phonemics, where we were able to ignore gradations of meaning—'bet' and 'bat' were simply 'different words with different meanings'. If we wish to treat intonation also from this general point of view—in terms of 'phonological units' to which individual pitches or pitch-sequences 'belong', or which they 'realize', then we shall have to accept a substantial degree of arbitrary simplification. With this in mind, and for the sake of brevity, we shall assume here that 'Yes' and 'No', etc., generally occur with only four significantly different intonation-patterns: falling to a low pitch; rising from a low pitch; rising from a fairly low pitch, then falling back to low; and falling to low, then rising again. The following represent typical varieties:

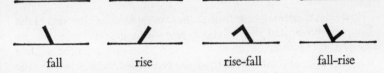

| fall | rise | rise-fall | fall-rise |

If we now increase the length of the utterance by adding unaccented syllables after the accented one, ('*Yes*, Mary', '*No*, thank you', etc.), we can show that the pitch of these is automatically dictated by the nature of the pattern chosen on the accented syllable. Thus in '*Yes*, Mary' the two (unaccented) syllables of 'Mary' will be low and level if there is a *fall* on 'Yes', or on ascending steps if there is a *rise* starting there. If the pattern is a rise-fall or a fall-rise, the two unaccented syllables as it were 'carry' the shape of the pitch movement up or down:

| fall | rise | rise-fall | fall-rise |

(The accented syllables are represented by the mark ○.) In utterances like these, the accented syllable is called the NUCLEAR SYLLABLE and any unaccented syllables following it comprise the TAIL. The nuclear syllable, together with any tail-syllables, comprise the NUCLEUS of the intonation-pattern. So 'Really, Mr. Jones!', one of our earlier examples, can now be seen as having an intonation-pattern consisting of a nucleus, which itself consists of a nuclear (accented) syllable ('Real-') followed by four (unaccented) syllables in the tail ('-ly Mister Jones'). Also, our monosyllabic examples like 'Yes' and 'No' can be seen as having patterns consisting of a nucleus with only a nuclear syllable, and no tail.

If we go on to look at still longer utterances, we shall find that for practical purposes they *all* have a nucleus at the end. That is, they (or rather their intonation-patterns) will finish with an accented syllable, with or without unaccented syllables following it, which behaves just like the examples above. So in 'Was he *really* allowed that?' the nucleus begins on the accented 'real-' and is continued by the tail syllables '-ly allowed that'; i.e. from 'really' onwards the pattern is just the same as in '*Really*, Mr. Jones?' If the accented syllable begins in the middle of a word, then the nucleus still starts there—English intonation seems to have very little respect for word-boundaries; thus in 'It's *enormous*' or 'That's *ridiculous*' the nuclear syllable is the second one in the prominent word. So an English intonation-pattern always ends in one of a limited number of sub-patterns—nucleus-types; we have assumed four such types here.

However, there may be syllables *before* the nucleus, as in several of the examples above; and one of these, or more than one, may also be accented. If the utterance does have more than one accented syllable (which implies of course more than one prominent word), then it is the *last* of these syllables which will begin the nucleus. For instance, in '*I* don't know *why* he's *coming*', where 'I', 'why' and 'com-' are all accented, 'com-' is the nuclear syllable (and '-ing' therefore the tail). Now in cases like this, an important point is that we can vary the type of nucleus (e.g. from rise to rise-fall) *without* altering what precedes it; and, vice-versa, this pre-nuclear sub-pattern, or HEAD, can be varied *without* altering the nucleus-type. Furthermore, a change from one type of head to another will bring a different attitudinal meaning, just as in the case of a change of nucleus-type.

All the ways in which various sequences of accented and unaccented syllables may be disposed on the pitch-scale, in each type of head, are too complex to be displayed here. The following are no more than examples of four common types; the only variable is the pitch of the head-syllables, yet each of these utterances would carry a different attitudinal meaning in the same situation:

74

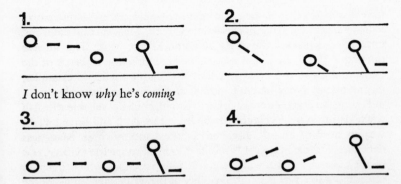

I don't know *why* he's *coming*

There remains a further sub-pattern to be discerned —the PRE-HEAD. This comprises any unaccented syllables before the first accented one. In 'It's a *terribly hard job*', for example, the head begins on the third syllable, and the first two—'It's a'—make up the pre-head; in 'That's *lovely*', the nucleus begins on the second syllable, and the first is the pre-head. It will be found that the pre-head too can vary independently (of both the head and the nucleus), and vary meaningfully. In the following two examples, only the pitch of 'It's a' differs, hence can be responsible for a change in attitudinal meaning:

1.

2.

It's a *terribly hard job*

So our intonation-pattern may consist of a nucleus alone, e.g. 'No-one'; or the nucleus may be preceded by a pre-head: 'There was *no*-one'; or by a head: '*Robert said* there was *no*-one'; or by both pre-head and head: 'But *Robert said* there was *no*-one'. Cases like these, and all the others discussed above, are comparatively simple ones—indeed, perhaps they give a misleading impression of a rather mechanical neatness; but there is no denying the subtlety and complexity of the way we use intonation and stress in English.

The choice of which words to make prominent, and of which into-nation-pattern to use, is of *crucial* importance in our everyday use of the language, yet we are seldom explicitly aware of the role these choices play in our conversations. We say, 'It's not what he said, it's the way he said it that annoyed me', but this type of remark is the nearest we usually come to referring directly to the intonation-system—we lack a vocabu-lary for describing it. Our writing and printing, too, are largely inadequate for representing the non-segmental features—the use of italics, a question-mark, an exclamation-mark, a sequence of full stops, underlining and so on are rarely sufficient. The examples we have been quoting in this discussion of intonation were of course chosen to make maximum use of these typographical devices, but even so they are not unambiguous. Novelists find they need other means, in addition, of indicating stress and intonation, e.g. 'He said, coldly', 'She remarked, in a wondering tone', 'His voice sounded oddly flat', and so on. Playwrights need to include directions to the actors, such as 'Mary (*enthusiastically*):' or 'Inspector (*sounding official and pompous*):'; indeed, one of the reasons for the wide range of interpretations which different actors bring to a part lies in the inability of the written medium—of the author's words—to specify intonation. Students of modern foreign languages need contact with native speakers of the language they are learning, since there is probably little to be found in textbooks on its intonation; and because the role of intonation is so little appreciated, the foreign learner of, say, English will not often be judged by English speakers as having a foreign accent, if he uses the wrong pattern, but rather as having the wrong attitude—a much more serious matter, in most situations. All in all, there seems little doubt that we tend to underestimate grossly the part played by non-segmental features in English; and in the linguistic description of those features and how they work, an enormous amount still remains to be said.

We have now come to the end of this discussion of the 'sounds of English'. It has necessarily been brief, but little attempt has been made to gloss over the difficulty and complexity of the task which faces the descriptive linguist, in this area of language as indeed in any other. It should be clear that, to deal with even the limited examples we have chosen from the phonetics and phonology of English, we need to use our tools—the technical terminology—as precisely as possible. The everyday vocabulary for describing the sound-systems of a language tend far too often, as we have seen above, to vagueness and ambiguity. To do the job of even partial description properly, there seems little alternative to a painstaking, sometimes laborious regard for technicalities; otherwise we risk doing less than justice to an involved but fascinating subject.

NOTES

1. The transcription used here is that devised by Professor A. C. Gimson and exemplified in his *Introduction to the Pronunciation of English*—see the bibliography at the end of this chapter.

2. Diachronic observations further support the division: in the history of English, there is no sound-change that involves both what we have called vowels and what we have called consonants.

3. There will be fewer of these if we allow borrowing from other languages such as 'Gwen' from Welsh; or non-R.P. forms like /tl, dl/ (instead of /kl, gl/) found in e.g. Ulster; or rare examples of a pattern, like 'gule' for /gj/, or 'dwarf', 'dwindle' for /dw/.

4. From now on, the *prominent word(s)* in examples like these will be *italicized*.

BIBLIOGRAPHY

The most comprehensive and up-to-date description of the phonetics and phonology of English (R.P.) is that by A. C. Gimson, *An Introduction to the Pronunciation of English* (London, 1962). An earlier work, standard for many years all over the world, is D. Jones, *An Outline of English Phonetics* (Cambridge, 9th ed. 1960); Jones' approach to the phonological side of the language is perhaps less satisfactory than more modern studies, and the sections on intonation and stress are open to basic objections; but the book as a whole is full of acute phonetic observation, and is still very useful. Another work by Jones, *The Pronunciation of English* (Cambridge, 4th ed. 1956), and one by I. C. Ward, *The Phonetics of English* (Cambridge, 4th ed. 1948) are shorter, but aimed more specifically at native speakers of English.

The most useful introductory treatment of English intonation appears in the first section of a handbook for advanced learners of the language—J. D. O'Connor and G. F. Arnold, *The Intonation of Colloquial English* (London, 2nd ed. 1963). Part III of Gimson's book is more technical, but covers more ground among the non-segmentals than O'Connor and Arnold. (The approach to this topic in the second part of this chapter owes a great deal to both these works, without completely following either.)

All the above works have sections on phonetic categories, and on the phoneme, as have the general introductions to linguistics mentioned in the bibliography to Chapter I of this book. There is a good deal of variation in terminology, however, particularly in the case of the American publications; most of this conceals basic agreement, or reflects only trivial differences, but in intonation there are certainly two distinct approaches—that exemplified in this chapter, and that (mainly American) in which the notion of the phoneme is extended to the non-segmental features. In these general introductory works by American linguists, perhaps the most readable section on phonetics and phonology is in Part I of R. A. Hall, Jr., *Introductory Linguistics* (Philadelphia, 1964). The relevant section in Robins' work (see bibliography to Chapter I) is also useful for a more comprehensive look at different approaches to phonology.

3

MORPHOLOGY: THE FORMS OF ENGLISH

D. J. Allerton with M.A. French, University of Manchester

I. Introductory

1. WORDS AND MORPHS

In this chapter we shall present an outline sketch of English morphology and discuss some of the problems involved in our analysis. Morphology studies the forms of a language, in particular the forms its words take. By 'form' here we mean not simply the phonetic make-up of words but rather their structure in terms of grammatical or meaningful units.

The two-level nature or 'duality' of human language (as compared with, say, traffic signals) has already been discussed: if we are to describe a language adequately, we need a set of basic units or building blocks for each level. This means we need a grammatical equivalent to the phoneme or phonetic distinctive feature.

Words themselves clearly have meaning and are used to build up sentences, but we cannot consider them as basic units because they are not always minimal—they are often susceptible to further analysis. Consideration of the words *clerk, tramp, worker, writer* reveals two words which are grammatically indivisible and two words, *worker* and *writer*, which can be analysed into meaningful parts *work, write* and *-er* 'person who undertakes the activity in question'. Since these parts are not themselves further analysable they are minimal meaningful elements or MORPHS.

Words like *clerk, soldier, work, write* which are not further analysable can be said to consist of a single morph and therefore to be SIMPLE words; further examples are *log, radio, delight, parliament, shine, one, for, red, exotic*. Words like *worker, writer* which consist of more than one morph are said to be COMPOSITE; further examples are *boys, loved, lovable, inexpensive, football, dentist*. Since, as we indicated, morphology studies the way words are grammatically built up, it will have no direct interest in simple words: in fact the field of morphology can be defined as the structure of composite words.[1]

The first task of the morphologist, therefore, is to establish the morphs of the language: this is not without its problems. The principal characteristic of the morph is its meaningfulness, but how are we to decide whether elements are meaningful or not? It is not necessary that we should always be able to describe exactly the meaning of morphs—it is difficult enough to describe the meaning of some words, e.g. *the*, *than*, *to* (in *I want to*)—but we should insist that the contribution of each morph to the overall meaning remains constant in different environments. Thus while it is easy to recognize an element with recurrent semantic value in *re-establish*, *redevelop*, *recharge*, *re-cover* (= 'cover anew'), it is difficult to see any consistent meaning for the *re-* of *receive*, *relax*, *respect*, *recover* (= 'reacquire; resume normal state').[2] Similarly there is no semantic justification whatever for regarding *cartridge* as *cart* followed by *ridge* despite the virtual identity in phonetic form.

Our test of RECURRENT semantic value meets difficulties in face of the so-called UNIQUE MORPHS: these elements always occur in the company of another element, from which they are, therefore, strictly speaking, inseparable; the elements they accompany, however, demonstrate their morph status by occurring freely with the same meaning in other contexts. For example, although we recognize a recurrent element *-berry* /-bərɪ/ in *blackberry*, *strawberry*, *raspberry*, *cranberry*, etc. what are we to say of *rasp-* /rɑːz-/ and *cran-* /kræn-/,[3] which occur only with *-berry*? Similarly, do we accept an element *-ation* in *ovation* on the grounds that this is an abstract noun and parallel to *protestation*, *quotation*, *starvation*, etc.? If so, what do we do with *ov-*, which has no independent existence whatever? Certainly *rasp-*, *cran-*, *ov-*, etc., are not fully-fledged morphs—at best they are unique morphs or quasi-morphs; nor are these normal occurrences of *-berry* and *-ation*. On the other hand we seem to be missing something, if we regard *cranberry*, *ovation* and their fellows as nothing more than simple morphs.

2. MORPHS AND MORPHEMES

We have defined morphs without explicit reference to their phonological form, but it is natural to expect that any linguistic sign should have a consistent form so that the language may function efficiently. We do find, however, that the same functional element varies in form from one context to the next: thus the terminal *-(e)s* of *cats*, *dogs*, *horses* has the regular meaning 'more than one' yet has three different phonological forms, /-s, -z, -ɪz/. The three forms never contrast, having identical semantic value, and they may be regarded as members of the same morph-class or MORPHEME. The different morphs of a single morpheme are said to be its ALLOMORPHS. The vast majority of English morphemes have a single allomorph, and for them there is no real necessity to make a difference between MORPH and MOR-PHEME.

The allomorphs /-s, -z, -ɪz/ are phonologically conditioned in their occurrence, but if we view the *-en* /-ən/ of *oxen* as a member of the same plural morpheme, then its occurrence is morphologically conditioned, i.e. it is determined by the presence of the neighbouring morph *ox*.

Sometimes we meet morphs which are free variants (allomorphs) of the same morpheme: the word *plaque*, for example, has the variant forms /plæk/ and /plɑːk/ which are completely interchangeable; similarly the morpheme *-ness* with its alternative pronunciations /-nɪs/ and /-nəs/, e.g. *kindness* /ˈkaɪndnɪs, ˈkaɪndnəs/.

Where the difference in form between morphs is more marked, linguists are less inclined to class them as belonging to the same morpheme. And very often, in such cases, this decision can be justified by finding a context where the two morphs contrast. Thus, although *un-* and *dis-* appear to be identical in meaning and morphologically determined in *unethical* and *dishonest*, they nevertheless contrast (at least for some speakers) in the environment *-interested*. (It could be maintained that in such cases we are dealing with two different words *interest(ed)*, each of which selects a different prefix.)

This leads to a further problem in morphemic analysis, viz. homonymy, or, to use a more precise word, HOMOPHONY. We shall, for instance, meet some occurrences of the phonological sequence /reɪs/ (*race*) with the meaning 'competition in speed'; other occurrences will have a quite different meaning, roughly 'ethnic group'. In this case we are clearly justified in analysing two separate morph(eme)s, both having the same phonological form. On the other hand, the two senses of (*a*) *paper*, '(an) academic lecture' and '(a) newspaper' would probably be regarded by most speakers of English as specializations of the same basic element, an example of POLYSEMY. But what of the many problematical intermediate cases, e.g. *dressing* 'sauce; manure; bandages; stiffening agent', *chair* 'professorial appointment; seat', *suit* 'set of garments; legal action; set of playing cards'? Similarly for purely grammatical morphs: how many different elements do we recognize in the *-ings* of *walking, meeting, towelling*?

3. FREE AND BOUND

Having appreciated, if not solved, some of the problems of morphs and morphemes, let us return to the question of morphological structure. We are, as we said, mainly concerned with composite words, and occurring in these we find two kinds of morph: some morphs occur elsewhere independently as simple words, e.g. the first part of *boy-s*, *love-d*, the second part of *in-expensive* and both parts of *foot-ball*; other morphs occur only within composite words, e.g. the second part of *boy-s*, *love-d*, the first part of *in-expensive*. The first class of morphs are generally referred to as FREE, the latter as BOUND.

This whole definition rests, of course, on an understanding of the term WORD, which is largely given to us by an orthographical tradition that is unsure in many crucial cases, particularly compound words, e.g. *matchbox*, *horse-box*, *telephone box*. This means that the concept WORD really needs to be redefined in a more satisfactory way, something we unfortunately have no space for here. But we should state that the essence of word-ness is not so much the ability to stand alone (this is more a requirement for SENTENCE status); rather it is a question of the 'separability' of a morpheme in context. This can be tested by the operations of (1) insertion between it and its neighbours, (2) freedom of re-ordering with its neighbours, (3) omission of its neighbours.[4]

Since it is individual morphs which are bound, it is quite possible for a morpheme with more than one member to have (a) all allomorphs free, e.g. /græf, grɑːf/ *graph*, (2) all allomorphs bound, e.g. /-s, -z, -ɪz, etc./ 'plural', (3) one or more bound, one or more free, e.g. the free morph /tʃaɪld/ *child* and the bound morph /tʃɪld-/ (or /tʃɪld-/) *child-* (as in *children*) are both members of the same morpheme.

4. *ROOTS, STEMS AND AFFIXES*

Morphemes in most languages fall into two classes, ROOTS and NON-ROOTS, depending on whether they are primarily lexical or grammatical in function. If their lexical value is paramount (in which case they normally belong to relatively open classes, and the range of possible substitutions for them is large), they are termed ROOTS and generally have a clearly definable meaning, e.g. *boy*, *work*, *foot*, *love*, *dent-* (in *dentist*, *dental*), *Franco-* (in *Franco-German*, etc.). Non-roots, on the other hand, normally have a more abstract, less specific meaning and have a relatively important grammatical function; they belong to relatively closed classes, e.g. *un-*, *-er*, plural *-(e)s*, *the*, infinitival *to*. AFFIXES may be defined as bound non-roots.

English affixes are always morphs belonging to a morpheme with no free allomorphs, and at least one of the morphemes to which they are added (to form a word) must have a free allomorph. Thus the *un-* of *unkind*, the *-er* of *worker*, the *-s* of *boys* and also the *-ren*[5] of children will all be affixes. The *-ist* of *violinist* will also be an affix of course, and it remains an affix even when it is added to another bound element like *dent-* in *dentist*.

The elements to which affixes are added are generally termed STEMS (an alternative term is BASE). Roots may be regarded as minimal stems. For instance, although we recognize *boy-*, *worker-*, *football-* all as stems in the plural forms *boys, workers, footballs*, of these stems only *boy* is a root, the other two being further divisible.

In English most roots are free, but we have already met some which are bound, viz. *child-*, and *dent-*. An overall picture of the three types of morph might be presented thus:

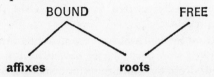

where each of the three lines corresponds to a class of morph. Strictly speaking, however, a fourth class would be necessary to account for the so-called 'structural words' like *the, of,* infinitival *to*, etc., which are free and yet have grammatical rather than lexical meaning. The following scheme might therefore be more appropriate:

	BOUND	FREE
GRAMMATICAL	**affixes**	**simple structural words**
LEXICAL	**bound roots**	**free roots**

5. WORD COMPOSITION

Amongst affixes there seem to be two fundamentally different kinds: DERIVATIONAL affixes, or simply DERIVERS; and INFLECTIONAL affixes, or simply INFLECTORS (also called INFLECTIONS[6]). DERIVED words (i.e. those formed with derivational affixes) may, in all contexts where they appear, be replaced by a simple word, to give a sentence of the same type, e.g. *untrue* may always have *strange, false, good, true* or some such word substituted for it; similarly *lovable* (*good, huge, dark*), *worker* (*clerk, man*). INFLECTED words, on the other hand, at least in some contexts, can only have their place taken by a word of similar structure. This is because inflectional affixes normally play a part in expressing syntactic relations between words and phrases while derivational affixes do not. Thus inflectors play a prominent part in such sentential co-occurrence relations as concord and government. Examples of English inflections are *-s* 'noun plural', *-ing* 'gerund/participle'. We may observe that neither *boys* nor *playing* may be replaced by a simple word of the same grammatical class in such an utterance as:

The boys were playing outside.

In other words: *boys* may not be replaced by a simple noun; *playing* may not be replaced by a simple verb.

Since their primary role is the expression of meaning and relationships at the phrase, clause or sentence level, inflectors are not usually regarded as forming new lexical items. No one, for example, would expect separate explanations in the dictionary for *ride, rides, rode* and *ridden* or for *fox* and *foxes*,[7] but they might do for *hope* and *hopeful* or for *green, house* and *greenhouse*. The study of the production of new lexical items is usually referred to as WORD-FORMATION and involves two processes:

    (i) **derivation:** by which derivers are added to roots (or stems) to give derived words, e.g. *hopeful, unkind, worker, gentlemanly*.

    (ii) **compounding:** by which roots (or composite words) are joined to other roots (or composite words) to give COMPOUND words, e.g. *greenhouse, football, washing machine, football player*.

Composite words with more than two elements may include both processes, derivation and compounding, as in our examples *gentlemanly, washing machine, football player*. Why have we classed *gentlemanly* as derived but the other two as compound? A brief answer to this question would be: because of the respective syntactic relations between the parts of each word. To explain this we must refer briefly to two basic notions of syntactic analysis, IMMEDIATE CONSTITUENTS and TRANSFORMATIONS

All languages have a hierarchically structured grammar, in the sense that each sentence can be said to consist of a sequence of elements, each of which in turn may consist of a sequence of elements and so on. Morphemes are of course the ultimate constituents, but each element at each level (or rank) may be thought of as a construction, i.e. a set of immediate constituents. An example of the organized constituent structure of a whole sentence is:

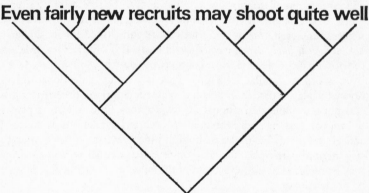

where, for instance, *fairly new recruits* has as immediate constituents *fairly new* and *recruits*.

A transformation[8] is the explicit statement of a relationship holding between two structures which differ in their status and/or sequence of elements. For instance *The castle is attacked* or *Someone/they attack(s) the castle* is clearly related to *the attack on the castle*, and they may be regarded as TRANSFORMS of each other.

To return to our examples: *gentlemanly* will be felt by most speakers to be related to *manly* or *friendly*, and there are no combinations of the type *gentle-brave*, *gentle-good* to compare it with; its immediate constituents are therefore *gentleman* and *-ly*, and it is a derived word with a compound stem. *Washing machine* already has a word division (at least an orthographical one), and certainly the relationship of *wash* to *-ing* must be closer than that of *-ing* to *machine*, as is evidenced by the transform *machine for washing*. Following similar procedures we must analyse *football bootmaking firm* (despite the orthography[9]) as:

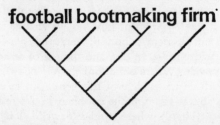

Thus the important point in studying word formation is not so much to classify words of different structure as to describe the processes by which they are built up, and, when words are classified, it is in accordance with their immediate constituents. It goes without saying that inflectional affixes also build up words (though not to form new lexical items), and some linguists have used the term COMPLEX WORDS to refer jointly to derived and inflected words, i.e. to non-compound composite words. An overall classification of the types of word we have described may be presented thus:

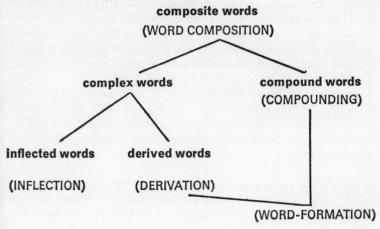

6. TYPES OF AFFIX

Affixes may be further classified according to the serial order in which they occur relative to the stem. PREFIXES precede the stem, SUFFIXES follow the stem, and INFIXES interrupt the stem. English has both prefixes and suffixes, but no infixes.[10] When infixes do occur, they have the effect of making discontinuous a stem (or root) which is normally an uninterrupted segment.[11] Some languages, e.g. Arabic, Hebrew, use infixation to such an extent that discontinuous roots are extremely common.

So far we have tended to assume that all our morphs will be concrete segments which are simply added together to produce words and sentences, as, for instance, *failure* /ˈfeɪljə/ may be described as an addition of *fail* /feɪl/ and *-ure* /-jə/.[12] But how do we analyse such words as *closure* /ˈkləʊʒə/ and *departure* /dɪˈpɑːtʃə/, where the /-j/ of *-ure* has, so to speak, blended with the /-z/ of *close* and the /-t/ of *depart* to give /-ʒ-/ and /-tʃ-/ respectively? Where is the cut between the two morphs to be made? Apparently in the middle of this consonant in each case. We are faced with almost the opposite problem in a word like *children* /ˈtʃɪldrən/ (also /ˈtʃɪ̩drən/), where /tʃɪld-/ (or /tʃɪ̩d-/) is clearly to be linked with *child* /tʃaɪld/ and where *-en* /-ən/ is identical with the /-ən/ of *oxen* and *brethren*. But what of the /-r-/? Presumably[13] it must be assigned to either the stem or the affix, but the choice is to some extent arbitrary.

Problems of a different type arise when we consider pairs of words like *shelf–shelve, sheath–sheathe, house* (Noun)–*house* (Verb). Let us assume, for the sake of argument, that the first word of each pair, the noun, constitutes a single morph, with the forms /ʃelf/, /ʃiːθ/ and /haʊs/ respectively, and that the second word consists of the noun form plus an affix meaning something like 'put into/on to a-'. How can the verb be segmented in each case? One solution would be *shelve* = /ʃel- + -v/, *sheathe* = /ʃiː- + -ð/, *house* = /haʊ- + -z/, where /ʃel-/, /ʃiː-/ and /haʊ-/ would be allomorphs of /ʃelf/, /ʃiːθ/ and /haʊs/ respectively, and /-v/, /-ð/, /-z/ would be allomorphs of the same morpheme 'put into/on to a-'. The drawback of this solution is that it ignores the fact that the verb is systematically formed from the noun by voicing the final (fricative) consonant. The question these data raise, then, is whether we should be prepared to assign morph status to phonetic features such as /VOICE/ rather than restrict ourselves to segments as we have done so far. Some linguists do accept morphs with such a form, calling this variety of affix SIMULFIXES.

Closely related to simulfixes are SUPERFIXES, which are said to occur when features or feature patterns extending beyond a single phoneme—over syllables and words—may be added or changed in a stem. English accentual patterns could be given this affixal status when they differentiate nouns from verbs, e.g. /ˈɪnsʌlt/ (NOUN) from /ɪnˈsʌlt/ (VERB) *insult*; sometimes changes in the phonemic sequence are also involved, e.g. /ˈsʌbdʒɪkt/ (or /ˈsʌbkʒekt/) (NOUN) beside /səbˈdʒekt/ (VERB) *subject*. Depending which (if either) we take as the stem, /ˈ- -/ 'noun' or /-ˈ-/ 'verb' could be regarded as a superfix.

7. OTHER KINDS OF MORPH

A further debatable practice in morphological analysis is the use of ZERO morphs and morphemes, which were first suggested by Sanskrit grammarians. A zero morph of the English noun plural morpheme has been assumed by some to occur in a word like *sheep* (PLURAL). It would be present in *The sheep are grazing* but absent in *The sheep is grazing*; it would be unclear whether or not it is present in *The sheep must graze*, since the sentence is ambiguous. Because of this difficulty some linguists prefer to say that the morpheme in question, e.g. 'plural', simply fails to occur with words of this type, e.g. *sheep*; for them this word would thus have neither a singular nor plural form but a 'numberless' one.

Zero morphs are at least normally members of morphemes with some positive manifestation. Zero morphemes, on the other hand, have a much more shadowy existence: they are by definition never realized. It is therefore with some apprehension that we view the possibility of a zero morpheme of singularity for English nouns. We would prefer to speak of the singular as being unmarked and the plural marked. English word-derivation offers some more plausible cases, viz. the identity in form of many nouns and verbs, e.g. *shame, fall*, considering the fact that many nouns are formed from verbs with an affix, e.g. *betray-al*, and vice versa, e.g. *fright-en*. But how is one to say in a purely synchronic account whether *shame*, for instance, is a verb and a zero-derived noun, or a noun and a zero-derived verb? Historical origins have no direct relevance in this matter.

Perhaps the most serious difficulties of description to confront us are those concerning such word-pairs as *foot-feet, dig-dug* and *heat-hot*. Foot /fʊt/ and *feet* /fiːt/ are clearly related, both semantically and grammatically, and to a certain degree they have a common phonetic form. At first sight, then, the best solution is to regard /f—t/ as a (discontinuous) root with two possible infixes, /-ʊ-/ 'singular' and /-iː-/ 'plural', but it obviously goes against the pattern of English nouns to have a singular morph—the singular is usually unmarked. It is, perhaps, preferable then to consider /fʊt/ as a single morph which is in conditioned variation with /f—t/ in the plural.

Both of the above treatments nevertheless depend on the acceptance of infixation and a discontinuous morph in the plural form *feet*. Some linguists argue that, since English does not have either of these phenomena except in this and other cases of vowel alternation, they are both unacceptable.[14] REPLACEMENT MORPHS or REPLACIVES have therefore been proposed. In the present case, for instance, *feet* could be said to consist of /fʊt/ plus /iː←ʊ/ (where ← is read as 'replaces'). It is clear, however, that replacement is an operation, not a segment, and thus cannot be added to other segments.[15]

8. WHAT MODEL OF DESCRIPTION?

Nevertheless we might instead regard replacement (also subtraction) as an alternative PROCESS to addition. This would presuppose a different model of grammatical description, in which, instead of describing formal items and the patterns they occur in, we rather list certain basic items and then give the operations or processes which they undergo. The former model of grammar has been termed ITEM AND ARRANGEMENT (I.A.) and the latter ITEM AND PROCESS (I.P.).

Whatever model of grammatical description we privately favour, however, we must constantly bear in mind that our aim is to present a picture that will render the complex phenomena of the English language intelligible. We shall endeavour therefore to give a straightforward account, our approach being uncommitted to any particular type of description and perhaps appearing ad hoc. In this way we hope to achieve a clear presentation of the material which leaves the choice of analysis to some extent to the reader.

II. Inflection

A. GENERAL

Some grammatical categories, e.g. noun plural, verb past tense, are obligatorily marked by the presence (or absence) of particular affixes; we have termed such affixes INFLECTORS. The inflectors of English are relatively few in number, so each has quite a high frequency of occurrence. It is therefore worthwhile giving an account of each individual affix.

From the functional pont of view, the inflectors of English fall naturally into two groups, NOMINAL and VERBAL; the only exceptions to this are the debatable cases of adjectival comparison (*-er*, *-est*) and adverbial *-ly*, both of which are partly derivational in character. The two groups are represented as follows:

nominal	**verbal**
$\{-Z_1\}$ 'noun plural'	$\{-Z_4\}$ '3rd person singular present'
$\{-Z_2\}$ 'possessive'	$\{-D_1\}$ 'past tense'
$\{-Z_3\}$ 'noun substitute'	$\{-D_2\}$ 'past participle'
(PRONOUN POSSESSIVES ONLY)	

{-m} 'oblique' {-ɪŋ} 'participle/gerund'
 (PRONOUNS ONLY)
{-self} 'reflexive; emphatic'

The braces { } mark a morpheme label. In the field of inflection we shall find it most convenient to refer to morphemes in this way, since some inflectors vary considerably in their phonetic (and orthographical) form. We have adopted as morpheme labels either the usual phonemic form e.g. {-ɪŋ} or (where there is phonologically conditioned variation) a morphophonemic formula e.g. {-Z_1}. In those cases where there is partial or complete homophony between affixes, we have used subscript numerals to distinguish the different morphemes. For instance all four morphemes {-Z_1}, {-Z_2}, {-Z_3}, {-Z_4} include the allomorphs /-s/, /-z/ and /-ɪz/; {-Z_1} and {-Z_3} also include other allomorphs.

The morphophonemic formulae /-Z/ and /-D/ stand for sets of (allomorphic) variants whose occurrence within the set is automatically determined by the sound system of English. Each set contains three members with the following distributions:

/-Z/	/-D/
(1) /-ɪz/ after sibilants and affricates (viz. /s, z, ʃ, ʒ, tʃ, dʒ/)	(1) /-ɪd/ after alveolar plosives (viz. /t, d/)
(2) /-s/ after other voiceless consonants	(2) /-t/ after other voiceless consonants
(3) /-z/ in all other cases (i.e. after all other voiced sounds)	(3) /-d/ in all other cases (i.e. after all other voiced sounds)

/-z/ is the variant selected when all three would give an English phonological sequence, e.g. the plural of /pen/ *pen* is /penz/ *pens*, not /pens/ or /'penɪz/ although these are perfectly acceptable English structures (the words *pence* and *pennies*); whereas /-s/ and /-ɪz/ only occur in environments where /-z/ would produce an impossible English sequence, e.g. /kæts/ not */kætz/ *cats*, /'hɔːsɪz/ not */hɔːsz/ *horses*. It is therefore reasonable to regard /-z/ as the morphophonemic base form, with /-s/ and /-ɪz/ replacing /-z/ when it is phonologically excluded; /-d/ may similarly be regarded as the morphophonemic base for /-t/ and /-ɪd/. We have therefore chosen /-Z/ and /-D/ as appropriate symbols for the whole morphophonemic alternance.

At this point we should note another important case of morphophonemic variation—this time one which affects the stems of inflected words:[16] each of the vowels /ɜː, ɑː, ɔː, ɪə, ɛə, ʊə, ə/ in stem-final position is automatically followed by a /r/ before {-ɪŋ}, {-ə}, {-ɪst} (the only inflectors with a vocalic onset which occur after vowels), e.g. /ˈpɜːrɪŋ/ *purring*, /ˈstɛərɪŋ/ *staring* /ˈpjʊərə/ *purer*, /ˈsɔːrɪst/ *sorest*. This rule applies only when there is an *r* in the spelling, i.e. in words which originally had a /r/. Pronunciations like /ˈdrɔːrɪŋ/ *drawing* are not generally accepted as standard. (All these remarks of course apply only to dialects which, like the so-called Received Pronunciation that we take as our norm, have no preconsonantal and word-final /r/.)

B. NOMINAL INFLECTION

1. {-Z₁} *'noun plural'*

The category of NUMBER is a feature of the noun phrase, being a potential characteristic of every one; it also appears in verbs but only when they are finite and then they are in concord with the subject noun phrase. In the noun phrase itself number seems to be marked in two ways:

(i) in the choice of determiners: singular *this, that, a(n), one, each,* etc., v. plural *these, those, two, three,* etc. (some determiners being neutral).

(ii) in the use of the {-Z₁} suffix in its various forms.

The regular (in the sense of productive and most frequent) form of the noun plural morpheme is morphophonemic /-Z/.

Phonologically irregular forms of the plural morpheme may be placed in five groups:

(a) A couple of dozen words which end in a voiceless fricative but in the plural take /-Z/ with a voicing of the final fricative, e.g. with /f-v/ *shelf-shelves, knife-knives*; with /θ-ð/ *mouth-mouths; sheath-sheathes*; with /s-z/ only *house-houses*.

(b) The word *penny* has a plural with /-s/ viz. *pence* /pens/. (This has an abstract meaning beside the regular *pennies* which has a concrete meaning.)[17]

(c) Seven words are marked for plural purely by a change of vowel phoneme (in one case two changes): /æ-e/ *man-men*; /uː-iː/ *goose-geese, tooth-teeth*; /ʊ-iː/ *foot-feet*; /aʊ-aɪ/ *louse-lice, mouse-mice*; /ʊ-ə–ɪ-ɪ/ *woman-women*.

(d) Three words take /-ən/ or /-rən/ with vowel change: *ox-oxen*; *child-children*; *brother-brethren* (the latter in the restricted sense of 'members of a religious fraternity').

(e) Learned and foreign formations of various types. These are virtually all words which occur predominantly in the written language, and consequently pronunciation varies in a number of cases. Examples are *alga-algae, stimulus-stimuli, crisis-crises, stratum-strata, criterion-criteria, phenomenon-phenomena* (all Latin and Greek patterns).

Nouns are often divided into two classes, COUNT nouns and MASS nouns, according to whether they have a number distinction or not. Count nouns like *table* have a plural form (*tables*) and co-occur with determiners like *a, one* in the singular, and *two, three, many* in the plural, while mass nouns like *furniture* have no plural form and collocate not with *a, one* but with *some* (/səm/ 'a certain quantity of') in the singular. But the division is not without its complications.

For one thing some nouns like *sheep, aircraft* may be plural or singular without any change in form; others like *cattle, police* are always plural as is clear from their verb concord (*the cattle are eating, the police are coming*) but have no sign of plurality in their form. On the other hand, there are words which have an apparent plural form i.e. end in /-s, -z, -ɪz/ but which have no equivalent singular form: some of these behave like singulars, e.g. *news, billiards*; others like plurals, e.g. *trousers, premises*. In other cases again, we are faced with apparent singular-plural pairs, e.g. *ash–ashes, content–contents* which do not exhibit the regular meaning relationship.

Further problems occur in the lack of concord of certain singular nouns with a collective meaning (*the Government believes–the Government believe*) and in the apparent irregularity of *sort, kind* in such locations as *these sort of books*. (In fact *sort of* and *kind of* might be best regarded as inserted word phrases with a meaning '... and its/their like'). An overall classification of nouns with respect to the number morpheme might be represented as shown on p. 92.

2. {-Z₂} 'possessive'

This morpheme is sometimes described as GENITIVE rather than POSSESSIVE. In fact almost all the principal meanings of *John's X* (where X is a noun) can be glossed, if not by 'the X possessed by John', then at least by 'the X belonging to or appertaining to John'.

In the case of nouns derived from transitive verbs which require a human object, *John* is normally construed as the object, e.g. *John's defeat, arrest, education*; but where the verb is intransitive, or transitive with the possibility of non-human objects, then *John* is taken as the subject, e.g. *John's arrival, death, discovery, attack*.[18] But if subject and object are unambiguously marked by prepositions, these rules may be relaxed, e.g. *John's defeat of the champion, John's discovery by the talent-spotter* (the latter type being less normal).

When the X element in a phrase *John's X* is a de-adjectival abstract noun, we can generally reconstruct an underlying proposition *John is/was/etc. A*, where *A* is the adjectival stem of X. For instance, *John's happiness* implies *John is/was/etc. happy*.

Certain uses of the {-Z₂} extend beyond animate nouns. Time expressions are particularly amenable to 'possessivization'. Singular

NUMBER IN THE ENGLISH NOUN

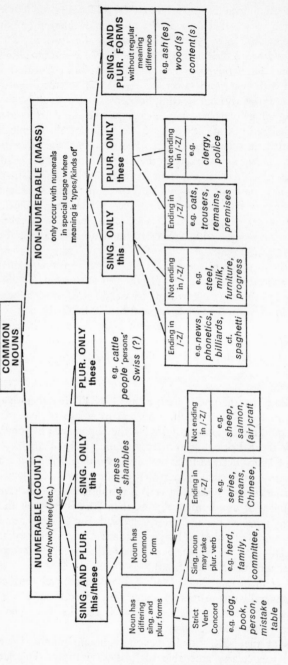

N.B. (1) MASS nouns occurring in a singular form normally collocate with *some* /səm/ while COUNT nouns in the singular do not.

(2) A whole group of nouns have dual membership of the MASS and COUNT groups e.g. *stone, crime virtue, paper, rubber* (the latter two with a specialized COUNT meaning). As a result usage with the numerals (and indefinite article) is ambiguous, e.g. *two stones* = (1) 'two pieces of stone', (2) 'two types of stone'.

(3) Some count nouns are sometimes marked for number, but sometimes not—particularly with quantity expressions and verbs of sporting activity, e.g. *four million, two foot (six), (to hunt) duck.*

quantity time expressions appear in this form when the head word is a mass noun, e.g.

one/a day's travel, (in) one/a week's time;

when the quantity is plural, of course, the possessive form is not marked in the spoken language but is traditionally written, e.g. *two hours' sleep, four weeks' notice*. Expressions which name a specific time may also be possessivized, e.g. *today's Guardian, last week's match*.

Apart from these cases $\{-Z_2\}$ occurs in some fixed phrases like *for (John)'s sake* (which means little more than 'for (John)'), *out of harm's way*, etc.

$\{-Z_2\}$ is identical in form with the main varieties of the $\{-Z_1\}$ 'plural' morpheme, viz. /-s, -z, -ɪz/, but it differs from $\{-Z_1\}$ in being perfectly regular with nouns, there being no other form possible than these three. This means of course that, at least in the spoken language, $\{-Z_1\}$ and $\{-Z_2\}$ will be homophonous for the large majority of nouns. The written language keeps them apart, e.g.:

	SINGULAR	PLURAL
PLAIN	*boy* /bɔɪ/	*boys* /bɔɪz/
POSSESSIVE	*boy's* /bɔɪz/	*boys'* /bɔɪz/

But wherever there is an irregular plural formation, the possessive singular and the plain plural are kept apart:

	SINGULAR	PLURAL
PLAIN	*wife* /waɪf/	*wives* /waɪvz/
POSSESSIVE	*wife's* /waɪfs/	*wives'* /waɪvz/

In this case the possessive plural has the same form as the plain plural, but in the case of nouns with uniform singular and plural like *sheep* the possessive plural is homophonous with the possessive singular (*sheep's*). Where the plural morph is not of the /-Z/ type at all, all four forms are distinct, e.g.

	SINGULAR	PLURAL
PLAIN	*man* /mæn/	*men* /men/
POSSESSIVE	*man's* /mænz/	*men's* /menz/

cf. *child, children, child's children's*.

We hinted earlier that $\{-Z_2\}$ is not a normal inflector. Normal inflectors may be thought of as being added to a single word. $\{-Z_2\}$, however, applies to a noun phrase rather than to a noun. For example in *the intelligent boy's marks* it is clear that *intelligent* modifies *(the) boy* not *marks* and that the *'s* therefore applies to the whole phrase not just to *boy* as is evidenced by the related structure *(the) marks of the intelligent boy*. As a consequence it is perfectly possible for $\{-Z_2\}$ to be separated from its noun, whenever the noun is followed by a modifier. It may be instructive here to compare $\{-Z_2\}$ with $\{-Z_1\}$:

The boys across the road
The boy across the road's bicycle.

In certain cases (referred to by Zandvoort as the 'classifying genitive') {-Z₂} may function not with a noun phrase but with a simple count noun (even though this could not alone form a noun phrase). Thus *a doctor's degree* in the context *He's working for . . .* can be regarded as an expansion of *a degree*, so that *doctor's* is simply a modifier like *doctoral*.[19]

Although, as we have seen, possessive complexes do have functions parallel to those of determiners and adjectives, they also appear in nominal positions, particularly as predicates of the verb *to be*. Sometimes this use may seem elliptical, although often it would be unusual to use the 'omitted' noun, e.g. *in the butcher's (shop)*, *at my uncle's (house)*. *He met her at St. John's* could be expanded with *Church* or *College* but could also be meant and interpreted as the name of a town (in Canada), when it would not be expandable.

In such instances the noun to be supplied (if any) is inferred from the context of situation, but it may be clear from the linguistic context, either within or outside the sentence: *You may not like this hat, but have you seen my sister's? That book is Colin's.* Closely related to this use is the use after *of* in *this hat of my sister's* and *that book of Colin's*. The relatedness of all these structures is demonstrated by the fact that all of them select the *mine-yours* form of pronouns, e.g. *That book is mine*, whereas all other uses we have examined of the possessive have been replaceable by the *my-your* form, e.g. *my book, her generosity*.

{-Z₂} has various phonological values with the pronouns including /-Z/, /ə(r)/ and suppletion combining with them to give the following forms:

I/me-my	it-its
you-your	we/us-our
(thou/thee-thy)	they/them-their
he/him-his	who/whom-whose
she/her-her	one-one's

Of these, *its* is perfectly regular, *whose* and *his* regular apart from the fact that the vowel is fixed for the possessives /huːz/, /hɪz/ but variable for the plain forms /huː, hʊ/, /hiː, hɪ/ (the /h/s are obligatory only in stressed positions). In addition, regular pronoun possessives exist for *one* (*one's*) and for compounds with *one* and *body*, e.g. *someone's, nobody's*.

3. {-Z₃} *'noun substitute'*

Only the personal pronouns distinguish in form between a determiner form and a nominal form of the possessive, the latter marked by {-Z₃} which has the variant form /-n/ in *mine, thine*. Thus, although

94

This is John's book is reducible to *This is John's*, *This is my book* appears as *This is mine*. *His* is unmarked for nominalization and *its* lacks a nominal form for most English speakers.[20] Since the form with {-Z₃} appears as a complete noun phrase in such occurrences as *It's mine, better than mine, mine seem good*, it is best regarded as a pronoun.

4. {-m} 'oblique'

{-m} is a second inflection limited in its use to pronouns. From the formal point of view it is difficult to carve out separate morph segments for the personal and case elements in *we* /wi:/ and *us* /ʌs/.[21] On the other hand, the two are perfectly parallel in function to the more clearly demarcated /hɪ- + -m/ *him*, /hu: + -m/ *whom*.

In order to avoid these difficulties of segmentation it might be more profitable simply to list the stressed forms in an ordered way:

Personal Pronouns and Determiners

SUBJECTIVE PRONOUN	OBLIQUE PRONOUN	POSSESSIVE DETERMINER	POSSESSIVE PRONOUN	REFLEXIVE EMPHATIC
aɪ	mi:	maɪ	maɪn	maɪ'self
I	*me*	*my*	*mine*	*myself*
ðaʊ[22]	ði:[22]	ðaɪ[22]	ðaɪn[22]	ðaɪ'self[22]
thou	*thee*	*thy*	*thine*	*thyself*
hi:	hɪm	hɪz	hɪz	hɪm'self
he	*him*	*his*	*his*	*himself*
ʃi:	hɜ:	hɜ:	hɜ:z	hɜ:'self
she	*her*	*her*	*hers*	*herself*
ɪt	ɪt	ɪts		ɪt'self
it	*it*	*its*		*itself*
wi:	ʌs	aʊə/ɑ:	aʊəz/ɑ:z	aʊə'selvz/ ɑ:'selvz
we	*us*	*our*	*ours*	*ourselves*
ju:	ju:	jɔ:	jɔ:z	jɔ:'selvz
you	*you*	*your*	*yours*	*yourselves*
ðeɪ	ðem	ðɛə	ðɛəz	ðəm'selvz
they	*them*	*their*	*theirs*	*themselves*
hu:	hu:(m)	hu:z	hu:z	(hɪm'self, hɜ:'self, ðəm'selvz)
who	*who(m)*	*whose*	*whose*	(*himself, herself, themselves*)
wʌn	wʌn	wʌnz	(wʌnz)	wʌn'self
one	*one*[23]	*one's*[23]	(*one's*)[23]	*oneself*[23]

As regards the uses of the {-m} form of the pronoun, we may today go so far as to call it the normal, general form, although historically it represents the accusative case (chiefly used to mark verbal and prepositional objects). Now, the subjective case is the exception rather than the norm: in fact it only occurs regularly with all speakers as a simple subject preceding the finite verb. Cases where vacillation[24] is common include: *It's ME/I*; *We looked for a job, Tom and I/ME*; *It was I/ME who looked for a job*; *It was ME (that) they were looking for*, and the ambiguity of *You know John better than ME*, where *I* is possible but pedantic in the subjective meaning. It is interesting to note that because the prevalent pattern *Tom and ME were* . . . has been prescribed against, some speakers have by overcorrection extended the use of *I* to non-subject cases of co-ordinate noun phrases, e.g. *You know Bill and I, between you and I.*

5. {-self} 'reflexive/emphatic'

{-self} combines with all the personal pronouns, including *one* but not *who*, as illustrated in the figure on p. 95. Words like *myself* do not look particularly like inflected forms of *me*, etc., but, on the surface, more like compounds consisting of possessive determiner plus noun.[25] However, from the point of view of function and meaning they cannot be interpreted in this way in typical uses like *I made myself do it*; here *myself* contrasts not with *my arm*, *mind*, *son*, etc., but simply with *him*, *you*, *George*, etc.—nor does it contrast with *me*, of which it may therefore be regarded as an inflectional variant. In *I did it myself/I myself did it*, *myself* functions like subject modifiers such as *alone, with my colleagues*.

{-self} pronouns have, in fact, two quite separate roles which are usually termed 'reflexive' and 'emphatic'. The REFLEXIVE pronoun must be used in the following positions, whenever the person referred to is identical with the subject:

(a) object	*I hurt myself*
(b) indirect object	*I did myself a favour*
(c) predicative	*He isn't himself*
(d) subject of downgraded ('infinitivized') clause	*I told myself to do it*
(e) object of downgraded ('infinitivized') clause with zero subject (= identical with main subject)	*His wife threatens to kill hersel*

96

(f) nominal element in
prepositional phrase
provided it is not a clear
locative

She has no confidence in hersel
Are you staying by yourself?
They saw it for themselves

Contrast (f) with (g):

(g) *I looked behind me,*
He took his camera with him.
He felt his blood tingle inside him.

Variable cases include some prepositions of direction:

I pulled the bedclothes over me/myself.
He moved the chair towards him/himself.

In its EMPHATIC uses, {-self} may accentuate any pronoun or noun phrase in the sentence. These emphatic uses differ from the others in that the pronoun is an optional modifier (meaning something like 'as opposed to others') and if omitted leaves behind a grammatical sentence, e.g.

The King himself made the request
The King made the request himself.
Did they give the present to you yourself?
In the house itself were a number of nice items.

When the subject is thus modified, the pronoun may either directly follow it, as in the first example, or appear at the end of the sentence, as in the second.

A final use of the {-self} pronouns is as simple replacements for *I/me*, etc., wherever there is vacillation between subjective and oblique form. Compare these examples with the ones quoted above for *I/me*:

We looked for a job, Tom and myself.
It was myself they were looking for.
You know John better than myself.

C. VERBAL INFLECTIONS

1. {-Z₄} '3rd person singular present'

This morpheme is used to form the 3rd person singular form of the present tense of all verbs, including verbal auxiliaries except the modals *will* (*would*), *shall* (*should*), *may* (*might*), *can* (*could*), *must*, *ought* (and sometimes *need* and *dare*), all of which use the bare stem in such cases. The form of this morpheme is consistently /-Z/ with a mere four verbs having a change of stem viz. *is* /ɪz/, *has* /hæz/ *does* /dʌz/, *says* /sez/.

The functions of {-Z₄} are manifold:

(i) It marks the verb as finite through its concord and sequential relationship to the subject, which is thus limited to a third person pronoun or noun phrase.

(ii) It marks the verb as singular.

(iii) It marks the verb as present tense.

$\{-Z_4\}$'s marking of 'singularity' is of course usually redundant, since the singularity of the subject is usually clear by itself.[26] However, when this is not so, the normally redundant $\{-Z_4\}$ may assume a distinctive role; cf.

> His sheep grazes in the meadow.
> His sheep graze in the meadow.

$\{-Z_4\}$ also signals the category of present tense; in non-3rd person singular forms this category is of course unmarked. The 'presentness' is actually a matter of non-pastness, since, most commonly, general habits or (relatively) permanent states of affairs are referred to.

2. $\{-D_1\}$ 'past tense' $\{-D_2\}$ 'past participle'

As with $\{-Z_1\}$ and $\{-Z_2\}$, the regular forms of the past tense and past participle morphemes are identical in form. However there are more irregularities and more cases of differences for $\{-D_1\}$ and $\{-D_2\}$. It is true that the two morphemes do not usually come into opposition since $\{-D_2\}$ must normally be preceded by an auxiliary or copular verb to make it finite, whereas $\{-D_1\}$ is finite in its own right. However the two morphemes may contrast in such sentence pairs as:

> I can imagine the boy *hid/froze*.
> I can imagine the boy *hidden/frozen*.

In these cases two different types of grammatical construction are involved, and it is the occurrence of $\{-D_1\}$ or $\{-D_2\}$ respectively that signals which construction it is.

We now come to the complex question of the forms of these suffixes. We shall deal with both morphemes together, mentioning specially all cases where they differ.

I: /-D/

The regular form for both suffixes is morphophonemic /-D/, e.g. *called* /kɔːld/, *passed* /pɑːst/, *waited* /'weɪtɪd/. This form of the affix occurs with the vast majority of English verbs and is automatically taken by all new verbs entering the language.

IA: Some verbs take /-D/ but vary the vowel of the stem, e.g. *say–said* /seɪ–sed/, *sell–sold* /sel–səʊld/, *hear–heard* /hɪə–hɜːd/, *sleep–slept* /sliːp–slept/, *weep–wept* /wiːp–wept/.

IB: Some verbs take /-D/ but are subject to a consonant change (loss) in their stem, e.g. *have–had* /hæv–hæd/, *make–made* /meɪk–meɪd/.

IC: Some verbs take /-D/ having first undergone both vocalic and consonantal change (devoicing), e.g. *leave–left* /liːv–left/, *lose–lost* /luːz–lɒst/.

II: /-t/

A whole group of verbs which ought regularly to have /-d/, in fact take /-t/. These verbs mainly end in /-n/ and /-l/, e.g. *burn–burnt* /bɜːn–bɜːnt/, *learn–learnt* /lɜːn–lɜːnt/, *smell–smelled/smelt* /smel–smelt/, *spell–spelt* /spel–spelt/, *spoil–spoilt* /spɔɪl–spɔɪlt/, *dwell–dwelt/dwelled* /dwel–dwelt/.

IIA: Some verbs change their vowel and add /-t/, e.g. *feel–felt* fiːl–felt/, *lean–leant* /liːn–lent/, *dream–dreamt* /driːm–dremt/, *buy–bought* /baɪ–bɔːt/.

IIB: Some verbs make both vocalic and consonantal changes in their stem, then add /-t/, e.g. *bring–brought* /brɪŋ–brɔːt/, *think–thought* /θɪŋk–θɔːt/, *catch–caught* /kætʃ–kɔːt/.[27]

III: Devoicing

This only applies to verbs ending in /-d/; their past form ends in /-t/, e.g. *bend–bent, build–built, lend–lent, spend–spent*.

IV: Vowel Change

This is the major irregular category for English verbs, and it is anything but homogeneous. There are many classes and subclasses which we try now to present in an organized way. We shall classify these verbs firstly according to whether the vowel of the past participle agrees with that of the past tense, with that of the present, or with neither; and secondly according to whether the past participle has the ending -(*e*)*n* /-(ə)n, ŋ/. Within each group we list the various vowel alternation patterns, some of which only apply to a single verb.

(1) Past Participle agrees with Past Tense, i.e. {-D₁} and {-D₂} are homophonous:

/iː–e–e/	*bleed, meet, read,* etc.
/e–ɒ–ɒ/	*get* (not in American)
/ɪ–ʌ–ʌ/	*dig, win, fling, stick,* etc.
/ɪ–æ–æ/	*spit, sit*
/æ–ʌ–ʌ/	*hang*
/uː–ɒ–ɒ/	*shoot*
/aɪ–ɪ–ɪ/	*slide, light* (also regular)
/aɪ–ʌ–ʌ/	*strike*
/aɪ–ɒ–ɒ/	*shine* (also regular)
/aɪ–ɔː–ɔː/	*fight*
/aɪ–aʊ–aʊ/	*find, bind, grind, wind*

99

(1a) Past Participle has same vowel as Past Tense but adds -(e)n, i.e.
{-D₂} = {-D₁} + -(e)n:

/iː–əʊ–əʊ/	steal, speak, freeze, etc.
/e–ɒ–ɒ/	tread, forget (get in American)
/uː–əʊ–əʊ/	choose
/eɪ–əʊ–əʊ/[28]	break, wake
/aɪ–ɪ–ɪ/	hide, bite, etc.
/aɪ–eɪ–eɪ/	lie ('recline')
/ɛə–ɔː–ɔː/[28]	bear, swear, tear, wear

(2) Past Participle has same vowel as Present stem, i.e. {-D₂} has a zero value or is absent. There are two examples of this without -(e)n, viz. each has a different vowel in the past tense:

/ʌ–eɪ–ʌ/	come (also be-, overcome)
/ʌ–æ–ʌ/	run

(2a) Past Participle has same vowel as Present stem, but adds -(e)n; thus {-D₂} is realized simply as /-(ə)n, -n̩/:

/iː–e–iː/	eat (ate = /et/)
/iː–ɔː–iː/	see
/ɪ–æ–ɪ/	bid ('command') forbid
/ɪ–eɪ–ɪ/	(for)give
/ɔː–e–ɔː/	(be)fall
/ɔː–uː–ɔː/	draw (also over-, withdraw)
/eɪ–ʊ–eɪ/	shake, forsake, take, undertake, etc.
/eɪ–uː–eɪ/	slay
/əʊ–uː–əʊ/	grow, blow, throw
/əʊ–juː–əʊ/	know

(3) Past Participle has a vowel different from both the Present and the Past Tense. Only one pattern exists without -(e)n:

/ɪ–æ–ʌ/	drink, ring, swim, begin, etc.

(3a) Past Participle has individual vowel and in addition -(e)n. Only two types occur:

/aɪ–uː–əʊ/	fly
/aɪ–əʊ–ɪ/	write, ride, drive, (a)rise, etc.

V: /-D/——(e)n

A category of 'mixed' verbs also exists which have a regular past tense but which normally have a past participle in -(e)n (-ed is a less frequently used alternative). Examples are mow–mowed–mown /meʊ–məʊd–məʊn/, hew–hewed–hewn /hjuː–hjuːd–hjuːn/, saw–sawed–sawn /sɔː–sɔːd–sɔːn/, cf. also sow/sew, show, strew.

VA: One verb is of this pattern but has vowel change in the past participle, viz. shear–sheared–shorn /ʃɪə–ʃɪəd–ʃɔːn/.

One verb has a different vowel in all three forms, viz. *do, did, done* /duː–dɪd–dʌn/; it is thus a blend of types IV and V.

VI: Zero

A complete series of verbs has no difference at all in form between present tense, past tense and past participle. We may say either that these verbs take a zero variant of the {-D₁} and {-D₂} morphemes or we can say (perhaps more realistically) that these verbs simply do not take {-D₁} and {-D₂}. Most of them end in /-d/ or /-t/, e.g. *bet, bid* (at an auction), *burst, cast, cost, cut, hit, hurt, let, put, rid, set, shed, shut, slit, split, spread, thrust.*

  VIA: A special case is *beat* which has an unchanged past tense but a past participle *beaten* /ˈbiːtn̩/. Thus while {-D₁} is not realized overtly, {-D₂} has the form /-n̩/.

VII: Suppletion

Our final category contains two verbs which use a completely different form in the past tense compared with present and past participle. They are:

  be—was/were—been /biː/ (unstressed: /bɪ/) –/wɒz, wɜː/ (unstressed: /wəz, wə/) –/biːn/
  go–went–gone /ɡəʊ–went–ɡɒn/

The verb *be* is idiosyncratic in other ways too: it is the only verb to have a special form for 1st person singular present tense, to have a different form for all singular as against plural past tense forms, and to have separate forms for plural present and infinitive. Its full conjugation is:

	PRESENT	PAST
1st. Sing.	*am* /æm, (ə)m/ ⎫	*was* /wɒz, wəz/
(Obsolete 2nd Sing.	*art* /ɑːt, ət/ ⎬	*wert* /wɜːt /)
3rd Sing.	*is* /ɪz, z, s/[29] ⎭	*was* /wɒz, wəz/
Plural	*are* /ɑː, ə/	*were* /wɜː, wə/
Participle	*being* /ˈbiːɪŋ/	*been* /biːn (bɪn)/
Infinitive	*be* /biː, bɪ/	

The function of {-D₁} is simply to mark PAST TENSE, The function of {-D₂} is slightly more complex.
Its most important functions are in its combining:
  (1) with *have* to produce 'perfect'
  (2) with *be* to give 'passive'
Alone it acts as an adjective, occurring both attributively and predicatively, when it usually carries with it the meanings of 'perfect' and/or 'passive', e.g.

  The illustrated article was rather protracted.
  He looked exhausted.

3. {-ɪŋ} 'participle/gerund'

Although the functions of this morpheme are varied and complex, its form is simple to describe: it consistently has the form /ɪŋ/.[30]

We have glossed {-ɪŋ} as 'participle/gerund', but it has other important functions:

(1) In conjunction with the verb *be*, it produces the 'progressive' forms, an integral part of the tense-aspect system of the verb.

(2) It functions as an affix which is partially or wholly derivational in character.

In fact the range of functions of {-ɪŋ} is unusual, in that it is neither wholly inflectional nor wholly derivational; it forms words which are neither wholly adjectival (participles) nor wholly substantive (gerunds): hence the common use of the neutral expression *ing*-form. Other major European languages have no comparable single form.

The unequivocally inflectional occurrences of *-ing* forms include the usual nominal, and, adjectival, slots, e.g.

(1) NOMINAL   (a) **subject:** Winning (matches) helps team morale.

    (b) **object:** He loves winning (matches).

    (c) **agent:** He is encouraged by winning (matches).

(2) ADJECTIVAL   (a) **prenominal attribute:**
His winning shots were superb.

    (b) **postnominal attribute of subject:**
He spent hours in the Casino winning (pounds) every time.

    (c) **postnominal attribute of object:**
I saw him winning (the race).

However, in all these cases the *-ing* form retains its verbal character, and, except in prenominal attributive position, it may always take a noun as object, as indicated in parenthesis above.[31] Moreover, while the subject of the *-ing* verb may be understood in a general sense ((1)(a)) or construed from the context ((1)(b), (1)(c), (2)(b)), it may also be made explicit by the use of nouns and pronouns (sometimes in the possessive form), e.g. *us/our, John('s)*, in all nominal cases. In cases like (2)(c) the subject is obligatorily expressed.

The *-ing* form is very similar in one of its uses to the infinitive with *to*: indeed *to smoke* is nearly interchangeable with *smoking* in a verbal complex such as *I like . . . a cigar after dinner*. While some verbs such as *like, intend, start*, do not discriminate between infinitive and *-ing* form, others require the one (e.g. *hope, manage*) or the other (e.g. *finish, risk*). An interesting subclass including *want* and *need* makes a contrast between the active use of the infinitive and the passive use of the *-ing* form, e.g.

The girls will need to scrub
The girls will need scrubbing[32]

When the *-ing* form has lost its characteristic verbal qualities of taking a subject, object (transitive verbs only), adverbial modifier, etc., and has become a pure noun or adjective, then we can say that {-ɪŋ} is acting as a derivational morpheme. In these cases {-ɪŋ} occurs with some lexical items but not with others. Examples are: *warning, meeting; coating, ironing; gardening*, which are all nominal in character. A border line case is the adjectival {-ɪŋ} of *a frightening affair, an interesting scheme*, where the form may, like ordinary adjectives, be modified by *very, more*, etc., but may be regarded as a transformation for verbs which take a human object and designate mental processes.

We have so far left aside the uses of {-D_1}, {-D_2} and {-ɪŋ} within the voice-tense-aspect system of the English verb. {-ɪŋ} combines with *be*, while {-D_2} may combine with either *have* or *be*; these combinations along with {-D_1} give us four optional modifications for any verb viz. PROGRESSIVE, PERFECT, PASSIVE and PAST, of which any one, two, three or even all four may be selected, to give such forms as: *has been seeing, had been, has been seen*.

D. OTHER INFLECTIONS

We mentioned earlier that apart from nominal and verbal inflections there exist some others which are of more debatable inflectional status:

(a) **adjectival comparison**—the two morphemes {-ə} 'more' and {-ɪst} 'most' as in *weaker, weakest*.

(b) **adverbial** {-lɪ} as in *quickly, strangely*. Let us examine the status of each of these in turn.

{-ə} and {-ɪst} may be said to be derivational in the sense that they form new adjectives, the COMPARATIVE and SUPERLATIVE forms, which may occur in many ordinary adjectival positions, e.g.

The tall boys had an advantage in the line out.

taller
tallest

In such contexts {-ə} and {-ɪst} are clearly derivational in character, since they can be replaced by a single form. On the other hand, such sentences as:

Michael's boy is *taller* than his teacher
Michael's boy is the *tallest* in his form

illustrate clearly inflectional uses of *taller* and *tallest*, since each is occurring in a context where the other is impossible (as is also the simple form *tall*).

The forms of the two morphemes are simple to state and have been given in our name for them. The comparative is regularly manifested as /-ə/ (/-ər/ before vowels). The superlative is regularly realized as /-ɪst, -əst/.[33] Some changes in the final phonemes of the stem take place:

(i) final /-ŋ/ in *long, strong, young* alternates with medial /-ŋg-/ in *longer, longest*, etc. It might be most appropriate to regard the /g/ as part of the comparative/superlative inflection, since it is not required in this position by the phonological system. Moreover other formations from these adjectives do not take /g/, e.g. /ˈlɒŋɪʃ/ *longish*.

(ii) syllabic /l/ alternates with non-syllabic /l/ in *simple, able*, beside *simpler, abler*, etc.

(iii) as always before a vowel the potential linking /r/ of the adjectival stem itself occurs, e.g. *dear* /dɪə/, beside *dearer, dearest* /ˈdɪərə, ˈdɪərɪst (ˈdɪərəst)/.

(iv) *far* inserts /ð/, with an optional change of vowel i.e. *far* /fɑː/, *farther/further* /ˈfɑːðə, ˈfɜːðə/ *farthest/furthest* /ˈfɑːðɪst, ˈfɜːðɪst/ (also /-əst/).

{-ə} and {-ɪst} may not be used with all adjectives: they are restricted to monosyllabic and common disyllabic forms. The alternative is a phrase *more/most* + adjective, which is used whenever a longer or less common adjective is involved, either alone, or in company with the {-ə}/{ɪst} forms e.g.:

He is the most honest man I know
She is prettier and more intelligent than her sister

Two sets of comparative and superlative forms correspond to a pair of adjectives rather than a single one:

good, well[34]	better	best
bad, ill	worse	worst

A similar phenomenon is apparent for two pairs of determiner-like adjectives of quantity which distinguish singular and plural in the simple form but not in comparative and superlative forms:

little, (a) few[35]	less	least
much, many	more	most

As Jespersen points out, the difference between comparative and superlative is not a difference between a comparison with one and a comparison with many or all; nor does the superlative indicate a higher degree. Consider the sentences:

Margaret was happier than all of her six sisters put together
Jean was the happiest of the three girls

The criterion for choice of comparative as against superlative is whether the entity compared is thought of as separate from the group with which it is compared or as part and parcel of it.[36]

Adverbial {-lɪ} is our other border-line inflection—border-line in the sense that it might also be thought of as a derivational affix. If we apply the test of replaceability by a simple word with the same function, we shall see that our attitude will depend on how strictly we insist that the function must be the same. The adverb is a complicated, even amorphous word-class containing widely-differing subclasses which nevertheless have just about enough members in common to justify setting up a single class ADVERB, e.g. *naturally* (sentence adverb and manner adverb), *slightly* (degree adverb and adjective intensifier).

Some types of adverb have most or all members without *-ly* (e.g. place adverbs like *here*, *down*, *near*), but within the major subclass of MANNER ADVERBS only *well*, *hard*, *fast*, *loud*, *right*, and a few others regularly occur without *-ly*. If we regard these as cases of suppletion or zero realization, *-ly* could be regarded as obligatory for manner adverbs and therefore akin to an inflection.

The phonological form /-lɪ/ is used absolutely consistently subject to the following modifications:
  (i) after syllabic /l/ just /ɪ/ is added, and the /l/ loses its syllabicity— there is no doubling of /l/, e.g. *possibly* /ˈpɒsəblɪ/, *nobly* /ˈnəʊblɪ/. After ordinary non-syllabic /l/ the doubling is optional, e.g. *coolly* /ˈkuːl(l)ɪ/, *wholly* /ˈhəʊl(l)ɪ/; but *fully* can only be /ˈfʊlɪ/.
  (ii) after the etymological ending *-ic* /-ɪk/ (which often does not have morpheme status) the written language requires *-ally*; this is sometimes pronounced /-əlɪ/ although /-lɪ/ is more normal, e.g. *linguistically* /lɪŋˈgwɪstɪk(ə)lɪ/.

The suffix {-lɪ} may be used with virtually any adjective with the exception of those mentioned above which form adverbs unmodified or by suppletion. An odd case is the word *difficult* which seems to have no adverbial equivalent except phrases like *with difficulty*. An unusual use of {-lɪ} is with noun stems, e.g. *namely*, *partly*, *purposely*, where there is no adjective equivalent and the adverb seems equivalent to a prepositional phrase involving the noun, i.e. 'by name', 'in part', 'on purpose'. Apart from these cases the meaning of {-lɪ} might be glossed as 'in a – way'.

III. Derivation

A. GENERAL

Derivation differs from inflection in a number of ways, the chief one being, as we have said, the grammatical role of the affixes involved. Whereas inflectors are predominantly grammatical in character, most derivers stand closer to the vocabulary and its root morphemes. The inflectional affixes of English are relatively few in number and fairly regular in their use, having a very general application; English derivational affixes, on the other hand, are greater in number and, with few exceptions, much more limited and sporadic in their distribution. Although the generally lexical character of derivers might be expected to give them more semantic precision, in fact their meanings are often vaguer and more diffuse than those of their inflectional fellows; indeed derivers frequently overlap and compete with each other.

The different nature of derivers necessitates a difference in their treatment. Rather than consider their form and function one by one, we intend to discuss in a general way the important characteristics of derivational affixes as a group.

B. FORMS OF DERIVATIONAL AFFIX

1. Prefixes

Derivational prefixes in English are either monosyllabic or disyllabic, with the sole exception of the /n-/ of *neither, never, nor, none* (and archaic *nought*).

Monosyllabic prefixes may be exemplified by: /ə-/ *ahead*, /riː-/ *re-occupy*, /priː-/ *pre-arrange*, /ʌn-/ *unhappy*, /nɒn-/ *non-payment*.

Disyllabic prefixes may be exemplified by: /ɔːtəʊ-/ *autosuggestion*, /semɪ-/ *semi-conscious*, /ɪntə-/ *inter-city*. There are fewer disyllabic than mono-syllabic prefixes; amongst the former rare and learned words tend to predominate.

Stress. Prefixes either take the stress or leave the stress of the stem undisturbed. In particular:

(i) The prefixes /ə-/ as in *afire*, /bɪ-/ as in *befriend*, and /ɪn-, en-/ 'put into a; make into a', as in *enrol/enslave*, are always unstressed.

(ii) Some prefixes occur both stressed and unstressed, e.g. /priː/ in *preconception* (stem stressed), *preview* (prefix stressed), *Prehistory* (variable).

(iii) Some prefixes are generally stressed when they occur with a noun stem, especially if it is short, e.g. /baɪ-/ (*by-product*), /kaʊntə-/ *counter-attack*, /fɔː-/ (*foreshore*), /aʊt-/ (*outpatient*).

Prefixes have no important effect on the phonemic structure of the stems they occur with.

2. Suffixes

English has asyllabic, monosyllabic and disyllabic suffixes, and one that is trisyllabic.

Asyllabic suffixes are limited to /-θ/, /-t, -d/ and /-ŋ/. /-θ/ occurs only [37] in the words *warmth, strength, length, breadth, width, depth* (all except the first having vowel alternation) and now seems incapable of being extended. A morpheme which may be referred to as {-D₃}[38] has /-t/, /-d/ and /-ɪd/ as allomorphs, e.g. *moustached, moneyed, spirited*. /-t/ is also found as a noun-forming suffix in *height* and *weight*. /-n/ occurs as a variant of the suffix *-n/-an/-ian*, e.g. *Zambia-n*.

Monosyllabic suffixes may be represented by: /-ə/ *runner*, /-ɪdʒ/ *wastage*, /-aɪz/ *localize*, /-ənt/ *contestant*, /-sɪ/ *captaincy*, /-ʃɪp/ *friendship*, /-səm/ *quarrelsome*, /-mənt/ *establishment*.

Disyllabic suffixes may be represented by: /-ɪtɪ/ *sincerity*, /-'ɛərɪən/ *authoritarian*, /-əbḷ/ *debatable*.

The only **trisyllabic** suffix found in English is /-iːˈaːnə/ *-iana* as in *Shakespeariana*.

Stress. Derivative suffixes seem to fall into three main categories with respect to stress:

(i) The majority of suffixes are unstressed and leave the stressing of the stem unchanged, e.g. /-ɪdʒ/ in *anchorage, percentage*, /-fḷ, -fəl, -fʊl/ in *beautiful, successful*.

(ii) Some suffixes are unstressed but shift the stressing of the stem, generally to the last syllable. Among others there exist the suffixes /-ɪtɪ/, /-ɪk/, /-əl/, /-jən/, as in *agile–agility, metal–metallic, accident–accidental, assimilate–assimilation*. A different pattern is observable in a few cases with /-əbḷ/ and /-əns/ which can shift the stress back to the first syllable as in *comparable* beside *compare, preference* beside *prefer*.

(iii) Suffixes which are usually stressed include: /-ˈɛərɪən/ (*Parliamentarian*), /-ˈeɪʃṇ/ (*exhortation*), /-ˈɪə/ (*mountaineer*), /ˈiːz/ (*Japanese*), /-ˈesk/ (*statuesque*).

Affixal combinations. Certain suffixal sequences seem to be analysable from the point of view of function, although there is not a straightforward realization of the two components. The following morph equations would seem to hold good:

/-ˈɪsɪtɪ/ = /-ɪk/ + /-ɪtɪ/ e.g. *electric-ity*
/-ɪʃṇ/ = /-ɪk + /-ɪən/ e.g. *electric-ian*
/-ɪfɪˈkeɪʃṇ/ = /-ɪfaɪ/ + /-ˈeɪʃṇ/ e.g. *electrify–electrification*

Stem variations. Certain stems, particularly those of Latin origin, vary in their final consonants before particular suffixes. Stems with final /-k/ in their free allomorphs have /-s/ before Latin-type suffixes beginning with /ɪ/, e.g. /əʊˈpeɪk/ *opaque* /əʊˈpæsɪtɪ/ *opacity*, but contrast *opaquish* with /k/. We can formulate tentative rules like:

/-Vt/[39] + /-jən/ → /-Vʃṇ/ as in *translation*
/-Vd/ + /-jən/ → /-Vʒṇ/ as in *persuasion*
/-Vnd/ + /-jən/ → /-Vnʃṇ/ as in *suspension*
/-Vz/ + /-ɪv/ → /-Vsɪv/ as in *abusive*

but these generalizations apply only to words of Latin origin.

Vowel variations also occur in some stems before suffixes. Many are concomitant with the alternation between stress patterns. Vowels and diphthongs are likely to be reduced in unstressed syllables as follows:

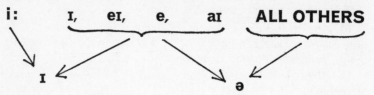

The unreduced syllables may have either primary or subsidiary stress.

Examples of such alternation are

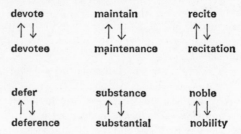

Other stems vary in their vowel phonemes even though the stress pattern remains constant. Certain suffixes, notably /-ɪtɪ/, /-ɪk/, /-ʃn̩, (*-tion*) seem to prefer preceding vowels to belong to the short series,[40] cf. these variations: /iː–e/ *redeem–redemption*, /eɪ–æ/ *tenacious–tenacity*, /aɪ–ɪ/ *bronchitis–bronchitic*, /əʊ–ɒ/ *ferocious–ferocity*, /(j)uː–ʌ/ *resume–resumption*.

Common to all stems (native and Latin) is the principle, found equally in inflection and compounding, that the vowels /ɜː, ɑː, ɔː, ɪə, ɛə, ʊə, ə/ take a following /r/ before a vowel. Examples are /stɑːrɪ/ *starry*, /'kjʊərəbl̩/ *curable*. But wherever there is no historical justification for the /r/—and no *r* in the spelling—it is avoided by many educated speakers, e.g. /'rɔːɪʃ/ not /'rɔːrɪʃ/ *rawish*, /'sɔːəbl̩/ not /'sɔːrəbl̩/ *sawable*.

3. *Final Replacives*

Certain word-final consonantal differences between otherwise identical words correlate with the difference between grammatical classes. In one important type we find a noun ending in a voiceless fricative and a related verb ending in the homorganic voiced fricative, e.g.:

-f/-v	-θ/-ð	-s/-z
belief–believe	mouth (N.)–mouth (V.)	advice–advise
half–halve	teeth–teethe	house (N.)–house (V.)
proof–prove		use (N.)–use (V.)
shelf–shelve		

The two most common meaning relationships are for the verb to mean (1) 'have, experience, give —', or (2) 'put into/on to a—'.

In some cases it is an adjective to which the verb is related:

–f/–v	**–s/–z**
safe–save	diffuse–diffuse

The meaning of the verb is in each case factitive.

There is a similar alternation between voiceless and voiced sounds in the case of a few noun–verb pairs, ending in the plosives /t/ and /d/, e.g. *intent–intend, ascent–ascend*. In some instances the noun ends instead in /s/, e.g. *expanse–expand, pretence–pretend*. All these types seem to be restricted to cases where /t, d, s/ follow /n/.

A rather different category is formed by adjective-noun pairs like *violent–violence, different–difference*. The /–s/ of such nouns may be analysed in two ways: as a final replacive; or as a suffix added to adjectives in /-ənt/, this latter solution being possible because pronunciations like /ˈvaɪələns/ and /ˈvaɪələnts/ are in free variation for many speakers.

The words *speak* and *speech* now seem to provide the only example of alternation between /k/ and /tʃ/. This was formerly a quite common pattern.[41]

4. *Medial Replacives*

Vowel alternation also used to play a much more significant role in English, but is now limited to verb inflection and the derivational relationship between certain verbs and (usually) nouns. The marginal nature of medial replacement in derivation is illustrated by the fact that only a couple of vowel patterns have more than one representative, and that the meaning–relationship between the members of some pairs is becoming less close. Examples are: *abode–abide, band–bind, seat–sit, shot–shoot, song–sing, drop–drip, stroke–strike, sale–sell, blood–bleed, food–feed*. The noun meaning may be defined in terms of the verb as 'an instance of -ing', or 'that which -s', or 'where one -s'.

A few factitive—non-factitive verb pairs are still related in this way e.g. *fell* 'cause to *fall*', *lay* 'cause to *lie*'.

One adjective–verb relationship is indicated in this way, viz. *full–fill*. A similar pair is *hot–heat*, where the latter may be either noun or verb. An adjective–noun pair also occurs: *proud–pride*.

Some monosyllabic words exhibit a combination of final and medial replacements, in that both the final consonant and the vowel alternate. The group includes *glass–glaze, grass–graze, bath–bathe, choice–choose, breath–breathe*. We may note that the consonant alternations involved here, viz. /s–z, θ–ð/ are also found in the cases of final replacives we discussed above.

5. Stress Shift

A whole set of pairs of related words have their members differing from each other solely in respect of their stress pattern. Most usually, again, the related words are noun and verb. They are usually disyllabic with the noun taking its stress on the first syllable, the verb on the second. The following are examples:

> abstract, digest, discount, import, increase, inlay, insult, offset, overhang, torment, transfer, transport.

The word prostrate is stressed initially when an adjective and finally when a verb.

It is, however, more common for the members of a pair to be differentiated by stress shift with simultaneous vowel alternation. Vowels are reduced to /ə/ and /ɪ/ in unstressed syllables in the manner described above for stems under the influence of suffixation. Examples are:

NOUN or ADJECTIVE		VERB
absent	/ˈæbsənt/	/əbˈsent/
combine	/ˈkɒmbaɪn/	/kəmˈbaɪn/
conduct	/ˈkɒndəkt/	/kənˈdʌkt/
contrast	/ˈkɒntrɑːst/	/kənˈtrɑːst/
export	/ˈekspɔːt/	/ɪksˈpɔːt/
perfect	/ˈpɜːfɪkt/	/pəˈfekt/
produce	/ˈprɒdjuːs/	/prəˈdjuːs/
progress	/ˈprəʊgres/	/prəˈgres/
rebel	/ˈrebl̩/	/rɪˈbel/
record	/ˈrekɔːd/	/rɪˈkɔːd/
survey	/ˈsɜːveɪ/	/səˈveɪ/

This stress patterning, whether with or without vowel alternation, is typically found in two-syllable words of Romance origin. Yet many words of the latter type now have (or have always had) fixed stress for noun/adjective and verb, either on the first syllable, e.g. comment, exile, process, or on the second, e.g. advance, concern, display, preserve, respect, content, (the latter group being larger). All of these words are both noun/adjective and verb, and exemplify zero difference between the two grammatical classes.

6. Zero Affixes and Backformations

When we meet two words of different grammatical class which are identical in form and closely allied in meaning, for instance the noun–verb pairs love–love, fish–fish, it is possible, as we remarked earlier, to describe them in terms of ZERO-derivation. But, since most users of a language are unaware of its history, this kind of derivation is generally out of place in a synchronic account. In fact the semantic relationships between verbs which are historically derived from nouns can be quite similar to those between original verbs and nouns later derived from them, e.g. *to mother–a mother* beside *to cheat–a cheat* or *to loan–a loan* beside *to look–a look*. We feel that the best synchronic approach to such pairs of words is to regard them simply as instances of MULTIPLE CLASS MEMBERSHIP, whereby one lexical item belongs to two (or more) grammatical classes.

In some cases, however, there is only a partial extension of grammatical role. As examples of adjectives occurring in positions which are generally occupied by nouns, we may cite *the poor*, *the French*, etc.; examples of verbs in a position which has some nominal characteristics are *have a shave/listen/try/chat*, *go for a walk/run/drive*. In neither case does the word under scrutiny have the full attributes of a (count) noun: it is just as unEnglish to say **the poors* or **a French* as it is to say **have the shaves* or **you have my listen*, In such cases it may be best to say that certain noun positions may be occupied by (a particular subclass of) verbs or adjectives.

Backformations are another phenomenon for which we must distinguish sharply between the synchronic aspect and the historical. From the diachronic standpoint it is clear that *beg* has been derived from *beggar*, and *donate* from *donation* by so-called BACKFORMATION, i.e. an originally simple word has been reinterpreted as a derived word, or, looking at it differently, a so-called UNIQUE MORPHEME (*begg-*, *donat-*) has been given full morphemic status. But what do we say about the state of the language once the process of backformation has been completed? In point of fact *beg–beggar* is then in no way different from *run–runner*, *read–reader*, or any other such pair. The native speaker is no more aware of the established backformation than he is of any other fact of linguistic history. There is no place here for subtractive morphemes.

C. FUNCTIONAL TYPES OF DERIVATIONAL AFFIX

1. Principles of Classification

To achieve an adequate description of derivation in English we must classify affixes according to their function as well as to their form. The range of grammatical functions of derived words is the same as that of simple words. In some cases the derived word is of broadly the same grammatical class as its stem, e.g. *lioness–lion*, *re-enter–enter*; in other cases the class of the derived word is clearly different from that of its stem, e.g. *enrich–rich*, *happiness–happy*. On this basis a distinction is usually made between CLASS-MAINTAINING and CLASS-CHANGING affixes. While recognizing this division, we should be aware of one or two difficulties.

Firstly some affixes are both class-maintaining and class-changing. An example is -*ist*, which may derive a noun either from a noun stem, e.g. *isolation-ist*, or from an adjective stem, e.g. *traditional-ist*. Similarly -*ly* may form adjectives either from nouns (*friendly*) or from other adjectives (*kindly*). We should note, however, that while it is quite common for English affixes to derive the same word-class from different stems, it is less common for the same affix to have words of different classes as derivatives.[42] It would appear, therefore, that the more significant property of affixes is the word-class they produce rather than the kind of stem they combine with.

The second question à propos of the class-maintaining versus class-changing distinction is how widely we define our classes. If it were argued that *whitish* is different in class from *white* because it does not form a comparative in -*er* (**whitisher*) but prefers *more whitish*, we would probably dismiss this difference as superficial, since it is determined mainly by the phonetic form of the adjective, in particular the number of syllables. If, on the other hand, we consider the difference between *manhood* and *man*, *priesthood* and *priest*, etc., we recognize that -*hood* combines with nouns denoting ANIMATE beings but forms ABSTRACT nouns. Moreover it seems to be a regularity of English that simple abstract nouns never serve as the direct stem for the formation of other nouns.

We shall find it useful, then, in our survey of suffixes to distinguish between animate, inanimate concrete, and abstract nouns.[43] We shall make our primary division of prefixes into class-maintaining and class-changing, but classify suffixes principally according to the class of word they derive. We give a fairly full but not exhaustive list of the affixes in each case: we include only the more widely-used of the learnéd affixes.

2. *Prefixes*

(1) **Class-maintaining** prefixes may be grouped simply according to their grammatical class, which is naturally the same for their stem and their derivative.

(a) NOUN: arch- (*arch-enemy*), demi- (*demi-god*), ex- (*ex-mayor*), micro- (*microgroove*), mono- (*monotone*), mid- (*mid-summer*), step- (*stepfather*), sur- (*surtax*), vice- (*vice-chancellor*).

(b) VERB: re- (*re-adjust*).

(c) ADJECTIVE: bi- (*bilateral*), extra- (*extra-marital*), hyper- (*hyper-sensitive*), intra- (*intra-molecular*), pan- (*pan-African*), uni- (*uni-lateral*).

(d) NOUN and VERB: counter- (*counter-attack*), fore- (*forefront, forewarn*), mis- (*misfortune, misspend*).

(e) NOUN and ADJECTIVE: anti-[44] (*anti-communist*), auto-

autosuggestion, autobiographic(al)), in- *(inexperience, inhuman),* multi- *(multi-millionaire, multilateral),* neo- *(neo-Catholic),* non- *(non-smoker, non-existent),* pro- *(pro-Consul, pro-British),* pseudo- *(pseudo-Liberal),* semi- *(semi-circle, semi-skilled),* trans- *(trans-Pennine).*

(f) NOUN, VERB and ADJECTIVE: inter- *(interrelate,* etc.), post- *(postnatal,* etc.), pre- *(preconception,* etc.), sub- *(subpostmaster,* etc.), super- *(super-charged,* etc.).

(2) Prefixes which are solely **class-changing** are only three in number. Two always convert NOUNS or ADJECTIVES to VERBS; they are:

be- *(befriend, belittle),* en-/em- *(enslave, embitter).* The third prefix is *a*- which has three slightly different functions: it may derive—
—PREDICATIVE ADJECTIVE from NOUN *(ablaze).*
—PREDICATIVE ADJECTIVE/ADVERB from NOUN *(aground).*
—ADVERB from ADJECTIVE *(aloud).*

(3) Three prefixes are both **class-maintaining and class-changing.** They all convert VERBS or NOUNS to VERBS. Examples are:

de- *(decompose, defrost),* dis- *(disbelieve, disillusion),* un- *(unwrap, unhorse).*

In addition the suffix *un-* may form ADJECTIVES from ADJECTIVES, e.g. *uncertain,* and *dis-* may form NOUNS from NOUNS, e.g. *distaste.*

3. *Suffixes*

The most revealing way to categorize suffixes is according to the class of word they derive. Within this grouping we subclassify the suffixes, according to the word-class(es) to which the majority of the stems belong. In some cases the stem is not a word, but a BOUND ROOT, i.e. a morph that belongs to a root morpheme which has only bound allomorphs. For example, the *horr-* of *horror, horrid* is a bound root, having no free variant; whereas the *metall-* /mɪ'tæl-/ of *metallic,* although a bound morph, is not a bound root, since it has the free variant *metal* /'metḷ/.

(1) **Derivers of animate nouns**

(a) from an ANIMATE NOUN stem: -ess *(baroness),*[45] -ette *(usherette).*

(b) from a NOUN stem of any kind: -arian *(Unitarian),* -n/-an/-ian *(Syrian, historian),* -eer *(engineer),* -ite *(Labourite),* -ster *(songster).*

(c) from a VERB stem: -ant *(informant),* -ee *(employee).*

(d) from an ADJECTIVE or NOUN stem: -ie/-y *(brownie, Johnny),* -ist[46] *(nationalist, Marxist),* -ling *(weakling, duckling).*

(e) from a VERB or NOUN stem: -er/-or *(rider, actor, hatter).*

(2) **Derivers of inanimate concrete nouns**

(a) from an INANIMATE CONCRETE NOUN stem: -ade (*orangeade*), -ing (*towelling*), -let (*booklet*), -ette (*kitchenette*).

(b) from an ANIMATE NOUN stem: -iana (*Victoriana*), -y (*stationery*).

(c) from a VERB stem: -ant/-ent (*consultant*), -ing(s) (*savings, building*).

(d) from a NOUN or VERB stem: -age (*vicarage, package, shrinkage*), -er (*freighter, boiler*).

(3) **Derivers of abstract nouns**

(a) from an ANIMATE NOUN[47] stem: -dom (*kingdom*), -hood (*motherhood*), -ship (*directorship*).

(b) from a NOUN or ADJECTIVE stem: -ism (*Calvinism, expressionism, colonialism*).

(c) from an ADJECTIVE stem: -ce (*violence*), -ness (*boldness*), -th (*warmth*).

(d) from a VERB stem: -al (*denial*), -ance/-ence (*assurance*), -ation (*temptation*), -ion (*assertion*), -ment (*establishment*), -ure (*failure*).

(e) from a NOUN or VERB stem: -age (*peerage, storage*).

(f) from a NOUN or BOUND ROOT stem: -itis (*tonsilitis, gastritis*), -(o)logy (*Kremlinology, sociology*).

(g) from an ADJECTIVE or BOUND ROOT stem: -itude (*exactitude, gratitude*), -ity (*agility, credulity*).

(h) from an ADJECTIVE, NOUN or BOUND ROOT stem: -(a)cy/-(e)sy (*sufficiency, infancy, adequacy, piracy, courtesy*).

(i) from a BOUND ROOT stem: -or/-our (*horror, splendour*), -y (*economy, scrutiny*).

(4) **Derivers of verbs**

(a) from a VERB stem: -le (*sparkle, crackle*).

(b) from an ADJECTIVE stem: -en (*darken, sadden*).

(c) from a NOUN or BOUND ROOT stem: -ate[48] (*assassinate, equate*).

(d) from a NOUN, ADJECTIVE or BOUND ROOT stem: -(i)fy (*glorify, simplify, quantify*), -ize (*computerize, legalize, colonize*).

(5) **Derivers of adjectives**

(a) from a NOUN stem: -ate (*passionate*), -en (*wooden*), -esque (*statuesque*), -ful (*sorrowful*), -less (*careless*).

(b) from a NOUN or ADJECTIVE stem: -ary (*fragmentary, secondary*), -ish (*bluish, boyish*), -ly (*masterly, deadly*).

(c) from a NOUN, VERB, or ADJECTIVE stem: -some (*awesome, tiresome, wearisome*), -y (*draughty, cuddly, greeny*).

(d) from a NOUN, ADJECTIVE or PARTICLE stem: -most (*topmost, outermost, inmost*).

(e) from a NOUN or BOUND ROOT stem: -al/-ial/-ual (*cultural,*

substantial, factual, federal, social), -ese (*Japanese, Maltese*), -ic
(*alcoholic, economic*), -ical (*farcical, identical*), -ous/-eous/-ious
(*poisonous, gaseous, superstitious*).

   (f) from a VERB or BOUND ROOT stem: -ive/-ative (*creative,
      informative, emotive*), -ory/-atory/-itory (*contradictory, auditory,
      confirmatory*).

   (g) from a BOUND ROOT stem: -id (*horrid, candid*).

   (h) from a NUMERAL stem: -th (*sixth, millionth*).

(6) **Derivers of adverbs**

   (a) from a NOUN or PARTICLE stem: -ward(s) (*forward(s),
      homeward(s), inward(s)*).

   (b) from a NUMERAL stem: -fold (*twofold, hundredfold*).

D. THE DISTRIBUTION AND SEMANTICS OF DERIVATIONAL AFFIXES

1. Irregularity of Distribution

In the previous section we classified affixes according to the types of
word they derive and according to the grammatical class of the stems
with which they appear. We listed -*eer*, for example, as a suffix which
forms animate nouns from noun stems, e.g. *engineer, profiteer*; there are,
however, no words **motoreer, *advantageer*. Similarly, although it is
perfectly acceptable English to say:

   I disbelieved what he said

it is not acceptable to say:

   I *disaccepted what he said

The distributions of -*eer* and *dis*- are defective in this respect. Again,
although there exists a word *provocative* 'likely to provoke', there
exists no word **incitative* 'likely to incite'. In such cases we may speak
of a derivational GAP.[49]

The distribution of derivers is irregular in another way. In many
cases a number of them with similar values are in COMPETITION
with each other, and it is impossible to give watertight rules for the
selection of the correct affix. If we consider the derivation of nouns
denoting persons engaged in an occupation, we find words like *con-
servation-ist, petition-er* and *grammar-ian*, all alike in having abstract
noun stems, and yet each with a different affix. Another set of affixes
with comparable values is to be found in the words *glad-ness, complex-ity,
efficien-cy, impertinen-ce*; again we see that, although every stem is an
adjective, each one selects a different suffix to form an abstract noun.

A final example is to be seen in the formation of deverbal abstract
nouns with the meaning 'act/process of -ing', where the main competitors are -*al*, -*ance*, -*ation*, -*ment*, -*ion* and zero. The case of *provocative*
and **incitative* seemed to indicate that semantically parallel stems do not
necessarily select the same affixes. The following examples show that

phonologically similar stems (in this case verbs) may select different affixes:

arrive–arrival	derive–derivation
assess–assessment	confess–confession
debate–debate	abate–abatement
deny–denial	defy–defiance
expect–expectation	elect–election
impose–imposition	disclose–disclosure
neutralize–neutralization	chastise–chastisement
perform–performance	deform–deformation
utter–utterance	better–betterment

Yet despite the similar meanings of these affixes and their apparent complementary distribution, we are still faced with pairs like *excitement–excitation, remittal–remittance*.

Although, as we have illustrated, there are many cases where affixes combine with stems in an apparently irregular way, this is not to deny that certain tendencies and, in some cases, even regularities of distribution are to be observed. It is convenient to recognize three types of regularity: phonological, semantic and inter-affixal (the latter being discussed in our next sub-section).

One example of phonological regularity is to be seen in polysyllabic verbs which end in the phoneme sequence /-eɪt/: a high proportion of such verbs form abstract nouns by the addition of the suffix *-ion*, e.g. *illustration, creation, alienation, dehydration*. In other cases, stems which select a given affix are characterized by a particular stress pattern: for instance, most verbs taking *-ee* to derive a noun meaning 'one who is -ed' are disyllabic, with the main stress on the second syllable, e.g. *detain, employ*. Features of both stress and phonemic form characterize nearly all stems which select *-eer*: such stems end in /n/ or /t/ and are disyllabic with stress on the first syllable, e.g. *engineer, profiteer, musketeer*.

We can frequently discern phonological features applying only to a smaller subgroup within the stem-class of a particular affix. A considerable number of verbs which select *-ment*, for instance, have a first syllable of the form /ɪn-/ or /bɪ-/ and have stress on the second syllable, e.g. *enchantment, embarrassment, bereavement, bewilderment*. Again, amongst those verbs which add *-al* to form abstract nouns, we find the rhyming group *arrive, deprive, survive, revive*.

The case of a stem-class characterized by common semantic features may be illustrated by stems which derive noun–adjectives with the meaning '(person) of ——' by the addition of *-i*. Most of these stems denote places in the Muslim cultural sphere, e.g. *Iraq, Pakistan, Zanzibar*. As a minor tendency we may cite the semantically akin *haul, cart* and *freight* which all select *-age*.

2. Inter-affixal relations

When derivers are added to stems which themselves are already derived, two (or more) affixes may come to stand next to each other. We sometimes find that when stems derived with a particular affix take a second affix, they generally select a particular one out of a number with similar values. In such cases it seems reasonable to speak of a LINK between the two affixes concerned.

A derived adjective in -less, for example,[50] may only form an abstract noun in -ness, e.g. *carelessness*, *weightlessness*; the sequence *-lessity is impossible. Similarly a derived verb in -ize must form its abstract verbal noun in -ation, e.g. *dramatization*, *legalization*. There is a strong tendency for verbal nouns in -ion to form agentives in -ist and adjectives in -al, e.g. *exhibitionist*, *conservationist*, *exceptional*, *occupational*.

The sequence in which derivers occur relative to each other is of course fixed: a prefixed deriver must precede any prefixes already contained in the stem, and a suffixed deriver must follow any suffixes already contained in the stem. It is difficult to place any upper limit on the number of derivers to be used in a word. The number of prefixes does not usually exceed two, but words like *re-dis-en-tangle* do occur. Suffixal combinations reach larger proportions, but such giants as *(de-)nation-al-iz-ation-ist-ic*[51] tend to be avoided.

3. Productiveness

Those affixes which are currently used to form new words are traditionally termed PRODUCTIVE. The suffix -ism, for example, is constantly occurring in new formations such as *revisionism*, *Gaullism*, while a suffix like -th is limited to a dozen or so words and seems incapable of further extension. We should not, however, give the impression that productiveness is an all-or-nothing matter: affixes might, in fact, be arranged roughly in a rank order of productiveness, e.g. -ism > -hood > -th.[52]

The degree of productiveness of an affix appears to be strongly influenced by its present distribution, i.e. by the number of words in which it already occurs. In general, affixes with a wide distribution tend to have a high degree of productiveness. A further factor is the number of clearly productive competitors an affix has; for instance, -ster (as in *pollster*) is limited in its productiveness partly by the fact that it has to compete with suffixes like -er, -ist.

When a deriver is subject to phonological restrictions on the stems with which it combines, this may be thought of as acting in two ways at once: on the one hand a suffix like -ion is limited in that it largely occurs with stems in -ate, etc.; on the other hand, whenever a stem in -ate needs a noun derivative, it most naturally selects -ion.

Affixes which have a clear-cut lexical meaning are influenced by a factor additional to those mentioned above. One stimulus for the coining of new derived words is what Hockett has referred to as 'the need-filling motive'. The productiveness of a suffix like *-ade*, for example, may decrease or increase according to whether or not society extends its production and consumption of (fizzy) fruit-flavoured drinks.

Since elements with the widest distribution and most frequent occurrences are likely to have very little specific lexical meaning, their function must be mainly grammatical. We would therefore expect the most productive affixes to be grammatical in character, and it is certainly true that inflectional morphemes are virtually 100 per cent productive. It is not surprising, then, that the most productive derivers of all, *-er* and *-ness*, are partly inflectional in character. This is most clearly seen in their occurrence in transformations of whole sentences.

If we compare the three sentences:
(1) Mozart composed this symphony
(2) This symphony was composed by Mozart
(3) Mozart was the composer of this symphony
we will notice that whatever changes we make in the subject, verb or object of the first sentence, we can produce not only a corresponding passive sentence like (2), but also an *-er* sentence of type (3). The *-er* here seems to be maximally productive.

However, recalling that derived words are by definition replaceable by simple words, we may find it worth asking what words could replace *composer* in sentence (3). They are virtually all *-er*-derivatives (e.g. *writer, arranger, editor*), a partial exception being *author*. In other words *-er* in such positions is really inflectional while elsewhere, e.g. in

Mozart was a great composer (figure/man/Austrian, etc.)
it is derivative in function. We should also observe that whereas the 'inflected' *composer* could mean 'of a poem, crossword puzzle, etc.', *composer* as a pure derivative is limited semantically to the field of music (cf. also *writer*).

Something similar applies to the *-ness* of *I'm worried about Simon's happiness*, which is generally equivalent to ... *whether Simon is happy*. Moreover, an unusual coining can take place spontaneously as a transform, even when it would be accepted very reluctantly as a normal item of vocabulary:
A. The play's very slow moving.
B. It's the slow-moving-ness of it that I like.

4. Meaning

It is difficult to generalize about the semantic value of derivers, because they in some ways form a bridge between syntax and the vocabulary and thus vary in character between these two poles. The more grammatical an element is, the less lexical meaning it has. We are not surprised, therefore, to find that class-changing affixes like *-ness*, *-er*, *-ment*, *-ation*, *-ic*, have largely abstract or grammatical meanings like 'person, thing, action, etc., connected with . . .'; exceptions include *-ism* 'cult, philosophy of . . .', adjectival *-en* 'made of . . .' and adverbial *-wards* and *-fold*.

Class-maintaining suffixes, on the other hand, must have some lexical meaning if they are not to be redundant. In English they might be classified under headings like:

FEMALE	-ess, -ette
DIMINUTIVE	-ette, -let
COLLECTIVE	-age, -(e)ry

The *-le* of *sparkle*, *crackle*, etc., might be regarded as a verbal intensive or iterative, and *-ish* as a kind of adjectival 'diminutive'. The suffixes *-ology* 'study of', *-itis* 'illness' and *-ade* 'drink' have unusually specific meanings.

Prefixes are, as we have observed, mainly class-maintaining and might be grouped under the following semantic labels:

NEGATIVES	a-/eɪ-/, in-, non-, un-
SPATIO-TEMPORAL	pre-, post-, intra-, extra-,
RELATIONSHIPS	mid-, trans-, sub-, super-
NUMERATIVES	hemi-, demi-, mono-, uni-, bi-,
	tri-, multi-
PREFIXES OF DEGREE	super-, arch-, micro-

semi- might be placed in either of these latter two categories, since it is not always so literally numerical as *hemi-* and *demi-* (cf. *hemisphere* with *semi-conscious*).

IV. Compounding

A. PROBLEMS OF DESCRIPTION

1. What are compound words?

Although differences of distribution and meaning[53] exist between inflectional affixes on the one hand and derivational affixes on the other, the two classes agree in having a strictly limited number of members. Compounding differs from inflection and derivation in that it does not involve affixes at all, but simply the adding together of any two roots or stems. The roots of a language are not subject to the same numerical limitation as its affixes; it is not only that there are more of them, but also that their number may be increased at any time by borrowings from another language or dialect (e.g. *sputnik*, *hippy*), or by deliberate fabrication (e.g. *ovaltine*).

It is thus impossible to discuss the components of compounds individually, and our approach here must be different from that used in either inflection or derivation. We shall discuss the problems of delimiting and describing compounds in English, and then give a tentative typology.

Our first problem is to decide exactly what we are to understand by the term COMPOUND WORD. We defined compounding as the process whereby two stems (simple, i.e. roots, or composite) are joined to form a word. But most English roots are free and therefore, in a sense, already words: thus *rail* and *way* are words, but *railway* is normally considered a single word, not a sequence of two words. Why is this?

As we indicated earlier, spelling is a poor guide to word status in the case of compounds. Certainly we should like to treat *firewood, fire-engine* and *fire insurance* in a similar way, despite the inconsistent use of word spaces and hyphens in our orthographical system.

Phonological patterning has been suggested as a criterion for distinguishing compounds from free collocations of words. In particular, main stress on the initial component has been taken as the deciding factor: and certainly the majority of what are usually considered compound words exhibit this feature, whereas word sequences like *red apples* or *wooden bench* generally have the main stress on the final element.

However, a purely phonologically based division would make *'blackberry* a compound but *black 'pudding* a free sequence,[54] *'blacklist* a compound but *black 'market* a free sequence; and yet the members of each pair are similar in their grammatical and semantic structure. Equally striking is the fact that whereas *Oxford 'Road* (also *Oxford 'Avenue*, etc.) would be a free collocation, *'Oxford Street* would be a compound. These inconsistencies underline the fact that the category of COMPOUNDS is a grammatical one, and that, although there is a tendency for it to be phonetically marked in a certain way, such marking is not perfectly regular.

What, then, are the defining characteristics of compound words as opposed to free collocations?

If we take the case of adjective-plus-noun expressions, we see that all free syntactic collocations are equivalent to noun-*that*-be-adjective, e.g. *green leaves = leaves that are/were green, cunning plans = plans that are/ were cunning*.

The compound word *madman*, however, involves a specialization in meaning of *mad*, limiting it to 'lunatic', while *mad* can otherwise also mean 'enthusiastic', 'angry' or 'frantic'; we may also note that the *mad* of *madman* cannot be qualified by *quite, rather*, etc.

The compound nature of the word *blackhead*, moreover manifests itself both in the meaning specialization of *head* and in the fact that it is not a 'head' at all but a pimple or a bird WITH a black head. Similarly, a *redcap* is not a 'cap' but a person; hence, whereas *cap* is an inanimate noun, redcap is a human animate noun.

Let us go on to consider such noun-plus-noun sequences as *cotton shirt, cotton socks*, which can be glossed as 'shirt/socks made of cotton'. These combinations differ from, say, *cotton mill* or *cotton reel* in being relatively free syntactically. It seems to be a productive pattern of English for a mass noun M denoting a material to precede and modify another noun X with the expression meaning 'X made of M'; further examples are *stone wall, iron bridge*. We may freely exchange the 'material' noun for any given head noun, e.g. *gold/silver/steel watch, brick/stone/concrete wall*. If we compare this state of affairs with compounds like *cotton mill, cotton reel*, we see that *wool mill and *plastic mill are just as unlikely as *nylon reel or *string reel. Moreover, although it is perfectly possible to expand *gold watch* to *24 carat gold watch* or *steel watch* to *stainless steel watch*, it is impossible to expand *ironmonger* or *goldsmith* in a similar way. We conclude that *cotton shirt, gold watch, brick wall*, etc., are free collocations, while *cotton mill, goldsmith*, etc., are compounds.

In summary we may say that:

(a) **free collocations** have an extensive syntactic potential (in terms of substitutions, transformations, etc.) that is strictly parallel to other collocations of the same grammatical structure. All free adjective-noun collocations, for example, have a similar syntactic potential.

(b) **compound words** usually have components, the meanings of which are more specialized in the compound than in other environments; moreover the syntactic potential of the components is more limited than elsewhere.

2. *Classifying compounds*

In isolating compounds from other morpheme sequences we have mentioned one criterion for distinguishing between different types of compound, namely, whether the compound as a whole is grammatically and semantically equivalent to (at least) one of its parts. When this is the case, we term the part in question its CENTRE and call the compound as a whole ENDOCENTRIC; in all other cases the compound is referred to as EXOCENTRIC. Endocentric compounds may be subdivided according to whether only one or both of the parts have functions equivalent to the whole compound. Examples of the three types are:

—ENDOCENTRIC—**one centre (subordinate)**: *gunpowder* 'powder for guns', *garden party* 'party in a garden'.

—ENDOCENTRIC—**two centres (co-ordinate)**: *pathway* 'path which is a way = way which is a path', *hosepipe* 'hose which is a pipe = pipe which is a hose'.

—EXOCENTRIC: *runaway* 'person who runs away', *outbreak* 'a breaking out'. A special subclass is the so-called BAHUVRIHI[55] type, where there is a modifier-modified type of relationship but the latter is not equivalent in meaning to the whole compound, e.g. *bluestocking*. We shall use the term HEAD in the restricted sense of 'that which is modified', reserving the term CENTRE for an element which is equivalent to the compound as a whole. Thus exocentric compounds have no centre but may have a head.

The vast majority of compounds are of the one-centred endocentric type, where the non-centre element (which is a modifier) restricts the meaning of the centre (which is a head) in some way. The ways in which a modifier affects the meaning are diverse, as is clearly illustrated by some of Jespersen's examples:

a goldfish = 'a fish *of the colour* gold'
a golddigger = 'a digger *for* gold'
a goldsmith = 'a smith *who works in* gold'
a gold mine = 'a mine *from which people obtain* gold'.

Although we are tempted to agree with Jespersen's conclusion that 'compounds express a relation between two objects but say nothing of the way in which the relation is understood', we feel that it is worth making some attempt to catalogue the types of meaning relationship to be found. It goes without saying that this cannot be done in the limited space available without omissions and over-simplifications.

The main framework for our classification of compounds must, however, be grammatical. In English we find compound nouns, adjectives and verbs, besides a few adverbs and the numerals. Aside from the grammatical class of the compound as a whole, we must also take account of the grammatical classes of its constituents. In the case of endocentric compounds, where the compound and its head word belong to the same class, there may be different classes of modifier.

Before we proceed to our classification we should mention one special type of compound. As we stated in our introductory section, some root morphemes have bound allomorphs; but as roots they form compounds when they combine with other roots. In the learnéd vocabulary of English some root morphemes may have a special variant in *-o* /-əʊ/ when they occur as the first element of a compound. Examples are: *Franco-German, Anglo-Norman, Anglo-Indian, electro-magnetism, socio-linguistic, politico-economic, astro-physics.*

In most cases only Latin and Greek elements occur as the first element in compounds of this type, cf. *Franco-British* beside *Anglo-French*. All such words may be regarded as having an adjective in first position, whether they are co-ordinated adjectives[56] like *Anglo-German* = *English-German* or adjective-noun combinations like *astro-physics* =

astral physics. The element *-o* is thus in some ways a kind of adjectival pseudo-suffix, being equivalent, for example, to *-ish* (*English*), *-ic* (*electric*), *-al* (*political*).

In some cases we may posit a compounding of two bound roots, e.g. *patri-cide,* since the *-(i)cide* recurs in *suicide, genocide,* etc., and the *patri-* in *patrilineal, paternal,* etc., and since neither form fulfils our requirements for affix status.

B. TYPES OF COMPOUND

1. *Compound Nouns*

(1) **Endocentric—Single noun centre,** which generally appears in second position[57]:

   (a) ADJECTIVE or PRONOUN MODIFIER (Y) + NOUN HEAD (Z): only one type is possible:
   —'**Z that is Y**', e.g. *madman, greenfly, smallpox; he-rabbit, she-wolf.*

   (b) NOUN MODIFIER (Y) + NOUN HEAD (Z): various semantic relationships are possible:

     (i) '**Z that is Y**'. Noun modifiers are usually more specific in meaning than their head noun, e.g. *fighter-plane, oak-tree.*

     (ii) '**Z that belongs to/comes from Y**'. The first noun may be in its plain or possessive form, e.g. *arrowhead, apple core, folksong, cow's milk.*

     (iii) '**Z that has/contains Y**', e.g. *picture book, family man, bagpipe.*

     (iv) '**Z that is made (up) of Y**'. These differ from free collocations like *gold watch,* both in their grammatico-semantic restrictions and in having initial stress, e.g. *breadcrumb, snowball, fish cake, paper money, lump sugar.*

     (v) '**Z that V-s Y**', e.g. *car thief, sheep dog, fire engine, cotton mill,* the verbs understood being something like 'take', 'round up', 'extinguish' and 'spin' respectively.

     (vi) '**Z that is V-ed by Y**', e.g. *steamship, air brake, police dog, hayfever, inkblot, Davy Lamp,* where the verbs understood are something like 'drive', 'work', 'use', 'cause', 'invent', respectively.

     (vii) '**Z that V.-s or is V.-ed in/at/on (etc.) Y**', e.g. *gunpowder, Christmas tree, garden party, press conference, footlight, heart attack, aircraft, garage mechanic, cradle song, night club.* The meaning relationships involved clearly vary between time, location and purpose, the three often overlapping.

     (viii) '**Z in/at/on (etc.) which Y V-s/is V-ed**', e.g. *football pitch, law court, date line, saturation temperature.* Time or location is the relationship involved, but it is the reverse of the preceding type, in that here the head noun, not the modifier, denotes the time or place.

(ix) '**Z that is like Y**', e.g. *bulldog, fountain pen, T-square*. Here a particular subclass is distinguished from the rest of the class by comparing it with a different entity with which the subclass has some feature in common.

(c) NOUN MODIFIER (Y) + *DEVERBAL* NOUN HEAD (Z): These compounds could be thought of as forming a special sub-group of (a). A different set of relationships is possible because Z retains its verbal content. The head noun (usually derived) may be either agentive or abstract. The types are:

(i) '**Z by Y**' (Y being the actor, and only abstract nouns being possible for Z): *population growth, cloudburst, farm production.* (Cf. such sentences as: *The population grows.*)

(ii) '**Z of Y**' (Y being the goal): *shoemaker, pastry cook; sightseeing, cost reduction, book review.* (Cf. such sentences as: *He makes shoes/Shoes are made by him; The sight is seen.*)

(iii) '**Z in/at/on (etc.) Y**' (Y being the location, destination, time, instrument, etc.): *sleepwalker, babysitter, nightworker, play-going, colour photography, stage whisper.* (Cf. such sentences as: *He walks in his sleep; He goes to the play.*)

(d) VERBAL MODIFIER (Y) + NOUN HEAD (Z): Three types seem to occur:

(i) '**Z that Y-s**' (i.e. the noun names the performer(s) of the verbal activity): *dancing team, hangman, watchdog, demolition gang.*

(ii) '**Z that is Y-ed**' (i.e. the noun names the goal of the verbal activity): *blowpipe, plasterboard, eating apple, smelling salts.*

(iii) '**Z in/at/on/with (etc.) which Y-ing takes place**' (i.e. the noun names the location, time or instrument of the verbal activity): *grindstone, playground, filling station, firing pin, freezing point, retirement age.*

(e) PARTICLE MODIFIER (Y) + NOUN HEAD (Z): These only differ from each other in the nature of the understood verb:

(i) '**Z that is Y**': *outhouse, outpost, inside.*

(ii) '**Z that V.-s Y**': *overlord, down train, undercurrent, afterthought* (where the understood verbs might be thought of as 'rule', 'travel', 'flow', 'come').

(f) NOUN HEAD IN FIRST POSITION (Y): This type is extreme-ly rare. The second element is usually a noun, e.g. *tiptoe* 'toe-tip' tip belonging to the toe' (cf. *arrowhead, apple-core*, where the head noun is in second position).

(2) **Endocentric—Co-ordinate noun centres:** two different types are possible:

    (a) EQUATIVE:

        —'Z that is a Y = Y that is a Z'. This type is not uncommon, e.g. *girlfriend, prince regent, pathway*.

    (b) ADDITIVE:

        —'Y and Z combined'. This simple type does not exist in English except in geographical names like *Schleswig-Holstein*. However forms with *and* do occur, e.g. *bread-and-butter, fish-and-chips*.

(3) **Exocentric noun compounds** have no centre but may still involve a modifier-head construction:

    (a) ADJECTIVE MODIFIER (Y) + NOUN HEAD (Z):

        —**he who or that which has (a) Y Z'** (the pure BAHUVRIHI type); *blackhead, bluebell, dimwit, recap*.

    (b) NOUN MODIFIER (Y) + NOUN HEAD (Z):

        —'he who has (a)Z like (a)Y': *hawkeye, butterfingers, egghead*.

    (c) VERB HEAD (Y) + PARTICLE MODIFIER (Z):

        (i) '**he who or that which Y-s Z or is Y-ed Z**': *stand-by, go-between, pullover*.

        (ii) 'the act of Y-ing Z': *get-together, splashdown*.

    (d) PARTICLE MODIFIER (Y) + VERB HEAD (Z):

        (i) '**that which Z-s Y or is Z-ed Y**': *income, offprint, offshoot*.

        (ii) '**the act of Z-ing Y**': *outbreak, afterglow, downfall*.

    (e) TYPES WITHOUT A CLEAR HEAD:

        (i) Verb (Y) + Noun object (Z):

            —'**he who or that which Y-s Z**': *pickpocket, scarecrow, stopgap*.

        (ii) Noun subject (Y) + Verb (Z)

            —'**that which Y Z-s**': *household* (a rare type).

        (iii) Noun object (Y) + Adjective object complement (Z):

            —'**a sufficient quantity to make Y Z**' (a rare type): *mouthful, spoonful*.

2. *Compound Adjectives*

(1) **Endocentric—Single adjective centre,** which always occurs in second position. Under adjectives we also include present and past participles in their adjectival role. Some types of meaning relationship apply only to participles, some only to non-participial adjectives; this should be clear from the examples cited:

    (a) NOUN MODIFIER (Y) + PLAIN ADJECTIVE HEAD (Z):

        Various semantic relationships occur:

        (i) '**Z on account of Y**' (i.e. Y is the cause): *seasick, lovesick, snowblind*.

    (ii) **'Z in respect of Y'**: *homesick, colour blind, waterproof.* These compounds might also be interpreted in terms of the prepositions *for, to, against,* respectively.

    (iii) **'Z of Y'**: *blameworthy, carefree.*

    (iv) **'Z like Y'**: *sea-green, stone-cold, dog-tired, pitch-black.*

    (v) **'Z as far as Y'**: *brimful, knee-deep, world-wide.* These are all double-stressed with the nuclear accent on the second element.

    (vi) **'Z as found in Y'**: *hunting pink, navy blue, Lincoln green.*

(b) NOUN MODIFIER (Y) + PARTICIPLE HEAD (Z):
Different verbal relationships are possible:

    (i) **'Z by Y'** (Y the agent of the verb stem of the past participle Z): *man-made, strife-torn, spellbound.*

    (ii) **'Z Y'** (Y the object of the verb stem of the participle Z): *soul-destroying, self-denying, all-embracing.*

    (iii) **'Z in/at/on/to (etc.) Y'** (Y location or prepositional object of the verb stem of Z): *home-made, factory-produced, seagoing, law-abiding.*

(c) ADJECTIVE MODIFIER (Y) + PLAIN ADJECTIVE HEAD (Z):

    (i) **'Z of the subvariety called YZ'**: *dark green, light-blue Roman-Catholic, Irish-American.*

    (ii) **'Z enough to be (also) Y'**: *icy cold, scalding hot, red hot.*

(d) ADJECTIVE (ADVERB) MODIFIER (Y) + PARTICIPLE HEAD (Z):
In these cases the construction is equivalent to an adverb + verb construction; in fact sentences containing such a compound adjective might also be expressed by a **verb plus adverb** or **verb plus adverbial phrase** construction, e.g. *he works hard* beside *(he is) hard-working.* Other examples are: *high-born, clean-cut. Ever-* also occurs as an initial element, representing the adverbial *for ever,* e.g. *everlasting,* also with a plain adjective, *evergreen; all* also occurs, being equivalent to *for/over all* in adverbial position, e.g. *allpowerful, almighty.*

(2) **Endocentric—Co-ordinate adjective centres**: these are relatively rare. Both possible types occur, but the line between them is sometimes hard to draw. The EQUATIVE type may be illustrated by *Anglo-Norman, blue-green* (cf. *dark green*). The ADDITIVE type is seen in *Franco-Prussian, bitter-sweet* (a special case is *French-German (dictionary)* where the order is relevant, a contrast being made with *German-French*).

(3) **Exocentric adjective compounds.** In both of the following types the compound has a head (which is not, of course, the centre since it cannot stand for the whole compound).

(a) NOUN HEAD (Y) + ADJECTIVE ADVERB MODIFIER (Z):

This is the adjectival equivalent of the BAHUVRIHI type like *blackhead, dimwit.* It is distinguished from the latter by having the adjective or adverb in second position and meaning 'having a Y which is Z' (rather than 'he who . . .'). Examples are: *footsore, heartsick, heartbroken, inside out, upside down.*

(b) ADJECTIVE MODIFIER (Y) + NOUN HEAD (Z):

This appears to be a fairly recent type which has arisen from noun phrases first occurring prenominally as a noun modifier, e.g. *a first-class player*, and then being shifted to predicative use as in *he's first class*. The meaning of the compound in its adjectival use might be described as 'of that type which V.-s (a/the) YZ'. Examples are: *commonplace, everyday, long-distance, high church, top quality.* A currently very productive model is with the noun *type*, e.g. *Russian-type, new-type*, but this is still rare in predicative position.

3. *Compound Verbs*

With the exception of a few exocentric types like *coldshoulder* 'give/ show . . . the cold shoulder', compound verbs are all of the single-centred endocentric type. Three kinds of first element occur, giving us three such types:

(a) NOUN MODIFIER (Y) + VERB HEAD (Z):

Three types of semantic relationship may be distinguished:

   (i) '**to Z (a/the) Y(-s)**' (where Y is the object): *househunt, thoughtread, flagwave.*

   (ii) '**to Z in/at/on/ (a/the) Y**' (where Y is the location or time): *globetrot, springclean, sunbathe, eavesdrop.*

   (iii) '**to Z like a Y**': *henpeck, manhandle, chainsmoke.*

(b) ADJECTIVE MODIFIER (Y) + VERB HEAD (Z):

the meaning is always 'to Z Y' (where Y is the adjectival complement), e.g. *roughride, whitewash.*

(c) PARTICLE MODIFIER (Y) + VERB HEAD (Z):

the meaning is again always 'to Z Y' (where Y is an adverbial particle), e.g. *downgrade, overstep, outstretch, underprop, uphold.*

4. *Other Types of Compound*

The only other substantial group of compounds is to be found in the NUMERALS. Such compounds as *twenty-four* are additive in the strictest sense: they represent straightforward additions. But compounds like *two hundred* are endocentric with a single head viz. *hundred*. The same contrast is seen at the derivational level in the difference between *forty* and *fourteen*, the suffix *-ty* meaning 'times ten' and *-teen* meaning 'plus ten'. A combination of the two types occurs in more complex numbers, e.g. *two thousand five hundred.*

Apart from the case of the numerals we only find a few compound prepositions, e.g. endocentric *into* and *on to*, and exocentric *out of*. The adverbial sequences *at once*, *of late*, etc., are probably best considered as full idioms and are therefore best left unanalysed.

5. Structures formed by compounding

The linguistic process of compounding may apply in theory to any kind of stem: even bound roots appear in compounds. Most of our illustrations have been of the compounding of simple words either with other simple words or with derived (or inflected) words, e.g. those inflected with {-ɪŋ}, {-D₂} and {-Z₂} 'possessive'. It is also perfectly possible for complex words (for the most part, derived ones) to be compounded with each other, and for a compound itself to be a constituent of a further compound.

Examples of some of the different types are:
—bound root + simple word: *Franco-German*
—simple word + simple word: *gatepost*
—simple word + derived word: *colour photography*
—derived word + simple word: *retirement age*
—derived word + derived word: *population growth*
—compound word + simple word: *steamship company*
—compound word + derived word: *blackboard duster*
—simple word + compound word: *council workman*
—derived word + compound word: *conference timetable*
—compound word + compound word: *railway timetable*

Thus different layers of word-formation may be built up to produce lengthy composite words, of which an extravagant example is Zandvoort's (*the*) *Empire Air Raid Distress Fund Flag Day Committee*.

Compounds themselves of course also form constituents of derived and inflected words. Compound words may behave in the same way as simple words with regard to inflection (e.g. *girlfriend*, *girlfriends*, *girlfriend's*, *girlfriends'*; *springclean*, *springcleans*, *springcleaning*, *springcleaned*); otherwise they are not true compounds. But compounds may also form the stem of a derived word, e.g. *schoolmaster-ly*, *un-seaworthy*, *greenfinger-ed*. In some cases where both derivation and compounding are involved, it is not clear whether a word is best regarded as derived or compound. For example, is a word like *householder* better analysed as *household-er* 'one who has a household', than as *house-holder* 'one who holds a house'?

6. Other factors affecting compounds

The tendency towards the 'clipping' of string compounds, i.e. omission of one of their elements, gives rise to some interesting semantic developments. The loss of medial elements may produce compounds with unusual semantic relationships between the components: for example, a *newsboy* is a boy concerned with news only in an indirect way; the word is presumably a 'clipped' form of *newspaperboy*. When a final element is lost, the result is that the remaining element acquires a new range of meaning and, in some cases, a new grammatical class, e.g. *Underground* 'Underground railway'. Sometimes a two-morpheme compound is 'clipped' in this way, e.g. *alarm* 'alarm clock', *life* 'life sentence' (whence the new derivative *lifer*).

Finally, compounds are just as susceptible as other words to the development of multiple class membership. Thus from the adjective *waterproof* a factitive verb *waterproof* has been formed. Further examples are *blackmail, steamroller* (verb from noun), *evergreen* (noun from adjective); this last example may well have involved 'clipping', some such word as *tree* or *bush* having been omitted.

NOTES

1. It should be noted that we distinguish between composite, compound and complex words. See below p. 84–85.

2. Note that whereas the first group (*re-establish*, etc.) normally has initial /riː-/ the second group (*receive*, etc.) usually has initial /rɪ-/ (or even /rə-/).

3. Not to mention the question of whether this *black-* and this *straw-* are the same as the ordinary words *black* and *straw*, or, for that matter, whether *-berry* is the same as the independent word *berry*.

4. In this respect cf. the 'separability' of English *I work*, French *je travaille* with Latin *labor-o*.

5. This morph is an affix in accordance with the definition, since, although the /tʃɪld-/ *child-* to which it is attached is not free, the same morpheme does have a free allomorph /tʃaɪld/ *child*.

6. This term has the disadvantage of also being used to name the process by which inflectional affixes are used.

7. Such groups are often described as LEXEMES.

8. We here use the term in the narrower sense proposed by Z. S. Harris *Language* 33, 283–340. We exclude mere realization or exponence relationships and do not necessarily presuppose a generative framework.

9. We give the form used in *The Guardian* 23rd August, 1968 (back page). We personally would prefer *football-boot making firm*.

10. At least no straightforward additive infixes. All cases of internal change might be said to manifest replacive infixation (e.g. *hang–hung*), and *stand–stood* might be described as a case of subtractive infixation (of the /n/). Cf. below.

11. A language in which additive infixes occur is Tagalog (spoken in the Philippines). We may cite Bloomfield's examples (*Language*, p. 218) viz. Tagalog /um/ and /in/ in the words /suˈmuːlat/ 'one who wrote' and /siˈnuːlat/ 'that which was written' compared with the root /ˈsuːlat/ 'writing'.

12. Leaving out of account the question of stress.

13. Hockett has proposed analysing an EMPTY MORPH /-r-/ in this case. But so long as we define a MORPH as a minimal meaningful unit, a meaningless morph like /-r-/ appears unacceptable. For cases where a single sound (or phoneme) seems to represent two morphemes, e.g. French *au* /o/ = 'à + le' Hockett has suggested the term PORTMANTEAU MORPH. *Departure*, *closure*, etc., could be said to involve OVERLAPPING realization.

14. A solution which avoids these difficulties, but is unsatisfactory in other ways, is to posit a zero morph in the plural.

15. SUBTRACTIVE morphs have also been proposed, e.g. for French adjectives for which the masculine form may be extremely simply derived from the feminine—by the subtraction of the final consonant, e.g. /plat—pla/ *plate—plat*, /lɛd—lɛ/ *laide—laid*, /frɛʃ—frɛ/ *fraîche—frais*, etc.

16. This applies equally to derived and compound words and to phrases.

17. At one time *die–dice* followed a similar formal pattern, but now *dice* is usual for both singular and plural.

18. Cf. also the triple ambiguity of *George's photograph is in the paper*. (1 = 'taken of George', 2 = 'taken by George', 3 = 'owned by George'.)

19. Jespersen regards such cases—citing *ship's doctor* beside *statesman*—as a special type of compound noun, and they certainly do have a tendency to be limited in range and to favour stress on the first element —both features of compound nouns.

20. Is the following acceptable English? *Both the boy and his dog have brown eyes but his are darker than its.*

21. Usual reduced forms /wɪ/ and /əs/.

22. Now restricted to religious and poetic use as is the even less used plural *ye* which otherwise behaves like *you*.

23. In some forms of English the forms *him, his*, etc., are more common here. The possessive pronoun *one's* is extremely rare.

24. The form appearing to be more common is given first.

25. Except for *himself, themselves*, which represent the older pattern.

26. {-Z₄} may also have a subsidiary distinctive role in other cases, e.g. with collective nouns like *committee* in such a sentence as *The committee finds it acceptable*, compared with *The committee find it acceptable*.

27. Some of these verbs end in a voiceless consonant in their present form, but the /-t/ is still irregular in the content of the past form base which ends in a vowel, e.g. /θɔ:-/ in *thought*. This irregularity, like most others, can of course be explained historically.

28. For speakers of dialects with postvocalic /r/, these two groups would form a single class.

29. This behaves as though it were morphophonemic /-Z/, except that it is always /ɪz/ when stressed. We have thus observed six different morphemes with the forms /s, z, ɪz/, viz.:

(1) (noun) plural
(2) possessive
(3) noun substitute (with possessive pronouns)
(4) (verb) 3rd sg. pres.
(5) verb *be* 3rd sg. pres.
(6) his (unstressed)

30. However we should note that, as with all other cases of /ŋ/ following an unstressed vowel, {-ɪŋ} is realized as /-ɪn/ in most local and regional dialects, and in the rapid colloquial style of many RP speakers. We should also note the occurrence of /r/ in stem-final position.

31. As a result, the sequence *-ing* form + noun may represent either (i) a noun modified by the *-ing* form or (ii) an *-ing* form used nominally followed by its object, or (iii) an *-ing* form used adjectivally followed by its object, as in:

(i) He played tiring games
(ii) He played (at) driving trains
(iii) He played wearing gloves

32. In this example *the girls* is simultaneously the subject of *need* but the object (or passive subject) of *scrub*. Some Northern English speakers extend this use of the *-ing* form to cases where there are two different noun phrases filling these roles, e.g. *I want it cleaning* instead of *I want it cleaned*.

33. The variation between /-ɪst/ and /-əest/ for the superlative form is not merely a result of the lack of an /ɪ/ $\neq$ /ə/ contrast in unstressed position: some speakers pronounce the superlative *oddest* as /'ɒdəst/ but the plain adjective *honest* as /'ɒnɪst/.

34. Both adjectival *well* ('in good health') and adverbial *well*. *Soon*, *cheap*, and a few other deadjectival adverbs also have comparative and superlative forms.

35. The form *fewer* is used by some speakers and indeed insisted upon by pedants, but in colloquial English *less* tends to replace it, presumably under the analogical influence of *more*, i.e. *more/less beautiful*, *more/less cheese* → *more/less books*.

36. It is therefore quite natural for speakers of English to use the superlative when there are only two members in the group, so long as the entity compared is one of them, e.g.

Jean was the happiest of the two girls

although such sentences are usually condemned as 'incorrect'.

37. *health* and *wealth* are probably best viewed as simple morphs.

38. It differs from the homophonous {-D₁} and {-D₂} in that it forms adjectives from nouns.

39. Here, and in the other transcriptions, V means 'any vowel' (but V alongside a word in conventional spelling means 'verb').

40. viz. /ɪ, e, æ, ʌ, ɒ, ʊ/.

41. Cf. *bake–batch*, *drink–drench*, etc., where the members of each pair are no longer felt to have a close semantic relationship with each other.

42. One example is *-ary* which produces *evolutionary* (adjective) beside *revolutionary* (noun or adjective).

43. We could go on to make other divisions such as PROPER–COMMON, COUNT–MASS, but we lack the space here. Even the division we have adopted gives us difficulties when we come to describe some noun-forming suffixes. Consider the range of different meanings exhibited by *-age* in *orphanage*, *postage*, *acreage*, *drainage*, or by *-(e)ry* in *yeomanry*, *jewelry*, *snobbery*, *creamery*.

44. *anti-* and *pro-* may also form adjectives from nouns, e.g. (*He's very*) *pro-Labour*, *anti-liquor*.

45. With the exception of *lion* and *tigr-* all stems with which *-ess* combines denote human beings. Such words as *murderess* might be regarded as being derived either from the male agentive, *murderer*, or from the root itself, *murder*.

46. In some cases a word in *-ist* derived from a noun stem is in free variation with one derived from an adjective stem, e.g. *educationist–educationalist*, *agriculturist–agriculturalist*.

47. Exceptionally, these suffixes are added to adjectives, e.g. *freedom*, *falsehood*, *hardship*.

48. Pronounced /-eɪt/, as compared with the adjectival suffix *-ate* pronounced /-ɪt, -ət/ as in *passionate*.

49. There are very few inflectional gaps. Note that, for example, the vast majority of verbs are inflected for past tense.

50. Cf. also *-ed*, *-ful*, *-ing*, *-ish*, *-ly*, *-some*, *-y*, all of which are native English suffixes.

51. Observe the class-changes brought about by these suffixes:

$$\text{nation} \; — \; \text{al} — \text{iz} — \text{ation} \; — \; \text{ist} \; — \; \text{ic}$$
$$\text{NOUN} {\rightarrow} \text{ADJ.} {\rightarrow} \text{V.} {\rightarrow} \text{N.}_{\text{ABSTR}} {\rightarrow} \text{N.}_{\text{ANIM}} {\rightarrow} \text{ADJ.}$$

52. $X > Y$ means 'X is greater (or more plentiful or more productive) than Y'.

53. Another difference is that the number of derivers greatly exceeds the number of inflectors.

54. Cf. *blackcurrant*, which would be a free collocation for most speakers but for some would be a compound according to this test.

55. A term coined by Sanskrit grammarians from one example of this type, *bahu-vrihi* ((man) possessing) much rice'.

56. *Anglo-Indian* may be either EQUATIVE (traditionally called APPOSITIVE) e.g. *the Anglo-Indian community*, or ADDITIVE (traditionally called COPULATIVE) e.g. *the Anglo-Indian treaty*.

57. Henceforth the symbol Y will be used to indicate the first element of a compound, and the symbol Z to indicate the second. V refers to an 'understood' verb.

BIBLIOGRAPHY

Treatments of morphology are to be found in the principal introductory works on linguistics; these include: L. Bloomfield, *Language* (London, 1935); H. A. Gleason, Jr., *An Introduction to Descriptive Linguistics* (New York, revised edition, 1961); C. F. Hockett, *A Course in Modern Linguistics* (New York, 1958); and R. H. Robins, *General Linguistics: an Introductory Survey* (London, 1964).

The most comprehensive work on the principles and methods of morphological study is *Morphology* by E. A. Nida (Ann Arbor, 2nd edition, 1949). A book by B. Bloch and G. L. Trager, *Outline of Linguistic Analysis* (Baltimore, 1962), contains a section on morphology.

Amongst major works devoted specifically to the morphology of English, both *The Categories and Types of Present-Day English Word-Formation* (Munich, 2nd edition, 1969) by H. Marchand, and Volume VI of *A Modern English Grammar* (London, 1946) by O. Jespersen, contain a wealth of detail. A book by R. W. Zandvoort, *A Handbook of English Grammar* (London, 2nd edition, 1962), contains chapters in which the main features of English morphology are briefly and clearly presented.

The last three works may be said to be traditional in approach; a different kind of treatment is seen in a book on English derived and compound nouns (as well as noun phrases): *The Grammar of English Nominalizations* by R. B. Lees (The Hague, 1963).

4

SYNTAX (AND ASSOCIATED MATTERS)

T. F. Mitchell, University of Leeds

Notwithstanding its title, this essay attempts to develop a little further the syntagmatic conceptualization of linguistic structure of the British linguist, J. R. Firth. Syntagmatics includes syntax but the reader already versed in linguistics may find more to interest him in the lexical content of the paper than in the treatment it has seemed appropriate to give to the sentence and its parts. Concern is principally with 'forms' of language and with the recognition and designation of categories with which to talk about texts. Although, therefore, meaning as such is not the present object of study, it is nevertheless recognized that language forms and functions are interwoven and meaning the ultimate objective. Consequently, a prefatory section has been included on aspects of meaning that the reader may need to be reminded of before he embarks on the close study of language. The essay concludes with a brief comparative account of the Firthianism informing it.

Meaning

One may approve of the Mad Hatter's intellectual misgivings, if not of his manners, when he tells Alice at the Tea Party that saying what she means and meaning what she says are not the same thing a bit—and he might have added that there is a good deal more than that to 'saying' and 'meaning'. One sympathizes less with more modern linguists who separate the domains of their professional concern into phonology, lexicon, grammar, and semantics without always explaining at all adequately how the separation is made and in particular how we are to recognize the scope of *semantics*, as if somehow meaning is known in advance, is given. Nor should we feel any more satisfied with the common enough view of semantics as concerning either the meaning of lexical items taken singly or that of a text over and above the meaning of its lexical items. This essay, it is hoped, will show that it is as unsatisfactory to regard what for the moment we may call 'word-meanings' as discrete, finite, and localized in advance as it is to see 'further' meaning as a kind of 'expressive' topping or dressing. If a somewhat scandalous example may be permitted at the outset, such an addressive sentence in English as *silly old b-----d*, may indicate the speaker's appreciation of a favour rendered by a close friend and impugn neither the addressee's intelligence, his vigour, nor his antecedents; rather would it mark gratitude and affection, the latter in a society in which close friendship or intimacy is shown less demonstratively than in other cultures, even western European ones close at hand. It is in fact the contravention of the linguistic taboo, the 'escape' from socio-linguistic constraints appropriate to other relationships between interlocutors, that marks the 'meliorative' meaning of affectionate gratitude in the circumstances. This is not to say, of course, that the same 'form of words' may not be used very differently elsewhere, 'pejoratively' by a student, let us say, in reference to his professor. And grammar is directly involved! Not only is *silly old* — recognizably an example of a 'meliorative-pejorative' type of adjectival compound in English[1] but, more generally, the example has just been shown to be ambiguous and ambiguity is rightly much to the fore today as a mode of demonstrating important meaningful distinctions and relationships that might otherwise go unobserved. The fact, however, remains that the type of ambiguity just illustrated goes by default and fails to engage the attention of influential linguists of the times. They would be likely to recognize the *pejorative* form of the example given, primarily because it illustrates the referential use of language, language 'at a distance', as it were, from the objects, people, qualities, etc. to which it may refer; from this standpoint, the example may plausibly be regarded as derivable from an amalgamation of such 'underlying' sentences as *he is silly, he is old, he is a b-----d*. But such a derivation makes little or no sense for the *meliorative* employment of the sequence in the face-to-face and ear-to-ear circumstances to which it is apt. Such contrasts, therefore, tend to be ignored, and one is left to wonder both why and how. At all events, meaning is clearly involved at all times in the close study of language forms; if nothing more, one is constantly asking oneself whether this or that sentence or part-sentence is meaningfully the same or different, and the important word here is 'constantly', such is the complexity of language. One cannot reasonably, then, examine sentences, the lexical items within them, and their possibilities of phonetic form, save at all times within a semantic framework or envelope. For a linguistic statement to have ultimate value, it must probably be a simultaneous statement of meaning and of form. It seems therefore appropriate to indicate as briefly and informally as possible important aspects of meaning that the observer and analyst may need to be aware of and take into account when studying language and perhaps especially spoken language. It might perhaps be said in passing that all linguists are at one in recognizing the primacy of speech over the essentially different manifestations of language in writing but far from all linguists adduce examples of recognizably spoken language in their work and the close study of conversation, for example – a functionally vital form of spoken language – has barely begun.

The English sentence *That'll do*, like an infinite number of other sentences in the language, is ambiguous in isolation and only disambiguated in extended discourse. With final rising intonation, say, it may be used homophonously for example by dad either to his erring small boy or to the shop assistant looking him out a tie, but a repetition of the form of words, this time with falling intonation, is adapted to the continued recalcitrance of the child but hardly to the requirements of the shop transaction. From such examples comes the recognition that language – and meaning with it – is not only contrastive but also ongoing. Dependency between sentences and in particular between elements of a sentence, otherwise the *syntagmatic* relations obtaining between parts of discourse, will be a recurring theme in this paper. Also on-going are the extralinguistic or situational circumstances of language use. It would be hard to better J. R. Firth's example – 'Now just take these. I'm sure they'll do you good. You'll feel much better in the morning. Good-night.' No doubt not all hospital sisters behave in this way, but some do, and the identification of the speaker as a night-sister, of the place as a hospital ward, of the activity as the distribution of medicine, is surely correct. In the way that one 'sees' the ward, its activity and the participants therein, so also one 'hears' the sister using rising intonation in more than one sentence-final place in order to reassure the patient. It is at once instructive and comic to ring impossible intonational changes on the sentence forms of such an example of living speech. Meaning therefore not only resides in contrastive relationships and in the on-going nature of language; appropriateness to the situation (also on-going) is a further inescapable condition of the meaningful use of language. This is not to say that the situation 'determines' the linguistic choices made or vice versa, but the proper rejection of the narrowly behaviourist view of us as creatures of purely conditioned linguistic reflexes should not entail the simultaneous rejection of 'situational context' as linguistically uninteresting.

It is, then, part of the nature of language to be on-going in on-going situations. What now is discernible of uses to which language is put? We might distinguish at least the functional, the emotive, the sociocultural, the topical, the ostensive, the referential, and the mnemonic. There are doubtless other distinctions that might be made, nor does the order of listing carry implications as to any priority of importance among the categories named, some of which may even overlap. It is not our concern, moreover, to consider for example the part played by language in the formation of concepts and vice versa. The difficult question of metaphor is also omitted. Deferring for the time being consideration of an aspect of language and its meaning which is of paramount importance for the linguist, namely the forms of language, let us look at what is intended by the seven named categories and at the same time remember that not only is the web of meaning made up of many strands but that more than one of them may meet at one node of the web, at a single place in discourse.

Functional meaning

Language, spoken or written, is used, for instance, to ask questions, make requests, promises, bids, to deceive, to silence an opponent, to give orders, testimony, advice, warnings, instructions, to count and calculate, to eulogize, mourn, recite, curse, compliment, congratulate, cajole, to greet and take leave of people, to celebrate, train and educate, tell stories, make jokes, gossip, play games, insult and quarrel, to pray, and the reader may add several other language functions of his own. The function is sometimes specialized in relation to its mode of production and perception. Radio or TV commentary, for example, is a form of spoken language in which the need to keep up with or to give the semblance of rapidity in the activity under commentary leads to the adoption of linguistic features, grammatical, lexical, and phonological, that are characteristic of this use of language. The circumstances of immediate confrontation in speech must also give rise to uses of language that are *sui generis*, as J. B. Pride has pointed out in the case of what has been termed 'reinforcement of the speaker', whom one seeks to encourage and reassure by a display of interest in and understanding of what he has to say; the use of appropriate interjections (including *mm* and *ah*), the exploitation of the intonational resources of the language, the occasional supply of a word or filling in of a gap, are among features that may give *prima facie* an impression of bare articulateness in a speaker who is in fact doing a competent job of keeping a conversation going. Elsewhere, of course, there are purely written forms of language use—say, on forms or public notices, in newspaper headlines or the preambles to insurance policies as well as in The Times Law Reports, and so on. French, if one may be permitted a minor digression, is full of eye-grammar; you may be asked in that language to fill in a form giving *vos nom, prénoms, âge, et qualité*, which contains interesting features of 'number concord' but which belongs to the written language only; in the same way, one should not call upon some imaginary feature of 'liaison' (nowadays, it appears, as much as anything a matter of the generation gap) to disambiguate *père et mère* and *pères et mères* occurring in the following two extracts from Articles 57 and 76 of the French *Code Civil*, relating to births and marriages: *Sur le registre . . . sont portés le jour, l'heure . . . de la naissance de l'enfant . . . et les prénoms des père et mère*, to be compared with *les prénoms . . . des pères et mères* from the *acte de mariage*. It is probably easier to distinguish in speech between *my uncle and aunt* and *my uncles and aunts* in English than it is between *mes oncle et tante* and *mes oncles et tantes* in French. It is not always a simple choice between written and spoken presentation, of course. Language may be read aloud, for instance, and although the implication of spoken utterance is less assured for some written functions than others, nevertheless rehearsals and performances of plays and similar entertainments, newsreading, lecturing and public address, though not 'colloquial' language, illustrate speech with the implication of writing and vice versa. In general, it should perhaps be said again that the linguist is ultimately interested in the relationship between forms of language and such language functions.

Emotive meaning

This aspect of meaning is more or less self-explanatory and need not detain us long. Emotive language is indicative of mood, anger, excitement, affection, cordiality, and so on. It is remarkable, for instance, how people tend to lose their educated hats when they get excited; the 'lapse' of an educated Arab from classical into colloquial forms of speech is a typical example, and the fact is used often enough for comic purposes in English plays and elsewhere; the use of 'diminutive' and 'augmentative' forms of nouns, adjectives, etc. in Spanish is more often a matter of 'affectiveness' than size. The 'affective' use of language is thus marked not only by such phonetic means as voice quality, for example, but also by the lexical and grammatical choices made by speakers. And, of course, to his interlocutor on the receiving end the fact of a speaker being angry may matter a good deal more than his reasons for being so.

Socio-cultural meaning

Here we are concerned, as we have already partly seen, with the linguistic aspect of who says what to whom and in which circumstances. An individual presents himself to his interlocutor/s in a variety of guises, largely translatable into terms of the relative roles and statuses of language users. One 'places' one's interlocutor and adjusts one's speech in accordance with various biographical assumptions. It should perhaps be said again that the aspects of meaning we are distinguishing intermesh and often meet in one text, in one sentence, even in one word or syllable. Thus, not only, say, deference, equality, superiority, reverence, etc. will enter into language seen from the standpoint of role relations but also such emotive categories as cordiality, affection, dislike, etc. Commands may be requests may be suggestions may be invitations, and, as Pride has it, can as easily involve advice as orders, entreaty as persuasion, tentativeness as positiveness, familiarity as unfamiliarity, and so on. As a simple illustration of language selected in response to the interrelationship of speakers, consider the vocative in English sentences and the case of the middle-class young Englishman, perhaps of public school background, addressing his mother. The often observable use of her Christian name may give offence to some but reflection shows that the options open to the young man are few. *Mum* has class connotations which he may not 'overcome', if at all, until he is a good deal older, *Mummy* becomes impossible for him to use from the age of 10 or 11 or thereabouts, and *Mother* might suggest to some a measure of old-maidishness or the status of bachelor living with his mother. There seem therefore to be few available choices other than the use of the Christian name or the adoption of a deliberately jocular form such as *Ma*. It is not only, then, the occurrence elsewhere of such phrases— whose putative semantic essence is frustratingly fugitive—as *Reverend Mother*, *Mother Mary*, *Mother India*, and *Old Mother Riley* that severely restricts the interest of the type of feature analysis by which *mother* will be analysed into semantic components corresponding to those of *bachelor*, whose meaning, we are told by some semanticists, comprises the features 'human', 'male' and 'unmarried'. Such analysis is explanatorily inadequate for one who wishes to come to grips with the fully meaningful use of language rather than simply with the 'ideal', logical implications of kin relations. Feature analysis has its place and the feature analyst is in any case hardly to be censured when the great majority of linguists to date have restricted their view of meaning to aspects which follow yet have not explained satisfactorily, if at all, how this is done. These aspects relate to the symbolic nature of language and to language at a remove from speech, *grosso modo* to the use of language to explain, refer to and remember artefacts, people, abstract concepts, etc. In the literature, at least the following terms are applied to these facets of meaning: 'cognitive', 'notional', 'conceptual', 'denotative', 'referential', 'representational', 'designative', terminological usage which, even if no more is involved, is decidedly confusing.

Topical meaning

Choices of language vary greatly with the subject-matter or topic. Technical jargons are an obvious example. Perhaps we can recognize individual words in Firth's *Tooth Ripple Losses in Unwound Pole Shoes* but that is about all, and most of us will be little wiser on being told that it is the title of an article in an electrical trade journal. Technical jargons, necessary as they are, belong at one end of a scale of choice according to topic, which would include less strictly codified differences, as between, say, intellectual and common-or-garden uses of language. More generally, much that comes under the heading of 'topical' can probably be regarded as a subdivision of 'referential meaning' (see below).

Ostensive meaning

'Specification' as a category of linguistic experience may encompass such varied grammatical classes as articles, ordinal numerals, and deictics (e.g. demonstrative *this/that, these/those*). It is perhaps particularly to the area of deixis that 'ostensiveness' belongs. In the world of the here and now with, say, flowers as objects of ostensive definition, we may point at a particular horticultural specimen and simultaneously say to our companion by way of explanation—'That is a japonica'. We are thus at one remove from the subsequent referential, *in absentia* use of language.

Referential meaning

We may ostensively define, for instance, 'a table' and can go on from there to idealize the concept 'table', even if we are uncertain whether, say, 'dressing-table' should be included within the same conceptual domain. It is noteworthy that not only objects, events, persons, and qualities can be conceptualized; the whole of meaning may be so, including all aspects already considered. There is some risk, however, of confusing as the object of linguistic analysis a metalanguage of explanation with the living language we encounter. Nor is there any compulsion to believe in the primacy of any subdivision of meaning, for instance in the referential 'table'-ness of 'table'. As will be shown subsequently, for example, an addressive sentence like *that's a good boy* in English cannot be dealt with in referential terms.

The explanation—often in their absence—of what things are, of how things work, of how people act, and so on, draws on our capacity for abstract conceptualization among other things. For referential reasons we should no doubt wish to regard *book* as the same item in *the book, the French book*, and *the accounts book*. It is the linguist's task to justify this equivalence overtly by adducing similarities of linguistic behaviour in extended contexts, if he considers it of interest to do so. In the same way, at a more abstract level than that of *book*, 'continuous spatio-temporal movement' may be used mnemonically to label or gloss the various associations of *run* with *men, engines, taps, noses, plays, films, trains, buses,* etc., while 'loss of intensity' is an appropriate gloss for *wear off* in *the pain/paint/enthusiasm/etc. wears off*. Be it said again that the linguist should be able to justify his acceptance of such similarity in terms of the analytical operations which he will subsequently be seen to perform—association with a similar range of adverbs, for example, may provide one criterion in the case of *wear off*. Intuitions as to the sameness or difference of items should always be capable of overt demonstration.

Mnemonic meaning

The mnemonic, perhaps better the 'naming' function of language should not be confused with that of ostensive definition. The human being seems endowed with a more or less discrete naming faculty, often sadly blurred by advancing years. The thesis is later put forward that words and word-classes are essentially names and classes of names serving at least two purposes: firstly, the mnemonic end of all abstraction, and secondly, the purpose of 'mention' or 'citation' for combinations of those abstract elements of linguistic structure which we shall subsequently call roots (or lexemes) and morphemes. Thus, for example, words 'figure forth' otherwise 'unmentionable' public notices, as *Please tender exact fare and state destination* in the British bus. Strictly, the root common to e.g. *tears* and *tore* is unpronounceable and so are the morphemes, e.g. *-s*, associated with it; associations, however, of roots and morphemes are utterable in speech or writing as 'words'. In a not wholly dissimilar way, the word *shall*, let us say initial in the sentence *shall we go?*, provides a means of referring *en bloc* to as well as separately identifying such greatly varied pronunciation forms as [ʃɪ, ʃə, ʃæ, ʃ̆, ʃl, ʃəl, ʃæl, etc.], just as the two words *is that* act in relation to a greatly varied range of phonetic possibility initially in the sentence *is that all you've got?*, variety by no means accounted for by the phonetician's styles (slow colloquial, rapid colloquial, formal, etc.). Such variation reveals that we do in fact resort to some tacit editing of our observations prior to presentation and that the contrasts we focus on are probably less often between single forms (uni-forms, so to speak) than between potential ranges of form. This, however, in passing; more central to the present approach to language is the view that so-called 'definitions' or glosses in dictionaries are not seen as 'the meanings' of the entries to which they correspond but rather as a somewhat mixed bag of essentially mnemonic extensions of the word-entry, in which an attempt, usually less than conscious, is made at summing up the entry's distributional 'privileges or occurrence', to use the current jargon. 'felis leo' or 'large, strong, flesh-eating animal indigenous to Africa and Asia', possible glosses for the entry *lion*, may serve as summations of the contextual occurrences of *lion* that are listed or might be listed in the dictionary article or, in the case of 'felis leo', as a referential switching device from one English style to another. The fact remains that neither gloss is of much if any relevance to, say, *L for lion* or *The Red Lion* in British English.

Such, then, is a general background of awareness against which linguistic form may be seen and evaluated. Much has been omitted from this summary and doubtless inadequate sketch of meaningful aspects of language. Its gaps and inconsistencies must, however, remain, so that we may proceed to that aspect of meaning which most centrally concerns this paper—*formal meaning*, the patterns and interrelations of linguistic form we use and respond to.

Formal meaning

The patterned arrangements of linguistic form, variously phonological, lexical, and grammatical, provide their own strand of meaning separable from all others yet intertwined with them. Valéry and also Eliot spoke, I believe, of their experience of composing first the formal rhythmic frame of a poem and letting the lexical and grammatical structures follow, but there are also discernible abstract arrangements of a lexico-grammatical order. It will be mostly with these that this paper will henceforth be concerned. The formal value of an item depends closely on (a) other items present in the text and the constraints and dependencies observable between them (b) the 'transformability' of the text in terms of the analytical operations of substitution, expansion or contraction as the case may be, interpolation (a form of expansion), and transposition. (a) may be termed *intra*-textual dependence and (b) *inter*-textual dependence; (a) is almost certainly consequent upon (b). A textual item is recognizable largely on the grounds of what may or may not be present in the text, all within a framework of judgment as to what is or is not meaningfully equivalent. For equivalence, as C. E. Bazell has said, there seem to be no truly rigorous tests; the linguist offers rather facts for or against by the application of his analytical operations. It has already been said that a linguistic item or class of items is meaningful not because of inherent properties of its own but because of the contrastive or differential relationships it develops with other items and classes. In an attempt to solve the difficult problem of presentation posed by this proportional nature of meaning, we posit items and classes as poles between which contrast seems reasonably to obtain and we name these end-points more or less extensively by the use of words, word-classes, dictionary- and other glosses. Meaning, however, is much less in the name than in the network of relevant differential relationships. The presence of *off*, let us say, in *the milk has gone off* (expansion) marks a different *gone* from that in *the milk has gone* (contraction), just as a different *off* is almost certainly 'determined' by the presence (substitution) of *John* in place of *the milk*. Many other features and distinctive linguistic behaviour will relate to ($go \pm off$) and, in turn, the lexicographer-grammarian must needs go on to consider ($go + off$) and to distinguish at least between *go off* (= *away*), *go off*

($\pm$ *the field*), *go off* (someone), *go off* ($\pm$ *bang*), *go off* (*one's head*), *milk go off*. It might be advantageous to illustrate the manner in which meaningfully distinct items are recognizable. Let us base our observations primarily on the ubiquitous spoken English category of 'particle' and, since we have started with it, let us stay mostly with the exemplar *off*, which—disregarding such occurrences as in the collocational frame *well/badly/comfortably/etc.* . . . or in such composite items as *come off* (= succeed)—may perhaps be glossed as referring to 'separation, release, removal, departure (e.g. from a location, an expectation, a norm of acceptability, etc.), unavailability'.

The term 'particle' is deliberately used since *off* is variously prepositional, adverbial, and adjectival. Moreover, it is sometimes difficult to distinguish between prepositional and adverbial (and even adjectival) *off* and all three grammatical subdivisions demand considerable further subdivision themselves. Notice in passing the reference to *grammar* in connection with general class names (particle; preposition, adverb, adjective). Other particles (e.g. *on, up, down, etc.*) behave similarly to *off*, so that generalization is possible having regard to facts subsequently indicated. Grammar is first and foremost generality in relation to lexical particularity, but this, it should be said, does not imply any denial of the essential one-ness of grammar, lexis, and meaning. Syntax, and more generally syntagmatic analysis, is concerned with textual dependencies and constraints. But to resume with *off*.

The category of 'preposition' in contradistinction to 'adverb' is usually recognized by its association with nominal and pronominal forms. Such forms frequently but not necessarily follow the preposition component of a 'prepositional phrase'. A noun follows, for example, in *he fell off his bike/rolled off the bed/ran off the field*, but not in *I saw him riding his bike but I didn't see him fall off/it's not the sort of bed to roll off*, although it is probably always possible to 'derive' the second type from the first. In certain circumstances the noun or pronoun may be optionally omitted and it may not be clear whether one is left with preposition or adverb. In cases where *away* may be substituted for *off* (cf. *he ran off*), most would regard *off* as 'adverbial' but there may be less certainty in response to the TV commentator's remark that *the players are running off*, to which *the field* may be optionally added; in the same way, when the restaurant waitress tells you that *the fish is off*, she is less likely to be saying that it is putrescent than that it is *off the menu*; again, is there any equivalence between the *off*'s of, say, *the wind blew the roof off the house* and *the wind blew the roof of the house off*? The omissibility of a following noun, moreover, is not limited to the 'intransitive' case, cf. *run someone off* ($\pm$ *your land*). It might seem plausible to regard the case of e.g. *he ran off the field* as a coalescence of 'prepositional' *off* and 'adverbial' *off* and thus derivable from *he ran off off the field*; it is also possible to consider *off* in *the wind blew the roof off the house* as a coalescence of *off* and *of*, which do occur together in regional speech (see also p. 148 below).

The case of verb + particle is interesting in numerous ways. Some verbs, for example, do not occur without aspectual (inceptive *off*, continuative *on*) or directional (*up, down, across, on to, etc.*) extension; *shamble*, for instance, requires the 'complementation' of *off, on/up, down, across,* etc., a fact to which its phonaesthetic overtones of *amble, shuffle,* and perhaps also *stumble* may or may not relate. Then again, there is the wider relevance of the fact of cognitive equivalence or difference of the verbal form in the context of particle extension. The inclusion of *off* simply provides 'adverbial' or 'prepositional' extension in the case of, say, *run off* ($\pm$ *the field*); one runs, whether or not off, so to say. Similarly, with the directional particle *down*, the ball 'rolled', whether or not 'down the road'. On the other hand, the verbal forms are greatly different in value as between *John tore down the poster* and *John tore down the road*. It is instructive to look at such examples a little more closely in order to demonstrate something of the complexity of intra- and inter-sentential dependency. The italicized portion of the sentence Noun + *tore down the poster* is ambiguous, 'interpretable' variously as 'ripped the poster violently from the surface to which it adhered' or 'rushed headlong down the poster'. In terms of the world of experience, the second interpretation relates perhaps to the activity of something mobile and smaller in size than the poster, for example an insect; on the first interpretation, *down* stands in similar relation to *tore* as the earlier example of *off* to *run* in *run off* ($\pm$ *the field*) and the particle and second noun (*poster*) are transposable, i.e. *John tore the poster down*. Therefore the first noun (*John, the centipede,* etc.) not only disambiguates *tore* but also 'determines' the prepositional or adverbial classification of *down* and thus the type of relationship between verb and particle. Thus, cf.

1. *John tore down the poster.*
2. *The centipede tore down the poster.*

But the second noun, also no less than the first, is relevant to the interpretation of both *tore* and *down*, severally and conjointly. Cf.

3. *John tore down the poster.*
4. *John tore down the road.*

Relationships so far discerned might be indicated in general terms by using initial letters for the noun, verb, and particle classes and different kinds of brackets as follows:

$$((N_1 \{[V] [P]\} N_2])$$

The conjunction of N_1 and N_2, taken as a discontinuous whole, permits or not the inclusion of post-verbal aspectual particles, notably *off* and *on*. When $N_2 = road$, then concomitantly $N_1 = $ e.g. *man* and $\neq$ e.g. *centipede* for *off* to be admissible; contrariwise, *off* is inadmissible where $N_1 = man$ and $N_2 = poster$. This relationship is indicated by the horizontal braces in

5. (a) *The man tore off down the road.*

   (b) *The centipede tore off down the poster.*

There must be added the relationship between verb and aspectival particle, indicated by the oblique stroke in the 'formula'

$$((\overbrace{N_1} /\{[V]\ \overbrace{P_1}/ [P_2])\}\ \overbrace{N_2}])$$

Finally for the present, with certain other comparable particles (e.g. *up*) substituted for *down*, the sentence
6. *John tore up the road.*
is ambiguous and may be glossed as (i) John brought a pickaxe to bear on the road surface or (ii) John rushed headlong up the road. In such cases, an aspectival particle (e.g. *off*) disambiguates the sentence. Cf.
7. *John tore off up the road.*
There obtains, therefore, a further relationship between the aspectival and the prepositional/adverbial particles. For the reader with the good-will, time and inclination to resolve the brackets, the relationships we have distinguished may be expressed *in toto* as follows:

$$((\overbrace{N_1} /\{[V]\ \overbrace{P_1}/ [P_2]\}/ \overbrace{N_2}])$$

The complexity of things is clear enough, as is the multiplicity of relationships developed by a single item, which derives its value from such relationships at the same time as it contributes to the 'definition' of other items in the text. This analytical circularity need not deter us; the important thing is to describe circles of sufficient size to meet the needs of descriptive adequacy. It will have been noted that no justification has been offered for or against the view of *tore* in *John tore down the poster* and *John tore down the road* as belonging or not to the same lexical root or lexeme. The answer to the question would hinge on the further extensibility of the texts and judgments as to similarity or difference between extensions. It is hoped, however, that the above exploitation of a small sample of comparable texts will suffice to reveal the arbitrariness and artificiality of attempts to separate, on the one hand, lexicon and grammar except in terms of generality, and, on the other, ultimately lexico-grammatical analysis and meaning.

The case of adjectival *off*, definable qua adjective on numerous grounds, among others by association with marks of comparison (*more, most, less, least*), with adverbial intensifiers (*very, completely, etc.*),

etc., may serve to reveal further the need to subdivide classes distinguished in analysis. There is insufficient space to attempt a detailed sub-classification of the uses of predicative *off* listed below but the reader might find it amusing and instructive to ask himself such questions as the following: (i) are there any constraints on the verbs which may precede *off*? (ii) what would be the corresponding 'transitive' verb or verbs in a given case (e.g. *the tap is off* (intr.): *turn off the tap* (tr.))? (iii) does *off* in the example stand in antonymous relation to *on* (cf. *the match is off/on* but *the milk is off/*on)? (iv) are there any limitations on the initial noun in terms, for example, of a distinction human/animate/inanimate (cf. *she looked decidedly off* vs. *the cat/the garden looked decidedly off*)? (v) does *off* require 'completion' within the phrase, as by *a long way* in *it's a long way off* or by *to the right* in *the house is off to the right*? (vi) may *off* be replaced by *away*? (vii) where does ambiguity occur and how may it be resolved (cf. *he is off today* = either (a) *hè is off-form today* or (b) *he is away from work today*. Cf. the relatability of (b) with *he has today off*, *a day-off*, *he is off ill today*, etc.) The reader will doubtless think of other questions to ask himself. Here are the examples—a random selection of what might be:

1. *The water/radiator/heating/etc. is/feels/seems off.*
2. *The tap/radio/switch/light is/seems off.*
3. *The brakes are off.*
4. *The milk/meat/fish/etc. is/smells/tastes/looks/seems/etc. off.*
5. *She was/looked/seemed off (to us).*
6. *His coat was off.*
7. *The match is off.*
8. *He is off today.*
9. *The door-handle is off.*
10. *The town is miles off.*
11. *The entrance is/lies off to the right.*

It will be seen that the earlier gloss (p. 144) was serving a genuine mnemonic purpose as an abstraction from such varied relationships.

By way of further illustration of the operations of formal linguistic analysis, let us stay with *off*, now variously associated with *take* in a 'transitive' verbal phrase. Consider the following examples:

1. *He took the money off John.*
2. *He took John off to tea.*
3. *He took off his coat.*
4. *He took John off to a T.*
5. *The wind took off the roof of the house.*

In (1) *off* is prepositional, the prepositional phrase is omissible, and the sentence is a transitive counterpart of e.g. *he turned off the road*. In (2) *off* is the motive-inceptive particle already noted and is omissible without prejudice to the meaning of the remainder. Omission, however, is only possible if the following prepositional phrase is not omitted at the same time. That *off* belongs here to a system of aspectual particles is shown by the substitutability of continuative *on* in *he took John on to tea*, wherein for practical purposes the remainder of the sentence is meaningfully the same. Other points of contrast with the other examples include the interpolability before *off* of the 'adverbial' forms *straight* or *right*, the substitutability of *away* for *off*, the irreversibility of the object noun (*John*) and *off* (i.e. *★He took off John to tea*; cf. (3), (4), and (5)), etc. In (3) *off* is inomissible and of a piece with *took*, is transposable with *his coat* (i.e. *he took his coat off*). *He took his coat off* is ambiguous since the personal reference of the pronominal forms *he* and *his* may not be the same; if *his* refers to a different person from *he*, then the sentence may be substituted by *he took his coat off him* but not in the 'reflexive' case when *he* and *his* are of the same personal reference. As to (4), the criteria which set off (3) from the other types also set off (4), but *take off* in (4) is an idiom. *Off* does not stand in antonymous relation to *on* as in (3) (cf. *he put on his coat*), nor can *took* be replaced by any other verbal form in the way that *took* in (3) may be replaced by e.g. *leave* without disturbing the cognitive equivalence of the remainder. *Took off* in (4), therefore, illustrates the characteristic non-productivity of the parts in relation to the idiomatic whole. Transposability of *John* and *off* is shared with (3) and so, too, is the stylistic substitutability of a single verbal form (e.g. *imitate, mimic*) for idiomatic *take off*. Notice, as a further illustration of syntagmatic dependency, how the introduction of the participial/gerundial form (perhaps better the *-ing* form) following *off* involves ambiguity (cf. *he took John off lecturing* = (a) he imitated John lecturing (b) he took John away to lecture (c) he relieved John from the duty of lecturing; see also Note 3 on pp. 173–4). In (5) the (verb + particle) complex is associated with a genitival phrase comprising two determined nouns separated by *of*, i.e. *the roof of the house*. The sentence type differs in many respects from the others. Thus, any of the following three sentence forms are possible for (5):

> *the wind took off the roof of the house*
> *the wind took the roof of the house off*
> *the wind took the roof off the house*

It is especially the third form that is interesting. *★off of* is regional English and *the wind took the roof off of the house* is dialectal, but cf. the case of *in* substituted for *off*, i.e.

> *the wind blew in the wall of the house*
> *the wind blew the wall of the house in*
> *the wind blew the wall in of the house*

The genitival phrases in such sentences, i.e. *the roof of the house, the handle of the door* (cf. *he took the handle off the door*) appear to exhibit a

148

relationship of the part to the whole. Although *took off* may be stylistically substituted by *removed* at both (5) and (3), there are clearly important differences between the two sentence types concerned. It may also be observed in passing that some of the five sentences (1, 3, 5) exhibit certain similarities of behaviour not shared with the others (2, 4). No attempt is being made in this essay to provide a complete, far less an explicit, rule-ordered formulation.

In the foregoing illustrations the operations of analysis clearly suggest grammatical generalizations. The same operations, however, are performed in 'defining' in formal linguistic terms even very particular items. Take *come off* (= succeed), for instance, which seems plausibly relatable to a corresponding transitive form *bring off*, an equation supported by the similar *come: bring* relationship in association with other particles cf. *come to* (= revive (intrans.)): *bring to* (= revive (trans.)), *come out: bring out*, etc. Supporting criteria include non-extensibility with a following noun or pronoun (contrast e.g. *come off it*), the inomissibility of *off* from *come off*, the non-transposability of *off* in contrast with adverbial *off* (= away) (cf. *off it comes*), and so on. In passing it may be noted that this transpositional front-shifting is an important criterion for the recognition of the inceptive-motive and directional categories of particle to which reference has already been made, cf. *off/on/away/up/down/in/out/over/etc., he went, off came his coat and down he got to work.*

Grammar and lexicon; syntax and morphology

Having seen something of meaning in general and formal linguistic patterning in particular, let us turn to grammar and related topics, staying with intra- and inter-textual constraint and dependency and with relationships of particularity and generality. Grammar is often divided into morphology and syntax, the former concerned with characteristics of words and their paradigms, the latter with patterned arrangements of words in larger stretches of language, typically sentences but also phrases and 'clauses'. It is not the purpose of this paper to discuss arrangements within word-boundaries of infra-word elements—the reader will recognize the composite nature not only of say, familiar compounds like *armchair* or *milk jug* but also of *unfashionable* and *disestablishmentarianism*. Nor shall we be much concerned with the grounds on which word-recognition may be based (for instance, transposability, uninterruptability, irreversibility, separability, criteria which are indeed employable on a broader linguistic front). The division between morphology and syntax is in fact a great deal less clear-cut than is often assumed and may even be otiose. Many of the roots and affixes, inflections and derivations of morphology have their implications as to choices made elsewhere in word+domains, and vice versa; *good* (with zero suffix) is by no means the singular of *goods* and will not therefore appear in such associations as *consumer*— or —*and chattels*, while *goodness* not only does not occur indiscriminately with any kind of following verb (cf. the impossibility of **goodness hates him*) but also excludes pronominal forms other than those of the first person singular from exclamations like *(my)*— and —*gracious (me)*. The view has already been expressed that words are names (of lexical items) derived from the combination of roots (or lexemes) and affixes (or morphemes). In addition, the traditional belief is endorsed by which linguistic awareness is divisible into more particular (lexical) and more general (grammatical) levels. By the exploitation of the human phonatory and scribal capacity, both levels may be given phonological shape in speech and variously graphic shape in writing. An important tenet of this paper, then, is the interdependence of grammar and lexicon. Lexical particularities are considered to derive their formal meaning not only from contextual extension of a lexical kind but also from the generalized grammatical patterns within which they appear, and, conversely, the recognition of general patterns is seen as justifiable only in response to selected comparisons of lexical combinations. Illustrations follow in abundance. It behoves us now to attempt at least working definitions of the related terms and concepts employed.

'Root' or 'lexeme', 'morpheme'; 'word', 'word-class'; 'collocation'

Rather as in the days of 'classical' phonemics much play was made of the 'minimal pair' in order to establish throughout a language such lexical differences as those between *pin, bin, tin, din, sin, thin*, etc., so today ambiguity informing sentences and sequences of words is greatly used as a presentational device and has already been sufficiently illustrated above. It should, however, be borne in mind, firstly, that—for reasons he does not explain but which derive from the on-going nature of speech—the analyst is apt to stuff his sentences to the tolerable limit with elements that more often than not in living discourse occur trans-sententially and, secondly, that if sentences are frequently ambiguous, then words and their parts are greatly more so. Consider a scatter of forms like the following, related to a lexical item *work*:

(1) (I) *work* (he) *work(s)* (he is) *work(ing)* (he) *work(ed)*
(2) (he is a/they are) *work(er/s)*
(3) (it is hard) *work*
(4) (good) *works*
(5) (a) *work(/s)* (of art, genius, supererogation, etc.)
(6) (a) (cement) *works*

Presumably, *-s* in (2) and (5) may justifiably be regarded as 'same' but cf. (1), (4), and (6), not to mention what one might find elsewhere in, say, *Marseilles, facilities*, or *linguistics*. Presumably, too, *work* at (3), (4), (5) and (6) is also the 'same' linguistic item, but at (3) it is not associable

150

with the indefinite article nor with 'pluralizing' -*s*, at (4) there appears at first sight to be no corresponding singular form without -*s*, (5) suggests that the indefinite article may not precede *work* unless in turn the latter is followed by *of* + abstract noun, while (6) does not admit a corresponding form without -*s* yet is regularly preceded by the indefinite article. That *works* at (6) is not to be equated with *works* at (4) is in part justified by the various associability of (6) with a following singular or plural verbal form, cf. *the works is/are on the other side of the road*, with which the obligatory plural contrasts in *good works are hard work*. *Works* at (4) may be relatable to *work* at (5) in terms of a regular correspondence of (plural) -*s* to (singular) (*a* + [*of*] + Noun], but there is more to it than this and -*s* at (4) must be regarded as part of lexical patterning that will be dealt with below under 'collocability'.

Note

It should not be thought that the above represents anything like an analysis or even a fully representative 'scatter' of *work* in English. The writer is also aware of the use of 'mass' and 'count' as terms relatable to distinctions between, say, *marvellous work* and *a marvellous work/ marvellous works* but finds more interesting the fact that the meaning of *work* derives from the several kinds of extension to which it is necessarily subject in the syntactical process. Adjectival extension, e.g. with *marvellous*, is one type, another is that of *of* + N; one can predicate of a work of art that *it is a marvellous work* or that *it is a work of art* but not that **it is a work*. The evident syntactical function of *a* and *of* in *a work of art* (pl. *works of art*) has led some linguists to take the view that the lexicon is divisible into 'full' words (e.g. *work*) and 'empty' (e.g, *a, of, the, for,* etc.), a view of relatively small merit. It is true that *a, of*, etc. do often act in the manner of morphemic flections elsewhere but any recognizable lexical item is capable of more particular meaningful employment in a language. Who is to say that the inclusion of *a* in e.g. *what sort of a dog is that?* may not warrantably be related to 'disparagement' in contrast with the case of the 'enquiry' after the canine species embodied in *what sort of dog is that?* In pre-ecumenical days, no Catholic would have regarded *the* as by implication meaningless in association with *faith*, just as the meaning of the French definite article *Le* in combination with *Chambertin* is that you find the wine in question towards the bottom of the merchant's list of burgundies and pay significantly more for it than in most other cases. But let us get back to *work*.

The 'ambiguity' of morphemic -*s* equally characterizes -*ing*, to name only one further flection. There has to be considered not only the -*ing*'s of *he is working* or *working long hours is bad for the health* but also those of *the working classes* and *hard-working*. Let us examine in turn the different questions posed by the last two examples. There are many kinds of adjectival or qualifying periphrases that follow nouns in English, cf. *men who work (for their living), men in the professions, people with money, men and women of leisure*, etc. In cases where shortened forms of such periphrases precede the noun, the appropriate lexical item is associated with one of a given selection of morphemes, cf. *work+ing men, profession+al men, money+ed people, leisure+ed men and women*. Such examples serve to illustrate not only the uncertain basis of the usual division between morphology and syntax but also the play of lexical constraint as well as the recognizability of semantic fields. On the last topic, if in the common phrase structure of Adjective + Noun, the noun selected is *classes*, then *working* is to be seen in relation to *lower, middle, upper, professional, moneyed, leisured*, etc. with subdivisions as appropriate. Within such a selection of phrases, *working* is definable as adjectival on the basis of the relationships it accretes paradigmatically (by substitution) with *lower/middle/etc.* and syntagmatically (by transposition and expansion) with *(men) who work (for their living)* as well as by its association with the noun *classes* in an Adj + N phrase. It has already been implied more than once that the recognition of semantic fields too often involves putting the cognitive cart before the formal linguistic horse and that it is the linguist's job to justify the fitness of the cart to ride in. It is true that much has often to be taken for granted, but it is in the questioning of such assumptions that advances are made. The earlier scatter of *work* rests on such assumptions, namely that careful analysis would reveal a basis of similar linguistic distribution justifying the scatter. No reason has been advanced for including *working* of *working classes* in the scatter. Even, however, if *a working man* is seen not to work but to be out of work, let us make the probably justifiable assumption that *working* belongs within the scatter of forms we have grouped together as belonging to some single lexical item labelled *work*. In other cases, decisions might be more difficult to arrive at—one not only *works* but also *works pumps, mines, tricks*, and even *miracles* and it may not be at all clear whether all these *work*'s should be included in the same scatter. The problem has been posed if not answered, and will arise again—and again, for the linguist's job is never done. Such questions are, however, relevant to the understanding of the use made in this paper of the concepts and terms of 'root' (or lexeme) and 'morpheme'.

The questions raised by the earlier compound *hard-working* are of a different though related kind, and concern the linguistic status of a composite element *hard work*. It will be seen that the inclusion of a single additional item serves to reduce in some measure the indeterminacy we have noted as attending the parts and the whole of words.

Invoking the inescapable condition of cognitive equivalence and considering that the same complex element is present in *he works hard*, *a hard worker*, *hard-working*, and *hard work*—the ambiguity of the last association of forms is immaterial—we see, firstly, that such a composite element comprises simpler elements occurring elsewhere in other company, i.e. *hard* and *work* considered separately, and, secondly, that the composite element can exhibit its own distribution qua compositum. Such an abstract composite element as *hard work* we shall term a 'collocation'. It is a particular member of a generalizable class of such associations, but we shall return to this aspect of collocability later. In the meantime we may notice that distribution is to be seen in both lexical and grammatical terms and that collocations are recognizable by their own extended 'distributional privileges of occurrence'. Thus, for example, men—specifically cement workers—work *in* cement works; others of different occupation work *on* works of art; others again, or both, *perform* good works. Not only are good works *performed* but cement works are *built* and works of art *produced*.

The concept and term of 'collocation' has to be seen partly in relation to that of 'root' or 'lexeme'. One may speak of the root $\sqrt{work}$, which exhibits the scatter, no doubt extensible, indicated earlier, and talk subsequently of the collocation of roots. 'Morphemes', typically flections but often words like *a, the, of, for,* etc. and including such less overt features as sequential order, are fused with roots as a result of dependencies within extended texts. Amalgams of flectional morphemes, including zero, and roots are 'words'. There are thus three homophonous words in *good works, cement works,* and *works of art,* all belonging to $\sqrt{work}$, which would supply the relevant dictionary entry. Collocations, therefore, are of roots, not of words, which are essentially means of reference. Collocations are at the particular end of the scale of particularity/generality within which analysis proceeds at all times. The recognition of paradigms of morphemes, such as those underlying the sub-divisions of the scatter of $\sqrt{work}$ on p. 150—for example, the verbal *zero/-s/-ing/-ed* associated with $\sqrt{work_1}$—also rests ultimately on collocability, but collocations are so infinitely numerous in such cases that observed regularities of association (e.g. of verbal with adverbial forms) may be generalized in grammatical terms. The analyst is constantly taking decisions as to where to locate his abstractions on the aforementioned scale; in contrast with the final flectional difference in the case of *facility* and *facilities,* forms whose virtually total dissimilarity of collocability suggests a need to ascribe them to separate roots, unlike, too, the case of *-s* in *(cement) works,* no collocational statement seems called for in relation to the verbal flections *zero/-s/-ing/-ed* or those of adjectival comparison (e.g. *zero/-er/-est* with *heavy*). A recognizably regular association of roots or a collocation nevertheless undergoes flectional variation which is accountable in terms of the extended context. For instance, the last two words of *he drinks heavily* severally contain marks of verbal agreement with a preceding third person singular subject (*-s* in *drinks*) and of an adverbial adjunct (*-ly* in *heavily*); comparable word forms are *heavy* and *drinker* in *he is a heavy drinker*, *heavy* and *drinking* in *he is putting in some heavy drinking*, and *drinking* and *heavily* in *he is drinking pretty heavily*. Notwithstanding this variation—cutting across paradigmatic borders—there is clearly involved a regular association between *heavily* and *heavy*, on the one hand, and *drinks, drinker, drinking*[1] and *drinking*[2], on the other. The common elements of each word form may be abstracted and labelled 'root' and associations of roots 'collocations'; the flectional accretions to roots, determined by the further context, form—in conjunction with roots—'words'. The latter are pronounceable and enable us to 'give shape' to particular texts and are in turn recognizable within them. In addition to flections, further morphemic accretions, as *a, the, of, as*, etc., or sequential order (cf. post-nominal *as white as snow* vs. pre-nominal *snow-white*) enable us to pronounce collocations. Although neither root nor collocation is strictly pronounceable as such, it often happens in English that a root and a word are—as in the case of $\sqrt{work}$—formally similar, but if we assume that the root of the word *heavy*, say, includes in its scatter such forms as *heave*, not to mention *heft* and *hefty*, then a postulated root $\sqrt{heav}$- might clearly appear as the unpronounceable abstraction it is, without our turning to the wholly suppletive evidence offered by, for instance, *go* and *went* or *I* and *me*. For most practical purposes, the root may be identified as the HCF of relata within a scatter, so that odd-looking roots like $\sqrt{educ}$- and $\sqrt{polit}$- are recognizable as contributing to the collocations ($\sqrt{educ}$- ∼ $\sqrt{system}$) (∼ = 'transposable with') in *an educational system* and *a system of education* and ($\sqrt{party}$ ∼ $\sqrt{polit}$-) in *political party, party politics, party politician* and *party political broadcast*. This is not, however, to say that there is no root recognizable on distributional grounds as common to e.g. *I* and *me* (or probably, for that matter, to e.g. *borrow* and *lend*).

Collocational analysis, then has at least two important objects. Firstly, to provide palpable identity for abstract roots, whose putative central cores or features are forever so stubbornly fugitive and which are so ill-defined by the application to them of vague aprioristic notions and glosses deriving in any case, however unconsciously, from the use of the root in extenso. To arrive at the meaning of any element of linguistic structure, it first behoves us to put it back where it came from and human beings do not speak in roots. To take the adjectival paradigm only of the root $\sqrt{heav}$-, there is clearly no other lexical item in English regularly associated *inter alia* with the roots of *cold/blow/dew/soil/ damage / damages / sarcasm / sky / drinking / breathing / make-up / hand /*

crop / rain / work / lorry / gun / accent / fall / heart / features / top-spin / humour / hydrogen / meal / going / etc. Roots themselves, however, are zero collocations and the second purpose of collocational study is to recognize the root+elements which discourse further comprises. A collocation is a composite structural element in its own right. If the reader takes the trouble to sift the foregoing collocations containing adjectival$\sqrt{}$*heav-*through their several grammatical distributions, he will find very little matching from one collocation to the next. Take, for instance, the examples I have used elsewhere—($\sqrt{}$*heav-* ~ $\sqrt{}$*drink-*) and ($\sqrt{}$*heav-* ~ $\sqrt{}$*damage-*); the first occurs in the grammatical patterns Adjective + Agentive Noun (*heavy drinker*), Verb ('intransitive') + Adverb (= Adj + *-ly*) (*to drink heavily*), Adj + Gerund (*heavy drinking*), and in the compound adjectival form involving adjectival *-ing* (*(a) heavy drinking (man)*): the second example, on the other hand, is distributed among Adj + Non-agentive Noun (singular) (*heavy damage*), Verb ('transitive') + Adverb (= Adj + *-ly*) (*damage heavily*), Adv + Passive Participle (*heavily damaged*). Any matching is clearly minimal. We may perhaps remind ourselves in passing that underlying all such present distinctions and those recognized in the subsequently extended frame of reference is the notion of contrast, by which a linguistic item or class of items derives its meaning from the place it occupies and the contrasts it develops within widely ramifying networks of differential relations, which it is unfortunately quite beyond the capacity of even the most sophisticated machinery to discern for us.

The term 'class' was used in the last sentence. Class-labels, 'noun', 'verb', 'adjective', etc. have already been used and the so-called paradigms of $\sqrt{}$*work* were namable in such terms. A great number of roots share the potentiality of association with the verbal set of morphemic flections, for example; others keep company regularly with such flections as *-ness*, *-ation*, *-er*, *-s*, etc. as well as with preceding articles and article-like words (*a/the/my/etc.*), preceding adjectival words, and so on. The latter class of words is termed 'nouns' for these and many other reasons of grammatical behaviour. A verb is not a 'doing' word, of course, or anything of the sort, for work in *hard work* or *good works* would equally merit such designation—it is a verb because for reasons of grammatical behaviour it is not a noun, an adjective, and so on. Such syntactically equivalent types of (root + morpheme) combinations are termed 'word-classes', which, like words but at the more abstract level of grammar, provide the means of giving shapes and names to generalized syntactic structures. As has already been said, both the word-name and the word-class name are further glossed as a rule, more or less memorably, in dictionaries and grammars; but we should not make the mistake of looking upon the gloss or the label as *the meaning* rather than as a more or less extensive summation of the distributional facts glossed or labelled. This is not, of course, to say that there is not a great deal in a name, but it is to say that the great deal may be of confusion, especially as far as the word-name is concerned. Linguistic analysis has been bedevilled by the use of 'word' as both several kinds of linguistic unit and as the names for those units, but the point is becoming unduly laboured.

Further collocational exegesis; 'colligation'; types of collocations; multi-directional dependency

Consideration of our earlier sentence *he tore up the road* shows that collocations not only cut across such word-class boundaries as noun and verb but also across such sentence parts as subject and 'predicate' (see below). For that matter they cut across sentence boundaries and in doing so provide apt enough illustration of the essentially on-going nature of language; cf. the collocation ($\sqrt{job} \sim \sqrt{apply}$) in, say, *He didn't want the job. I don't think he even applied.* (With or without a change of speaker between sentences.) A collocation is not a mere juxtaposition or co-occurrence; *off* or *on*, for example, though developing their own collocational relationships with *tore* in *he tore off/on up the road* do not belong to the collocation ($\sqrt{tVr} \sim \sqrt{up}$) ($V$ = vowel), between whose elements they are interposed. Moreover, as we have seen, more than one constraint is usually focused on a particular root; thus, in *he tore up the road, tore* will relate to other features of 'tense' in the context— cf., for instance, a narrative sequence of tenses as *The man rushed/rushes from the house. He stopped/stops for a moment, then tore/tears up the road.* Simultaneously, however, so to speak, much of the meaning of the form derives from its association with *up* and, as far as the collocation ($\sqrt{tVr} \sim \sqrt{up}$) is concerned, it is immaterial whether $\sqrt{tVr}$ appears as *tore* or *tears*. We shall see that the concept of a collocation has also to be considered in relation not only to 'root', 'morpheme' and 'word' but also to 'idiom', of which more subsequently. A collocation is not an idiom. An idiom resembles rather a root; it is a bloc or assemblage of roots, non-productive in terms of the substitution, transposition, etc. of roots within it. The collocation ($\sqrt{tVr} \sim \sqrt{up}$) is not an idiom because there is no such fixity of association between $\sqrt{tVr}$ and $\sqrt{up}$; $\sqrt{lope}$, $\sqrt{amble}$, $\sqrt{shamble}$, $\sqrt{race}$, $\sqrt{rVn}$, etc. may be substituted for $\sqrt{tVr}$ and $\sqrt{down}$, $\sqrt{across}$, $\sqrt{onto}$, $\sqrt{into}$, $\sqrt{along}$, etc. for $\sqrt{up}$, cf. *he ambled up the road, he tore across the road*, etc. ($\sqrt{tVr} + \sqrt{up}$) is clearly a particular member of a generalizable class of collocations involving in this case a sub-class of the word-classes 'verb' and 'particle', namable perhaps as 'motive verbs' and 'directional particles'. A class of collocations may be termed a 'colligation'. As collocations are namable by words, so colligations involve the use of word-classes to name the collocational class. Colligational labels often underline the necessary admixture of 'formal' and 'functional', as in the case of ('motive' verb + 'directional' particle)—a fact indicated in the example by the use vs. non-use of quotation marks. Again, as in the case of the individual collocations making up the class, the colligation is to be seen as an entity, and to this extent the measure of inescapable tautology involved between 'motive' and 'directional' is unfortunate and a better labelling might be ('motive' (verb + particle)). It will be seen that stress is being laid throughout this essay on the paramount importance of the *syntagmatic* relations obtaining between linguistic items in texts and differences of such relations between texts; 'syntagmatic' includes 'syntactic', a term usually reserved for the consideration of such relations at the general level of grammar. The unwarrantable artificiality of separating syntax from other pertinent aspects of syntagmatics has, I hope, been sufficiently demonstrated. At the same time, the descriptive categories recognized are available for the purpose of formulating structural statements and an attempt is being made to avoid the pitfalls involved—from the standpoint of meaning, the ultimate objective—in splitting unitary associations of various kinds and forcing fictitious parts of their meaning into word-size or word-class size 'jars of conceptual content'.

We have seen that the particular final noun in *he tore up the road* does not resolve the ambiguity of the sentence. If, say, *paper* is substituted for *road*, the latter can be seen to belong to at least two conceivable sub-divisions of noun: 'reducible' or 'destructible' in *he tore up the road/ paper/etc.* and 'travellable' in *he tore up the road/path/finishing straight/etc.* The ambiguity of *he tore up the road* is resolved rather by associability or not with 'inceptive' *off*, i.e. *he tore off up the road, off he tore up the road,* wherein *up* is identifiable unmistakably as the prepositional particle of a phrase (Preposition + N). The case of variously classifiable *road* in *he tore up the road* is simply one instance of an infinite amount of overlapping between linguistic classes, which reflects in part the infinite distinctions recognizable within the total aggregate of our experience of the world. There is little interest in trying to account for all such facts of distribution; the occurrence of *road* with *paper* is of no major significance and it is very easy to demonstrate the difference of linguistic value or distribution of the nouns. The infinity of experience and the fact that it is reflected in language could be further shown by the substitution of *the spider* for *he* in *the spider tore up the paper*, when *tore* clearly belongs to the class 'motive' verb. Of more fundamental linguistic interest, however, is the establishment of such a class as well as the recognition of such abstractions as collocations and their classes and of the fact that they spread across sentence parts. The decision as to whether the recognition of a set of relations is linguistically interesting or not must lie with the linguist as a human being, prompted by his own awareness of language organization and usually by a natural desire to make statements of as high a degree of generality as facts permit, as well as by his assessment of the 'habitualness' of collocational associations. His analytical purpose is also relevant. Use was made above of the highly specific collocation *come off* (succeed) to illustrate quite general modes of analytical procedure; it could also be used for the general purpose of distinguishing between collocations and idioms. Again, at a lower level of structural generality than that to which the association of $\sqrt{tVr}$ and $\sqrt{up}$ belongs, there may well be justification for recognizing classes of 'occupational' noun and 'employment-terminating' verb, when one notices the collocational constraints operating in the cases of *barristers* who are *disbarred*, *doctors* who are *struck off*, *solicitors* who are *struck off the roll(s)*, *officers* who are *cashiered*, *priests* who are *unfrocked*, *stockbrokers* who are *hammered*, *schoolboys* who are *expelled*, *students* who are *sent down*, *footballers* who are *suspended*, *working men* who are *sacked*, and *chairmen of regional gas boards* who are *sent on indefinite leave*. We are probably all aware of the operation of even weaker collocational constraints as we search for the 'right' choice among, say, *achieve, accomplish, effect, execute, implement, realize*, etc. to associate with *plan* or *project* or *proposal* or *ambition* or *object* or *objective*, and a certain inescapable 'prescriptivism' informing language choices is perhaps worthy of note in passing.

It should not be believed that texts are constructed according to a kind of linear successivity, that meaning diminishes in terms of a left-to-right or earlier-to-later unidirectional progression. As in the case of *he tore (off) up the road*, linguistic dependencies look from right to left, so to speak, as often as from left to right, and often enough in both 'directions' at once. Cumulate choices on the part of speaker and hearer are almost certainly the rule rather than the exception. Consider the collocational association of $\sqrt{green}$ and $\sqrt{grass}$ in *(as) green as grass*, where *(as)—as—* is a discontinuous morpheme appropriate to the collocational class concerned and where the bracket encloses an optionally omissible element. In contrast with the case of $(\sqrt{tVr} \sim \sqrt{up})$, in which the interpretation of each element is dependent on relations developed with further textual elements, the association of $\sqrt{grass}$ with $\sqrt{green}$ does not 'modify' the meaning of $\sqrt{green}$, any more than collocation with $\sqrt{green}$ 'modifies' $\sqrt{envy}$ in *green with envy*. The reversal of orientation in the dependencies observable in *(as) green as grass* and *green with envy* might perhaps be indicated by the use of arrows, thus $(\sqrt{green} \rightarrow \sqrt{grass})$ and $(\sqrt{green} \leftarrow \sqrt{envy})$, or by some device better known to the student of symbolic logic or the philosopher of rules than to the present writer. $(\ldots \rightarrow \sqrt{grass})$ is an intensifying extension of $\sqrt{green}$ and is one of a class of over a hundred of what might be termed 'similative intensifiers' in English. It has nothing to do with herbiage as such but (within the predicative adjectival phrase) is to be seen rather in relation to *very green, extremely green, greener than, as green as (that is)*, etc. The further 'proof' of the rightness of this interpretation is provided by the existence of such comparable intensifying elements as *a doornail/mutton (as dead as a doornail/mutton)* or *a post (as deaf as a post)*, which bear no cognitive resemblance to homophonous linguistic items employed elsewhere. There are numerous similar examples elsewhere in the language. For example, as $\sqrt{grass}$ is to $\sqrt{green}$ in *as green as grass* or $\sqrt{green}$ to $\sqrt{envy}$ in *green with envy*, so is 'intensifying' $\sqrt{up}$ to $\sqrt{tVr}$ in *he tore up the paper* (cf. *he tore the paper*). ($\sqrt{tear} \rightarrow \sqrt{up}$) is not to be considered an idiom any more than *as green as grass*, since *tore* may be recognized as equivalent in both *he tore the paper* and *he tore up the paper* and, in contrast with idiomatic immutability, we may substitute *across, down*, etc. for *up* and *ripped, bundled*, etc. for *tore*. *up* in *he tore up the paper* is one of a system of particles of aspect (see Note 3 on p. 173) involving concepts of timing and continuity in time; the others are importantly *off* and *on* and all three may be illustrated by *he started off* (inceptive) *running, carried on* (continuative) *walking, and finished up* (completive) *crawling. Tore up* in *he tore up the paper* and *tore off* in *he tore off up the road* both belong to the same generalized class of (verb + particle of aspect). We have already noticed that in *he tore off up the road*, 'he', 'off', 'up', and 'the road' all enter into their several grammatical relationships with *tore*; such is the intricacy of language organization.

A further example of 'fore and aft', cumulate linguistic dependency and one in which the usual referential approach to semantics is clearly not very helpful, is the sentence *that's a good boy*—commonly said to a small boy or perhaps a pet animal as a sign of approval of what he has just done or, with appropriate phonological adjustment, as a means of encouraging him to do what one wants. Now it is commonly believed that the difference between *this* and *that* is 'fully grammatical'[2], words that would be unobjectionable if based on different theoretical assumptions but which seem to imply a belief that one can always substitute *this* for *that* and vice versa without 'modifying' the textual remainder and while remaining presumably within a generally agreed world of deixis or ostensive definition. But outside the schoolroom and the somewhat lifeless examples of the kind *this/that is a book* or *that/this is a pencil*, one has to account not only for the somewhat 'odd' American use of *this* in *who is this?* to one's interlocutor at the other end of the telephone line or for the non-substitutability of *that* for *this* in storytelling (cf. *now this man I'm telling you about . . .*) but also, conversely, for the inadmissibility of *this* but admissibility of *there* in the addressive sentence *that's a good boy*. Now we may also substitute *naughty* for *good* in this sentence and say *that's a naughty boy* to a child or pet taken in misdemeanour, and we may label the language function involved 'approval/disapproval', but this is not the general linguistic point being made, which is rather that, apart from phonological features of intonation, voice quality, rhythm, etc., the language function in question is grounded in the choices that may be made *at one and the same time* in the ultimate nominal and penultimate adjectival positions as well as in the initial option between *that* and *there*. To see that one is not at all concerned with deixis and the facts of linguistic structuring that go with it, one need only substitute, say, *piano* for *boy*, whereafter we can point as well as substitute *this* for *that* and adjectives like *new* for *good*. Once again, then, it will be seen that a linguistic item derives its meaning from the total syntagm and the contrasts obtaining between it and other syntagms within our linguistic organization, so that, when it comes to the difficult task of formulating the facts, we can metaphorically speak of the use of *good/naughty* versus *good/new* and of *boy/girl* versus *piano/book* 'determining' the use of *that/there* in *that's a good boy*, all with a semantic framework that is built on more than just 'reference' as that term is commonly understood.

'Idiom'

We have now indicated what we mean by root, morpheme, word, word-class, collocation, and colligation. There remain to be noticed idiomatic and compounded types of composite element before we go on to consider other aspects of grammatical patterning and notably of sentence formation. For ease of reference we shall henceforth cite examples in the form of words, except where attention is specifically drawn to roots or morphemes. First, the idiom. Idioms (subsequently enclosed in square brackets) can occur as part of collocations (e.g. [*the nose on your face*] in *as plain as* [*the nose on your face*] or combine to form a collocation (e.g. [*take off*] (= imitate) + [*to a T*] (= perfectly) in [*to take (someone) off to a T*]). Some readers may have been accustomed to regarding as idioms certain of the collocations that have been specified earlier but the idiom belongs to a different order of abstraction. It is a particular cumulate association, immutable in the sense that its parts are unproductive in relation to the whole in terms of the normal operational processes of substitution, transposition, expansion, etc. This is presumably what is implied by the usual notional definition of an idiom as an entity whose meaning cannot be deduced from its parts—a definition, it should be said, that does not indicate how the parts are to be recognized. Thus, ($\sqrt{put}$ $\sqrt{down}$) in *he put down the book* is a collocation like ($\sqrt{tVr} \rightarrow \sqrt{up}$) in *he tore up the paper* but the comparable forms in *he* [*put down*] *the rebellion* constitute an idiom, the parts of which are so to say, both separable (cf. *he put the rebellion down*) and inseparable (cf., for example, the inomissibility of *down* in contrast with the case of *he put down the book* (on the table). In regard to this important type of association between verb and particle, it may be said in passing that the whole often corresponds to a cognitively similar single form which may replace it either optionally or obligatorily in certain functional (stylistic) contexts (cf. [*make up*] = *compose*, [*make it up*] = (*be*) *reconcile*(*d*), [*make up to*] = *flatter*, [*make it up to*] = *compensate*, etc.), but although such correspondences are usually suggestive, they are apparently not a necessary condition of idiomaticity and collocations are sometimes similarly replaceable (cf. *put down* (the book) = *deposit* (on the table), *come off* = *succeed*, etc.), while other idiomatic types may not be so substitutable (cf. [*take* (someone) *for*] (someone else), [*take it out on*] (someone), etc.).

Parts of idioms are subject to similar morphemic modifications as occur elsewhere, cf. the verbal flectional possibilities in *he* [*kick/s/ed the bucket*], which serve both to 'isolate' *kick* and to separate it from *the*, as well as the insertability of expletives to precede immediately the ultimate strongly stressed or tonic syllable (i.e. *he has kicked the—'Pygmalion'—bucket*), which not only serves to separate *the* and *bucket* but is also in parallel with the treatment in this respect of non-idiomatic lexical items (cf. *abso—'Pygmalion'—lutely*). Thus, separability and morphemic modification serve to identify the several roots comprising the idiom, notwithstanding its essential linguistic unity. Further support for the recognition of idioms is generally forthcoming from homophonous contrasts (much beloved of the punster), so that idiomatic (*he*) *kick*(*ed*) *the bucket* may be compared and contrasted with non-idiomatic (*he*) *kick*(*ed*) *the bucket* (*with his foot*), (*was that*) *the bucket* (*he*) *kick*(*ed*)? etc. Again, the component parts of idiomatic [*may as well*] in *he may as well go* are recognizable on such grounds as the optional insertion of *just* (i.e. *he may just as well go*) and the extensibility of the text to include a further infinitive before which *as* appears again but *well* is excluded (e.g. *he may as well go as stay*).

It should not be thought that an idiom bears no resemblance to any other idiom. Idioms are often members of highly productive grammatical classes. [*kick the bucket*], for example, together with [*sow wild oats*], [*see the light*], etc,. belongs to a type of verb-article/adjective-noun association commonly characterizing idioms, and [*go to the wall*], [*go by the board*], etc. belong to another such type. It will be seen therefore that collocations and idioms are similar to the extent that both are generally relatable to grammatical generalizations and that both cut across syntactic classes (e.g. verb and 'object complement' in *kick the bucket*, verb and 'adverbial complement' in *put off* = *postpone*, etc.). The principal difference has been sufficiently emphasized, namely that, in contrast with the collocation, there are no discernible parts of an idiom that are productive in relation to the particular whole. The semantic unity of the idiom corresponds to a 'tighter', often more immediately apparent distribution in collocation than in the case of the collocation. ($\sqrt{}$ *smoke* + $\sqrt{}$ *chimney*) in *to smoke like a chimney*, ($\sqrt{}$ *swVr* + $\sqrt{}$ *trooper*) in *to swear like a trooper*, ($\sqrt{}$ *blue* + $\sqrt{}$ *cold*) in *blue with cold*, etc. are not idioms but collocations; in the same way as *as green as grass* is 'intensified' *green*, so *swearing like a trooper* is 'intensified' *swearing*, and *smoking like a chimney* 'intensified' *smoking*. Again, the fact that any movement of manual rotation is often no longer necessary to the turning off of a light (in contrast with a tap or car-engine) does not prevent the identification as collocation rather than idiom of *turn off* in *turn off the light/tap/engine/etc.*; whatever the referential meaning of *turn*, *off* remains constant, formal evidence being provided *inter alia* by the uniformity of predicative transforms (sc. *the light/tap/engine is off.*) *turn off* thus contrasts with idiomatic [*take off*] (= imitate). The idiomatic type comprising verb + adverbial particle behaves in a substantially similar manner to its non-idiomatic counterpart (*turn off* (the light)) and both of them differently from the comparable structure comprising verb + prepositional phrase (cf. *turn* + *off* (the road)). Thus:

	A	B
non-idiom:	*he turned off the tap* *he turned the tap off*	*he turned off the road* (not **he turned the road off*)
idiom:	*he took off the Prime Minister* *he took the Prime Minister off*	
non-idiom:	*he turned it off*	*he turned off* (*it*)
idiom:	*he took him off*	
non-idiom:	**he turned suddenly off the tap*	*he turned suddenly off*
idiom:	**he took suddenly off the* *Prime Minister*	*the road*

Somewhat similar idioms are recognizable which comprise verbs and prepositional (as opposed to adverbial) particles, e.g. [*take to*] (= like) (someone), [*take* (someone) *for*] (someone else), others which involve more than one particle (e.g. [*do away with*] (someone/something)), others again which contain particles and the apparently pronominal form *it* (e.g. [*make it up*] (with someone), [*make it up to*] (someone)), others yet again which include nominal forms (e.g. [*put foot down*] in *they should put their foot* (*feet) *down*—for the case of a morphemically variable noun form where the verb either is or is not part of the idiom, cf. [*eat heart/s out*] in *they are eating their hearts out* and (eat) [*head/s off*] in *they are eating their heads off*), etc. Some idioms of this general verbal type further resemble collocations in exhibiting specifiable patterns of grammatical distribution, cf. [*make up*] (sc. with cosmetics or greasepaint) (verb) and [*make-up*] (noun), [*let down*] (verb) and [*let-down*] (noun), examples whose multi-componential character as idioms is partly revealed by the difference of tonicity (q.v. infra) corresponding to the grammatical distribution indicated. It must not, however, be thought that the recognition of idioms is any more straightforward than that of other linguistic categories; every supposed case must be considered on its own merits and will undoubtedly depend for its recognition on the type of relationship it accretes with other sentential features (cf., for example, the relevance of the 'reflexive' pronominal forms in e.g. *they are eating their hearts out/heads off*).

There occur also what might perhaps be termed 'functional' idioms (in the sense that 'language function' has been used in this paper), for example, the entreating *do you think you could . . .* in *do you think you could (possibly) do this (for me)?* (an example to which we shall return), the exclamatory *for (heaven's) sake!*, the military challenge *who goes there?*, aphoristic or proverbial comments like *waste not, want not* or *too many cooks spoil the broth*, and so on. It is noteworthy that such examples often cover whole sentences to the exclusion of all else. They have been termed 'ready-made expressions' but the label is not self-explanatory and this area of language remains to be explored effectively by the linguist. Part of the explanation for such 'pieces' of language may derive from the fact that we make use of a comparatively limited number of morphemes and morphemic patterns, of phonatory potentialities, and indeed of generalized formal patterns of grammar, even of sentential type, for the manifold functions of language. Thus, for instance, interrogative form considered in the abstract is as multivalent as the flection *-s* and is variously used, in addition to the challenging *who goes there?* above, for suggestions (*what about having something to eat?/wouldn't it be better if . . .?*), exclamations (*what did I tell you!/is it as late as all that!?/isn't it nice*), threats (*will you* (or *are you going to*) *do as you're told!*), gestures of politeness (*may I give you some water?/* (the shop assistant's) *can I help you?*), requests for instructions (*shall I phone them or what?*) requests for advice and help (*do you think . . .?/could you possibly . . .?*), retorts (B's *can't I!?* in reply to A's *you can't prove it*), and so on. Conversely, the myriad functional uses to which language is put day by day may confidently be expected to correspond to extensive appearance of idioms and collocations of the kinds illustrated. *do you think you could do this for me?* is apparently an expansion of *do this for me* and we should be even more unwise than elsewhere to rely in in cases like this or word-based referential meaning, applies here especially to *think* and *could*. The sentence form *do you think you could do that?* (pronounced with identical voice quality, rhythm, and intonation—let us say with an intonational rise from penultimate *do*) is wholly ambiguous. There is the interpretation we have just been considering, in which *do you think you could . . .* is an idiomatic formula of polite en-

163

treaty, and that in which an inquiry is being made as to the addressee's belief in his own capacity to perform whatever is in question. The ambiguity is easily resolved by transformational means, cf. *do you think you could (possibly) do that (for me)?*, where the inclusion of *possibly* and *for me* are inappropriate to the second interpretation.

'Compound'

So much—undoubtedly far too sketchily—for idioms. To turn—it is feared more sketchily still—to compounds, composite elements of texts that must be distinguished from both idioms and collocations. Compounds (subsequently doubly hyphenated) may occur within the scatter of a collocation (e.g. *bull=fight/-er/-ing*, which belong to ($\sqrt{fVght} \sim \sqrt{bull}$)) or even, though more rarely, of an idiom (cf. verbal [*make* (oneself) *up*] and its cognate nominal compound [*make= up*]). The same collocation occurs three times in *a bullfighter fights bulls at a bullfight*, twice in compound form and, of course, in verbal and nominal forms appropriate to the syntactic conditions of occurrence. The individual compound is essentially bipartite and uninterruptable, except by e.g. *and* in the special case of co-ordinate compounds (e.g. *knife=and=fork*, *brush=and=comb*, etc.).

(*a*) *high=chair* (*sc.* for the baby) is a chair and is high but is not to be equated with (*a*) *high chair* (*sc.* any sort of chair that is high). The proof of this particular pudding lies not only in the different phonetic potentialities of the two sequences (in matters of tempo and vowel quality, for example) but also in their contrastive 'operability'. The baby's *high= chair* is not only uninterruptable, it is also adjectivally 'incomparable' and 'unintensifiable'; thus, neither (*a*) *higher chair* nor (*a*) *very high chair* refers to the artefact in question and, having regard to the rule by which, other things being equal, colour adjectives occur in closer proximity to the noun than *high* in the Adj + N phrase, we find that (*a*) *high red chair* (in contrast with (*a*) *red high=chair*) is again not specifically for the baby. Similarly, *New=York* is a compound within a collocationally productive pattern of place names. Although the compound here refers to a particular city and its parts are unproductive in relation to the particular linguistic whole, nevertheless they are productive in relation to other directly comparable wholes (*York, London, New= London, New=Guinea*, etc.). *New=York* cannot therefore be regarded as an idiom (as it sometimes has been) and we should once again beware of the possibility of confusing the facts of reference with those of linguistic structuring.

Although *high=chair* and *New=York* do not enter into the same network of relations, they may perhaps both be reasonably seen as exemplifying a formative process of 'fusion' or 'welding'. This is not the only process of compounding in English and indeed other types of fused compound are recognizable. *Black=bird*, for example, noticeably differs from *high=chair* and *New=York* in respect of the placing of the tonic accent (a feature which is of considerable significance in English and which the reader will probably be familiar with from reference to it in the common run of grammar books in connection with such verbal/nominal distinctions as *convíct* (verb): *cónvict* (noun). The examples given of this tonic difference, however, rarely if ever include compounds but of *make úp* (verb): *máke-up* (noun), *run abóut*: *rúnabout*, *black óut*: *bláckout*, etc.). *black=bird* is identifiable with more certainty as a compound than, say, *blackboard*, not only on the grounds of contrast with uncompounded *black bird* but also of relatability to *humming=bird*, etc.; a blackboard may not be black or even a board, so that *blackboard* is less obviously relatable to *black board* than *blackbird* is to *black bird*. Perhaps, however, the relationship of synonymy between *blackboard* and *board* provides some justification for the view of *blackboard* as compound. We must not, however, allow etymology and orthographic conventions to confuse us. How do we justify the recognition of *ice-cream* as compound? *public housing* is certainly a compound but why should *public house* be? Once again, every text must be considered on its own merits in terms of plausible relations discernible within the contemporary (spoken) language.

An earlier 'structuralist' linguistics tended to take compounds (as it took *meaning*) as effectively given in advance and to restrict its interest to the fused type of compound illustrated by *blackbird*. It rather ignored therefore the linguistic relations of many kinds surrounding compounds and in particular the highly productive processes of transposition (cf. *snow=white* (hair) vs. (hair) *a. white as snow*, *bull=fight/-er/ing* vs. *fight bulls*, etc., etc.). Morphemic modification in the case of transposed compounds takes many forms; cf., for example, the presence and absence of *-s* in *a game of billiards* vs. *billiard=balls*, that of *as—as—* in *as white as snow* vs. *snow=white*, that of *the—of—* in *the hunting of big game* vs. *big game=hunting*, etc.; cf., too, the use of the flection *-al* in *(a) professional women* vs. *(a) women in the professions*. Sometimes particular collocational constraints may impose their somewhat frustrating limitations on generality, at least until further knowledge is acquired of regular processes that may be at work. Thus, cf. *medical book* (not *★medicine book*) vs. *book on medicine* vs. *law book* (not *★legal book*) vs. *medicine chest* (not *★medical chest*). While making these all too brief references to transpositional relationships, perhaps we should observe that the earlier non-compound *black bird* will be classified as 'phrase' and that its single form *black* is relatable to the relative periphrasis in, say, *(a(ny) bird) that is black*. As a corollary, relatives may not occur within compounds but the Adj + N phrase is nevertheless 'derivable' by formative process in a similar way to, say, *billiard=balls* and innumerable other examples of transposed compounding. The fact that *black bird* is labelled phrasally reflects, it seems, a combination of conventional practice, analytical convenience, and the ascribing of special semantic significance to this particular type of structural relationship.

Nominal compounds have usually come in for the lion's share of attention, but, among other types, adjectival compounds are extremely common, e.g. (*a*) *fine*=*big* (*boy*) = *adj*=*adj*, *pearl-grey* = *n*=*adj*, *long*=*legged* = *adj*=*n*, etc., and again illustrate the two main processes of compound formation, fused (*fine*=*big*) and tranposed (*snow*=*white*) in addition to contributing their own patterns of morphemic modification (for some of these, see perhaps 'Some English Phrasal Types' in the J. R. Firth Memorial Volume, *loc. cit.*). The reason for the greater prominence accorded to nominal compounds is suggested by the word 'nominal', underlying whose use in the context is reference to the contribution of the noun to the phrase and consequently to the formation of sentences. For the time being, however, we are concerned less with nominal compounds than simply with compounds. Verbal compounds rarely comprise two verbal forms (cf. *make do* (*with*)) but the compounded association of verb and particle, for instance, is of correspondingly high frequency. *Over*=*produce* and *over*=*production*, for example, are verbal and nominal transposed compounds belonging to the scatter of the collocation also illustrated in (*to*) *produce over* (*what is required*), and the particle component in this case is markedly productive (cf. *over*=*estimate*, *over*=*value*, *over*=*rate*, *under*=*estimate*, *under*=*value*, *under*=*rate*, etc.). On the other hand, verbal forms like *overcome*, *understand*, *undergo*, etc. resist efforts to divide them in any plausible way and are almost certainly unrecognizable as compounds on any but descriptively inadequate etymological grounds.

The individual compound, we have said, is characterized by uninterruptability but the compound process may be of compounds themselves. Thus, if *ivory*=*balls* is regarded as the compound transposed form of *balls made of ivory*, *ivory billiard balls* comprises two compounds, one of which is discontinuous. Perhaps in this case simplification might be achieved by regarding *ivory* as separable and adjectival (like *black* in *black bird* above) but other incontrovertible examples of discontinuous compounds are given below. The different feature of the coalescence of compounds is also very common. Thus, say, (*the*) *Roman Catholic Church* may be plausibly regarded as compounded by coalescence from *Roman Catholic* and (*the*) *Catholic Church*, with *Catholic* looking both ways at once, so to say. Similarly, in the attested example of (*a*) *young professional woman decorator* the compounds *professional woman* and *woman decorator* have coalesced, while *professional* is also compounded with *decorator* (cf. (*the*) *decorating profession*, (*the*) *profession of decorating/-or*) in the manner of *ivory* with *balls* in the earlier *ivory billiard balls*. Moreover, there are good reasons for considering *young* as compounded with *woman* (notice, for example, the fixed adjectival order in *a tall (promising, etc.) young woman/man*, not *★a young tall (promising, etc.) woman/man*, and the fact that in the compound *young* is not associable with, say, the marks of adjectival comparison). Thus, the whole *young professional woman decorator* can be regarded as the coalescent form of *young woman, professional woman, professional decorator*, and *woman decorator*, with *young* and *woman, professional* and *decorator* discontinuously associated. What has not yet been completely explained in the absence of further research are the factors governing sequential order in such cases. We may note in passing that the whole phrase may be enlarged to include a prepositional extension, as in *a young professional woman decorator of* (or *with*) *charm (and discernment)* and that such prepositional phrases are, as we have seen in other cases, inadmissible for transposition to the form *a charming (, discerning) young professional woman decorator*. The earlier example of *billiard balls* may be expanded to illustrate further coalescence resulting from the compounding of compounds. Thus, balls used for billiards are *billiard=balls*, the supply of billiard balls is *billiard=ball=supply*, and a company which supplies billiard balls is a *billiard=ball=supply=company*. Diagrammatically, coalescence here might be shown as follows:

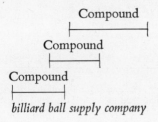

Discontinuity would require other means of diagrammatic representation, as, say,

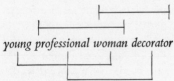

The compounding process is not an additive one, it seems, as in the case of, say, predicative adjectives of colour (e.g. *white* in *white (billiard balls)*), which permit 'modifications' of other kinds, e.g. adjectival comparison (*white/-er/-est*) or 'adverbial' intensification (*very white, etc.*). One may talk of some billiard balls as *whiter* than others but not of *★whiter wine* in relation to the compound *white=wine*. It is presumably considerations such as these and also those of sequential order (cf.

Spanish + *red*=*wine* but *red* + *Spanish* + *soil*) that underlie the recognition of *white* in *white billiard balls* and *charming* in *a charming young professional woman decorator* as essentially additions or extensions to a noun rather than as components of any particular type of compounded association.

Obviously, little has been said here on the complex subject of compounding. Some may indeed hold that, in view of the complexity of the topic, it would have been better to omit all reference to it than give it so summary a treatment. It has, however, seemed necessary to give the reader some idea of how compounds relate to the different syntagmatic concepts of collocation and idiom, not to mention phrase. Even if cut and dried aprioristic solutions for all cases have not been provided, perhaps at least some theoretical means has been suggested of enabling the reader to sort out relevant linguistic complexes as he meets them or at any rate to ask questions about them. One of the principal objectives of scholarship is to inculcate the ability to recognize interesting particularities, from which, it may be hoped, valid general conclusions will follow.

'Phrase'

Compounds, collocations, idioms, single forms, and much else besides can all constitute phrases, since the phrase belongs essentially to generalized grammatical patterning which we recognize as of a sentence and its parts.

The commonest phrasal types are traditionally nominal, verbal, and prepositional; in turn, nominal and verbal phrases have in the past been termed 'endocentric' and prepositional phrases 'exocentric'. These terms, which have loomed in the literature of linguistics probably larger than they deserve, refer to the reducibility or non-reducibility of a construction to a single form. Thus, *a high hard chair* or *a hard high chair* may be regarded as expansions of *chair* and *high*=*chair*, and *all those fifteen big black Maori chaps in white woollen jerseys* as an expansion of *chaps*, while—as to verbal phrases—*saw red* in *he saw red*, *came running* in *he came running* and *kept on running in and out* in *he kept on running in and out* are expansions of *saw*, *came*, and *run*. The single expandable forms are known as 'heads' of endocentric constructions and the remaining items are somewhat unsatisfactorily termed 'modifiers'. Expansion is not the only endocentric possibility; substitution by single pronominal forms (e.g. *it*, *what*, *that*) is one way of recognizing the noun phrase nature of, say, *For him to say so* (or *That he said so* or *His saying so*) *bothered me* (cf. *It bothered me (for him to say so, etc.)* or A. *What bothered you?* B. *For him to say so* or *That was what bothered me. For him to say so.*). The linguist is mostly preoccupied in such cases with the recognition of the subject of a sentence, and it does not seem possible to speak save in a subjective, impressionistic manner of the head and modifiers of such a construct as *For him to say so*, although it seems reasonable to regard the phrase as relatable to a single unitary linguistic form. Recent transformational-generative linguistics, it might be said, offers additional, more convincing criteria for the recognition of e.g. *For him to say so* as a noun phrase, and we shall return to the topic. In the meantime, all the preceding cases are of endocentricity. Exocentricity, for its part, was said to characterize, for example, the relationship between a preposition and its following (pro)nominal phrase in the prepositional construct and is illustrated in the foregoing examples by *in white woollen jerseys*. Such phrases appear indissoluble, so to speak, in terms of nuclear and satellite grammatical elements. The concepts and terms of endocentricity and exocentricity are characteristic of an earlier, though recent enough, structuralism developed in and from the work of the eminent American linguist Leonard Bloomfield (1887–1949), but many modern grammarians ascribe the difference between noun and preposition phrases, for example, to what is termed 'surface' structure (see below), the presence or absence of a preposition being determined by 'deeper' semantic considerations. For such grammarians, the distinction between endocentric and exocentric is unnecessary and the terms rarely appear in their work. We shall return to such topics later when considering transformational-generative linguistics; in the meantime, let us do a little preliminary clearing of ground.

Some constituents of verb phrases

Linguists have by and large tended to concentrate their phrasal attention on nominal phrases, so—not out of perverseness but rather from a wish to vary the diet as well as to facilitate subsequent discussion of sentence types—let us spend a little time looking at the *verbal* phrase and exploit it in passing for other purposes of linguistic appreciation and definition than the purely phrasal.

The English verbal periphrasis is more commonly spoken of in terms of main and auxiliary verbs than of head and modifiers, but the terminology is of little importance. To take as our example the root $\sqrt{ask}$ and to consider first the infinitival ('to'—) forms of the verbal phrase, on the basis of the minimal *to ask* and maximal *to have been being asked* we can delineate the phrase and recognize four possible structural components, a main verb (lexically *ask*, the phrasal 'head') and three discontinuous verbal elements ('modifiers') which, moving backwards from the main verb, comprise 'passive' (*be* (ask)*ed*), 'continuative' (*be* (be)*ing*), and 'perfective' (*have* (be)*en*)/auxiliaries. There are thus eight infinitival forms of the phrase as follows:

Table I

Auxiliary Verb			Main Verb	Legend
Perfective	Continuative	Passive		V = main verb
V-3	V-2	V-1	V	caps = lexical verb
have	been	being	ASKed	.... = perfective
—	be	being	ASKed	——— = continuative
have	been	—	ASKing	unmarked = passive
—	be	—	ASKing	
have	—	been	ASKed	
—	—	be	ASKed	
have	—	—	ASKed	
—	—	—	ASK	

to {

In addition to the positional interdependence of the auxiliary categories, it is worth noting the discontinuity by which any auxiliary verb is bound to the morpheme suffixed to the immediately following verb (auxiliary or main). Thus, for instance, the form *been* (usually somewhat unenlighteningly termed the past participle of *be*) 'looks both ways' in the syntagm, irrespective of whether *be* is *be1* or *be2*.

It will be seen that the 'modifying' forms in the above table comprise the infinitives *have*, *be1* and *be2*, the perfective morphemes (*be*)*en* and (*ask*)*ed*, the continuative morpheme *-ing*, and the passive morpheme (*ask*)*ed*. Forms like *have*, *be*, *been*, *being*, *asking* are termed 'non-finite', whether infinitival, gerundial, or variously participial, and in order to complete the classification as far as the scope of this paper permits, it is now necessary to introduce the 'finite' verb forms, i.e. those which for instance are preceded in the declarative sentence by the 'subject' forms of the personal pronouns (sc. *I*/*he*/*she*/*we*/etc. in contrast with *me*, *my*/*him*, *his*/*her*, *her*/*us*, *our*/etc.). *like* and *likes* are finite forms in *I like her* and *she likes me*. Finite forms (whether of auxiliary or main verb) always occur first in the verbal phrase. To both of the *be*-infinitives correspond the finite forms *am*, *are*, *is* (present tense)/*was*, *were* (past tense); *have*, *has* (present)/*had* (past) are the finites related to infinitival *have*. We must also include the finite forms of the main verb, i.e. *ask*, *asks* (present)/*asked* (past) in the example. In addition, there is to be recognized for the first time a further class of auxiliary verb (finite only) which is characterized not only by its similar manner of association with the 'subject' pronouns but also by the fact that it precedes the infinitival periphrases of Table 1. This class is that of the 'modal' auxiliaries *can*/*could*/*shall*/*should*/*will*/*would*/*may*/*might*/etc.

Now all the finite forms are importantly involved in the recognition of English sentence types. They are, for instance, specially 'conjugated' with the negative particle *not* in the negative sentence (e.g. *he hasn't asked him, he isn't being asked, he won't be asking him, etc.*) and 'front-shifted' in interrogative sentences, positive and negative (e.g. *has(n't) he asked him?, is(n't) he being asked?, will/won't he be asking him?, etc.*). With the notable exception of the copula *be* (cf. *he isn't fat, is(n't) he fat?, etc.*), the main verb can neither be 'conjugated' with the particle *not* in negative sentences nor 'front-shifted' in interrogative sentences, and this introduces the last auxiliary category we shall notice at present, namely the 'suppletive' *do, does* (present)/*did* (past), which—in the absence of any other auxiliary—supplies the appropriate negative and interrogative 'prop' corresponding to the positive-declarative appearance of the main verb without auxiliary. Thus, in the same way that *do* may be (pro-verbally) substituted for any main verb in the language (cf. *A. What is he doing? B. Eating/Sitting down/Screaming his head off/etc.*), so *he doesn't/ didn't think so, does(n't) he think so?, did(n't) he think so?* fill the gaps that might theoretically have been filled by such putative negative and interrogative forms as **he thinks not so, *thinks he so, *thinks not he so?* in relation to the positive-declarative *he thinks so*. There are other uses of the suppletive auxiliary in relation to the main verb but enough has been said to demonstrate the relationship and to permit us now to tabulate all relevant forms as follows:

Table 2

INFINITIVAL AND OTHER NON-FINITE ELEMENTS	ASPECT AND VOICE															
	NON-CONTINUATIVE								CONTINUATIVE							
	NON-PERFECTIVE				PERFECTIVE				NON-PERFECTIVE				PERFECTIVE			
	ACTIVE		PASSIVE		ACTIVE		PASSIVE		ACTIVE		PASSIVE		ACTIVE		PASSIVE	
INFINITIVAL AUXILIARY	zero		be2		have		(have)		be1		(be1)		(have)		(have)	
OTHER NON-FINITES	(ASK)		(ASK)ed		(ASK)..ed		(be)..en (ASK)ed		(ASK)ing		(be)ing (ASK)ed		(be)en (ASK)ing		been being (ASK)ed	
TENSE	PRES	PAST	PRES	PAST	PRES	PAST	PRES	PAST	PRES	PAST	PRES	PAST	PRES	PAST	PRES	PAST
FINITE FORMS																
(a) (i) lexical verb flections	zero/	-ed	—	—	—	—	—	—	—	—	—	—	—	—	—	—
(ii) suppletive auxiliary (+infinitive of lexical verb)	do/ does	did	—	—	—	—	—	—	—	—	—	—	—	—	—	—
(b) aspectival and voice auxiliaries (replacing appropriate infinitive)	—	—	am/ are/ is	was/ were	have/ has	had	have/ has	had	am/ are/ is	was/ were	am/ are/ is	was/ were	have/ has	had	have/ has	had
(c) modal-auxiliaries (+ any infinitive form)	shall/should/will/would/can/could/may/might/must/ought to (/need/dare/used to)															

172

(1) Flections like *-ed* and *-en* are multivalent within the paradigm of one lexical verb (cf. *I asked* (past), *I have asked* (perfective), *I was asked* (passive)) and also do duty in the Table for other modes of formation (cf. *I took/have taken/was taken, etc.*). The association of a root with given flections is, of course, part of its scatter.

(2) There is a noticeable tendency in modern spoken (and increasingly written) English to replace *be2* (passive) by *get* (cf. *he's getting asked, the house must have been getting burgled while they were watching television, etc.*).

(3) *be1* (continuative) is to be seen in relation to other aspectival auxiliaries that may be substituted for it, e.g. *keep* ((on) *-ing*), *start* ((off) *-ing*), *finish* ((up) *-ing*), *leave* ((off) *-ing*), etc. We have already briefly noticed the aspectival or aspectual relevance of the particles *off*, *on*, and *up* and perhaps the opportunity may be taken of commenting a little further on the associated behaviour of the auxiliaries of aspect, the particles of aspect, and the infinitival and *-ing* forms of the main verb. *He started off laughing* is an example of (*laugh* + 'inceptive' aspect) in both of the possible interpretations (i) he started to laugh (but stopped himself) and (ii) he started off laughing but finished up crying. In the second case *to laugh* may not be freely substituted for *laughing* and the contrast is therefore in parallel with e.g. *he stopped to smoke* and *he stopped smoking*, but cf. elsewhere e.g. *to laugh* (or *laughing*) *is good for you*. Aspectival meaning is rarely if ever attributable solely to the particle, which is to be considered rather, for example, from the standpoint of its omissibility or otherwise. Thus the same particle *up* appears in the antonymous *he gave up running* and *he took up running*, and the elsewhere antonymous *up* and *down* occur in the synonymous sentences *why doesn't he slow up? why doesn't he slow down?* It may fairly be said that the verb is of greater relevance to aspect and that it is *start–finish* that provides the antonymous contrast in *he started off laughing and finished up crying*, whence—provided that intonational form, notably in respect of *finished*, is appropriate—both *off* and *up* are omissible. Again, 'inceptive'—'iterative'/'continuative'—'completive' belongs rather to *start-keep-finish* than to *off-on-up* in *he started off running, kept on running, and finished up crawling*, whence—with appropriate safeguards as to intonation—all the particles are omissible. The particles serve mainly, it seems, to 'reinforce' the auxiliary of aspect, to disambiguate otherwise ambiguous sentences, and to 'complement' certain verbal forms, e.g. *set*, cf. *he set off walking* (not *★he set walking*). As an example of the disambiguating part played by particles, *he finished crying* is variously interpretable as 'he was crying as he

finished' and 'he completed his crying'; *off* unambiguously marks the latter 'completive' aspect in the more realistic example *he finished off painting the house* (notice in passing the superficially antonymous use of the same particle for 'inceptive' aspect in *he started off laughing*). It is, however, also important to distinguish between *-ing* forms, for example between the verbal act of participial *-ing* and the verbal activity of gerundial *-ing*, as another instance of the complexity of dependencies within sentences. A clearer example of the contrast is *he left off lecturing* vs. *he left lecturing*; in the former case the lecturer stopped in mid-lecture, in the latter he renounced his career as a lecturer. Similarly, *he gave up running*, in which *up* is an inomissible element of the composite *give up*, variously relates to the race he was in the act of running or to his athletic career; in such a case, disambiguation will rest on appeal to other criteria, e.g. difference as to transposability (cf. *he gave running up*). One final illustration in this brief exposé is capable of threefold interpretation: *he went off playing football* = (i) he was playing football as he went, (ii) he went off (in order) to play football, (iii) he no longer liked playing football. Space is limited but the inomissibility of *off* in (iii) only, the substitutability of *to play* for *playing* in (ii) only, are among the means by which such 'homologous' forms of sentence can be interpreted.

The above tabulation involves, of course, little more than a first recognition of formal verbal distinctions in English. The categories labelled in the table are justifiable on syntactic grounds but it remains for the linguist to look in detail at the distributional characteristics of items, classes and categories relevant to the verbal phrase, for example at other features of aspect, at the facts pertaining to so-called 'sequence of tenses', at the tense relationship if any between such modals as *can* and *could* (cf. *I hope he can* vs. *I hoped he could*, and the like), at the various uses of *will* in, say, *will you do as you're told* (to the difficult child) and *she will go on so* (in reference to the loquacious lady) as well as *she'll be coming round the mountain when she comes*, and so on. In particular, the twofold distinction of tense is imposed by the contrasts that inform the table in order to account for (unstated) differences of linguistic accompaniment as well as of morphemic modification between e.g. *I ask/he asks*, on the one hand, and *I/he asked*, on the other, a distinction paralleled in the other finite forms tabulated. This is not to say that numerous other linguistic distinctions relating to concepts of time should not be recognized but, as far as the verb is concerned, it would be unfortunate to recognize other categories of tense. There is, of course, strong temptation arising from some not very clear temporal concepts to distinguish more than two tenses in English, but meaning is ever the ultimate object of inquiry and 'present tense' and 'past tense' are little more than labels helping to focus the attention on linguistic form; 'tense 1' and 'tense 2' might well have been better terms to pick. We have already seen how constantly we extrapolate from distinctions recognized in response to a given selection of data, so that exclamations like *what did I tell you!* or threats like *are you going to pick it up or not?* are quite properly termed interrogative *as to form*, even when no contrast obtains with corresponding declarative forms of sentence. Just as there are discernible patterns of, say, English rhythm, so there are patterns of the English verbal phrase and that is where tense belongs. If one looks for categories of tense in relation to conceptual distinctions of temporal meaning, the number of English 'tenses' will greatly exceed two but the price paid will almost certainly be confusion. In the field of stylistics, some linguists argue quite plausibly that there is no coherent correlation between tense and time and would rather relate tense distinctions to speech function and attitude. For such linguists (see, for example, H. Weinrich, 'Tense and Time', *Archivum Linguisticum*, Vol. 1 (New Series), 1970), present tense would indicate not present time but discursive attitude (i.e. one of tension, as in the case of conference discussants, radio or TV commentators, etc.) and lack of perspective (either retrospection or projection). A so-called pluperfect tense in a narrative (vs. discursive) situation would indicate retrospection, while a future tense in discursive function, like a conditional tense in the narrative-counterpart, would indicate projection. The recognition of such distinctions, which involve little explored trans-sentential relations, may be justifiable or not but the questions raised are certainly interesting and cannot sensibly be dismissed as 'mere stylistics'. It would, however, perhaps be confusing to call such differences distinctions of tense, if one adopts the classificatory scheme of the above table, which envisages no such divisions of tense as 'conditional', 'future', or 'pluperfect'.

Sentence types; 'subject', 'predicate', 'object'

We have seen that a sentence like *isn't that nice* pronounced in certain intonational forms, is ambiguous, either directly relatable or not to a sentence *that isn't nice* and as a consequence variously 'interpretable'. It is noticeable, too, that certain sentence elements 'block' the free convertibility of the sentences of which they are part or to which they are adjoined; thus, *oddly enough*, say, in *oddly enough, he wouldn't tell her* does not 'permit' a corresponding interrogative sentential form *(oddly enough,) would(n't) he tell her?*. Little work has been done on such matters but it is notable that the 'loose-knit' sentence is as necessary for the ringing of changes on the way to the recognition of general patterns and regularities as the grammatical mould is essential to stylistic particularities, as if the grammarian's *you left your hat on the table* is the obverse of the poet's coin of *a room so loud to my own*.

We have also seen that by introducing the negative particle *not* in association with an auxiliary verb as well as by including an auxiliary *do/does/did* and alternating the sequential order of (pro)nominal phrase and finite verb, it is possible to produce the following four sentences, classifiable as labelled. The regular interrelationship of sentence form they exhibit is basic to English and from it countless similar contrasting sentences are generated:

(1) (Declarative-Positive)   *you left your hat on the table*
(2) (Declarative-Negative)   *you didn't leave your hat on the table*
(3) (Interrogative-Positive)   *did you leave your hat on the table?*
(4) (Interrogative-Negative)   *didn't you leave your hat on the table?*

Other sentence types are recognizable, e.g. imperative (positive and negative), but we shall defer reference to them for the time being and concentrate on the parts of sentences that can be distinguished on the basis of contrasts within the above and similar sets of sentences. We shall deal first with more or less traditional categories like subject, predicate, object, adjunct, complement, and clause, and subsequently, in order to give the reader some acquaintance with the present 'state of the game', relate what is said about them to the contemporary approach to language study known as 'transformational-generative' or TG for short.

The (pro)nominal phrase *you* in the above examples precedes the textual remainder in the declarative sentences and occurs within it in their interrogative counterparts. It has been the practice not only to recognize sentence types on the basis of such criteria but also to sub-divide sentences into S(ubject) (*you*) and P(redicate) (the remainder). Used in such a way, subject and predicate are clearly not semantic categories but rather parts of sentences discernible in the process of recognizing certain sentence patterns. Predicate is an ill-defined entity to which we shall return; for the moment, let us say that it consists typically of a verb phrase $\pm$ additional elements. The latter, though highly diversified as to constituency, have often enough been classified broadly into two categories, A(djunct) and C(omplement), a distinction resting largely on the inomissibility or non-deletability of C and delet-ability of A in any given instance. In these terms, *you left your hat on the table* would be analysed as SPCA, *on the table* (A) being omissible (in contrast with *your hat* (C)), without prejudice to the cognitive equiva-lence of the remainder. We shall also return to complement and adjunct, but first let us look at subject and object.

Subject and object are mutually definable by such distinctions as that between *Tom hit Bill* and *Bill hit Tom* and both are even more clearly distinguished by specialization of pronominal form, cf. *I hit him, he hit me, they hit them, etc.* Again in contrast with the subject, the object does not occur 'within' the predicate and develops no concordial relations with the finite verb, cf. *he hates them, he hates him, they hate them, they hate him,* etc. *him* in *everybody likes him* is object not because of some 'objective-ness', 'person-ness', 'thing-ness' or 'passive-ness' about it but because of such facts as that the second pronominal form is *him* as opposed to *he* and *his* elsewhere; *him* and *he* clearly have the same personal reference in *everybody likes him* and its passive synonym *he is liked by everybody* but in the first case *him* is object and in the second *he* is subject. A distinction is sometimes drawn between grammatical subject and logical subject; in the example, *everybody* would be the grammatical subject of *everybody likes him* and the logical subject of *he is liked by everybody*. The distinction has little to recommend it, for logical subjects are all too often extremely fuzzy. What is the logical subject of, say, *the boat's rocking* or of that celebrated example of ambiguity— *flying planes can be dangerous?* Whether we interpret *flying* as adjectival or gerundial, we cannot be clear as to who or what is dangerous, and to whom—is it the practice of flying? planes? the act or manner of flying planes? pilots? etc.? Nor would it seem that any such distinction as that of grammatical and logical subject is of very great relevance to the analysis of such relations of synonymy as are intuitively felt to obtain between e.g. *John lent the book to Tom* and *Tom borrowed the book from John*. Initial *John* and *Tom*, however, are both necessary to the constituency of the two sentences in a way that *to Tom* and *from John* are not and it is for such reasons that subject is felt as a rule to occupy a special place among sentence constituents.

Whatever the deeper 'truths' of linguistic organization, subject and object are among terms that can be usefully employed as means of reference to constituents of particular sentences as they occur. It is not certain that as much can be said for P(redicate), whose limits and constituency are often by no means easily defined. Thus, such sentences as *leave your hat on the table, would you!?*, *left his hat on the table, hasn't he?*, *he left his hat on the table and so did John* (with final ellipsis of *leave his hat on the table*), etc. suggest that e.g. *you didn't leave your hat on the table* should be divided *you* (subject) + *didn't* (auxiliary + negative) + *leave your hat on the table* (predicate?). But, apart from the object *your hat*, is *on the table* part of the predicate in e.g. *on the table was where you left your hat?* Perhaps we should be well advised to abandon 'predicate' in favour of, say, 'verb phrase' with or without further accompaniment, separately specified.

There are, of course, too, a great number of spoken English sentences that either do not lend themselves to analysis in terms of subject and 'predicate' or have first to be 'filled in' in order to submit to such analysis. It will not do to dismiss, say, *what about a drink?* variously as 'a ready-made expression' or 'a sentence fragment' or, in the absence of proof, as one of a finite number of 'odd men out'. Again, from the evidence already provided, there seems little point in attempting to analyse *that's a good boy* in terms of the usual subject–'predicate' division, unless it is to underline the way in which we use syntactic patterns for multifarious purposes. As to ellipsis, it is not only necessary to recognize it as part of human linguistic capacity in general but we should also attempt to specify the uses to which it is put. Even if we assume it to be reasonable to regard as elliptical subject–'predicate' structures the landlord's *Time, gentlemen, please!* or the artillery detachment commander's *Detachment rear!* or the TV commentator's *Bremner* (pause) . . . *Madeley breaking on the right* . . . *a cross to the far post* . . . *a catch made to look so easy by Bonetti*, the point must also be made that the 'full' subject–'predicate' structure is inappropriate to such language functions where 'time is of the essence'.

'Adjunct' and 'complement'

On the table in *you left your hat on the table* has been commonly termed an 'adjunct', the main criterion for whose recognition has traditionally been that it may be deleted without the meaning of the remainder being affected. The adjunct *on the table* is thus a kind of optional extension to *you left your hat*. But such a category, as well as the oppositive 'non-deletable' complement (e.g. the 'object complement' *your hat* in the example, *a shame* in *that's a shame*, *ten stone twelve* in *he weighs ten stone twelve*, both *him* and *unhappy* in *it made him unhappy*, etc.), is too often incapable of application to the same linguistic element when it is considered within sets of contrasting and related structures beyond the simple oppositions implicit in the single sentence $\pm$ complement/adjunct. Certain verbs like *shamble, put, set, etc.* have already been noticed as necessitating extensions of some kind in order to be meaningfully employed within a verb phrase; thus, if we take the sentence *they put peas in cans*, not only is *peas* not deletable but so, too, is *in cans*. Are therefore both *peas* and *in cans* to be termed complements? If they are, the use of the term is probably only justifiable as far as very early, rather superficial, contrasts are concerned and will in all likelihood have to be abandoned as soon as other types of relationship are discerned with their implications for the modification of grammatical rules. Thus, it seems reasonable to regard *they put peas in cans* and *they can peas* as similar and to identify *put in cans* and *can*. If this is so, clearly *peas* in *they put peas in cans* differs categorically from *in cans* and it seems preferable to call it 'object' in preference to 'object complement' and perhaps even in general to look with some suspicion at 'complement'. Similarly, it will be recalled that *on the table* might be seen as 'adjunct' in *you left your hat on the table*. But consider the implications of regarding

178

this sentence in a transformational-generative manner as an amalgam of two sentences, *you left your hat* and *your hat was on the table*, the latter being incorporated or embedded in the single sentence *you left your hat on the table* by the application of (transformational) rules to delete *your hat* and *was* from the second (underlying) sentence. If such an interpretation of the original sentence is accepted, then at a deeper level *on the table* in the underlying *your hat was on the table* was a complement, not an adjunct. This would hardly be a satisfactory state of affairs. In fact, *on the table* was recognizable as adjunct because of the verb *leave*; if we substitute *put* for *leave*, i.e. *you put your hat on the table*, the same problem arises as was posed by *they put peas in cans*. In the same way, *remarkably* is adjunctive in *he does it remarkably well* but complementary in *he not only does it well but remarkably well*. It seems therefore to many modern grammarians that adjunct and complement—at least in the manner of their traditional and sometimes quite recent linguistic employment— are indistinct categories and perhaps even likely to block progress towards a deeper awareness of such relationships as between *John lent the book to Tom* and *Tom borrowed the book from John* and conceivably towards sentence analysis generally. The criticisms made of 'complement' might seem less applicable to the case of those elements which, while recognizable as separate items, lack the independent status of apparently comparable entities; the nominal form *going*, for example, must be collocated within the noun phrase with e.g. *the* and/or certain attributive adjectives (cf. *what's the going like?*, *he likes the going (to be) firm/hard/soft/etc.*); again, *shamble* is a verb but necessitates extension in the verb phrase by an aspectival particle (*off*, *on*) and/or a directional preposition (*up*, *down*, *across*, *along*, etc.); similarly, to say that *off* is 'of a piece' with *switch* in *he switched the light off* is not to say that *switch off* is not properly relatable to e.g. *be/go off* in *the light was/went off* or even to *switch* (noun), but rather to recognize the difference between *switch the light off* and *switch* (= exchange) *the light*. But it seems that the relevant facts of distribution can be handled by collocations as these have been envisaged in this paper without appeal to 'complementation'. The traditional use of adjunct and complement recognizes the fact of syntagmatic dependency and constraint but are bound to be insecure if based on a single criterion of deletability or non-deletability. The term 'adjunct' is much more satisfactorily used, it seems to the present writer, in contrast with 'conjunct' and 'disjunct' and with reference to English adverbial forms and their syntagmatic implications for discourse.[3]

'Clause'

'Clause', for its part, is characterized by sentential structure and by being included within sentences and phrases. *When I want to* in *I'll do it when I want to, to please her* in *he did it to please her,* and *however late* in *he'll still come, however late* are all clausal in form, respectively a finite clause, a non-finite clause, and an elliptical clause. *Where we get off* in *this is where we get off* and *me to go* in *is it me to go?* are also examples of finite and non-finite clauses. Non-finite clauses, for example *to please her* in *he did it to please her,* are convertible to related structures containing finite verb forms, e.g. ... *(so that) he might please her/she might be pleased,* and such conversion assists in the recognition of the sentential nature of clauses, which is what essentially distinguishes them from phrases. At the same time, clauses are said to be distinguishable from sentences by the possibility of their occurrence within sentences and phrases.

Traditionally, distinction is made between simple and complex sentences, the latter involving clauses in association. In such combinations of clauses, one is usually termed 'main' and accompanying clauses 'dependent'. Clausal dependence may notably take the forms of either co-ordination (marked in particular by conjunctions, e.g. *and, but, or,* cf. *he is going and so is John, will you go or shall I?*) or subordination as in the case of the relative clauses contained in *he's someone [whom] I didn't know [that he] existed.* Some have distinguished between compound sentences (mostly of the co-ordinated type) and complex sentences (comprising main and dependent clauses). There is, however, more to the consideration of clauses than mere nomenclature, and indeed the concept and terminology are perhaps superfluous, once the process of embedding sentences within other sentences is recognized. We shall return to the topic of embedding when briefly considering transformational-generative linguistics. Although practice varies among TG linguists, there is in their work a noticeable diminution in the use of the term 'clause' and a corresponding gain in the economic formulation of facts.

Transformational-generative grammar

It would perhaps be surprising today if the reader had not already heard of transformational-generative grammar. There are currently recognizable subdivisions of TG but there can be no doubt that they all derive from and owe much to the work of N. Chomsky, whose seminal *Syntactic Structures* appeared in 1957.

Human linguistic capacity

TG sets out to describe in the form of explicit rules what we know intuitively about a language and healthily admits that so far it has only discovered things in the barest outline and that its hypotheses are at times probably over-extended. Our grammatical knowledge, then, is not directly accessible from overt forms of utterance; the grammatical principles in terms of which we speak and write and also respond to language are largely unconscious. 'Grammar' for the TG grammarian is another name for linguistic knowledge. We are able to recognize whether a string of elements is a sentence or not, and this fact needs explaining, since such strings are clearly infinite in number. We understand elliptical sentences like *I'd go if I could but I can't*, we interpret the foreigner's *you not go please*, we say that e.g. *thleemstta* is unintelligible and we find some distorted sense in *tomorrow the kangaroo sauntered rapidly upstairs into the basement*, which we might render more non-sensical by omitting the *to* of *into*. The TG grammarian would probably describe such a nonsense sentence as well-formed grammatically but ill-formed semantically, but the dichotomy may be misleading. The sentence can be reasonably held to illustrate our general capacity to extrapolate and analogize, and since grammatical well-formedness may quite reasonably be considered to depend on semantic well-formedness, the grammatical and the semantic may be seen not as opposed but as complementary. Be this as it may, the sentence is classifiable with, say, Jabberwocky nonsense (sc. '*Twas brillig and the slithy toves . . .*'), which retains recognizably English patterns of sequential order, affixation, and phonaesthesia (with *slithy*, cf. *slimy*, *slither*, *slippery* and other forms that are comparable phonetically and semantically), as well as with *sincerity admires John*, with which Chomsky is concerned to demonstrate the fact of selectional dependencies between classes of nouns and verbs that co-occur. To the extent that we understand such a sentence as *tomorrow the kangaroo sauntered rapidly upstairs into the basement*, we are presumably comparing and contrasting it by some internal process with e.g. *then he walked rapidly upstairs into the bedroom* and, however nonsensical, it con-tains clear indications as to its own constituency and that of sentences in general. We might notice in passing the particular relevance of sequential order, since no conclusion like that just drawn could have been reached from a point of departure provided by such penultimate anagrammatic nonsense as *sauntered basement upstairs the rapidly kangaroo into the*, beyond which lies the possibility of jumbling the constituents of roots and morphemes and removing any indications as to lexical divisions. As already said, the fact of our ability to recognize the ultimately ungrammatical has also to be accounted for, as well as our capacity to perceive the multiple ambiguity of *it's too hot to eat*, the synonymy of *I seldom go* and *I don't go often*, and the omission finally of *leave my hat on the table* from *he left his hat on the table and so did I*. All such abilities must arise from our knowledge of the grammar of a language and as grammarians we shall in all probability wish to look more closely, for instance, at *he left his hat on the table and so did I* in order to understand the reasons for the presence of '(pro)verbal' *so* and the auxiliary *did*, for the positional relationship of *did* and *I*, and also at the implications of *and* both for this sentence and for the ways in which we conjoin sentences more generally.

Deep and surface structure

The fact of our appreciation of the ambiguity of many sentences and part sentences is one means by which we know that relationships must be involved between elements of sentences that are not revealed directly by the overt form of the individual sentence. This has led to the recognition of two levels of relationship, deep and surface, the latter corresponding to the overt form of a sentence, the former to its 'placings' within the linguistic organization of the brain and nervous system. An ambiguous sentence will have one surface structure and a minimum of two deep structures, the number depending on the range of interpretation the sentence may be given. The ability to structure sentences at both deep and surface levels belongs to what the transformational-generative linguist speaks of as the fluent speaker's *competence*, which enters into its own contrastive relationship with *performance*, a dichotomy which is discussed briefly elsewhere.

Transformations

Deep structures, at the level of which meaning is considered, are converted by means of *transformations* into the surface structures by which 'meaning is communicated'. Deletion or ellipsis is one kind of transformation. So-called 'identical noun phrase deletion', for example, has occurred in the sentence *I want to go*. The contrast with *I want him to go*, etc. indicates that *I want to go* contains *I* as the 'deep' subject of *go*; thereafter, since *I* has already occurred as subject of *want*, it is transformationally deleted. Similarly, *I'd go if I could but I can't* exemplifies the deletion of the identical verbal *go* from a deeper *I'd go if I could go but I can't go*. 'Reflexivization' is another example of relationship between deep and surface structure: the ungrammaticality of e.g. **I fancy myself, *you fancy themselves, *they fancy ourselves, etc.* against the grammatical *you fancy yourself, he fancies himself, etc.* imposes the recognition of the special behaviour termed reflexivization when two identical noun phrases occur as subject and object. Thus the deep structure of *John fancies himself* or *you fancy yourself* is seen as *John fancies John, you fancy you*. For the reflexive pronoun to occur the two noun phrases must be within the same single sentence, cf. *he said he would go*, not **he said himself would go*. Reflexivization provides further evidence for the 'existence' of a deep subject *I* for a second sentence *to go* in the earlier *I want to go*, since we find such contrasts as *I want him to go himself* and *I want to go myself*. These examples also illustrate the embedding of one sentence within another, a topic to which we shall return presently. The transformational approach, then, provides a framework within which to handle many of the dependencies we have already seen to obtain between textual elements. Selectional constraints are at present largely introduced with lexical items into deep structure by means of the feature-specification of such items which has been criticized elsewhere in this paper.

Both deep and surface relationships are spoken of in terms of constituents and functions. A sentence is structured in the sense that its elements fall into groups. The comparison and contrast we have already made between *you left your hat on the table* and *did you leave your hat on the table?* revealed the divisibility of the sentences into a noun phrase (*you*) and a verb phrase+, at any rate on the surface of things. As we have seen, structure at the surface level is derived by transformational rules rearranging and/or deleting deep structure constituents. Thus, for instance, *today* has been 'shifted' and 'replaced' by *it* in *it is early closing today* (cf. the synonymous *today is early closing*). There is, too, a regular interrelation of intonational form between such sentences, at least in British English. Transformational tests help to isolate constituents: for example, passivization delineates the noun phrases (NPs) flanking the verb in *everyone likes him* (passive: *he is liked by everyone*); the reflexive transformation also identifies NPs like *the man* in *the man shot himself*; the so-called cleft sentence in which, for practical purposes, an NP must occur after *was* in e.g. *what bothered me was his appearance*, corresponding to *his appearance bothered me* and serving to define *his appearance* as NP. Sentence-like constituents are identified as NPs by similar means, e.g. *for him to go* in *what was silly was for him to go* (cf. *for him to go was silly*), or (*the fact*) *that he should take that line* in *what was odd was* (*the fact*) *that he should take that line* (cf. (*the fact*) *that he should take that line was odd*). Verb phrases (VPs) seem less clearly discernible but the 'identical verb deletion test' provides one means of recognition, cf. *he left early and so did I* (*leave early*). Most TG grammarians agree on the presence of noun phrases in deep structure but there is less agreement on the presence of verb phrases and even less on that of such constituents as auxiliaries. Some speak of NPs, VPs and AUX(iliaries) in deep structure, others of Predicates and Arguments, the latter perhaps deliberately in order to mark deep structure off terminologically from its surface counterpart. Terminological usage, moreover, is not always uniform among TG specialists, notwithstanding substantial agreement on fundamental issues. The use of 'clause', for example, varies quite noticeably; some will speak of main and subordinate clauses in a more or less traditional way, others only of relative clauses.

Noticeable differences and a properly scientific uncertainty exist also, for instance, over the status of prepositions. There seems good reason to believe that at least some semantic relations between deep structure constituents are often rendered explicit by prepositions. Thus, *in, at, with, etc.* are frequently associable with location or instrumentality, rather in the manner of the cases in whose terms some of us may have been brought up to decline Latin nouns. For example, in the sentence *we arrived at* (more colloquially, *got to*) *the ground after the kick-off*, it seems defensible to suppose that *the ground* stands in the same relation to the verb as it does in *we reached the ground, etc.*, from which *at* or *to* is absent. If this is so, it seems also defensible to suppose that the prepositions should somehow be recognized in the common deep structure of these cognitively equivalent sentences. Accordingly, a number of TG grammarians take the view—tentatively, it should be said, as is appropriate to any hypothesis—that prepositions originate as features of deep structures, in particular as features of noun segments thereof, and that they are introduced into sentences by transformational means. Such evidence as is provided by e.g. *I'll see you at 5/in December/on December 12th/(during) next week/etc.* is taken to support the view of the close association of prepositions and nouns. It is likewise considered that e.g the preposition *by* in *he is liked by everyone* is 'there all the time' in deep structure, though deleted in the un-transformed sentence which has *everyone* in subject position (i.e. *everyone likes him*). In the same way, prepositional *of* in *John's acceptance of the challenge*, which is termed the 'nominalization' of *John accepted the challenge*, is associated by some with a deep structure object. But, per contra, prepositional phrases often do not behave like noun phrases and the choice of preposition seems to depend as often on verbs or adjectives as on nouns and may even vary between cognitively equivalent nouns and adjectives. It is by no means immediately apparent why *with* appears in *she was pleased with thè flowers* (cf. *the flowers pleased her*) but *of* in *she was terrified of him* (cf. *he terrified her*), nor why *for* accompanies *affection* in *to feel/have affection for someone* when *towards* appropriately accompanies the adjectival cognate in *to feel affectionate towards someone*. It is plausible to regard *the wall* as objective in *he looked over the wall* (where *look over* = inspect) and to consider the preposition *over* as part of the object. But, as far as I am aware, no one has offered any explanation for the contrast between the absence and presence of the preposition *of* in, say, *the Senate approved the budget* (?nominalization: *the Senate's approving (of) the budget*) and *the Senate approved of the budget* (?nominalization: *the Senate's approval of the budget*), which might even be co-ordinated in *the Senate approved the budget without approving of it* or even, somewhat jocularly, *the Senate approved the budget but not of it* (with *of* stressed, of course). Again, *John looked for him* is ambiguous, variously interpretable as 'searched him out' and 'looked on his behalf'; thus, the two *for's* develop different relations with *look* in the unambiguous *John looked for it for him*. Even if it is reasonable to regard *it* and *him* here as direct and indirect objects with their prepositional concomitants, how are we to consider *for* in *John went for it in a big way*? Though prepositional, *for* here forms an idiomatic whole with *go* in the same way that e.g. *at* is associated with *get* in *what is he getting at?* (cf. *what is he looking at?*) or *on* with *count* in *you shouldn't count on him* (cf. *you shouldn't count on your fingers*) or *by* with *come* in *it's hard to come by* or *he comes by a bargain almost every day* (vs. *he comes by the house almost every day*). The object is therefore inomissible with the idiomatic type in contrast with the non-idiomatic counterpart. Finally, although TG can offer a plausible deep structure for e.g. *I took him to be someone else*, I am unaware of any explicit account of the substitutability of *for* in place of *to be*, sc. *I took him for someone else*. But although there are doubts, considerable gaps, and even dubious proposals, the spirit of grammatical enquiry is today much in evidence among transformational-generative linguists and the times are exciting for the serious research worker, even if he is not always sure how among other things to consider prepositions.

We should perhaps observe before leaving the deep: surface contrast and transformations that 'interrogative', for example, has been used in this paper to refer to a certain kind of surface sentence pattern corresponding to a variety of language functions. It is the latter which belong incontrovertibly to the semantic base of linguistic form. Although the ultimate interest of the linguist is, or should be, in meaning and the relationship between meaning and form, he nevertheless needs a set of terms in which to talk systematically about particular texts and their parts at the surface level. This paper has not concerned itself greatly with consideration of elements of deep structure and indeed there is disagreement among linguists as to what should be understood by deep structure. This could even turn out to be something very like 'meaning' and to comprise language functions-cum-forms such as those distinguished earlier under the headings of 'approval/disapproval', 'melioration/pejoration', etc. as well as those of a referential kind (time, place, instrumentality, etc.), which at present figure more prominently in the literature.

Sentence functions

The native speaker of English knows that the two sentences *Tom hit Bill* and *Bill hit Tom*, in spite of their identical lexical constituency, meaningfully differ in a regular way. The positional interrelationship of items is clearly important and is referred to in terms of 'functions' rather than constituents. *Tom* in *Tom hit Bill* is said to fulfil the function of subject and *Bill* that of object. Whether or not these functions belong to deep or surface structure is also under debate. Object seems exclusively a surface category while subject is usually seen as belonging to both deep and surface levels. Be this as it may, the subject of a sentence, deep or otherwise, is not a constituent like an NP; it is a function fulfilled by a constituent. It is the surface subject that determines concord (e.g. the agreement of *he* and *shouts* in *he shouts*) and, as we have seen, the subject is often transformationally deleted, as *I* from *I want (I) to go* or *you* from the imperative *(you) wash yourself*. That the distinction between subject and object is probably exclusively a matter of surface structure appears to be strongly indicated by the fact that the kind of semantic relationship obtaining between *boat* and *rock* is identical in both *the boat's rocking* and *you're rocking the boat*. Again, 'reciprocity' seems to involve the same meaningful relations between the constituents of our earlier example *John lent the book to Tom* and its synonym *Tom borrowed the book from John*. Subject and object, it should be said, are not the only functions to be recognized. Relative clauses, for example, are a function of what are called embedded sentences. We will illustrate sentence embedding fairly fully but before this is done, attention should perhaps be directed to what is known as recursion or recursiveness as a property of language.

Recursiveness; sentence embedding

There is theoretically no limit to the size of sentences, for example to the number of sentences that may be embedded in or conjoined with others. The fact is made use of in nursery rhymes like *The House that Jack Built* and in folk and community songs like Burl Ives' *There was an old lady who swallowed a fly* and, rather more subtly, in the type of 'adverbial' intensification illustrated by *she went on chattering away to her heart's content ninety to the dozen all day long* (which is presumably related to *she chattered, she chattered away, she chattered to her heart's content, she chattered ninety to the dozen, she chattered all day long, she went on chattering*). The device that permits such immeasurable sentence length is known as recursion.

The embedding of sentences in others takes many forms and we may observe again in passing that if we speak of 'embedded sentence', then 'clause' appears to be a superfluous term. Sometimes the embedded sentence is more apparent than others. The subject-verb-object pattern of *he'd done it* in *John thought he'd done it* seems immediately to mark it as sentential, perhaps because it also functions as an object constituent of an including sentence also having the subject-verb-object pattern. But it may be equally plausible to regard comparative sentences, let us say, like *my face was redder than his* or *Frenchmen are more conservative than Englishmen* as surface amalgams of two sentences in deep structure, namely something like *my face was red. His face was red* and *Frenchmen are conservative. Englishmen are conservative* to which comparative features are added. A transformational rule (identical noun phrase deletion) might delete the second noun from *my face was redder than his face* just as identical verb phrase deletion deletes *was red* from *my face was redder than his face was red* and *are conservative* from *Frenchmen are*

186

more conservative than Englishmen are conservative. (We may in passing notice the dependency between *Frenchmen* and *Englishmen* in the example —selection is restricted on either side of comparative *than*; comparison must be between the comparable and e.g. **Frenchmen are more conservative than houses* will not do. But to return to sentence embedding.) Noun phrases may contain, in addition to head nouns, not only articles, numerals and the like but also sentences; verb phrases may contain, in addition to main verbs, not only auxiliaries of various kinds, aspectical particles and the like, but again also sentences. *I'm delighted that you've been able to come* contains the two sentences *I'm delighted* and *you've been able to come*, the second marked by an omissible *that* preceding it and underlying the synonymous nominalization (*I'm delighted by*) *your being able to come*. Often enough, a noun preceding *that* underlines the nominality of the whole, as *fact/idea/thought/recollection/etc.* in *she was pleased by the fact etc. that he'd passed*, which can also be 'rendered' by *she was pleased for him to have passed* (infinitive) or . . . *by his having passed* (gerundial). Such embedded sentences are sometimes known as noun phrase complements but terminological usage varies quite widely. One important type of sentence embedding in noun phrases is illustrated by *he's the man I met the other day*, derivable from *he's the man* and *I met the man the other day* with the application of appropriate transformations moving the second *the man* to the front of its sentence prior to deleting it and replacing it by a 'relative pronoun' *who(m)* or *that*. When the latter is associated with the verb *be*, they are both commonly subject to further deletion, cf. *John always buys cars* (*which* or *that are*) *expensive to run*. If subsequently again the post-adjectival element *to run* is deleted, i.e. *John always buys cars expensive*, then the adjective must be transformationally moved into the position preceding the noun. Adjectives in noun phrases are therefore seen to be derivable from sentences containing *be*.

The processes of deletion or 'collapsing' can be very complex. How, for example, shall we analyse *he's a man I didn't know existed*? Additional lexico-grammatical constraints will almost invariably be operative at some point or points, as can be seen from the following examples of double reduction or deletion in which *know*, *see*, and *find* clearly differ as to potential accompaniment: *he's the man I knew existed//he's the man I saw go(-ing)//he's the man I found going/gone* or again *I knew (that) he existed* vs. *I knew that he went/had gone/was going* vs. *I saw (that) he went/ him go/him going* vs. *I found (that) he had gone* (or *him gone*)/*he was going* (or *him going*). Moreover, verbs of sensory perception seem to show meaningful differences relatable to the form of an accompanying embedded sentence. Thus, *hear* and *see* exhibit a similarity of distribution in e.g. *I hear/see that he goes* (disregarding *see* = ensure) and *I hear/see him go/going*, but a different manner of auditory perception, say, corresponds to the use of the finite (*that*) *he goes* in *I hear that he goes* from the non-finite case of *I hear him go/going*. It can be seen, too, that the infinitival particle *to* is not 'devoid of meaning', as it is commonly said to be, when we notice it serving in part to mark the difference of verb type between *like/want* and *see/hear* in such contrasts as *I like/want him to go* vs. *I see/hear him go*. It is hardly surprising that TG linguists are often modest in their claims for the coverage provided by TG grammars to date. All the examples of embedding so far adduced have been of sentences within noun phrases; examples within verb phrases are *he'll agree to go* (derivable from *he'll agree* and *he'll go*), *he awoke to find it still dark* (*he awoke* and *he found it still dark*, the latter being further analysable), *we stopped to rest* (*we stopped* and *we rested*), and so on. But let us look rather at co-ordination, which provides interesting and complex examples of 'sentences within sentences'. Once more space does not allow very detailed treatment but consider the following illustrations of co-ordination with contrastive *but*:

*John left his hat on the table but I did
John left his hat on the table but I took mine
*John left his hat on the table but didn't I?
John left his hat on the table but I didn't
John left his hat on the table but did I?

From such evidence it not only appears that there are restrictions on the co-occurrence and sequencing of sentence types (in terms of e.g. declarative-interrogative, positive-negative contrasts) but, more generally, that *but* does not seem to permit more than one contrast between the verb phrases of the contrasted sentences, i.e. lexical verb vs. lexical verb, negative vs. positive, interrogative vs. declarative. One needs, of course, to be constantly on guard against the danger of drawing premature conclusions from insufficient data, and the foregoing tentative statement should, for example, be understood not to include the context in which the second sentence contains *too*, i.e. *John left his hat on the table but I did/didn't I, too*. *too* neutralizes the earlier contrast and *but* now marks such a distinction (expressed or implicit in the extra-linguistic situation) as that between the bracketed portions of *John left his hat on the table* (and there it still is) *but I did/didn't I, too* (and where is mine?). Co-ordination, it seems, can be a complicated process and involves more than the simple juxtaposition of sentences. Similarly, we must be wary of making too facile phonetic assumptions. We might wish to cite *what are you saying and come in* as an example of the general unacceptability (in one sentence) of the sequence interrogative-imperative but discourse analysis proper would require attention to be drawn to the acceptability of the sequence if a pause of sufficient length is made after

188

saying, whereafter we should probably wish to recognize the sequence as containing two separate sentences. Again, a sentence like *John is a musician but Tom plays the piano* has led some to categorize it as unacceptable on the grounds that a hierarchical relation of inclusion exists between *to be a musician* and *to play the piano* and that contrastive *but* cannot be interpolated between elements related in such a way. Nevertheless, by using suitable decelerando rhythm and a falling-rising tone on *musician* and an 'emphatic' (high-) falling tone on *plays*, it is perfectly possible to render the sentence to 'mean' *John is a musician of sorts but Tom plays the piano really well*. There is, it must be said, an unwarrantable tendency to ignore such things.

Enough has no doubt been said about sentence embedding and specifically about the comparatively recent and fruitful form of linguistic analysis known as transformational-generative grammar. The concept of transformation and the explicitness of their formulation of grammatical rules are the two major contributions of TG grammarians —and these are considerable by any standards. The manner in which TG formulates its grammatical findings has not been exemplified in this essay, which has focused rather on transformations, and the reader may wish to pursue matters further by reference to the works listed in the concluding bibliography. Transformations have led to the making of insightful comparisons that were too often missing from the earlier structural linguistics as from still earlier 'traditional' grammars and they also lead to a greater explicitness and generality of rules accounting for many related constructions. It ought perhaps to be said that the writer finds himself much in sympathy with the aspirations and aims of TG, especially when they are allied with the spirit that prompts the practitioner to believe that many linguistic relationships are at present only intuitively felt and therefore not completely or successfully formalized and that many others have not yet been perceived at all. Reservations, however, are expressed elsewhere over, for instance, the TG conception of *competence* and the limited view of meaning that at present implies. Moreover, a limited view of the relevance of phonetic form would tend to lead the TG specialist away from much that is meaningful in spoken language proper. There does not, however, seem to be any theoretical reason why a desirable extension of interest should not be brought about within the framework that transformational-generative grammar provides.

Hierarchies and matters arising

Hierarchical relationships of inclusion are of more than one kind in linguistics. There is, for instance, that by which the individual speaker is a member of a speech community, whose generalized speech habits are likely to be of greater interest than the possibly idiosyncratic behaviour of the individual. The analyst, therefore, needs to be aware and wary of what may intrude of his informants' and (especially) his own personal forms of language. The necessary percipience is not easily acquired. More central to our present concern, however, are the hierarchies of generality and size within what may be taken to be a linguistically homogeneous group. Collocations may serve to illustrate both. The collocability or compatibility of textual elements is perhaps our highest relevant order of abstraction and grammar attempts to capture as much of it as possible in its own network of generalized concepts and terms. Collocations themselves, however, are particular members of generalized classes of associations that we have labelled 'colligations'. The relationship between 'collocation' and 'colligation', then, is on a scale of *generality*. As we have seen, moreover—for example, in the case of the noun phrase— classes may include classes. The relationship between collocation and root, however, is of a different kind, namely one of *size*. It will be recalled, for instance, that the root $\sqrt{green}$ occurs in the collocation ($\sqrt{green} \rightarrow \sqrt{grass}$), with concomitant morphemic 'infilling' by (*as*)—*as*—. Now, until recently linguists have devoted much time, some may say far too much time, to hierarchical relations of size. This preoccupation may possibly be shown to derive from the central and associated concepts of 'phoneme' and 'morpheme' in American structural linguistics of the Bloomfieldian and post-Bloomfieldian kind. We shall return to the view of morphemes as the smallest meaningful units of language, often so-called 'simpler' words but also parts of words (e.g. affixes), made up of one or usually more than one meaningless phoneme. In the meantime, the linguist's notable 'urge to segment' has often taken the form of segmentation in terms of hierarchical ranks or layers, with units of one rank typically composed of units from the rank below, while not very long ago linguists devoted their whole syntactical attention to demonstrating the hierarchical nature of sentence structure in terms of what were named immediate constituents or ICs for short. In accordance with the method and terminology proposed by Bloomfield, a sentence was divided and subdivided into two components at a time (ICs) by a series of binary cuts until ultimate constituents were reached that would yield no further binary division. Bloomfield's example was *Poor John ran away*, divisible first as *Poor John///ran away*, subsequently as *Poor John///ran//away*, thereafter as *Poor/John///ran//away*, with or without the possibility of further cutting *a-way* on the analogy of *along*, *aboard*, etc. C. C. Fries (in *The Structure of English*) was among others to propose cutting rules (not invariably successful) and the sequence of their application, while much thought was devoted to the theoretical basis of IC analysis (see, for example, Rulon S. Wells, 'Immediate Constituents', *Language* 23 (1947), pp. 81–117; reprinted in *Readings in Linguistics I* (ed. M. Joos),

Chicago University Press, 1966) as well as to such questions as the divisibility of co-ordinates like *pitch and toss, fits and starts, etc.* Rather different uses of hierarchical layering in sentence analysis have been developed by several 'schools' of linguistics, among others by the British neo-Firthianism associated with M. A. K. Halliday, the American tagmemics of K. L. Pike and R. E. Longacre, and the American stratificational grammar of S. Lamb. For example, tagmemics (based on the *tagmeme,* which is neither the function or 'slot' nor the class of forms filling the slot but rather the correlation between them, as for example the tagmeme namable as 'subject slot filled by nominal phrase') insists on cutting the sentence into many parts simultaneously in contrast with the binary procedure of IC analysis, but the difference may not be fundamental and the approach also recognizes levels or ranks at which tagmemes occur; these are—for the tagmemicist— sentence, clause, phrase, word, and morpheme, which are to be seen basically as in descending order of size. These approaches recognize 'shifting' between levels; for example, words act as clauses, and clauses may be part of (usually smaller) phrases; cf. *I was bothered by the fact that he was there,* wherein the clause (*that*) *he was there* is part of a nominal phrase (*the fact that he was there*) which is in turn part of the prepositional phrase *by the fact that he was there.* This behaviour is termed 'rank-shifting' by linguists adhering to theories in which our linguistic organization is seen as stratified in this way. It will be realized that fundamental importance is not attached in this paper to the possibility of such layering and also that 'morpheme' and 'word', for instance, are here very differently defined.

The current notion of 'generation' is relatable to generality rather than to hierarchy in the immediately foregoing sense of layering. Most grammars today claim to be 'generative', whether they are subsequently also 'transformational' or not. The native speaker of a language has the capacity to utter and recognize an infinite number of sentences by the use of what seems by comparison to be few internalized regularities. To the extent that a grammar duplicates this capacity it can be said to generate from a finite number of rules and an accompanying lexicon an infinitely large number of sentences. Generative grammars identify sequences as grammatical sentences in a language and describe a set of observed utterances in such a way as to account for an indefinitely greater number of potential utterances. This is in marked contrast with the philosophy of IC analysis and similar subsequent procedures, which, at least in their origins, were concerned to provide an analysis for a fixed textual corpus (however large) in terms of a set of preconceived categories. The risk to be avoided is the forcible imposition upon a text of a predetermined grid, into whose mould facts may all too often be unjustifiably forced—it is of no consequence, after all, whether the mould is that of, say, Latin applied to English, or one of an apparently more objective, modern, 'scientific' kind. Insofar as certain prominent linguistic theories today—notably TG—permit the text rather to 'prompt' the analyst towards comparisons leading to the refinement of rules and a greater depth of meaningful appreciation, modern linguistics is much indebted to such theories, although they too may have their weaknesses.

A generative grammar is not necessarily a transformational one. The latter is essentially characterized by the recognition of 'deep' vs. 'surface' structures, although it is true that systems of grammar that do not answer to the name 'transformational' are increasingly claiming that they recognize the same twofold distinction; this is perhaps hardly surprising when the notion of depth is not too clear. For practical purposes, ambiguity (cf. *he went off playing football*) provides a useful means of indicating the difference between deep and surface structures. Appearances are only skin-deep but one can look for 'explanations' from a variety of sources. Ultimately, it is the individual linguist's philosophy of language and his views on the contribution he has to make to knowledge of meaning that shape his interpretation of the concept of 'depth'. For our present purpose, however, the important thing is the understandable view of the transformational-generative linguist that, to take tagmemics as an example, there is no reason to formulate grammatical rules in such a way as to generate words from morphemes, phrases from words, clauses from phrases, and sentences from clauses. The application of rules to the deep structures of transformational grammar is totally unconstrained by considerations of level or hierarchical rank, which is considered to be relevant to surface structure only. The TG linguist, then, would be more interested in the relatability and interpretation of the three earlier synonymous sentence forms (*the fact*) *that he was there bothered me, his being there bothered me, I was bothered by the fact that he was there* than in the occurrence of a clause as part of the nominal phrase component of a prepositional phrase in the last example. As J. Lyons puts it, 'it is only recently that linguists have made any progress in accounting for [transformational relationships between sentences] in an explicitly generative framework. Any grammar that claims to assign to each sentence that it generates both a deep structure and a surface structure analysis and systematically to relate the two analyses is a transformational grammar'.

It is, however, over what is chosen to relate that one may experience misgivings, and it is the present writer's view that there are serious gaps among both the semantic and the phonetic features that transformational-generative grammar seeks to bring together. The transformational element in TG linguistics has led to some very interesting insights into the structure of English and desirably away in some measure from the earlier structuralist tendency to take meaning as given. At the same time, practitioners of TG themselves often tend to over-simplify, partly perhaps as a result of espousing the somewhat jejune view of language as 'doubly articulated', with semantics on the one side and phonetics on the other. One not only needs to broaden the scope of one's semantic enquiries but also to 'free' phonetics from a word- and segment-based phonology in order to help in the process. Phonetics (or phonology, if preferred) as the branch of linguistic research most concerned to sharpen our awareness of meaningful aspects of pronunciation has nothing whatever to do with orthoepy. While therefore generally in considerable sympathy with the lexico-grammatical aims of TG linguistics and its desire to formulate the highly complex facts of linguistic structure in terms of explicit rules, the writer is *un*sympathetic to the TG profession for what is tantamount to abhorrence of what is called 'performance'—language 'on the air'. We may agree that the speaker/hearer's internalized 'competence' is the object of enquiry, but this should not entail a view of 'performance' as quite devoid of interest, since, in a situation wherein much still remains unknown, the study of 'performance' is 'the only way in'. Failure to observe closely the full detail of meaningful *spoken* language must lead to inadequacy and impoverishment of accompanying semantic statements. To demonstrate his interest in spoken language the TG linguist might perhaps be expected to adduce such examples of ambiguity as our earlier *do you think you could do that?* At present the impression is given that one is expected to go straight to the 'referential heart' of a spoken sentence, but no explanation has yet been given of the manner in which we are to dispose beforehand of the manifold non-referential aspects of speech nor of any reason for ignoring them.

The grammarian has, for example, tended, when dealing with imperative sentences, to confine his attention to those respects in which the sentence type differs from the declarative and interrogative, in the same limited terms that the latter distinction was earlier drawn. (The following 'uniquely grammatical'(?) features serve to establish the imperative type: (1) restrictions on subject—may be *you*, quantifier + *of you* (*all of you, two of you*, etc.), indefinite pronoun (*everybody, nobody, somebody, anybody*), or zero; (2) restrictions on verb—no tense distinction, no association with perfective or modal auxiliaries; (3) *don't* precedes the subject—*don't anybody go*; (4) special behaviour of *be*—*don't be silly* (imp.) vs. *aren't you silly* (interrog.), *you be here early* (imp.) vs. *you are here early* (declar.), *everybody be quiet* vs. *everybody is quiet*;[4] (5) behaviour with 'tags' and other extensions—*you eat it, will/would/won't you* vs. *you eat it, don't you, you eat it, please* (imp.)). But what is the justification for placing such restriction on the forms of imperative sentence that are selected for examination? The following seven possible forms and extensions of *leave your hat on the table* are randomly chosen from a much greater range of possibilities. They represent comparisons that are makable within what appears to be a homogeneous meaningful area of commands and requests, on a scale of politeness.[5]

1. *Leave your hat on the table.* (spoken as a brusque order; 'clipped', staccato, very rapid)
2. *Leave your hat on the table.* (a polite invitation; drawling, decelerando, much reduced overall speed in relation to 1. Intonational form of 1 and 2 may be identical)
3. *Do leave your hat on the table.* (again ambiguous; insistent, even impatient if the invitation is being repeated, otherwise polite; intonational and other variation)
4. *Please leave your hat on the table.* (ambiguous once more, varying from pleading to peremptory; intonation and rhythm much involved)
5. *Would you leave your hat on the table.* (probably more polite than 4 but by no means certainly so)
6. *Won't you leave your hat on the table.* (almost certainly more polite than 4)
7. *Would you care to leave your hat on the table.* (distinctly polite; all elements to the left of the verb *leave* in 3–6 may be shifted to the end of the sentence, but this is not true of 7, which leads into a whole gamut of quasi-idiomatic pre-verbal elements)

The writer is only too well aware of the insufficiency of the bracketed comments, an insufficiency which may serve to indicate the inadequacy of our present knowledge and parallel descriptive apparatus, as well as the need to undertake seriously what Z. S. Harris called 'discourse analysis', although in rather different terms from those he had in mind. Even such a fragmentary first selection may, however, show how unsatisfactory it is either to label, say, polite formulae of greeting and leave-taking as 'meaningless' since 'predictable' (it is surely meaningful to be polite) or to wrap such distinctions as are adumbrated above in the blanket term 'expressive' before throwing them overboard. We have already referred to the reluctance of many linguists to consider such an ambiguous sentence as *do you think you could do that?* Why have I just written a question mark, I wonder? In what sense is such a sentence 'interrogative'? Is it 'imperative'? It seems reasonable to recognize a single area of commands and requests, and even plausible in the writer's view to relate the foregoing example in its 'request'-ful sense to the 'unequivocally' imperative form *do that*, and certainly more consequential, one might think, than to analyse the earlier part of the sentence in terms of 'subject and predicate'. The extensibility of *do that* is noticeably different from that of *leave your hat* (*on the table*)—*I suppose you couldn't . . . (or I don't suppose you could . . .)* is hardly associable with the latter, for instance—and conceivably such differences relate to the distinction hinted at between 'command' and 'request'. But the point to be made is that semantics should not stay with the 'be'-ness of *be* or the *'red'*-ness of *red* and it is to be hoped that semanticists will shed their preoccupations with the apparent havens of kin and colour, where idealization is perhaps feasible and colour differences at any rate 'explicable' electronically in the last resort, for the deeper, rougher, often uncharted seas of meaningful speech. 'Ideals' may often have little to do with language and by the same token the 'universals' we all long to know are undoubtedly there for the discovering, although the somewhat uninteresting nature of those at present available suggests that we should be looking beyond the mere referential and existential at what men do with language the world over. But this is by-the-way.

The relevance of phonological features

It is very widely accepted among linguists that language is 'doubly articulated', a view endorsed by linguists as far apart as N. Chomsky in America and A. Martinet in France. In order to see what may be implied by the double articulation of language, perhaps we could profitably follow through an example of phoneme-morpheme analysis in 'classical' structuralist terms, since it is to such a source that the concept is probably traceable in the short term. One would start with phonemics and notice, for example, that the different 'k'-sounds in /ki:p/ ('keep'), /bækt/ ('backed'), and /kɔ:d/ ('cord, cored, cawed') occur in mutually exclusive positions in relation to other features of the phonetic environment and are therefore in complementary distribution. One thus has various *phones* in different contexts or environments, so that if x is the environment, then $k1:x1: :k2:x2: :k3:x3$ ... Thereafter one sets up an abstract class of phoneme and the erstwhile phones become allophones of a phoneme. Going further, one finds, for example, the forms /kæt-s/ ('cats'), /dɔg-z/ ('dogs'), and /hɔ:s-iz/ ('horses'). These pose a problem, since although the differences between the final sibilant elements are clearly relatable to the nature of the preceding consonant (voiceless /-t/ in /kæt/, voiced /-g/ in /dɔg/, sibilant /-s/ in /hɔ:s/), the phonemic difference between /s/ and /z/ has already been recognized elsewhere (cf. /su:/ ('Sue, Sioux') vs. /zu:/ ('zoo')) and, in the American structuralist view, archiphonemes and the neutralization of phonemic distinctions in the Prague-school manner were inadmissible. The problem is 'solved', however, when it is seen that the final elements 'have the same meaning', namely 'making the plural'. Now we are with morphology and can re-write the final element as {-Z}, re-christen 'morphs' what up to now have been phones, and classify them together on the basis of their mutual exclusion as allomorphs of a morpheme.

One looks therefore at a word, sees or hears a symbol for a morph, which must have a phonic realization—each allomorph has a pronunciation, a morph with a sound. The morpheme, then, in contrast with the phoneme, has meaning, and it is basically the relation of the meaningful morpheme and its included meaningless phonemes that constitutes double articulation. Now, there is more than one reaction to record in the terms of this paper. First, according to the syntagmatic view of things taken here, 'plural' would have no sound in English but be one of a system of number categories that take multiple form. Second, the urge to segment and give shape to morphemes—which led in the past to much anxiety, for example, over the lack of sound difference between *sheep* in singular syntagms and *sheep* in plural syntagms, and again, over how to deal with *take* (present tense) vs. *took* (past tense)—belongs with the need we feel to provide palpable means of reference to linguistic abstractions. Thus, phoneme belongs with word and word-class as seen in this paper, and the continuing orthoepic basis of most phonemics seems to lend support to this view. This is not to say, then, that to give phonemic shape to roots and morphemes is not a *useful* thing to do but it contributes little or nothing to analysis and in any case it does not seem that it can be done in advance of the necessary syntagmatic analysis of sentences without begging the questions this paper has tried throughout to pose. It might be useful to distinguish between phonemics in this practical sense and phonology as meaningful phonetics. Third, one either accepts the contrastive basis of analysis or not—one cannot have it both ways, it seems to me. If one does not accept Bloomfield's 'minimum same of vocal feature' as the means of identifying phonemes, if one does not believe, that is, in the 'k'-ness of /k/, one can still believe firmly in the meaningfully contrastive basis of phoneme recognition by which such words as /kɪn/, tɪn/, pɪn/, etc. are given acceptable shape at the same time as the rest of the lexicon. On this view, to draw attention to the supposed meaninglessness of the phonemic components of, say, roots and morphemes in our terms, would be something of a red herring. In speech one is using the human phonatory apparatus to give shapes of many kinds to meaningful distinctions; it is hardly surprising, therefore, that phonetic differences are often found to reinforce the recognition of generalized grammatical categories. In one sense, the analysis of meaning in speech is 'all phonetic' and lexico-grammatical categories and classes useful shorthand devices. At bottom, one feels that double articulation could well be based on acceptance of phonemes as 'minimum sames of vocal feature' and of a word-based semantics of a more or less traditional kind. Feature analysis—semantic and phonetic—seems in effect to carry the process further, to segment the segment, and can involve the turning of deaf ears to the innumerable phonological dependencies and constraints of a syntagmatic kind that are to be observed within and without the boundaries of roots and morphemes. This paper does not therefore accept that it is 'a primary fact that sentences consist of pairings or associations of information about meaning with information about pronunciation'. The view of spoken language as meaningful pronunciation seeks rather to give its rightful place to the close phonetic study of spoken language. TG's 'phonetic representations' are said to be 'a system of instructions governing the movements of a physical system— the speech apparatus', and, with due adaptation of metaphor, 'classical' phonemics could probably claim to be the same thing.

Obvious phonological areas of close relevance to the understanding of sentences are intonation, tonicity, and rhythm, and we shall exemplify them fairly fully subsequently. Yet often enough, vocalic and consonantal features require close consideration—from the different potential forms of *had* in the ambiguous *they had explained to them the rules of the game*, through the length differences in the -*t(t)*- preceding the final tonic vowels in (1) *they had a settee* (2) *they had a set-to* (3) *they had a set, too*, to include the comparison of -*sn't*- and -*sant*, which, though alike in *isn't* and *pleasant* as pronounced in isolation, are subject to noticeably different possible treatments in *it isn't to taste* vs. *it's pleasant to see* (cf., for good measure, *its pleasanter taste*). The English negative conjugation, so to speak, is marked phonetically in numerous ways—the reader might wish to see what he can do with -*n't b*- in *I can't be bothered* and contrast what might be done with his *Aunt Belinda*. But let us turn to examples of tonal differences.

In the sentence ⌄*John, lend me your ₍book*, the use of the falling-rising tone on the vocative *John* and of the rising tone on *book* is 'request'-ful enough; with the book withheld, repeated falls on *John* and *book* in ₍*John, (don't be a ₍bore,) lend me your ₍book* are indicative of exasperation. Trans-sentential dependencies are no less noticeable phonologically than lexico-grammatically. In this case the form of words is neutral as to the distinctions that may be carried in this way by intonational means. In the case of *you might at least have said so*, expostulation is already present in the form of words and intonation may be used to add incremental recrimination, as by the use of three falling tones, equally spaced rhythmically, sc. *you ₍might at ₍least have ₍said so*; the falling tone so used syntagmatically throughout the sentence might seem to be on a par with such concordial devices as final -*a* in E. Sapir's Latin example *illa alba femina* 'that white woman'. Firth's already quoted example *Now just take ₍these. I'm sure they'll do you ₍good. You'll feel much better in the ₍morning. Good-₍night*, illustrates the use of the rising tone (more or less passim and certainly more than once) for reassurance. As has been said, comic play can be made of using inappropriate intonation patterns for individual sentences of the total text and thereby providing an inappropriate con-tonation pattern for the whole. Linguists have so far preferred unrealistically to confine themselves, however, to the somewhat artificial limits of the sentence and have all too often settled for some illusory meaning attached to particular tones (falling, rising, falling-rising, rising-falling, level, etc.). In fact, tonal features are as a rule interwoven into the whole formal complex and only regarded as totally separable from the remainder (phrases, sentences, even roots, etc.) at the cost of dulling our analytical awareness of meaningful distinctions. There is proof enough of this in the number of times that it has been necessary in this paper to hedge lexico-grammatical statements around with phonological caveats. Moreover, as scholars, we cannot be satisfied with coarse descriptive nets that may catch distinctions metaphorically the size of tunny while allowing many sizable fish to slip through unobserved. The resources of the human mechanism of utterance may well be exploited to provide distinctions that are phonological *tout court* but we should be rash to dissociate such resources from 'forms of words' and generalized grammatical patterns. Distinctions of the kind we have just recognized may be relatable in particular to 'emotive' (?'expressive') meaning, but not only is it unjustifiable to regard such meaning as unimportant but tonal distinctions have in fact much wider relevance. Let us consider some meaningful differences of a tonal kind relevant to the interpretation of the following ambiguous sentences:

1. *What's your name, Barbara?*

   The use of the lower part of the voice register for a rising tone associated with *Barbara* marks *Barbara* as vocative as well as the fact that the speaker is addressing a small child called Barbara and inviting her to tell her name to a third person or persons present. This interpretation, like any other, derives from contrast with other possibilities, such as the use of the higher part of the voice register for the rising tone on *Barbara*. In the latter 'appositive' case, 'Barbara' may be of any age and the speaker seeks confirmation that her name is indeed 'Barbara'. The portion *what's your name* need exhibit no variation.

2. *Chelsea 2 Leeds 2*

   If you are a football pools punter and this is the final draw you need in order to win the big dividend, then should the radio announcer pronounce the final *2* on anything other than a monotone, you will— to put it mildly—wish him elsewhere. Draws demand the use of one intonation pattern only; here a falling tone on *Leeds* and a low level (monotone) on *2*. A falling-rising or rising tone on *Leeds* would indicate disparity between the scores of the two teams but a falling tone can only mean equality.

3. *I didn't do it on purpose*

With the falling-rising tone associated with (*on*) *purpose*, the sentence may be glossed 'it wasn't on purpose that I did it'. Otherwise, the ambiguity of the sentence is probably to be resolved only by appeal to the further context. Grammatically, contrast is between negation of the main verb (sc. *not do*) and negation of its 'modifying' accompaniment (sc. *not on purpose*). Other examples would be *I didn't go because I was ill, I didn't do it deliberately, he couldn't do it if you paid him.* Notice that the composite *on purpose* and sentential *because I was ill* are not transposable but that the single 'adjunctive' form *deliberately* may appear pre-verbally in *I deliberately didn't do it*, which of course is unambiguous.

4. *They're pretty good usually*
He'd gone by the time I got there

A falling tone on *good* and *gone* is typically accompanied by a rise on or from the accented syllable of *usually* and *got* (*there*). So-called 'adjuncts' in the declarative sentence are commonly marked in this way and may often also be front-shifted; if so, and if a noticeable pause may occur after the 'adjunct' when initial, then there is a fairly regular tonal correspondence between the two sentence forms (with 'adjunct' initial or final), cf. *usually, they're pretty good* and *by the time I got there, he'd gone.*

5. *I thought he was*

With the final portion of the sentence pronounced with rising intonation, cf. the subtle potential difference of pitch range employable between the two cases where the sentence = (1) 'now what you say confirms my earlier view' and (2) 'now what you say makes me less sure of my earlier view'. Cf., too, say, *you said he was coming* = (1) 'and there he is coming through the gate' and (2) 'where is he?' The first sentence of both pairs is exclamatory, the second contrastive (contrast is between the form of one's expectancy and the form of events). The verbs (e.g. *think, say*) that permit such a contrast within appropriately extended structures, are few in number but frequent in occurrence.

6. *I like that*

The common rising tone on *that* does not preclude an interpretation of positive liking, but the sentence may also be rendered to mean 'I like that but I'm not mad about it', so that a contrast partly comparable with that under 5 applies. Notice in passing the extremely common use of the falling-rising tone for contrastive purposes and its frequent correlation with an extension introduced by 'contrastive' *but* . . ., as in the present example. Contrast both of these possibilities with that of the same form of words used as a protest, when a falling tone is typically associated with *that*.

The phonological features of tonicity (i.e. the placing of the tonic, nuclear, stressed, accented, or prominent syllable) and rhythm (i.e. the distribution of utterances and part-utterances in time, which is partly dealt with under such headings as 'juncture' and 'stress' in the literature of linguistics but still remains to be fully studied in any language, including English) are also very important, possibly more so even than intonation, for the understanding of syntactic combinations. As a rule in speech, it is a simultaneous complex of these and other phonological features with which one is concerned. Thus, for example, to take the example above of *what's your name*, not only would a rising-falling tone on *your* be appropriately used by the immigration officer addressing a small child but inappropriately in the case of an adult applicant for a visa or travel permit but, in addition, in the latter case and in the absence of other interlocutors with whom contrast could be made, the tonic syllable would typically be *name* rather than *your*. Let us look a little more closely at tonicity, about which, in comparison with tonality, more still can be meaningfully said within the frame of the sentence and even of the phrase, compound, idiom, etc. A. E. Sharp has rightly remarked that if English is not a tone language, then at any rate it is a tonic one.

The usual grammar-book references to tonicity are confined to pointing out the difference between such pairs of words as *súbject* (noun) and *subjéct* (verb) but in fact this type of meaningful distinction permeates the whole of English speech. The *búllfighter/fíghts búlls/* (at a) *búllfight*, the man who *pícks póckets* is a *píckpocket*, one who *blacks óut* has a *bláckout*, another who *runs abóut* in a jalopy owns a *rúnabout*, the ladies *make úp* with *máke-up*, *toy fáctories* may be produced in *tóy factories*, and so on. Tonicity is not only relevant to compounding in English. It concerns the reflexive, for instance, so that one may *fáncy onesélf* to win but if one *fáncies onesélf*, then one is a vain, conceited fellow; similarly, the man who *shot himsélf* committed *felo de se* but the

200

one who *shot himself* should probably have passed the ball instead of taking a shot at goal. Again, the meliorative adjectival construction illustrated by *a prétty lìttle house* does not permit the association of tonicity with *little*; if it is so associated, then *pretty* 'modifies' *little*, sc. *a pretty líttle house* = a not very big house. Yet again, the constituency of sentences extended by such frequently occurring 'end-pieces' as *either* or *too*, cf. *I can't swim, either/I can swim, too*, is indicated by the place of the tonic syllable in the sentence preceding the extension; thus, *Í can't swim, éither* = any more than you can, *I can't swím, éither* = any more than I can ride, *Í can swim, tóo*, = as well as you, *I can swím, tóo* = as well as ride. One may find in tonicity, too, a means of recognizing the constituency of idioms, as for example that of *put up with* = tolerate, any of whose three constituents may be tonic in appropriate grammatical circumstances; cf. *A. You'll have to put úp with it. B. It's not the kìnd of thing you can put up wíth.* This is tonicity in a context of repetition or 'second mention' of a linguistic item. The same feature accounts for differences of tonicity between the pronunciation of lexical items in isolation and in the contexts of living speech; cf. *I sáid Sémitic, not Hámitic*, or *A. Hurry úp or he'll disappéar. B. Let him dísappear*. Grammatical generalization is by no means a prerequisite of tonic meaningfulness. It is a statement of considerable generality that any English sentence of given tonic pattern is almost certain to differ meaningfully from counterparts varying only in respect of this feature, cf., for example, *did you see him?*, wherein tonicity may variously be associated with *did, you, see*, or *him*. Similarly, *he's a góod man* is probably a moral judgment on a man; of another person it may be said that *he's a good mán* (sc. for the job, though a reprobate); someone who *isn't hálf mad* is utterly furious but if he or she *isn't half mád*, then he or she is wholly crazy; finally, by way of illustration, a man who *makes his money out of playing cárds* is a gambler, while the one who *makes his money out of playing cards* is an industrialist. Once again,the syntagmatic dependency of items in texts can be exemplified tonically. A clear example above was that of *a pretty little house*; in the same way, tonicity associated with *might* in e.g. *I might have known he was coming* (= someone might have informed me of the fact) marks a very different *might* and *know* from those apparently similar forms in *I might have known he was coming* (sc. he *would* be coming, what a bore!), and other features of a phonological kind will almost certainly be necessary for the interpretation of the sentence. Although, as has been said at the beginning of this paper, the study of genuinely spoken language (conversation) has barely begun, it should also be remembered that most written language has the implication of being read aloud at least and that in order to understand it we may have to rely on features like tonicity. The following recorded 'remarks' by James II at the end of a stormy interview in 1688 with seven Anglican bishops for long puzzled historians: 'I tell you that there are seven thousand men, and of the Church of England, too, that have not bowed the knee to Baal'. Once one realizes that the Catholic James may well accuse the bishops of apostasy ('bowing the knee to Baal'), all is clarified by the association of tonicity with *thousand* (sc. seven *thousand* in contrast with a mere *seven*), *England* (in contrast with *Rome*), and *not* (in contrast with the seven who *have* (bowed the knee)). (The example is owed to Hugh Ross Williamson, *Historical Whodunits*, London, 1955).

Is there further need to demonstrate the relevance of phonology to sentence structure? Perhaps brief mention should be made of 'timing' in relation to, say, *we need several more talented players* = (1) several more players of talent in addition to the talented players we already have, with *several* and *more* rhythmically fused (2) several players of greater talent than those we now have, with *more* and *talented* closely associated and *several* rallentando. The meaningful difference is not enormous in this case but cf., say, the possibly threefold association of the words *twenty, one, hundred, dollar, bills* with the various meanings (1) 20 100-dollar bills (2) 21 100-dollar bills (3) 2100 dollar bills and compare the rhythmic differences between them. We should recall that the distinctions we recognize are potentially multiform. *I like that* (protest) may occupy no more time than *I like that* (avowal of liking) but it *may* also be extended in time in a way inappropriate to the contrasted sentence. We should remember, too, that distinctions are rarely minimal, nor should we be misled by this fact into facile acceptance of so-called 'redundancies' in speech. The earlier sentence *John is a musician but Tom plays the piano* (quoted in a communication from P. R.

Hawkins of the Department of English, Victoria University of Wellington, New Zealand) was seen to be acceptable if 'properly spoken', with the use among other features of falling-rising tone and rallentando tempo on *musician* and (high) falling tone on *plays*. The example therefore was one of the combined distinctiveness of tone and tempo. Tonicity and tempo are associated in (1) *the New Building sub-committee* (*sc*. the sub-committee concerned with the New Building) vs. (2) *the new Building Sub-Committee* (*sc*. the freshly constituted sub-committee on building); contrast the timing of *new* and *building* in the two examples and compare tonic *sub-* in (1) with tonic *Building* in (2). But space and time is pressing and enough has surely been said to reveal the greater relevance of phonology to syntactic analysis than the mere provision of (ortho)phonemic shape for sentences and their parts.

Conclusion

In the English-speaking world of linguists little more than ten short years ago, the talk was of grammatical models labelled 'Item and Arrangement', 'Item and Process', and 'Word and Paradigm' (see, for example, C. F. Hockett, 'Two models of grammatical description', *Word* 10 (1954), pp. 210–34; reprinted in *Readings in Linguistics I*, ed. M. Joos, Washington, D.C. (1957), pp. 386–99, and R. H. Robins, 'In defence of WP', *Transactions of the Philological Society*, Oxford (1959), pp. 116–44).[6] Before and since, grammar was and is variously styled 'phonological', 'tagmemic', 'stratificational', 'systemic', or otherwise designated according to the theoretical stance of a particular linguist or group of linguists. Of recent years it is transformational-generative grammar that has undoubtedly called the tune, although here, too, diversification has 'set in'. These are times of turmoil in the affairs of men, no less in linguistics than elsewhere. From one's own coign of vantage—and there is much relativity in linguistics, let alone in language itself—one forms the impression that some linguists have temporarily retired to re-group, as it were, and who is to say what the picture will be a few years hence? In such circumstances it did not seem sensible to attempt in this paper to review theories that may or may not be in competition. The reader may well have discerned that the approach to language here outlined reveals the strong influence of H. E. Palmer and J. R. Firth. If a label has to be given to it, it should be called 'Firthian' and, since there exists or has existed what may be a better known 'Neo-Firthian' kind of British linguistics, it has seemed useful to conclude with a brief résumé of the Firthianism informing the paper and at the same time to bring its Firthian characteristics into focus by comparing them with relevant aspects of neo-Firthianism and, to a lesser extent, with those of the highly influential TG linguistics of the day. Any inaccuracies in the interpretation of these 'positions' are due to the writer, and it should

203

perhaps be said beforehand that, in these days of rapidly accelerated change, certain stated characteristics of neo-Firthianism may very recently have ceased to be such. There appear to be three salient features of Firthianism and we shall confine our comments to them:
(1) insistence on the centrality of meaning in all its aspects
(2) adoption of a basically inductive approach to language study
(3) recognition of the priority of syntagmatic analysis.

The centrality of meaning

With insistence on the centrality of meaning goes a greater willingness to face up to meaning in all its aspects. Although the TG position is not entirely clear, it seems to have, or at any rate potentially to have, more in common semantically with Firthianism than with Bloomfieldianism, wherein meaning was taken as given; TG, however, has been too preoccupied so far with its understandable rejection of the earlier view of us as speaking automata to attend to the many aspects of meaningful speech that at present it ignores and thus fully to live up to its proclaimed and laudable object of asking and answering important questions about language which 'center upon the nature of the abilities displayed by human beings in acquiring and using a language'. Firth, however, went further than most TG grammarians in explicitly rejecting the separation of semantics from phonological, lexical, and grammatical study. To some extent in common with TG, Firthianism dislikes the earlier division of linguistic analysis into watertight levels, and this is reflected, for example, in the use of the term 'lexico-grammatical' and associated concepts in this paper. In this respect, the present approach differs quite sharply from neo-Firthianism, which regards lexical study as separate and separable from grammar. It will be recalled, for example, that the view taken here is that collocations are to be studied within grammatical matrices and that the latter in turn depend for their recognition on the observation of collocational similarities, including similarities of difference. Neo-Firthian collocations, however, have been taken to be determinable statistically, for example by the use of computers. For J. R. Firth, 'the business of descriptive linguistics is to make statements of meaning'; for the neo-Firthian, descriptive linguistics has been predominantly concerned with 'the description of linguistic patterns in the abstract, without reference to how, where, when ... they are used'; for some neo-Firthians, but notably not including M. A. K. Halliday, linguistic patterns seem to be relatable to features of referential meaning only—the rest is not strictly a matter of meaning proper but belongs rather to an all-embracing 'significance'. Firth rejected the concept of 'central cores of meaning' for words, which leads logically on to notions of 'deviation', which in turn implies the existence of some central language core whence deviation is measurable. This may underlie the use of computers to count mechanically what occurs on either side of a lexical item focused in one's attention. The Firthian view is rather that more interesting results are likely to follow from the use of one's own knowledge for the comparison of texts and that the apparent objectivity of such quasi-mathematical procedures is illusory. Neo-Firthians have in the past claimed that they study language 'for its own sake', which—it has been pointed out—is an unhappy form of words since language has never existed for its own sake; that they, like other linguists, understandably wish to study the forms of language objectively and in terms that recognizably belong to linguistics, goes without saying, and perhaps this is how one should understand the reference to studying language 'for its own sake'.

Inductive vs. deductive

Insistence on a basically inductive approach to analysis should not, of course, be thought to involve rejection of the need for theoretical expectations and for predictive power in the classes and categories recognized in analysis. One can never be wholly inductive or exclusively deductive but it is possible at a given time to be more one than the other, and when there is still so much to know of meaning and its formal linguistic aspects around the world, then it seems reasonable to believe that it is at least for the time being desirable to treat texts and part-texts on their own merits. This is all that is implied by a 'basically inductive' approach, namely that free rein should be allowed to the development and exploitation of contrasts arising out of close observation and textual analysis. This does not run counter to the need for objectivity and rigour of statement but, in their understandable wish to meet these requirements, some linguists have shown a tendency to jump to general conclusions ahead of time. Many linguists in the past have wished to limit their linguistic statements to those based on a corpus of collected texts, in the belief that a sufficient number of such texts will capture all that is worth capturing. This procedure not only denies by implication the value of what in fact is an inescapable introspection in the analytical process but has in the past led to what seems excessive reliance on aprioristic grids of hierarchically ordered categories, imposed *deductively* on texts and carrying all the 'risks' that linguists in what one might almost call 'the old days' fervently recognized in their unanimous condemnation of forcing English facts into a Latin mould. In the present paper, as has been said, the recorded utterance is seen rather as a device to prompt the observer towards the making of 'worthwhile' comparisons and contrasts. Clearly, one starts with all sorts of expectations, which noticeably obtrude, for example if instead of leaving the first recording of spoken utterance to a machine, one immediately seeks to reduce it to writing in whatever form, including phonetic transcription. Clearly, too, one must avoid the oddities and particularities of speech 'on the air', but the meaning of a text and its parts does not lie *in* the text itself but rather in the networks of differential relations between texts; meaning is not part of the text but part of the linguistic organization of the speaker-hearer, who most of the time is the observer-analyst. Meaningful distinctions are not in any absolute sense 'signalled' in utterance as per an older structuralist view—it does not seem reasonable to believe that one hears absolutely and on any particular occasion a given level of pitch, let us say, or a value of 'junctural time' between words; more plausibly, one locates what one observes in relation to other comparable features in their absence. This view is more in accord with the competence-performance distinction of the TG linguist (itself directly relatable to the older 'langue-parole' dichotomy of F. de Saussure); it does not, however, share the TG 'abhorrence' of performance, which, as was said earlier, is 'the only way in', at any rate for someone who does not take meaning as given. Moreover, to the extent that 'competence' as so far exemplified in transformational-generative linguistics does not account for many meaningful aspects of language, it seems to stand in need of modification and extension. There is no obvious theoretical reason why this extension cannot be encompassed and a deeper awareness of language achieved in terms of transformational grammar and its manner of explicit formulation. In order to confront more of language than at present, TG almost certainly needs among other things to face squarely up to the facts of a 'performance' that comprises more than hesitations, changes of direction, and the like. Furthermore, as we have seen, the Firthian view of spoken language as meaningful pronunciation and of the phoneme as essentially an orthoepic concept, is at variance with the widely accepted doctrine of the 'double articulation' of language.

It is noticeable that among the most insightful work in TG terms is that which is usually described as 'fragmentary', i.e. based on selections of bits of language that are presumably felt to cohere meaningfully, notwithstanding the impression one is given that a monolithic TG grammar will one day follow. When it does, will it contain chapters, one wonders? Firth advocated what he called 'partial studies', e.g. the study of newspaper headlines *per se*, in which attention would be drawn to features of the 'restricted language' itself as well as to contrasts between it and other restricted languages. There is much in common between 'restricted language' and the neo-Firthian 'register', now fairly generally accepted qua term. What is shared at bottom is the willingness of both Firthians and neo-Firthians to look at more aspects of meaning than most other kinds of linguist. Yet there remain important differences of approach. For the neo-Firthian, linguistic form is paramount and logically prior to all else; a change of linguistic form involves a potential change of register. The linguist, therefore, among all specialists with an interest in language, is seen as best equipped to recognize meaningful variation in language, since language variety is before all else formal variety. Such a view naturally follows from neo-Firthian acceptance of the form: meaning dichotomy and differs markedly from Firth's own willingness to treat on equal terms what scholars in other disciplines had to say about language from their standpoint. As J. B. Pride has observed, it is precisely because language is more than just form that the notion of 'register' is a useful one. It follows from the neo-Firthian view of the priority of linguistic form that linguistics is the prior discipline among those with an interest in language, but such pre-eminence is no more tenable than that claimed for psychology by the statement, *pace* Chomsky, that 'linguistics is a branch of cognitive psychology'. The fact that our meaningful uses of and responses to language are organized in the brain (perhaps better, the nervous system) is of no special relevance to the diverse areas of scholarship to which language is of concern. In to-day's situation in which such different disciplines as linguistics, anthropology, sociology, psychology, philosophy, communications engineering, computer science, etc., as well as the very many particular language disciplines, all have their contribution to make to linguistic knowledge, no one discipline can be considered prior. Although most linguists, conscious of their own limitations and anxious to welcome the insights of other specialists, nowadays very properly seek the occasions to hear other points of view, it is nevertheless highly unlikely that many will achieve Chomsky's own mastery of a whole congeries of disciplines and more probable that they will be obliged to remain content with a thorough acquaintance with one or at most two specialized areas of study. In such circumstances, an inductive approach of a somewhat different kind is indicated—is indeed a practical necessity—namely that by which the individual scholar may hope to make his own contribution according to his own lights. The claim is often made by linguists today that the particular theoretical model of their allegiance is in fact an all-embracing reflex of the brain or nervous system. It need hardly be said that no such claim is made here. Firthianism was decidedly more on the 'hocus-pocus' side of the formerly current dichotomy that had 'God's truth' as its other half.

The paramountcy of the syntagm

In the manner of its emphasis on the syntagm, Firthian linguistics is very much on its own. Syntagmatic analysis aims at avoiding, for example, what are seen as errors and pseudo-problems that attend the splitting of unitary associations like collocations and the forcing of parts of the meaning of such wholes into fictitious 'sememes', to use the Bloomfieldian term, which are then attributed in particular to words and bits of words. Recognition of the on-going nature of language and that of sentences as at least in part definable on the basis of trans-sentential relations also reveal this syntagmatic orientation. It is necessary to separate the 'appreciation' of what is meaningful and how it is so from the subsequent manner in which findings are formulated; it is only in the latter less fundamental, though probably more practical domain that we can, for instance, metaphorically ascribe meanings to words and word-classes. These should first be shown, however, within the syntagmatic associations whence their meanings derive. In any other sense, once syntagmatic analysis has been completed, it is, strictly speaking, otiose to deal again in a narrow paradigmatic way with the discriminations recognized. It is perhaps because of a preoccupation with 'units' and their relevance to formulation that linguists to date have not yet considered at all closely the facts of linguistic patterning within supra-sentential domains. Why, one wonders, should the sentence not continue to suffice as the principal unit of statement? Why should we need some unit like the written paragraph before we undertake the study of language functions in discourse? Perhaps again our semantic predispositions are at the bottom of things. In phonology, too, it should be said in conclusion, the Firthian view was to reject the phoneme in favour of a syntagmatic concept, which was termed—perhaps not too happily—the 'prosody'. The mainspring of prosodic analysis in phonology was the recognition of phonetic features whose domains extended beyond those of the phoneme as well as of constraints and dependencies which, as in the case of lexico-grammatical study, had to be examined first before deciding what, if anything, was left to be dealt with paradigmatically under 'phonematics', a term which bears only etymological resemblance to 'phonemics'). Subsequently, the syntagmatic basis of the prosody came to be confused rather with other aspects of Firthian thinking and especially with the need not to identify—in the phonemic manner—terms in what was recognizable as one system with those in another. A polysystemic approach to language analysis is wholly justifiable but belongs rather with those features of Firthianism that were dealt with under the previous heading. But this is not the place for discussion of Firthian phonology in general, nor of its relations to lexico-grammatical study, nor indeed for any further emphasis on the syntagm. It is, in fact, the time and place to end. Perhaps this paper has asked as many questions as it has has provided answers. At all events the debate will continue—and continue to continue. At present all we can say with certainty is, with the Latin poet, that *Grammatici certant, et adhuc sub judice lis est* ('The grammarians are at variance, and the matter is still undecided'). And this is no bad thing.

A SHORT BIBLIOGRAPHY

These times of rapid change and development would make it difficult to provide a fully representative bibliography of books and articles matching the contemporary 'state of the game'. Fortunately, this is not what is required for the present purpose, which is rather to help the general reader who has the time, facilities, and inclination to familiarize himself to some degree with characteristics of discernibly different American and British 'schools' of linguistics that have been explicitly or implicitly mentioned in the foregoing paper. Certain other suggestions for further reading have been made from time to time in the text and are not necessarily repeated below. The number of titles under any one head has also to be seen in the light of emphases made in the paper rather than as an indication of the 'importance' to be attached to a particular school. Choice of titles has been invidious and, although some attempt has been made to provide reasonably comprehensive cover, one's own favourite titles are often missing and the list should not be regarded as, say, prescribed reading for an intensive course in linguistics. It is thought that for the average reader, who will probably not wish to delve too deeply, eight titles of comparatively short works will suffice. This has posed an even more difficult problem of selection but the eight works suggested are starred in the subsequent list. The order of presentation is roughly chronological; the transformational-generative point of departure has been taken as the year in which Chomsky's *Syntactic Structures* appeared. Where reference is made to selected chapters or pages of *books*, it is for their special relevance to the subject of the paper or for the contribution they make to defining the characteristics or the 'school' concerned.

Strange as it may seem, it is not possible to make very specific reference to the grammatical writings of J. R. Firth. It is not only that Firth devoted more of his energies to phonology but also that the recognizably Firthian notions of the present paper are such that permeate the whole of Firth's writings without being easily detachable from them. It may also be the case that one derived more from conversation with Firth on grammatical topics than from the little he wrote on the subject. It certainly cannot be said that those who are Firthian among British linguists have established any clearly agreed approach to grammar, at least in its syntactic and syntagmatic aspects. There is perhaps, however, more of Firth's influence than might at first seem in F. R. Palmer's *Linguistic Study of the English Verb* (London. Longmans. 1965). The book in which it is most marked is Heinrich Straumann's *Newspaper Headlines* (London. Allen & Unwin, 1935). In general, however, one can only suggest perusal of relevant articles in the two volumes of Firth's collected papers, *Papers in Linguistics* 1934–51

(Oxford. Oxford University Press, 1957) and *Selected Papers of J. R. Firth* 1952–59 (London. Longmans, 1968). The heading 'Firthian' is therefore missing from the list that follows.

'*Traditional*'

H. Sweet, *A New English Grammar* (Oxford, Clarendon Press, 1891 (Vol. 1) and 1898 (Vol. 2)

H. Poutsma, *A Grammar of Late Modern English (Part I, The Sentence)* (2nd ed.) (Groningen, Noordhoff, 1928)

O. Jespersen, *Essentials of English Grammar* (New York, Holt, 1933; and University of Alabama Press, 1964)

O. Jespersen, *Analytic Syntax* (Copenhagen, Munksgaard, 1937; and New York, Holt, Rinehart & Winston, 1969)

H. E. Palmer, *A Grammar of English Words* (London, Longmans, 1938)

H. E. Palmer (with F. G. Blandford), *A Grammar of Spoken English* (2nd ed.) (Cambridge, Heffer, 1939)

'*Structuralist*'

L. Bloomfield, *Language* (especially Chapters 10, 11, 12, and 16) (New York, Holt, 1933; and (latest re-printing) London, Allen & Unwin, 1967)

★B. Bloch and G. L. Trager, *An Outline of Linguistic Analysis* (Baltimore, Waverly Press, 1942)

★C. C. Fries, *The Structure of English* (New York, Harcourt Brace, 1952)

C. F. Hockett, *A Course in Modern Linguistics* (especially Chapters 17–23) (New York, Macmillan, 1958)

C. F. Hockett, *The State of the Art* (The Hague, Mouton, 1968) (Review by F. R. Palmer in *Language*, Vol. 45, No. 3 (1969), pp. 616–21)

'*Tagmemic*'

K. L. Pike, *Language in Relation to a Unified Theory of the Structure of Human Behaviour* (originally printed in 3 parts in the period 1954–60, now in one volume; The Hague, Mouton, 1967)

R. E. Longacre, *Grammar Discovery Procedures* (The Hague, Mouton, 1964)

B. Elson and V. Pickett, *An Introduction to Morphology and Syntax* (Santa Ana, Summer Institute of Linguistics, 1964)

★W. A. Cook, *Introduction to Tagmemic Analysis* (New York, Holt, Rinehart & Winston, 1969)

'*Transformational-Generative*'

N. Chomsky, *Syntactic Structures* (The Hague, Mouton, 1957)

N. Chomsky, *Current Issues in Linguistic Theory* (The Hague, Mouton, 1965)

N. Chomsky, *Aspects of the Theory of Syntax* (Cambridge, Mass., M.I.T. Press, 1965)
(Review by P. H. Matthews in *Journal of Linguistics*, Vol. 3, No. 1 (1967), pp. 119–52)

J. Lyons, *Introduction to Theoretical Linguistics* (Cambridge, Cambridge University Press, 1968)
Note—An excellently clear, non-polemical book, which, notwithstanding its own distinctive features, contains what is perhaps the best introduction to TG. It has, however, been considered too compendious for starring purposes.[7]

C. J. Fillmore, 'The case for case', in *Universals in Linguistic Theory*, eds. E. Bach and R. Harms (New York, Holt, Rinehart & Winston, 1968), pp. 1–89

*R. A. Jacobs and P. S. Rosenbaum, *English Transformational Grammar* (Waltham, Mass., Blaisdell, 1968)

*D. T. Langendoen, *The Study of Syntax* (New York, Holt, Rinehart, & Winston, 1969)

'*Stratificational*'

*S. M. Lamb, *Outline of Stratificational Grammar* (Washington, D.C., Georgetown University Press, 1966)
(Review by W. L. Chafe in *Language*, Vol. 44, No. 3 (1968), pp. 593–603)

'*Neo-Firthian*'

M. A. K. Halliday, 'Categories of the theory of grammar', *Word*, Vol. 17 (1961), pp. 241–92

*M. A. K. Halliday (with A. McIntosh and P. Strevens), *The Linguistic Sciences and Language Teaching* (London, Longmans, 1964), pp. 21–55

M. A. K. Halliday, 'Lexis as a linguistic level' in *In Memory of J. R. Firth*, eds. C. E. Bazell *et al.* (London, Longmans, 1966), pp. 148–62

M. A. K. Halliday, 'Notes on transitivity and theme in English', *Journal of Linguistics*, Vol. 3, Nos. 1 and 2 (1967) and Vol. 4, No. 2 (1968)

R. M. W. Dixon, *What IS Language?* (London, Longmans, 1965), pp. 91–7

J. McH. Sinclair, 'Beginning the study of lexis' in *In Memory of J. R. Firth*, eds. C. E. Bazell *et al.* (London, Longmans, 1966), pp. 410–30

J. Ellis, 'On contextual meaning', *ibid.*, pp. 79–95

G. N. Leech, *English in Advertising* (London, Longmans, 1966), pp. 8–22 and 67–101

G. N. Leech, *A Linguistic Guide to English Poetry* (London, Longmans, 1969), early chapters on general linguistic aspects

'Serial Relationship'

*R. Quirk, *Essays on the English Language Medieval and Modern* (London, Longmans, 1968), pp. 148–83. The chapter 'Descriptive statement and serial relationship' also appears in *Language*, Vol. 41, No. 2 (1965), pp. 205–17

S. Greenbaum, *Studies in English Adverbial Usage* (London, Longmans, 1969)

Note—'Serial relationship', especially associated with R. Quirk and the *Survey of English Usage* at University College, London, was not specifically mentioned in the paper but nonetheless noticeably shares features with the approach outlined in it.

NOTES

1. Criteria for the recognition of such compounds can be found in the volume of essays *In Memory of J. R. Firth* (London, Longmans, 1966), p. 349.

2. Thus, for example, M. A. K. Halliday, Angus McIntosh, and Peter Strevens, *The Linguistic Sciences and Language Teaching* (London, Longmans, 1964), pp. 32–3.

3. See S. Greenbaum, *Studies in English Adverbial Usage* (London, Longmans, 1969).

4. Perhaps the interesting baby-talk example of *Tommy drink it* is to be related in some way to *everybody be quiet*. *Tommy drink it* is said to a baby by its mother or other adult, very frequently with encouraging intonation, rising from *drink.* Intonation and rhythm are usually equally appropriate to declarative sentence form, sc. *Tommy drinks it.* No pause occurs after *Tommy*, in contrast with that which is potential at the place indicated by the pre-verb comma in, say, *Odd numbers, prove* (military command), *any boy absent last Tuesday, step out to the front*, or *my dear woman, sweet as you are, do shut up.*

5. Vocative and appellative forms are not considered but would clearly also reflect the manifold interrelations of role and status that influence addressive language but which lie outside the scope of this paper, cf. *I say, John, lend me your bike; hey, the man in the yellow shirt, mind yourself; you people over there who look as if we've got all day, get a move on*, etc. We may notice in passing that vocatives, though often associated with the imperative, are not necessarily so and may even stand alone as the whole of a conversational exchange.

6. For a recent *mise au point*, see also P. H. Matthews' 'Recent developments in morphology' in *New Horizons in Linguistics* (ed. J. Lyons) (Penguin, 1970).

7. A recent collection of essays edited by the same author—under the not wholly satisfactory title of *New Horizons in Linguistics*, (Penguin, 1970)—is also useful for the balanced assessment it provides in easily assimilable form of the current state of transformational-generative linguistics.

5

LEXIS: THE VOCABULARY OF ENGLISH

C. J. E. Ball, Lincoln College, Oxford

The *Oxford English Dictionary* contains 450,000 entries. But the words of a living language can never be precisely numbered. Grammar is concerned with closed systems, such as 'number' or 'tense', but the lexical stock of a language is arranged in open sets which, by definition, cannot be finally delimited. The delimitation of the English vocabulary is further complicated by the various lexical distinctions typical of the different varieties of English. Some words are restricted to a particular dialect of English (e.g. *beck, sidewalk, dinkum*), others to a particular register (e.g. *belly, pussy, teeny*). In another dimension, some words are dropping out of use (e.g. *martial, weary, betrothal*), others are recent innovations (e.g. *teenager, hovercraft, motel*). Even the boundary between languages is partly blurred in the case of vocabulary; by what criteria do we decide whether the following are English words or foreign words quoted in English sentences: *baroque, bourgeois, bouillabaisse*?

The illustration (following page) showing page xxvii of Volume I of the *Oxford English Dictionary* aptly summarises the difficulty of delimiting the English vocabulary. But if we cannot draw a line around the vocabulary of English we can certainly indicate its core, the common stock of words which are neither literary nor colloquial, neither foreign nor dialectal, neither novel nor obsolescent, neither scientific nor technical.

'Indeterminacy' is one of the most important features of vocabulary and needs to be discussed a little further. It is a commonplace of language study that two different types of definition are often needed: sometimes we can delimit successive chunks of material much as a cartographer draws boundaries around contiguous countries on a map; at other times the material is indeterminate and can only be usefully analysed by indicating the centre of each chunk, rather than its borders. In the latter case our model might be the definition of a group of partially overlapping magnetic fields. Clearly, the English vocabulary must be defined in this way—by indicating its core, rather than by attempting to map its boundaries. But the contrast between determinacy and indeterminacy is important throughout the study of vocabulary: for instance, we may say that the opposition between the senses of *male* and *female*, or *sister* and *brother*, is determinate, while that between the senses of *large* and *small*, or *red* and *yellow*, is not. In general, grammatical oppositions are determinate: vocabulary is largely indeterminate.

It follows that, while the linguist can usually state decisively whether a sentence is 'grammatical' or 'ungrammatical', questions of lexical acceptability are more difficult to answer clearly. *This men listened musics* is ungrammatical in three obvious respects; *the woolly hedgehog swore a hearty thought* is lexically unacceptable—or is it? We find ourselves searching for possible contexts, such as a fairy story, and conclude that the collocations *woolly/hedgehog*, *hedgehog/swear*, *swear/thought*, and *hearty/thought* are extremely unusual rather than totally unacceptable. Grammatical questions can be answered 'yes' or 'no': lexical questions are typically answered by 'more or less'.

Vocabulary, then, is indeterminate, and lexical questions can often not be answered decisively. A third respect in which the study of vocabulary differs from that of grammar (and phonology) is that the synchronic and historical dimensions of language cannot be altogether separated from one another. Native speakers of English learn the grammar and phonology of their language during their early childhood, but they add to their vocabulary throughout their lives. Languages change at all levels, but lexical change seems to occur most freely and frequently, so much so that we all learn and use the processes whereby new words may be formed. Any study of vocabulary must recognize that it is dynamic, not static.

Because of these special problems it is not possible simply to list the items in the English vocabulary, explain the various relations between them, and describe the way in which they refer to the world of experience. The indeterminacy of vocabulary prevents us from even attaining the first step of drawing up an exhaustive inventory of items. All dictionaries necessarily select merely a portion of the theoretically infinite vocabulary of English. Because the internal organization of the vocabulary is so difficult to describe precisely, until recently linguists have been content to compile alphabetical lists of words, treating each one separately and largely disregarding the relations between them. All dictionaries do this, though the best ones give a lot of implicit information about the organization and use of the vocabulary by exemplification. An alternative method of presenting vocabulary is found in the thesaurus, which attempts to display some of the semantic relations of words by arranging them according to their similarity of meaning.

The words we are concerned with are the members of the four great form-classes—nouns, adjectives, verbs and adverbs. The remainder of the form-classes are within the domain of grammar. (The class of interjections is a special case, not easily handled in either grammatical or lexical terms. Typically, interjections do not contract syntagmatic relations, though forms which may be used as interjections may also be members of other form-classes: e.g. *damn, God, blast*. They require separate treatment, and will be largely disregarded in what follows.) It is one of the interesting features of English that words rarely betray their form-class by their structure, and that it is common for the same form to appear as a member of several classes: e.g. *table* (noun, verb), *forward* (noun, verb, adjective, adverb), *round* (noun, verb, adjective, adverb, preposition). As we shall see this feature is exploited in one of the processes of word-formation.

The definition of 'word' in English need not detain us, so long as we remember that the word as a grammatical, or phonological, unit will not always or necessarily coincide with the word as a lexical item. The grammar of *Union Jack*, for instance, is noun-modifier+noun-head, but it is convenient to treat it as a single lexical item for the statement of meaning. But this is a special and relatively rare case: most of the time the grammatical word and the lexical word are one and the same. In English, moreover, the word is institutionalized: the convention of showing word-divisions in the written language gives us an obvious and convenient method of definition, and it is in this conventional sense that 'word' is used here.

In this chapter I shall attempt in a sketchy way to describe the English vocabulary and to indicate its internal organization and external relation to the world of experience. This will not be done by offering exhaustive lists, but by touching on the sources of the vocabulary, both historical and contemporary, the strata into which it may be divided, the organization of the vocabulary, both formal and notional, and its external reference.

In comparison with many other languages the vocabulary of English is of very diverse origins. Old English was a member of the West Germanic group of languages, which was one of the descendants of Primitive Germanic, itself one of many related Indo-European languages. Historical linguistics cannot reconstruct an earlier form of language behind Indo-European, but there is no doubt that there must have been an earlier history stretching back many thousands of years. Much of the English core-vocabulary is of Indo-European (or earlier) origin: the numerals, kinship terms like *father, mother, brother,* parts of the body like *arm, tooth, foot,* personal and other pronouns like *me, who, that,* animal terms like *hound, goose, ox,* common verbs like *do, sit, fall,* and many others. Some words cannot be traced back beyond the Germanic stage, and must therefore have been formed or adopted at that period: *God, earth, house, hold, rain, sea, drink,* and others. A smaller group of words are specifically West Germanic, like *beer, sheep, learn.* It is a universal feature of languages that they adopt, or 'borrow', foreign words to a greater or lesser extent, and English is no exception. Borrowing has occurred at all periods and continues today. The earliest loan words that can be traced (though there must have been still earlier ones) are some cultural borrowings of the Germanic period, like *hemp, rich, iron.* A considerable number of Latin words were adopted in West Germanic: *street, mint, wine, cheese, mile, cup, kitchen,* and others. Old English also borrowed from Latin: *school, sponge, lily, disciple, offer, fiddle, paradise,* and others. A small number of words entered Old English from other languages: e.g. (Greek) *devil, church;* (Celtic) *bin, dun, brock;* (Norse) *thrall, law, fellow, wrong;* (French) *proud, capon, sot.* But most of the new vocabulary which was created in the Old English period was formed by compounding and affixation, rather than by borrowing: *almighty, gospel, shepherd, rainbow, eventide, seaman, Sunday* etc.; *crafty, thankful, friendless, overcome, understand, inward, wisdom,* etc.

These two processes of compounding and affixation have remained the major sources of new words in Middle and Modern English, though there are also other internal methods of word-formation in use which will be discussed later. But English has also adopted a vast number of foreign words from many sources since the Conquest. In the Middle English period the French and Scandinavian loanwords are naturally the most numerous and important. Loanwords are a rough and ready index of the degree of contact between two linguistic communities; the number and direction of the loans also provide a measure of the (real or assumed) cultural superiority of one community over the other. From the Norse settlers in the north and east Middle English adopted a surprising number of words that belong to the core-vocabulary today: *they (them, their), both, ill, die, egg, knife, low, skill, take, till, though, want,* and many more. The complete assimilation of these Norse words into English, so that few native speakers are aware that they are adoptions, can be partly explained by remembering that English is more closely related historically to Norse, a Germanic language, than to French or Latin; it also suggests that the Norse-speaking community must have become fused with the Old English community soon after the Conquest.

The importance of the French element in the English vocabulary is only matched by Latin among the external sources. Many of the French words borrowed into Middle English have been completely assimilated into the core-vocabulary: *aunt, people, debt, lodge, common, pray, war, fruit, table, front, touch, manner, peace,* etc. Others still perhaps betray their foreign origin: *messenger, purchase, pavilion, concord, trespass, challenge, venison, peril, liquor, vengeance, medicine,* etc. French adoptions are found in almost every part of the vocabulary: law, (*justice, evidence, pardon,* . . .), warfare (*conquer, victory, archer,* . . .), religion (*grace, repent, sacrifice,* . . .), rank (*baron, master, prince,* . . .), clothing (*collar, mantle, vestment,* . . .), architecture (*castle, pillar, tower* . . .), finance (*pay, rent, ransom,* . . .), food (*dinner, feast, sauce,* . . .), and many others. As an indication of the tremendous influx of French words in Middle English we may note that, discounting proper names, there are 39 words of French origin in the first 43 lines of the Prologue to Chaucer's *Canterbury Tales.*

Although the French and Scandinavian languages, together with Latin, were the most important sources of Middle English adoptions, they were not the only ones. There are a number of borrowings from Low German (*poll, dote, booze, luff, huckster,* etc.), from Italian (*florin, alarm, million, ducat, brigand,*—though some of these seem to have reached English through French), and from Irish (*kern, lough*). In addition we may add a number of indirect borrowings (through other languages, such as Latin or French) from Greek (*centre, fancy, logic, rhetoric, treacle, allegory, comedy, halycon, theme,* and others), from

Gaulish (*gravel, quay, skein, valet,* etc.), and from Arabic (*saffron, admiral, alchemy, cotton, amber, syrup,* etc.).

A large number of words were adopted in Middle English direct from Latin: *diocese, conviction, legitimate, formal, index, orbit, concrete, equator, lupin, locust, implication, compact, admit, discuss,* and many others. Most of these were learnéd words when they were adopted and have remained outside the core-vocabulary. But already in Middle English we see the beginning of the development whereby Latin, and later Greek, were to contract a special lexical relationship with English. It is an interesting feature of some living languages that they are able to tap the lexical resources of a dead language to create neologisms with the same freedom that they have to produce new internal formations. A number of Indian languages have such a relationship with Sanskrit. In the case of English, not only the vocabulary but also many of the derivational affixes of Latin and Greek are available to create new forms. In the present century English has borrowed from the classical languages or rather created out of Latin and Greek elements, the following words, among many others: *aerodyne, ambivert, androgen, antibiotic, astronaut, audio-visual, autolysis, barysphere, cacogenics, callipygous, chromosome, cartology, cartophily, cryotron, cyclorama, dendrochronology, dromophobia, ergatocracy, hypnotherapy, hypothermia, isotope* ... Because the lexical resources of Latin and Greek are treated as if they belonged to English, many neologisms combine elements from different sources: *aqualung, television, microgroove, sonobuoy,* etc. Although all these Latin- and Greek-derived words are distïnctly learned or technical, they do not seem foreign, and are very different in this respect from the recent loan-words from living languages, such as *montage, angst, cappuccino, sputnik, kibbutz,* etc. Thus, for the Modern English period a distinction must be made between the adoptions from living languages and the formations derived from the two classical languages.

Latin has provided English with a large number of productive affixes, such as *de-, ex, pre-; -al, -ate, -ous.* Many of these can now be used to form new words with roots of any origin. During the modern period a considerable number of words have been borrowed direct from Latin, such as (16th century) *genius, area, circus, codex, stratum;* (17th century) *premium, squalor, focus, complex, tedium;* (18th century) *ultimatum, nucleus, alibi, extra, prospectus;* (19th century) *opus, ego, animus, aquarium, consensus;* (20th century) *exemplum, gravitas, mores, persona, continuum.* We have borrowed many words from Greek through the medium of Latin, and a smaller number direct, such as: (16th century) *rhapsody, crisis, topic, pathos, stigma;* (17th century) *coma, tonic, cosmos, nous, dogma;* (18th century) *bathos, phlox, philander, triptych, neurosis;* (19th century) *phase, pylon, myth, agnostic, therm;* (20th century) *topos, euphoria, enosis, schizophrenia, hamartia.* From Greek also comes a wide range of learnéd affixes, such as *bio-, chrono-, geo-, hydro-, logo-, auto-, hemi-, hetero-, homo-, mono-, neo-, epi-, meta-, para-, -ism, -ist, -ise, -logy, -graph, -phile, -meter, -gram*, and many others.

While the influence of Latin and Greek on the English vocabulary has been steadily increasing, the number of adoptions from living foreign languages has rather been diminishing in the modern period, although the number of languages which have provided items in the English vocabulary has grown enormously. Naturally enough, apart from the two classical languages, the chief influences have been the major languages of western Europe. French has continued to provide a considerable number of new words, for example (16th century) *trophy, vase, grotesque, machine, moustache*; (17th century) *brigade, unique, attic, soup, routine*; (18th century) *terrain, canteen, brochure, corduroy, police*; (19th century) *acrobat, blouse, beige, chef, prestige*; (20th century) *montage, voyeur, camouflage, questionnaire, chauffeur*. The Italian element is particularly strong in the fields of art, music and literature, for example (16th century) *model, sonnet, madrigal, traffic, bandit*; (17th century) *opera, vista, burlesque, balcony, manifesto*; (18th century) *soprano, quartet, costume, lava, arcade*; (19th century) *flautist, studio, scenario, tirade, spaghetti*; (20th century) *scampi, cappuccino, aggiornamento, timpani, quattrocento*. There is also a considerable Spanish element in English; it is interesting to note how many of these words have their origin in the New World: for example, (16th century) *sherry, cannibal, banana, potato, comrade*; (17th century) *cargo, parade, avocado, vanilla, piccaninny*; (18th century) *cigar, hacienda, bolero, stevedore, quadrille*; (19th century) *rodeo, stampede, mustang, patio, canyon*; (20th century) *cafeteria, tango, marijuana, supremo, incommunicado*. Low German, especially Dutch and later Afrikaans, and High German have been fertile sources of loanwords in the modern period: for example, (16th century) *dock, yacht, frolic, beleaguer; landgrave, carouse, younker, kreutzer*; (17th century) *brandy, smuggle, cruise, sketch; plunder, zinc, hamster, sauerkraut*; (18th century) *schooner, roster, mangle, springbok; iceberg, shale, waltz, nickel*; (19th century) *trek, spoor, boss, commander; poodle, lager, yodel, paraffin*; (20th century) *apartheid, autobahn, ersatz, angst, strafe*.

The other European languages have not been nearly so important as sources of vocabulary for English as were French, Italian, Spanish and German. But, nevertheless, Modern English has adopted a few words from almost every European language: (the Scandinavian languages) *link, rug, scrub, troll, smut, cosy, ski, fjord, slalom, ombudsman*; (Irish) *brogue, leprechaun, galore, banshee, colleen, céilidhe*; (Welsh) *crag, coracle, cromlech, gorsedd, eisteddfod, hwyl, corgi*; (Portuguese) *padre, flamingo, madeira, buffalo, macaw, caste, pagoda, verandah, albino, commando*; (Russian) *rouble, czar, steppe, mammoth, ukase, balalaika, pogrom, troika*, *samovar, soviet, commissar, sputnik, intelligentsia*; (Hungarian) *shako, paprika, goulash*; (Finnish) *sauna*; (Lapp) *tundra*; and so on.

The loanwords we have been considering have all, except where otherwise stated, been directly borrowed into English. Many more have reached English indirectly from a wide variety of languages. An example of the intricacies of indirect adoptions is provided by *veneer*, borrowed in the 18th century from German *furnieren*, itself an earlier adoption from French *fournir*, which is derived from a Common Romance word borrowed from Germanic. In the Old and Middle English periods a number of words reached English in this way from non-European languages, and they have continued to do so in the modern period. But, with a growth of international trade and the urge to explore and dominate the unknown world, English has made a number of direct adoptions from languages spoken outside Europe. As with the borrowings from the less important languages of Europe, few of these words have entered the core-vocabulary, and most are material nouns referring to culturally distinct objects. Some examples are: (American Indian languages) *moccasin, wigwam, squaw, mugwump, pemmican*; (Arabic) *sultan, sheikh, roc, hashish, fakir, harem, hookah, ghoul, shadoof, yashmak, bint, shufti*; (Australian languages) *dingo, wombat, boomerang, budgerigar, billabong*; (Chinese) *litchi, ketchup, kaolin, sampan, typhoon, loquat, tong*; (Eskimo) *kayak, igloo, anorak*; (Hawaian) *hula, lei, ukulele*; (Hebrew) *shibboleth, kosher, kibbutz*; (Hindustani) *guru, pundit, pukka, sari, khaki, swami*; (Japanese) *kimono, tycoon, judo, haiku, karate*; (Indonesian) *proa, amok, sarong, orang-utang, raffia*; (Persian) *cummerbund, purdah, shah, dervish, divan, caravan, bazaar, shawl, houri, howdah*; (Polynesian) *taboo, tattoo, kiwi*; (Sanskrit) *avatar, suttee, yoga, nirvana, swastika, soma*; (Swahili) *bwana, safari, uhuru*; (Tamil) *pariah, catamaran, anaconda*; (Tibetan) *lama, sherpa, yeti, yak*; (Turkish) *caftan, yoghourt, kiosk, fez, bosh*; (Yiddish) *schlemozzle, schmaltz*. There are many others.

Two special forms of word-borrowing should be briefly mentioned. The first, loan-translation or 'calque', is exemplified by *loanword* itself, which was formed on the pattern of German *Lehnwort*; other examples are *shock-troops* (German *Stosstruppen*) and *gospel* (Greek *euaggélion*). Internal borrowing is more important: this occurs when one dialect of a language adopts words from another. During the history of English this must frequently have happened, but the details are often unclear. Contemporary Standard British English borrows a large number of words from American English (*movie, jazz, blurb, gimmick, cagey, egghead, heel* 'cad', *grassroots, rib* 'tease', *sit-in, teach-in, supermarket, tearjerker*, and many others); *gormless* and *gawp* are recent borrowings from English regional dialects, but dialects of English overseas seem to be more important sources of vocabulary nowadays: e.g. (Australian English) *outback, cobber, bushed, fossick*.

Loanwords are the most immediately obvious additions to vocabulary, but they are rarely the most important or numerous. Certainly in Old English and in the later Modern English period the internal processes of word-formation have been responsible for the bulk of new words. The two most important processes in English are compounding and affixation.

Compounds must be carefully distinguished from phrases on the one hand (*greenfinch/green grass*), and from affixed formations on the other (*paratroop/paratyphoid*). As opposed to phrases, compounds typically have a single stress (*'greenfinch*), are inseparable (*green hand-sown grass*), and do not allow modification of the first element (*very green grass*); but *green fingers* and *grass-green* (both of which have two stresses) must be treated as phrase and compound respectively, because, while the first has the two-stress pattern of a normal syntactic group (adjective-modifier + noun-head) as opposed to *'greenfinch*, the latter has the syntactic pattern (noun-modifier + adjective-head) found only in compounds (*'waterproof, 'carefree, 'seasick*, and *'dirt-'cheap, 'pitch-'black, 'brand-'new*). The boundary is, however, indeterminate, as is shown by examples like *ground floor, hand grenade, home town* (*ground-floor*, etc.) which occur variously with one or two stresses. Equally indeterminate is the border between compounds and affixed forms. Typically, affixes are not independent words (*epi-, un-, -ation, -ous*), whereas both elements of compounds are normally free forms. Moreover, it is usually possible to make a generalized statement about the function of an affix, especially if it is still productive, whereas in compounds the same element may function in a variety of ways. Compare *pre-elect, prejudge, prepay, prearrange, precook*, etc., with *puppydog, bulldog, watchdog, policedog, lapdog, sheepdog*, etc. In the first group *pre-* adds the sense 'before' to the verb; in the second no such general statement is possible.

Compounds are usually either nouns or adjectives, although verbal and adverbial compounds are often secondarily derived from primary (nominal or adjectival) compounds: e.g. *to belly-ache, to weekend; sickmakingly, self-importantly*. There are a wide variety of adjectival compounds of the types *carefree* (noun + adjective: *pitch-dark, lovesick, world-wide, self-secure*), *bitter-sweet* (adjective + adjective: *greeny-blue, Franco-Prussian, Indo-European, shabby-genteel*), *breath-taking* (noun + participle: *earth-shattering, self-propelling; hand-made, airborne, self-taught*, and others e.g. *hard-working, far-fetched*).

The nominal compounds fall into two main groups, endocentric and exocentric. Examples of endocentric compounds are *frogman, atom-bomb, woman-hater*, where each compound has the same grammatical distribution as one of its elements (*man, bomb, hater*); neither element of an exocentric compound (*spoilsport, bighead, fallout*) can replace the compound in this way. There are several different types of endocentric compounds in English: noun + noun (*lipstick, dustman, clothes-line, girl-friend, fighter-bomber, self-contempt, batsman, beeswax, dining-room, inkstand, fox-hunting, shopkeeper, nanny-goat*); verb + noun (*treadmill, flick-knife, sob-sister*); participle + noun (*mocking-bird, serving-woman*); adjective + noun (*blackboard, sick-room*); pronoun + noun (*he-man, she-devil*); noun + adjective (*court-martial, heir-apparent*). Likewise, the exocentric nominal compounds can be sub-divided: verb + noun (*spendthrift, stopgap*); verb + adverb (*diehard, stowaway, setback, frame-up, take-off*); adjective + noun (*redhead, loudmouth, blue-bell, green-shank*). It will be obvious from the examples that several of the sub-types of compounds can be further differentiated; for example, in *lipstick* the first element modifies the second, while in *fighter-bomber* the two elements are co-ordinate.

Before turning to affixation, we should consider one further, rather odd, type of compound. The reduplicative compound is rare and recent; examples occur in all the main word-classes: noun (*goody-goody, chuff-chuff, never-never*), adjective (*hush-hush, pretty-pretty*), adverb (*fifty-fifty*) and verb (*clop-clop*). Some of these are similar to expressive formations, which will be discussed later. This particular type of compound is especially common in nursery language: *yum-yum, bye-byes, din-din, woof-woof, ta-ta, Papa*, etc.

English affixes can be immediately divided into prefixes and suffixes, for English has no infixes. There are more than 60 prefixes and more than 80 suffixes. Few of these are native forms: of the prefixes, only *a-, be-, un-, fore-, mid-,* and *mis-* are found in Old English, though rather more suffixes have survived (e.g. *-dom, -er, -ful, -hood, -ish, -less, -ling, -ly, -ness, -ship, -y,* etc.). Some suffixes have the effect of converting members of one word-class into another (*laugh/laughable, willing/willingness*); others merely modify without converting (*cartoon/cartoonist, star/starlet*). Most suffixes and some prefixes are confined to particular word-classes. Many affixes are no longer productive, for example *cis-* (*cisalpine*), *preter-* (*preternatural*), *sur-* (*surname*), *-th* (*warmth*), *-ton* (*simpleton*), *-et* (*freshet*), but a surprising number can still be used to create new formations.

Some of the most important productive prefixes are: *anti-* (*anti-Communist, anti-submarine, anti-semitism, antifreeze*); *counter-* (*counter-espionage, counter-demonstration, counter-threat*); *de-* (*deodorise, dehydrate, derate, declutch, decompression*); *dis-* (*disassemble, disincentive, discontinue, disown*); *inter-* (*interracial, interbreed, inter-war, interdependence*); *non-* (*non-skid, non-starter, non-believer, non-stick*); *pre-* (*preshrunk, predigest, prenatal, pre-school*); *re-* (*rethink, repaper, rebirth*); *semi-* (*semi-transparent, semi-skilled, semi-educated, semi-starvation*); *un-* (negation: *unconventional, unfunny, unforeseen;* reversal: *unmake, unfreeze, unsighted*).

Some of the most important productive suffixes are: *-able* (adjectival,

from verbs and nouns: *available, adaptable, favourable, marriageable*);
-age (substantival, from verbs and nouns: *shrinkage, breakage, orphanage, voltage*); *-ate* (verbal, from nouns: *assassinate, vaccinate, chlorinate*); *-ation* (substantival, from verbs: *verification, neutralisation, ruination, visitation*); *-dom* (substantival, from nouns: *bumbledom, stardom, muddledom*); *-ee* (substantival, from verbs: *evacuee, examinee, detainee*); *-er* (substantival, from verbs and nouns: *consumer, poser, geographer, probationer, lowlander, honeymooner*); *-ery/-ry* (substantival, from nouns: *snobbery, punditry, creamery, rookery, rocketry*); *-ish* (adjectival, from nouns: *Lettish, sheepish, tallish, bluish, fiftyish*); *-ist* (substantival, from nouns and adjectives: *racist/racialist, revisionist, stockist, orientalist, nominalist*); *-ite* (substantival, from nouns: *Bevanite, vulcanite, ammonite, Pre-Raphaelite*); *-ize* (verbal, from nouns and adjectives: *americanize, terrorize, galvanize, bowdlerize, hospitalize, finalize, denuclearize*); *-less* (adjectival, from nouns: *spineless, strapless, humourless*); *-ness* (substantival, mainly from adjectives: *promptness, shortsightedness, willingness, nothingness*); *-ship* (substantival, from nouns: *membership, studentship, censorship, showmanship*); *-y* (adjectival, from nouns, verbs and adjectives: *sexy, spidery, matey, trendy, wriggly, weepy, pinky, crispy*). These lists, long as they are, hardly do justice to the variety of productive affixes and the wealth of affixed formations.

Simple conversion, or 'zero-derivation', is a process of word-formation closely related to affixation. From *tape* (noun) we have produced *tape* (verb, 'make a tape-recording'); from *tease* (verb) we have *tease* (noun, 'one who mocks'). Just as the pattern of root and affixed derivative (*lead/mislead*) can be extended to produce new forms (*derive/misderive, analyse/misanalyse*), so the simpler patterns of *bed* (noun and verb) or *walk* (verb and noun) can also be extended. Adjectives and adverbs seem to resist this type of formation but both nouns and, especially, verbs are often formed by simple conversion. There are four common types and two rarer ones: verbs from nouns (*garage, audition, baby, process, wolf, torpedo,* etc.); verbs from adjectives (*tidy, best, short, gentle, pretty, wise,* etc.); verbs from particles (*up, down*); nouns from verbs (*sweep, bore, sell, must, have,* etc.); nouns from adjectives (*lovely, natural, short, inferior, tiny,* etc.); nouns from particles (*over, down, out, off*). A special type of simple conversion is the process whereby proper names become common nouns. English has a number of words like *wellingtons*, named from the Duke of Wellington, or *cardigan*, named from the Earl of Cardigan. This process, though never very common or important, continues to operate in contemporary English: e.g. *waterloo, boycott, diesel, mae-west, primus, bikini, quisling,* etc.

Back-formation is another related process of word-formation. Just as the relationship between *write/writer, read/reader* encourages the development of new affixed formations like *consumer, trafficker,* so by a reverse derivation we get *scavenge* from *scavenger* and *swindle* from *swindler.* Although this is not a very common process a number of words have been produced by back-formation. The main types are: *scavenger/scavenge (peddle, burgle, hawk, beg, sculpt, ush,* etc.), and *resurrection/resurrect (automate, pre-empt, televise, vivisect, emote, electrocute,* etc.); but there are also a number of other isolated examples, such as *reminisce, enthuse, laze, salve, jell, liaise.*

Affixation, simple conversion and back-formation all have in common the principle of pattern-extension. In a few rare cases the pattern which is extended is itself due to a misconception. The word *hamburger* was borrowed from German where it is a derivative of the city-name *Hamburg*; in English it was misinterpreted as a compound of *ham* (though ham is not used in making hamburgers) and *burger,* and on the basis of this false analysis were formed such new compounds as *eggburger, cheeseburger,* and many others.

Abbreviation is a process of word-formation particularly associated with the spoken language. In 1710 Swift wrote a letter to *The Tatler* objecting to the abbreviations *mob (mobile vulgus), rep (reputation), phiz (physnomy,* a variant of *physiognomy)* and *pozz (positive).* It is instructive to note that of these one *(mob)* has become thoroughly established in spoken and written usage, one *(pozz)* is still found in spoken usage only, one *(phiz)* is only met with in literature from the late 17th century to the 19th century, and one *(rep)* has disappeared altogether, although a new *rep* has been produced from both *representative* and *repertory* (theatre). Three types of abbreviation may be distinguished, depending on whether the beginning, the middle, or the end of the original word is retained. Like *deb* (from *debutante)* are *fan, pub, sub, trog, intercom, mike, polio, perm, bra, prop, mod, pop, prom, pram, zoo, lino, undergrad, exam, prefab,* names like *Al, Ben, Sam,* and many others; sometimes the abbreviated word is provided with a suffix: *cabby, nappy, bolshy, nighty, undies, granny, compo, ammo,* etc. Like *bus* (from *omnibus)* are *taters, phone, plane, drome, cello, brolly, van,* names like *Bella, Bert, Tina,* etc. Like *flu* (from *influenza)* are *tec, fridge,* and names like *Liz*; this is by far the rarest type. Compounds are also sometimes formed with abbreviated elements: *paratroop, conrod, telegenic, heliport, oxyacetaline, microfilm,* etc.

Blending and acronymic formation are two minor processes of word-formation which arise more from the fancy of an individual than the structure of the language. Lewis Carroll's blends like *slithy (slimy* and *lithe), mimsy (miserable* and *flimsy),* and *chortle (chuckle* and *snort)* are well known from *Through The Looking-Glass*; the last one has become completely established as an independent word. Other examples are: *squarson (squire* and *parson), mingy (mean* and *stingy), chloral (chlorine* and *alcohol)*, *motel, brunch, smog, subtopia, chunnel, spam (spiced ham), shamateur, motourist, fantabulous, slanguage,* etc. *Absquatulate* 'decamp' is a remarkable triple-blend in American English formed from *abscond, squattle* 'decamp', and *perambulate*.

An acronym is a word formed from the initial letters of other words: the classic English example is *radar* (*r*adio *d*irection-finding *a*nd *r*ange). Most of the new words formed in this way remain proper names (e.g. *Naafi, Unesco, Nato, Zeta, the Raf, Seato, Shape,* etc.), but a few have been assimilated more deeply into the language: *derv* (*d*iesel-*e*ngined *r*oad *v*ehicle), *ufo* (*u*nidentified *f*lying *o*bject) and *radar*. *Futhorc*, the name of the Old English runic alphabet, is formed from the first six letters of that alphabet. Rather similar to the acronym is the word produced by pronouncing the initial letters of a phrase or compound: *T.V., G.I., Y.M.C.A.,* etc. The development of blends and acronyms is a recent phenomenon in English; no certain example of either is known before the 19th century.

To these seven processes of internal word-formation, compounding, affixation, simple conversion, back-formation, abbreviation, blending, and acronymic formation, must be added one other, expressive formation, which is especially interesting. The forms of words normally have only a conventional relationship with what they refer to, as can easily be shown by a comparison, such as *horse, Pferd, cheval, equus, hippos,* etc. But a small part of the vocabulary is onomatopoeic: the sounds of such words as *cuckoo, ding-dong, swish, buzz,* seem to be appropriate to their senses. As a result of the undoubted existence of the small number of onomatopoeic words speakers of a language tend to associate certain sounds and sound-sequences with certain senses in an expressive relationship. An English example is *-ump*, which has the, sense 'protruberance' in *bump, chump, clump, dump, hump, lump, mump(s), plump* (adjective), *rump, stump, tump,* and of 'heavy fall' in *bump, dump, crump, clump, flump, jump, plump* (verb), *slump, stump, thump.* We can therefore distinguish between two types of expressive formation, direct onomatopoeic formation, and the extension of such expressive patterns as *-ump* above. There are many possible, even probable, examples of either type, but it is difficult to find certain examples since in many cases other explanations of the neologism are also admissible, and often multiple origin is to be suspected.

Examples of simple onomatopoeic formations are: *pom-pom* (gun), *plop, ping, whoosh, swish, whoop, coo, twang, thrum, clash,* etc. The expressive formations are more complex; we may distinguish two types, depending on whether the expressive element is initial or final. For example, initial *spl-* is found in *splash, splodge, splotch, splurge, splutter, splatter, splosh, splat,* all of which have developed in the modern period and are either of directly expressive origin or are expressive variants of other words (e.g. *plash*, *sputter*); initial *sn-* links a group of words, all probably of ultimate expressive origin, but some very old, having a central meaning 'nasal sound': *sneeze*, *sniff*, *snigger*, *sniffle*, *snivel*, *snicker*, *snore*, *snort*, *snuffle*. Of the words ending in *-ump* listed above, more than half are probably of expressive origin; the expressive value of final *-ing* reinforced by *sing* and *ring*, has produced the modern formations *ping*, *ting*, and *whing*. There are many other patterns, both initial and final, as the following examples indicate: *zoom*, *scurry*, *chuff*, *fizz*, *fizzle*, *biff*, *yatter*, *squawk*, *flunk*, etc. In some cases expressive doublets are formed by altering the stem-vowel of a word: e.g. *jibber/jabber*, *snip/snap*, *jiggle/joggle*, *splash/splosh*, *putter/potter*, etc.

A similar type of formation is seen in words like *chitchat* and *super-duper*, where two elements, which show either vowel-alternation or rhyme, are compounded. Sometimes both elements are independently meaningful (*lovey-dovey*, *singsong*, *dripdrop*, *teenyweeny*), sometimes one (*crisscross*, *mishmash*, *fuzzy-wuzzy*, *rolypoly*), and sometimes neither (*riffraff*, *zigzag*, *hurdy-gurdy*, *hugger-mugger*). Fairly recent formations of this type are: *hifi*, *pingpong*, *walkie-talkie*, *heebie-jeebies*, *lilo*, *flower-power*, *hokey-cokey*, *itsy-bitsy*, *swing-wing*, etc.

This brief survey of the history of the English vocabulary and its living processes of word-formation shows very clearly the extreme diversity and variety of English words. Intuitively, we feel that the vocabulary is divided into an indefinite number of different sections, though we would be hard put to it to map them. Although dictionaries make no attempt in their general layout to separate the various strata in the vocabulary, yet they often give helpful labels which classify some words: e.g. *tummy* (nursery), *bread-basket* (colloquial), *guts*, *belly* (impolite), *viscera* (learnéd), and so on.

There are many ways in which the vocabulary could be classified, and any classification may be applied broadly (as here) or in more and more minute detail. It is suggested that English words can be located on a number of dimensions stretching from the central core-vocabulary towards extreme neologisms or archaisms, totally foreign words, words confined to a particular regional dialect or appropriate to a particular occupation, medium, or register. We shall consider each of these dimensions in turn, but must remember that some words will be located significantly on more than one dimension: *Franglais*, for instance, is distinctively both foreign and novel; *mike* ('microphone') is novel and more appropriate to the spoken medium than the written; *amelioration* is formal and more appropriate to the written medium; and so on.

The dimension stretching from the neutral core-vocabulary towards extreme neologisms can be exemplified by pairs like *gramophone/record-player*, *reconsider/rethink*, *complete/finalize*, *adolescent/teenage*, where in each case the second example still seems distinctly novel. O course, as with all methods of classifying the vocabulary, we are dealing with a gradation between the unmarked core-vocabulary and the markedly neologistic word, and we can draw up sequences of roughly synonymous terms to show this: e.g. *modern, contemporary, mod, with-it, trendy*. Many examples of recent innovations have been given in the discussion of word-formation, but the following may be added: *grotty, telly, scrounge, supermarket, gimmick, discotheque, groovy, maxi, psychedelic, technocentric, merger, stopover, phoney, drip-dry, aerocrat, computerize, kinky*, and many others. Although much has been said about the processes of word-formation we have not yet discussed its motivation. It is often assumed that new words are created to handle new ideas or objects, but this is only partly true. One of the main functions of neologisms is simply to be new, and it is not surprising that when they are no longer new they often rapidly fall out of use. Words of this sort are time-bound, e.g. *spiffing, erk, lunik, spiv, prang*, etc. The up-to-date all too quickly becomes dated.

The dimension of archaism is similar to, though not the same as, the dimension of neologism. Again, it is simplest to exemplify archaism by pairs of words: e.g. *feather/plume, warlike/martial, hair/locks* (or *tresses*), *marry/wed* (or *espouse*), *engagement/betrothal, linguistics/philology, tired/ weary*, where in each case the second example seems distinctly archaic beside the first. Of course, the relationship between the pairs cannot be explained only in terms of archaism: in the case of *marry/wed*, for instance, we must recognize that in newspaper headlines *wed*, being shorter, is the preferred form. The gradation from the unmarked core-vocabulary towards the extreme archaism can be seen in a sequence such as *hate, loathe, detest, abhor, abominate*. Why do some words become obsolete? There is no single answer to the problem; a number of factors may be involved. Homophony certainly played a part in the gradual loss of *let* ('prevent', cf. *let and hindrance*), *quean* ('woman'— with derogatory sense) and *raze*: the homophones *let* ('allow'), *queen* and *raise* have related, but contrasting, meanings which could easily lead to confusion. Taboo will sometimes cause a word to disappear: *jakes, privy, latrine*, etc. Perhaps one of the most important factors is the tendency for words to fall into roughly synonymous pairs of which one is fashionable and the other unfashionable. We have seen how neologisms can often be paired with neutral words in this way (*teenage/ adolescent*); our attitude toward such pairs easily shifts from treating the first member as markedly neologistic, to stigmatising the second as archaic and obsolescent. Consider *stove/cooker, wireless/radio, cab/taxi, hasten/hurry, torment/torture, dish/plate, nay/no, hallow/bless, halt/lame, perfidy/treachery, peril/danger*, etc. Any dictionary is full of words which are no longer in active use but which are known from our reading of earlier literature: *abjure, abnegate, accouchement, aestival, afore, ague, ail, alack, amain, ambuscade,* and so on. The archaic element in the vocabulary must be very much larger than the neologistic.

The dimension stretching from the unmarked native vocabulary, which of course includes fully-assimilated loanwords, towards totally foreign words is particularly interesting. The borrowing of a foreign word is not a once-and-for-all matter but a gradual process. At one extreme we have fully-assimilated loanwords like *sky, send, cheese*; at the other the quotation of totally foreign words or phrases in English sentences: *inter vivos, salvete, déraciné, Aufklärung,* etc. Unless an English speaker is bilingual, he will neither use nor understand such foreign quotations. In the gradual transformation of a quotation into a loanword the first step is taken when monolingual native speakers begin to understand and use the new words; examples in contemporary English are *Abseil, cum laude, caritas, bouillon.* In the next stage, the assimilation of the originally unassimilated loanword, three types of change can often be observed.

First the phonology of the word is gradually adapted to conform to English patterns. *Restaurant,* a 19th century borrowing from French, has three common types of pronunciation: /'rest(ə)rɔ̃/ with nasalized final vowel as in French; /'rest(ə)rɒŋ/ with assimilation of the nasalized vowel to the nearest appropriate native pattern; /'rest(ə)rɒnt/ with a new pronunciation deduced from the spelling. In none of the pronunciations, it is worth noting, is the French /r/ retained. Until quite recently English did not have the sound /ʒ/ in final position, though it was common enough medially (*measure, seizure*); but it has established itself in French loanwords: *rouge, beige, collage, camouflage, montage, garage, prestige, decolletage, ménage,* and others. Although there are quite a large number of words in this group, there is some evidence that final /ʒ/ is unstable. *Garage,* the most widely-used example, has three pronunciations, /'gærɑːʒ/, /'gærɑːdʒ/ and /'gærɪdʒ/; the last two show assimilation of /-ʒ/ to the more usual English final consonant /-dʒ/, and /'gærɪdʒ/ has been further assimilated to conform to the *marriage, carriage* group of words (*montage* also sometimes occurs as /'mɒntɪdʒ/). A non-native initial consonant group is found in *schlemozzle,* but the development of the common alternative form *schemozzle* shows that phonological assimilation is in progress. Phonological assimilation sometimes takes the form of a reinterpretation of the spelling according to the usual English conventions: thus we have /'spʌtnɪk/ beside /'sputnɪk/ (*sputnik*), /'zɒlvəraɪn/ and /'zwiːbæk/ beside /'tsɔlfəraɪn/ and /'tsviːbak/ (*Zollverein, Zwieback*), / kwestɪə'nɛə/ beside / kestɪə'nɛə/ (*questionnaire*), and so on.

The second type of change which affects loanwords is that, as they become more closely assimilated into the borrowing language, they become capable of producing derivative formations: from *garage* (noun) have developed *garage* (verb) and *garageman*, from *trek* (noun) we have *trekker* and *trek* (verb). A similar, but rather rarer, process is seen in *au-pair*, which is an adverbial phrase in French but functions in English as a noun; *viva voce*, a Latin adverbial phrase, becomes in English a noun (and derivative verb) in its abbreviated form *viva*.

Thirdly, loanwords often undergo a marked change of meaning as they become assimilated into the borrowing language. *Café* means 'coffee' in French but 'restaurant' in English, the connection being through the sense 'coffee-house'. *Gentle* (13th century), *genteel* (16th century) and *jaunty* (17th century) are three independent borrowings of French *gentil*; *jaunty*, especially, has diverged a long way from the original sense of 'well-born'. *Rodeo* (19th century) seems to have meant 'round-up' when it was first adopted from Spanish, but later it came to refer to the place where the cattle were penned and from this it developed the sense 'cowboy sports'. The frequency with which such changes of meaning take place among newly-borrowed loanwords may seem surprising, since one might assume that a loanword would normally be borrowed to make good a specific deficiency in a language. But loanwords are a type of neologism, and it must be remembered that neologisms are often created as much for their novelty as their particular application. Moreover, a loanword is remarkably isolated: it has no derivational relationships within the borrowing language, nor semantic links with other words, and the network of relationships it contracted with words in the source-language is broken.

Repêchage (20th century) shows this rather well. The French word is a noun derived from *repêcher* 'to fish out again', which can be applied in various circumstances, e.g. to a drowning man, to torpedoes, to a candidate who is given a second chance at an examination. But the various meanings are held together and controlled by the obvious relationship of *repêchage* to *pêcher* ('to fish') and the prefix *re-* ('again'). In English the word is opaque: with the stress on the first syllable it cannot even be related to the common English prefix *re-* ('again'). The word is used for a supplementary race in which the best losers in earlier heats get a second chance to enter the final. A further example, *blank*, was borrowed from French in the 15th century. In French it means 'white, pale, pure, blank', and has a host of derivatives, such as *blanchir* 'whiten', *blanquette* 'veal stew with white sauce', *blanchaille* 'whitebait', and is part of a network of semantic relations with other colour-words, of which the most important is probably its opposite, *noir*. English *blank* has a basic meaning 'empty'; it has completely lost the colour-sense which is primary in French. While it has produced new derivatives (*blank* (noun) and *blankness*) it has lost contact with the words with which it has an etymological relationship (*blanch*, *blancmange*, *Blanche*), and it no longer has a relationship of direct opposition with any other word. These examples should make clear how important to the meaning of a word are its derivational and semantic relationships.

In some languages, such as Vietnamese, recent foreign adoptions constitute a more or less distinct section of the vocabulary for which a separate phonological description is necessary. Is this true of English? There is no doubt that at an earlier period, in Middle English, the French loanwords in particular constituted a distinct section of the vocabulary with a partially different phonology: the diphthong /oi/ was introduced into English through such adoptions as *choice, joy, join, noise,* etc. But Modern English has fully assimilated these earlier borrowings, and the more recent adoptions from French, though in many cases only partially assimilated, are too few in number to form an independent section of the vocabulary. There are, however, some grounds for claiming that the learned words formed from Latin and Greek elements constitute a special section of the vocabulary: prefixes like *hyper-, meta-, micro-, mono-, para-, poly-, proto-, retro-, ultra-, uni-,* and suffixes like *-ation, -ic, -ician, -ine, -ise, -ory,* are generally found only with elements of Latin and Greek origin. But such words are not phonologically distinct from the rest of the vocabulary, except in as much as they are generally polysyllabic in a language where monosyllables and disyllables are otherwise the majority type. Apart, then, from the possible isolation of a Graeco-Latin element in the vocabulary, the dimension stretching from the core-vocabulary towards fully foreign words cannot be easily broken down into various sections. The gradation from the centre towards the periphery can be exemplified in sequences like: (French) *vogue, valet, valise, velours, voyeur, vécu, vitrail* . . .; or (German) *plunder, poodle, pumpernickel, poltergeist, pretzel, putsch, privatdozent* . . .

The dimension of dialect, like that of foreign adoption, is complicated by the fact that there are many dialects of English, just as there are many foreign languages from which we borrow words. Standard British English may be imagined as the centre of a circle, around the periphery of which are ranged Scots, American English, Australian English, and so on. (However, it must be remembered that a similar study could be made of American English, for example, in which case British English would be one of the peripheral dialects.) Although we are once again dealing with a gradation we may distinguish four types of dialect words: words which are not understood by non-dialect speakers, e.g. *ashet* (Scots, 'dish'), *yat* (northern 'gate'), *mullock* (Australian, 'rubbish from a mine'), *meld* (American, 'merge'); the partially assimilated borrowing, which is recognized, but not used by the non-dialect speaker, e.g. *bairn, fash, cookie, checkers, dinkum, cobber*; the more fully assimilated word, which is both recognized and used by the non-dialect speaker, but still retains its dialect association, e.g. *dour, canny, lass, feckless, outback, movie, figure out*; and, finally, the fully assimilated adoption, which is of historical interest only, e.g. *vat, till, hale, raid, blizzard*. It is often forgotten how much of the English vocabulary is produced by intimate borrowing from its dialects. Most of us are aware of the stream of new words from American English, but the following list of Australian English words shows that English borrows from other dialects as well: *aborigine, also-ran, barrack, billy-can, booze-up, bushed, cobber, crook* (adjective), and so on. At present it is clear that British English is adopting many more words from overseas dialects, especially American English, than from the regional dialects of Britain.

In the discussion of the dimension of dialect, I have so far confined myself to spatially separate varieties of English; but the term 'dialect' can also be applied to forms of language appropriate to particular social classes. The situation is complicated in English by the fact that the standard language is both a regional and a class dialect at one and the same time. Standard English, defined as the form of language common to its educated speakers, is itself remarkably diverse; both members of such pairs as *mirror/looking-glass, toilet/lavatory, slip/petticoat, costume/suit,* or *notepaper/writing-paper,* in which some see a class-difference, are certainly part of it. But there are a number of words which can be located along the dimension stretching from the standard language to the speech of the uneducated: *chocs, telly, drawers* ('pants'), *bint, skirt* ('woman'), *Ma, fancy* (verb), *fag* ('cigarette'), *tanner* ('sixpence'), *neck* (verb), *char* ('tea'), etc. Some of these are also used in the standard spoken language, but usually with an intentionally humorous or vulgar effect. There are a number of other words in English which have a different social connotation, such as *varsity, footer, togs, Mama,* etc. But these words, which are used by members (or those who affect to be members) of a superior social group, are less common than the vulgarisms.

From the class-dialect it is but a short distance to the occupational dialect. All occupations develop their own vocabulary of technical terms: *hose* ('socks, etc.' in the clothing trade), *battels* ('bill for board and lodging' at an Oxford college), *lexis* ('vocabulary' in specialist books on language), and so on. In such cases, of course, it is very difficult to draw the line between the core-vocabulary and the occupational vocabulary. Once more, we can observe a gradation, as in the following lists of linguistic terms: *pitch, preposition, prefix, paradigm, phoneme, polysemy* ...; or *dialect, denotation, dative, diacritic, deixis, diathesis* ... What our dictionaries call learnéd words can also be grouped with other terms appropriate to particular occupations. Occupational dialects are distinguished almost entirely by their vocabulary; their grammar and phonology are rarely distinctive. When we remember how many occupational dialects may be distinguished it is easy to see that this is one of the more important dimensions by which the vocabulary can be classified.

Occupational varieties of language are roughly halfway between dialect, which refers to varieties of language distinguished by user, and register, which refers to varieties of language distinguished by use. To some extent it is true that each occupational variety is used only by a section of the speech-community as a whole, but most of us command more than one occupational variety—for example, the languages of our profession, our hobbies and sports; and we are able to switch from one to another as appropriate.

The most immediately obvious distinction within the field of register is medium. We can observe two main types of medium, spoken and written language (though we may note in passing the two intermediate types, reading aloud and scripted language). Clearly, the bulk of the English vocabulary can be appropriately used in both written and spoken English, but there are a number of words which are more often used in one or other medium: *decease, alight, commencement, authorization, appended*; *hey, ref, oopsy-daisy, telly, teeny, with-it, chewy, twee*, etc. There is a partial, but by no means complete, correlation between the archaic and the written sections of the vocabulary, and between the novel and the spoken portions.

The other dimensions which I have grouped together under the general heading of register are role and formality. The first of these, role, refers to the various types of language appropriate to different social roles: the language of the commentator differs from that of the lecturer; a letter to *The Times* and a letter to one's wife will not be alike. Some of the differences will be grammatical, but many of them are lexical, e.g. *cleanse* (language of advertising), *pussy* (language of the nursery), *hereinafter* (language of legal documents), *wed* (newspaper headlines). The dimension of role can be exemplified by a comparison of such sentences as: *the damn fool nearly ran over my bloody foot!* and *Darling, you must give me a teeny drink—I've had a simply frightful time!* What makes us think that the first sentence was spoken by a man and the second by a woman? We can distinguish a large number of different roles, and each one will have its own appropriate vocabulary. As before, there is a gradation from the core-vocabulary to the special words associated with each role, for example in this list of nursery words: *grumpy, grizzle, potty* (noun), *gee-gee, bow-wow* (noun). It may be objected that the dimensions of role and occupation are very similar, but the difference can be shown by a comparison of *copy, leader, par* (occupational language of journalism) with *probe, ban, bar* (verb) (role language of newspaper headlines).

The dimension of formality can be exemplified by pairs such as *right away/immediately, think/consider, photo/photograph*, etc. The well-known comparison of *low-income dress for dignified maturity* with *cheap clothes for fat old women* shows that a formal style is more appropriate for such a notice. Once again we must recognize a considerable degree of overlap between the categories of formal and written language and between informal and spoken language, but medium and formality are distinct dimensions. Compare the following notices: *visitors are kindly requested not to walk on the lawns/please keep off the grass*; or these letters—*Dear Bill, Thanks for your note. Next Wed. is O.K. See you then. Yours, Jack./Dear Mr. Smith, Thank you for your letter, Wednesday, 4th June, will suit me admirably, and I look forward to meeting you on that date. Yours sincerely, J. Brown.*; or these introductions—*Mrs. Johnson, may I introduce a colleague of mine—Mr. Jones?/Meg, this is Jimmy: he works with me.*

We have now seen how the English vocabulary may be roughly stratified along a number of dimensions—archaism, neologism, foreign adoption, dialect, medium, role, and formality. Any word may be located in the vocabulary by placing it on a scale stretching from neutral to extreme for each of these dimensions. Thus, *puissance* is distinctively archaic, foreign, formal and appropriate to written Englsih, but neutral as regards neologism, dialect and role; *weskit* is archaic, typical of a particular class-dialect, and more appropriate to spoken English, but it is neutral in other respects; *yum-yum* is more appropriate to spoken English and the role language of the nursery, and is very informal; *hors d'oeuvre* is foreign and typical of the occupational language connected with food; and so on. This is one way in which the organization of the vocabulary may be studied. Another way is to map the derivational relationships of words. We have already seen how the various processes of word-formation produce families of words, derivationally related, such as *father* (noun and verb), *fatherhood, father-figure, fatherland, fatherless*, etc., or *television, televise, telly, T.V., telly-mania*, etc. Most words are members of such word-families, although there are some, especially among the recent borrowings from foreign languages or dialects, which are isolated: *biennale, aficionado, ouzo, quorum, tontine, torso*, etc. But the vocabulary is organized in more ways than the two which have so far been mentioned (derivational relationships and lexical dimensions): we must now proceed to study collocational organization and sense-relationships.

The term 'collocation' is used to refer to co-occurrence of words. Adjective + noun is a regular grammatical structure, and examples of it may be multiplied: *blank look, molten glass, yellow tie; blank glance, molten butter, yellow wine*. We use the term collocation to describe the acceptability of the first group in contrast to the (relative) unacceptability of the second. To some extent the concept of collocation handles what is often called idiom, the apparently inexplicable phrases like *glad eye* or *glad rags*, and equally the non-occurrence of seemingly parallel phrases like *glad ear* or *glad clothes*. But these idiomatic examples are extreme cases of collocational restriction. All words have a range of acceptable collocations, and when we know a word's range of collocations we have gone a long way towards understanding its meaning. It may be objected that in many cases collocations (such as *blue leaf, molten feather, woolly hedgehog*) do not regularly occur for the very obvious reason that leaves are never blue, nor are feathers molten, or hedgehogs woolly. We may feel that it is not so much the words that are incompatible in such cases, as the referents. In other cases, such as *unmarried wife, female father, he ate his beer*, the incompatibility seems to be almost more a matter of grammar than of lexis: *wife* and *father* each belong to subclasses of noun which normally exclude adjectives such as *unmarried* and *female*, respectively; *eat* is one of a number of verbs (such as *chew, munch, gnaw*, etc.) which do not usually select as object such words as *beer, milk, orange-juice*, and so on. But although collocational restrictions sometimes border on grammatical and logical restrictions, the bulk of collocational patterning is clearly within the sphere of lexical organization. Moreover the study of the English vocabulary will be assisted more by an attempt to describe such collocational patterns than by explaining them away by an appeal to common sense.

It will be obvious that the question of lexical acceptability is not a straightforward one. Few collocations can be firmly excluded as impossible; they range from the unquestionably acceptable to the extremely unlikely. Context is often all-important: *woolly hedgehog* will be admissible in a fairy-story, *blue leaf* in some sorts of poetry, while it does not require much imagination to produce an appropriate context for *unmarried wife* or *female father*.

In order to bring out the reality and importance of collocational patterns we must discuss some examples in detail. The dictionary-definition of *hale* is 'healthy'; yet we all recognize that no single example of *healthy* can be replaced by *hale* in contemporary English speech or writing: *healthy child, healthy walk, healthy influence, healthy water, healthy state*, etc. In fact, *hale* probably occurs only in the collocation *hale and hearty* today. The knowledge of its restricted collocation is more important for the understanding of *hale* than is its dictionary-definition. But this is not all. We note that the collocational range of *hearty*, which is anyway considerably restricted, is further reduced by the addition of *hale*. With *meal, laugh, support, welcome, appetite*, for instance, *hearty* is acceptable, but *hale and hearty* inappropriate.

Soft, mild and *gentle* can all collocate with *voice, rebuke*, or *breeze*, for example, but each of them also has exclusive collocations with other words: *soft water, soft ground*; *mild ale, mild steel*; *gentle blood, gentle slope*. The example of *soft water* can be used to show how a collocational relationship will often hold good through a series of derivationally-linked words: *water-softener, she softened the water, the softness of the water*, etc.

Another word where collocational pattern is interesting is *rotten*. This has two closely related senses, 'putrid' and 'of poor quality'. How does the native speaker know which is intended in any particular case? *Rotten apples* is clearly ambiguous, but *rotten butter* must be 'butter of inferior quality'; in this case, the appropriate word for 'putrid' is *rancid*, which has a very restricted collocation, virtually confined to *butter, oil, fat (lard*, etc.), *taste* and *smell (flavour, odour, stink*, etc.). It is easy to see how large a part is played by collocational pattern in distinguishing such virtual synonyms as *putrid, rotten, rancid* and *addled*. *Addled*, which is confined to *eggs* and *brains (wits*, etc.), is like *hale* and many other, generally archaic, words which have very restricted collocations: *spick and span, chit of a girl, flitch of bacon, rood screen, serried ranks*, etc.

Of course, it is easier to point to the fact of collocational range and restriction and give a few fragmentary examples, than it is to undertake a full description of the collocations of even a few words. Our dictionaries normally list only the unexpected ones (*glad rags, glad eye*), and only give a full statement in the case of highly restricted words like *addled*. But the commonest words have individual collocational patterns which contribute to their distinctive meaning: *a quick glance* (but not *a fast glance*), *a black mood* (but not *a white mood*), *a new day* (but not *a novel day*), etc.

One of the most easily overlooked types of lexical change is the extension or restriction of a word's collocational range. Recently *key* has considerably extended the range of words with which it collocates: *key man, key component, key move*, etc. Adjectives of value very frequently undergo rapid collocational extension in colloquial usage, simultaneously exchanging their precise sense for a more general one, for example *gruesome party, revolting dress, wicked price, vicious remark, blissful idea, heavenly shoes, divine soup*, etc. The collocational range of words may also be restricted, as the following examples from *Pride and Prejudice* indicate: *happy manners, mean understanding, tolerable fortune, perfect indifference, indifferent imitations*, etc. These, though not impossible, would all be unusual collocations today.

Most of the examples of collocations which have been discussed have been within the grammatical structure, adjective + noun; but it has been stressed that the collocational relationship is not dependent on any particular grammatical structure. One of the problems in the study of collocation is how far a collocation may be extended before it becomes insignificant: e.g. *soft water; the softness of cool, fresh rainwater; use the water from the stream at the end of the field—the softness will be good for your skin*. Are each of these to be counted as collocations of *soft/water*? However, although there are obvious difficulties in making a collocational description of vocabulary, there is no doubt that the range of collocations contracted by any particular word is one of the important elements in its meaning. We must now turn from collocational organization to sense-relationships.

In discussing the meaning of words we are accustomed to assuming that each word will have one single meaning (or, at least, one basic meaning) more or less like proper names such as *Chaucer* or *Edinburgh*. I have tried to show that what we call meaning is a complex of different relationships, and we have so far considered the relationships of derivation, dimension, and collocation. Two types of relationship remain, sense-relations and reference. The latter is easily understood: it is the relationship between words and the world of experience. *Edinburgh* and *Chaucer* 'refer' to the city and the poet, respectively. Sense-relations are the semantic relations words contract with one another. Let us consider an example. We may say that *orange* (adjective) refers to the colour of oranges, but we should add that it is part of a lexical system (*red, orange, yellow, . . .*) and that its meaning largely depends on its position between *red* and *yellow*. Similarly, *cow* and *vixen* refer to female cattle and foxes, respectively, but a fuller understanding of their meaning is gained by observing that *cow* and *bull* are incompatible, but the sense of *fox* includes that of *vixen*: in other words, the utterance *I saw a fox today—I think it was a vixen* is perfectly acceptable, but *I saw a bull today—I think it was a cow* seems, at least, facetious.

We may broadly distinguish four types of sense-relationship: identity, inclusion, incompatibility, opposition. Few words contract all four types of relationship, but no word is completely without sense-relations. Identity of sense, commonly called synonymy, is easy to exemplify: *adder/viper, photo/photograph, hide/conceal, just/fair, telegram/cable, gramophone/record-player, football/soccer*, etc. It will be obvious, even from this short list of examples, that it is rash to claim that two words are synonymous without qualification. Two important qualifications must be made. First, identity of meaning commonly depends on context: *do* and *clean* are synonymous in a sentence like *have you done/cleaned your teeth?*, but not often otherwise. Secondly, the concept of synonymy of sense is not intended to handle the type of difference already discussed under the heading 'dimension'. For example, the meaning of *soccer* differs from that of *football* in that the former is both more informal and more colloquial than the latter: they share an identical sense, though once again, one should observe that they will not necessarily be synonymous in all contexts, e.g. *Rugby football is a brutal game.*

Identity of sense is closely related to inclusion. The latter refers to the relationship between *red* and *scarlet/crimson/magenta*, etc., or *fruit* and *apple/plum/lemon*, etc. English, like other languages, provides numerous examples of families of more specific words subsumed under a more general cover-term. In some cases the general terms are so general that they are able to embrace most of the rest of the vocabulary, e.g. *thing, do*. Inclusion differs from identity in that, while synonyms may freely replace one another, only the including term can replace the included, and not vice versa. The sentence *there's a plum-tree in our garden* implies *there's a fruit-tree in our garden*, but *fresh fruit for pudding!* does not imply *fresh lemons for pudding!* In some cases, the family of included words lacks a general including term, as, for instance, the group *tree, shrub, bush*. A thesaurus arranges the vocabulary of a language according to the two types of sense-relation so far discussed, identity and inclusion. The fact that the whole of the vocabulary of English can be accounted for in such a scheme indicates the linguistic importance of these sense-relationships.

Incompatibility handles the difference in sense between such members of a lexical set as *red, green, yellow, blue*, etc., or *lion, tiger, leopard, panther*, etc. Many words differ in sense without being incompatible; in the sentences *that lion is a joke* and *the sky is wide and blue* the pairs *lion/joke* and *blue/wide*, which certainly differ in sense, are applied to the same objects. Conversely, incompatible words are commonly similar in sense, and make up a family of words which are included in a higher general term. Thus in most contexts *coloured* includes *red, yellow, green*, etc., which are mutually incompatible; in turn *red* includes another incompatible set, *crimson, scarlet, vermilion*, etc.

In cases like *father/mother* or *brother/sister*, which are incompatible sets with only two members, we come to the fourth type of sense-relation, opposition. This is easily exemplified with pairs like *odd/even, wet/dry, father/son*. Several different types of opposite may be distinguished. Complementary pairs like *odd/even* or *male/female* differ from opposites like *good/bad* in that there is no gradation between the extremes. If a number is not odd, it must be even; if a person is not male, she must be female. Pairs like *good/bad, wet/dry, few/many, cheap/ expensive*, are, however, gradable. This is the commonest type of opposite. A third type is the converse pair like *husband/wife* or *mother/ daughter*, where there is a reciprocal relationship between the two terms. In the case of *mother* we may observe that it is a member of a complementary pair (*mother/father*) as well as a converse pair (*mother/ daughter*), and that, in turn, *daughter* is a complementary opposite to *son*.

It is worth noting that a word can be in opposition to two or more words in different ways. *Odd* and *even* are, as we have seen, a complementary pair, but *odd* and *normal* are in some contexts gradable opposites. A sentence like the following plays on this double relationship: *you may call eighty-eight an even number, but it's the oddest number I've ever seen.* On occasions complementary pairs may be treated as gradable pairs to gain a particular effect: *John seems rather more married than he used to be.* The flexibility of the sense-relations we have been considering cannot be emphasized too strongly. Certain linguistic contexts, or social situations, will neutralize some relations and generate others. *Red* and *white* are ungradable opposites when collocated with *wine*, though the system is slightly complicated by the third term, *rosé*. *Black* and *white* are two members of a large incompatible set when collocated with *horse*, but are complementary terms when applied to *magic* or *coffee*. *Good* and *bad* have been stated to be gradable opposites, but when a mother says to her child *David, you are not a good boy* she is implying a complementary relationship between them.

With the four types of sense-relation which we have discussed languages are able to map the world of experience. It is important to note that different languages do this in different ways. Even English and French (or German), which are closely related both historically and culturally differ in a number of instances, e.g. *know/savoir, connaître; cousin/Vetter, Cousine.* In the latter case German has a pair of complementary terms distinguishing sex, where English *cousin* is indifferent with regard to sex.

We have now completed our survey of the various ways in which the English vocabulary is organized. I have argued that a word's meaning, far from being a straightforward matter, is a complex of different relationships. Fully to understand the meaning of a word we need to know its derivational relations, its place on the various lexical dimensions, its collocational patterns, the sense-relationships it contracts with other words, and, of course, finally, its reference.

Some of these approaches to the study of vocabulary can be usefully applied to literature. For instance, the words of W. H. Auden's poem *Who's Who* seem to have been carefully selected from a particular section of the vocabulary: they are remarkably informal, colloquial and neologistic.

> A shilling life will give you all the facts:
> How Father beat him, how he ran away,
> What were the struggles of his youth, what acts
> Made him the greatest figure of his day:
> Of how he fought, fished, hunted, worked all night,
> Though giddy, climbed new mountains; named a sea:
> Some of the last researchers even write
> Love made him weep his pints like you and me.

239

With all his honours on, he sighed for one
Who, say astonished critics, lived at home;
Did little jobs about the house with skill
And nothing else; could whistle; would sit still
Or potter round the garden; answered some
Of his long marvellous letters but kept none.

We notice *life* ('biography'), *researchers, pints, jobs, potter, marvellous*.
The vocabulary (and the grammar, though this is not relevant here) are
carefully designed to imitate the language of the potted biography
mentioned in the first line. Not only the selection of the words but also
their collocation is appropriate to this scheme, e.g. *give/facts, climbed/
mountains, weep/pints, astonished/critics, sit/still, long/letters*. These, and,
some of the longer sequences, are markedly ordinary collocations and
give this poem its unoriginal, even banal, effect. A study of the vocabulary will take us so far: but one needs to go beyond the words to explain
why the poem, with all its clichés, is yet so moving.

At different periods in the history of English special vocabularies
have developed for certain literary purposes. In Old English the
vocabulary of verse was partially distinct from that used in prose,
which was no doubt closer to the spoken norm. A similar situation has
developed several times in the more recent history of English. In the
18th century poetry commonly used a rather formal vocabulary: e.g.
*abode, bounty, celestial, dread, dirge, dauntless, disdainful, fleeting, fretted,
graved, genial, heath, haply, hoary, inglorious, ignoble, jocund, lowly, nigh,
pangs, pore, ply, rill, rustic, rugged, sturdy, shrine, strife, strew, sequestered,
swain, turf, unfathomed, vale, wan, wonted, wayward, woeful, yon, yonder.*
These words, which as a group, if not individually, seem typical of 18th
century verse, are all drawn from Gray's *Elegy Written in a Country
Churchyard*. But other lists could be produced to exemplify the vocabulary typical of the later 19th century poetry (for example, such adjectives as *sweet, tender, dear, keen, . . .*), or of other periods or other literary
kinds. Of course, one can only isolate the distinctive vocabulary of a
period or genre in a very rough and ready way. Often a particular
author will have his own partially distinctive vocabulary, e.g. Hopkins
(*dapple, selve. comb, fond, fretty, juice, whelm, sear, . . .*), or Hemingway
(*bastard, crazy, yank* (verb), *bitch, plenty* (adverb), *awful* (adverb),
lousy, . . .), or Spenser (*ween, puissance, hight, darksome, loathly, doff, mazed,
wight, blithe, . . .*). But in the study of the selection of vocabulary one
should not concentrate solely on the eccentric at the expense of the
more normal. The choice of undistinctive vocabulary, as in this poem
by Robert Frost (*Stopping by Woods on a Snowy Evening*), is just as
significant a stylistic decision as, for example, Spenser's use of archaic
diction in *The Faerie Queene*.

Whose woods these are I think I know.
His house is in the village though;
He will not see me stopping here
To watch his woods fill up with snow.

My little horse must think it queer
To stop without a farmhouse near
Between the woods and frozen lake
The darkest evening of the year.

He gives his harness bells a shake
To ask if there is some mistake.
The only other sound's the sweep
Of easy wind and downy flake.

The woods are lovely, dark and deep,
But I have promises to keep,
And miles to go before I sleep,
And miles to go before I sleep.

Not only the selection but also the collocation of words may be distinctive and interesting. In the Auden poem quoted earlier the collocations were, on the whole, so predictable as to appear (intentionally) trite. In the Frost poem the collocation of, for instance, *little/horse, frozen/lake, easy/wind, downy/flake*, is not predictable, but they are in no way remarkable or unusual. Some of the most startling lines of verse achieve their effect by unexpected collocations, e.g. *Light thickens; A grief ago; Sweet rose, whose hue angrie and brave/Bids the rash gazer wipe his eye* . . .; etc. Some poets, such as Dylan Thomas, use the unexpected collocation almost as a stylistic device:

How soon the servant sun,
(Sir morrow mark),
Can time unriddle, and the cupboard stone,
(Fog has a bone
He'll trumpet into meat),
Unshelve that all my gristles have a gown
And the naked egg stand straight . . .

In verse like this it is not the selection of words which is distinctive but their collocation. By combining the notions of selection and collocation we can distinguish four lexical styles: distinctive vocabulary in unusual collocations, distinctive vocabulary in usual collocations, undistinctive vocabulary in unusual collocations, undistinctive vocabulary in usual collocations. This is, of course, a greatly oversimplified scheme, since, as we have seen, vocabulary can be distinctive in a large number of different ways, and the scale between the usual and the unique collocation is a gradual one.

A further point of interest is the question of lexical repetition. In Old English prose it was an acceptable rhetorical device to repeat words and their derivative relations in a way which now seems intolerable. The following passage by the homilist Aelfric, with its very literal translation, is a clear example of this practice.

'þæt folc, þa þe þæt wundor geseah, cwædon be Criste, þæt he wære soþ witega, þe toweard wæs.' Soþ hi sædon, sumera þinga: witega he wæs, forþan þe he wiste ealle towearde þing, and eac fela þing witegode, þe beoþ gefyllede butan twyn. He is witega, and he is ealra witegana witegung, forþan þe ealle witegan be him witegodon, and Crist gefylde heora ealra witegunga. þæt folc geseah þa þæt wundor, and hi þæs swiþe wundredon; þæt wundor is awriten, and we hit gehyrdon.

'The people, when they saw the wonder, said about Christ that he was the true prophet who was to come.' They spoke the truth, in some ways: he was a prophet, because he knew all things to come, and also prophesised many things which are without doubt fulfilled. He is a prophet, and he is the prophecy of all prophets, because all prophets prophesied regarding him, and Christ fulfilled all their prophecies. The people then saw the wonder, and they wondered at it greatly; the wonder is recorded, and we have heard it.

Now, there is no doubt that such a style seems offensive in Modern English. Far from lexical repetition being an acceptable rhetorical device, some authors clearly strive for its opposite, lexical variation. Consider this passage by Dr. Johnson (*Rasselas* chapter 44, 'The dangerous prevalence of imagination'):

'Disorders of intellect,' answered Imlac, 'happen much more often than superficial observers will easily believe. Perhaps, if we speak with rigorous exactness, no human mind is in its right state. There is no man whose imagination does not sometimes predominate over his reason, who can regulate his attention wholly by will, and whose ideas will come and go at his command. No man will be found in whose mind airy notions do not sometimes tyrannise, and force him to hope or fear beyond the limits of sober probability. All power of fancy over reason is a degree of insanity; but while this power is such as we can control and repress, it is not visible to others, nor considered as any depravation of the mental faculties: it is not pronounced madness, but when it becomes ungovernable and apparently influences speech or action.

'To indulge the power of fiction, and send imagination out upon the wing, is often the sport of those who delight too much in silent speculation. When we are alone we are not always busy; the labour of excogitation is too violent to last long; the ardour of enquiry will sometimes give way to idleness or satiety. He who has nothing external that can divert him, must find pleasure in his own thoughts, and must conceive himself what he is not; for who is pleased with what he is? He then expatiates in boundless futurity, and culls from all imaginable conditions that which for the present moment he should most desire, amuses his desires with impossible enjoyments, and confers upon his pride unattainable dominion. The mind dances from scene to scene, unites all pleasures in all combinations, and riots in delights, which nature and fortune, with all their bounty, cannot bestow.

In time some particular train of ideas fixes the attention; all other intellectual gratifications are rejected; the mind, in weariness or leisure, recurs constantly to the favourite conception, and feasts on the luscious falsehood whenever she is offended with the bitterness of truth. By degrees the reign of fancy is confirmed; she grows first imperious, and in time despotic. Then fictions begin to operate as realities, false opinions fasten upon the mind, and life passes in dreams of rapture or of anguish.

'This, sir, is one of the dangers of solitude, which the hermit has confessed not always to promote goodness, and the astronomer's misery has proved to be not always propitious to wisdom.'

There is obviously much of lexical interest in this passage. We note the selection of distinctive vocabulary—learnéd, formal, and typical of written rather than spoken English; on the other hand, the collocations, without being predictable, are rarely abnormal. Johnson often uses the sense-relationships of identity or opposition to produce such parallels as *fictions/false opinions* or *to promote/to be ... propitious to*, and such antitheses as *luscious falsehood/bitterness of truth*. But we are particularly concerned with the repetition of words. In this passage of over 400 words we are immediately struck by the rarity of the lexical repetitions and the variety of the significant vocabulary: *mind* (5 times); *imagination/ imaginable* (3 times); *ideas, attention, fancy, reason, fiction(s), conceive/ conception, intellect/intellectual* (twice); *will, notions, believe, insanity, mental, madness, speculation, excogitation, enquiry, thoughts, opinions, wisdom* (once). This is an extreme case of lexical variation, but to a greater or lesser extent all modern prose strives to avoid lexical repetition. It is interesting to note that the Old English vocabulary, which was more homogeneous than that of Modern English and contained many more and larger derivative families, was better designed for a style permitting lexical repetition; a style of lexical variation is, however, wholly appropriate to Modern English with its immensely diverse vocabulary providing such partial synonyms as *work, job, toil, employ-ment, occupation, labour*, etc., or pairs like *despise/contempt, mind/mental*, etc. It is perhaps not too much to claim that the structure of the English vocabulary is partly responsible for this feature of modern English prose style.

BIBLIOGRAPHY

The study of the English vocabulary cannot be undertaken without the aid of a good dictionary. There are a number of excellent shorter dictionaries to choose from, such as H. C. Wyld, *The Universal English Dictionary of the English Language* (London, 1932); *The Shorter Oxford English Dictionary*, ed. C. T. Onions (3rd edition, revised with addenda, Oxford, 1956); G. N. Garmonsway, *The Penguin English Dictionary* (London, 1965); but the serious student is advised from the start to refer to what is probably the greatest dictionary ever produced for any language, *The Oxford English Dictionary* (being a corrected re-issue of *A New English Dictionary on Historical Principles*), ed. J. A. H. Murray, H. Bradley, W. A. Craigie, C. T. Onions (Oxford, 1933). A thesaurus of English is conveniently available in the Penguin edition of *Roget's Thesaurus* (London, 1953). *The Oxford Dictionary of Etymology*, ed. C. T. Onions (Oxford, 1966) is valuable for the study of the origins of the English vocabulary. A useful historical study of loanwords is available in M. Serjeantson, *A History of Foreign Words in English* (London, 1935); A. J. Bliss, *A Dictionary of Foreign Words and Phrases in Current English* (London, 1966) provides a mass of contemporary material. The standard treatment of word-formation is H. Marchand, *The Categories and Types of Present-Day English Word-Formation* (Wiesbaden, 1960). No full treatment of collocation in English is as yet available, but the subject is usefully discussed in A. McIntosh and M. A. K. Halliday, *Patterns of Language*, pp. 183–199: A. McIntosh, 'Patterns and Ranges' (London, 1966); and *In Memory of J. R. Firth*, ed. C. E. Bazell and others, pp. 148–162: M. A. K. Halliday, 'Lexis as a Linguistic Level', pp. 410–430: J. Sinclair, 'Beginning the Study of Lexis' (London, 1966). An invaluable study of sense-relations and the general problem of meaning is to be found in J. Lyons, *Introduction to Theoretical Linguistics*, pp. 400–481 (Cambridge, 1968).

6

STYLE: THE VARIETIES OF ENGLISH

Dr. D. Crystal, University of Reading

Many of the terms used in the study of language are 'loaded', in that they have a number of different, sometimes overlapping, sometimes contradictory and controversial senses, both at popular and scholarly levels. The word 'style' is a particularly good example of the kind of confusion that can arise. The multiplicity of meanings which surround this concept—or, perhaps set of concepts—testifies to its importance in the history of English language studies, and indicates the magnitude of the problem facing any student of the subject. On the one hand, there are highly technical definitions of style such as 'the style of a text is the aggregate of the contextual probabilities of its linguistic items' (Enkvist); on the other hand, there is the loosely metaphorical, aphoristic definition of style as 'the man himself' (Buffon). Style has been compared to thought, soul, expressiveness, emotions, existence, choice, personality, good manners, fine clothing . . . and much more. How, one might well ask, is it possible to sort out such a semantic tangle? For sorting out there must be, if there is to be any clear discussion of this undeniably fundamental aspect of people's use of language.

One useful way into the tangle is to look at the most important senses in which the word 'style' is used at the present time, and see if there is any common denominator, or dominant use. There may be no single answer to the question, What is style?, but it should at least be possible to distinguish the main strands of meaning which would underlie any such answer.

The first, and possibly the most widespread use, is to take 'style' as referring to the distinctive characteristics of some *single* author's use of language—as when we talk of 'Wordsworth's style', or make a comment about 'the style of the mature Shakespeare'. There are a number of different areas of application for this interpretation: for example, we may want to clarify some comparative question (as when comparing the 'styles' of two poets in a given tradition), or we may be concerned with the study of some single author as an end in itself, or again we might be engaged in stylistic detection work—'linguistic forensics', as it is sometimes half-seriously called—as with the investigations into the 'style' of the Pauline epistles, to see whether one man wrote them all. But in each of these applications, the primary task is the same: to pick out from the totality of the language that an author has used those features which would be generally agreed as belonging to him, identifying him as an individual against the backcloth of the rest of the language-using world. And it is these idiosyncratic linguistic markers which are referred to by this first use of the term 'style'. If we beware of the metaphor, 'style is the man' is an appropriate summary of the focus of this view.

A second, and closely related use, is to talk about 'style' in a collective sense, referring to *groups* of literary figures, as when referring to the 'style' of Augustan poetry, or generalizing about the style associated with one particular genre of drama as opposed to another. This is a more general sense, obviously, but it is to be noted that the procedure for arriving at any conclusions in this area is precisely the same as in the study of individual authors: distinctive linguistic features have still to be identified and described—only this time the use of these features is shared by a number of people, and are not idiosyncratic in the narrow sense of the preceding paragraph.

These two senses are the most common in any discussion about literature, in view of the emphasis in literary criticism on defining the individuality of authors and tracing the development of genres; but in terms of the study of the English language as a whole, it should be stressed that these senses are extremely narrow. They are restricted largely to literary English, and to the written form of the language. But we can—and do—equally well apply the term 'style' to spoken English, whether literary or not, and to written English which has nothing to do with literature at all; and it is this more general use which provides us with a third sense of style. For example, when we refer (usually in a pejorative tone of voice) to the 'style' of Civil Service prose, or to 'business-letter style', or to the 'formal style' in which sermons or proclamations are given—or even to the 'style' of newspaper and television advertisements—we are referring to an awareness of certain features of English sounds and spellings, grammar and vocabulary, which characterize in a distinctive way these particular uses. And comparably familiar examples could be cited of people referring to the style of individuals, as well as of groups—'I do like John's lecturing style, don't you?'

In the light of these examples, the term 'style' can be seen to be applicable, in principle, to a great deal of language use other than literature; and on the basis of this we might well generalize and say that style seems to be a concept which is applicable to the language as a whole. The word 'distinctive' has occurred a number of times already in this chapter. If one of the bases of style is linguistic distinctiveness of some kind, then it is very difficult—probably impossible—to think up cases of uses of English in which there is no distinctiveness whatsoever. Even the most ordinary kinds of conversation have the distinctive feature of being 'most ordinary'. Non-literary uses of language must not be decried simply because they are non-literary. To refer to such uses as 'style-less' is to beg the whole question as to what style consists of, and to ignore a highly important perspective for literary study. Without an 'ordinary' style, or set of styles, which we are all familiar with and use, it is doubtful whether we would ever appreciate an extraordinary style, as in literary linguistic originality. This is a point I shall return to later.

Other senses of the term 'style' may be found, but they take us into a quite different dimension. These are mainly variants of a sense of style as a 'quality' of expression. When we talk about someone or something displaying 'style', we are making an intuitive judgment about a (usually indefinable) overall impression—as when Mr. X is said to 'have style', whereas Mr. Y has not, This is very near to the sense of 'style' as 'powers of lucid exposition or self-expression': Mr. Z. 'has no sense of style at all', we might say. Then there is a wholly evaluative sense, as when we talk of a style as 'pretty', 'affected', 'endearing', 'lively', and the like. These uses are very different from those described in previous paragraphs, as what we are doing here is making value judgments of various kinds about a particular use of language, passing an opinion about the effect a use of language has had. The difference between the phrases 'Shakespeare's style' and 'affected style', essentially, is that the first is a descriptive statement, referring to certain features of the English language which could presumably be pointed out and agreed upon in a reasonably objective way; the second is an evaluative statement, where a subjective judgment is passed about some aspect of a use of language, and where we are told more about the state of mind of the language critic than about the linguistic characteristics of the author being assessed. Any critical task will involve both elements, descriptive and evaluative, in varying degrees, corresponding to *what* we respond to and *how* we respond to it. What must be emphasized is the importance of placing our evaluative decisions in a thoroughly descriptive context: value judgments with no 'objective correlative' to support them may give us a great deal of personal pleasure, but they do not provide anything of permanent critical value. We can only resolve a debate as to the merits or demerits of someone's style if the parties in the debate are first and foremost objectively aware of the relevant characteristics of the language they are discussing. The descriptive, identifying task is quite primary, as it provides the basis for the response which any two critics might be arguing about. *Why* does X think that line effective, whereas Y does not? The descriptive analysis of a piece of language (I shall call this, whether written or spoken, a 'text', for convenience) is in no sense a replacement for a sensitive response to that language, as some critics of a linguistic approach to literature have implied—how could it be? It is simply an invaluable preliminary which is likely to promote clear thinking. What such a descriptive analysis might involve I shall outline below.

When such matters are considered, it becomes very clear that there is unlikely to be a single, pithy answer to the question 'What is style'. And perhaps therefore a more constructive question might be: 'What is there in language that makes us want to talk about "style", in any of its senses, at all?' This approach can be revealing: not only does it display the complexity of the concept of style very clearly; it also integrates this concept with that of 'language' as a whole, and thus produces a more general characterization than any of those so far reviewed. The approach is, briefly, to see 'style' in the context of the socially-conditioned *varieties* a language may be shown to possess—and this is the reason for the title of this chapter.

The idea that the English language can be—indeed, *has* to be—seen in terms of varieties is one of the themes underlying the first chapter of this volume. The phrase '*the* English language' is itself highly misleading, for there is no such animal. If we look at the use of English in all parts of the world expecting to find identical sounds, spellings, grammar and vocabulary on all occasions, then we are in for a rude shock. There is a great deal in common between 'American' and 'British' English, for instance—to take one example that regularly rears its head in the letter-columns of the press—but people are much more aware of the fact that there are differences. The English language is not a single, homogeneous, stable entity: it is a complex mixture of varying structures. The unfortunate thing is that so many people look upon this as an unsatisfactory state of affairs, and try to correct it. The English-speaking world is full of people who want to make everyone else speak as they do, or as Shakespeare did. It is a pity that the fact and fundamental role of variety in the English language cannot be accepted for what it is—an inevitable product of language development.

What, then, are these varieties? The kind of variation which most people are readily aware of usually goes under the heading of 'regional dialect'. It is not difficult to cite examples of people who speak or write differently depending on where they are from. This is one of the most well-studied aspects of language variety. The major rural dialects of Great Britain have all been studied in some detail, at least from the phonetic point of view, as have many of the dialects of the United States. Urban dialects—such as those of London, Liverpool, Brooklyn, and Sydney—have on the whole been less intensively studied, but their distinctiveness is as marked as that of any rural area. Take, for instance, the language of currency heard in parts of Liverpool: 'og' or 'meg' (halfpenny), 'two meg' (penny), 'joey' (threepence), 'tiddler' (silver threepenny piece), 'dodger' (eight-sided threepenny piece), 'sprowser' (sixpenny piece), 'ocker' (shilling piece), and so on. Terms such as 'kecks' (trousers), 'jigger' (back alley), 'ozzy' (hospital) and 'sarneys' (sandwiches); phrases such as 'good skin' (nice chap), 'to get a cob on' (to get into a bad mood) and 'that's the gear' (that's fine); sentences such as 'don't youse butt in with the men' (don't interfere with what we're doing) and 'I'll put a lip on you' (I'll hit you in the mouth): all these illustrate clearly the kind of language variation which can only be explained in terms of geographical place of origin.

Three points should be noted in connection with regional dialects. The first is that this kind of variation is usually associated with variation in the *spoken* form of the language. The existence of a standardized, written form of English which all people born into an English-speaking community are taught as soon as they begin to write means that modern dialects get written down only by their introduction into a novel or a poem for a particular characterization or effect. The speech of the gamekeeper in *Lady Chatterley's Lover*, or that of many of the characters of Dickens, or of the 'regional' novelists such as Joyce, indicates this point abundantly—but even here, only the vaguest approximation to the original pronunciation is made. (After all, if we tried to indicate this pronunciation with any degree of accuracy, it would mean devising some form of phonetic transcription, and this would make the text impossible to read without training.) In non-literary contexts, regional dialect forms are not common, though they are sometimes used in informal contexts, and there are a few predictable examples, such as the differing spellings of certain words between British and American English.

Secondly, despite the association of regional variation with speech, 'dialect' is a term which should not be identified with 'accent'. The 'regional accent' of a person refers simply to his pronunciation; his 'dialect', on the other hand, refers to the totality of his regional linguistic characteristics—idiosyncrasies of grammar and vocabulary as well as pronunciation. An accent is usually the most noticeable feature of a dialect. Whenever comedians wish to make a joke using dialect differences, they invariably get the effect they want by simply 'putting on' a new accent, and not bothering to introduce any grammatical or other features into their speech—but in many ways an accent is the most superficial feature also. Changes in syntax and vocabulary are much more relevant for defining the differences between two dialects than are variations in pronunciation.

Thirdly, we must remember that dialects are not just local matters. My only illustrations so far have been from the dialects of one country; but far more important in a way are the dialects of English which operate on an international, as opposed to an intranational scale. Whatever differences exist between the regional dialects of England, they have all a great deal in common when compared with those of, say, the West Indies or the United States. The term 'dialects of English' *must* be allowed to include these areas, whose importance will undoubtedly increase as regional forms of literature develop.

But regional place of origin is by no means the only kind of linguistic variation in a language. Just as important is the variable of *social* place of origin—where we come from in terms of a position on a social scale of some kind. The social background of an individual has a powerful and long-lasting effect on the kind of language he uses, and there are certain general linguistic markers of class which occur regardless of the particular region to which he may belong. For example, it is probably the case that people who come from (what is regularly referred to as) a 'working class' background have a more restricted command of grammar and vocabulary than those of other classes. Again, distinctions can often be pointed out in terms of the choices we make in the use of words referring to particular concepts—such as how we address someone or say farewell to him, or how we refer to various meals, relations, or the toilet. Terms like 'mate' and 'old man' have clear social restrictions in British English. Again, the use of 'received pronunciation' normally implies a degree of education which need not be present for any of the other accents used in Britain. 'Class dialects', as they might be called, exist. They are not linguistically as clearly definable as are regional dialects because the social correlates are not as readily delimited and defined as regional ones—it is not simply a question of kind and degree of education. Also, English has far fewer indications of position on a social scale than many other languages: in Japanese, for example, there are distinct, 'honorific' forms of words, which overtly recognize class distinction.

Before going on to relate these points to the notion of 'style', a third variable in English should be referred to, which is very similar to those already outlined, namely, historical variation. Our use of English indicates very clearly our historical place of origin, as well as our regional and social background—our place on a time scale of some kind. Whether we like it or not, the younger generations do not use the language in the same way as the older generations do. This affects vocabulary for the most part, but sometimes also grammar and pronunciation. Parents' complaints about the unintelligibility of their children are perfectly familiar. The macrocosmic counterpart to this is of course the phenomenon of language change over the centuries. 'The English language'

251

can hardly be restricted to that of today, but must be allowed to comprehend earlier states of the language. Of course the boundary-line between English and the language from which it came is by no means easy to determine (it is a matter of some delicacy as to whether Anglo-Saxon should or should not be included under the heading of 'English'), but there is no doubt that *some* earlier states can be legitimately included, which is the point to be made here. And just as there are different standards or norms for the various regional and class dialects, so there are different norms for the historical 'dialects' also, though this is often forgotten. We cannot talk about Elizabethan English, let us say, in precisely the same terms as Modern English, or vice versa. The man who tries to read a Shakespeare play without caring about the values that pronunciation, grammar and vocabulary had at that time is being just as unrealistic as the man who cries 'Preserve the tongue which Shakespeare spoke!' in present-day discussions about correctness. Shakespearian English, as the English of any other historical period, must be seen in its own terms, bearing in mind the usage of the Elizabethan period of language development, and no other. Without an awareness of linguistic differences between the various periods of English literature, a great deal which is of literary importance can be missed. To take just one example: without an understanding of the normal personal pronoun system in Elizabethan English (the meanings of the pronouns 'thou' and 'you', in particular), our appreciation of Hamlet's remarks to Ophelia (in Act 3 Scene 1), where there is a controlled alternation between the different forms of the second person, is much reduced.

These three types of variation, regional, social, and historical, are very important factors in accounting for the heterogeneity of the English language. There are other factors too, as we shall see shortly; but these three form a group on their own. The basis for this grouping is that they are all relatively permanent, background aspects of any individual's use of English. Most people normally do not talk as if they were from a different area, class or time from the one to which they actually belong. Of course, a few people have the ability to adopt a different dialect for humorous or literary reasons, as we have already seen in the case of regional variation; and there are also cases of people adopting what they believe to be a more 'educated' dialect of English in their quest for social betterment. The case of Eliza Dolittle in *Pygmalion* merely takes to extremes a process which is not uncommon. But these are nonetheless the exceptions: on the whole we do *not* vary our regional, social or historical linguistic norms. They are, essentially, a linguistic background against which we can make ourselves heard. They are, to put it another way, varieties of the language on the largest possible scale.

The relevance of these dialectal features to the study of the phenomenon of style should be clear from this paragraph: they have very much a *negative* role to play. Regional, social, and historical variations in a use of language have to be eliminated before we can get down to some serious study of what we consider to be 'style'. When we talk of 'Coleridge's style', let us say, we are not, in the first instance, thinking of his regional, etc. linguistic background; and people do not in fact generally make use of such phrases as 'the style of the Cockney', 'the style of Elizabethan English', and so on. Dialectal features are uncontrolled, unconscious features of our use of language; many people find it impossible to vary their usage deliberately in these respects. Consequently, if we hope to account for the relatively conscious, controlled use of language which can produce the distinctiveness referred to above, then it must be other elements of language than these which are being manipulated. What other kinds of variation exist in English, therefore, that could account for our awareness of a 'style'?

The short answer is that no-one is fully aware of *all* these other variables, but some have been given detailed study. Certain aspects of the immediate situation in which language is used have been shown to have a strong influence on the kind of linguistic structures which occur. One of the most important of these is the occupational role that a person may be engaged in at the time of speaking or writing: the job he is doing very often carries with it a probability that in normal circumstances certain linguistic structures will be used and others will not be. One way of speaking or writing is felt to be more appropriate to a specific professional activity than another, and the members of a profession tend to conform in their usage to produce a consistent expression. The reasons for this kind of behaviour are sometimes difficult to determine, but its extent is beyond dispute. One very clear example of occupationally-motivated use of language is in the technical vocabulary associated with various fields: scientists, for instance, make use of a range of vocabulary which precisely defines the phenomena they are investigating. This vocabulary does not normally occur outside of a scientific context, and alternative ways of expressing the same ideas do not normally occur within a scientific context—a particular substance may have a quite familiar domestic name, but in the laboratory this name will tend not to be used, because popularity carries with it looseness of meaning, and ultimately ambiguity. Similarly, the scientist, when he is not 'on duty', will not use his technical terminology to refer to everyday objects, for there is no need to introduce such a degree of precision into his language. The comic situation in which a scientist asks his wife at dinner to 'pass the $H_6C_{12}O_6$' is comic precisely because it is an abnormal, unexpected, incongruous choice of vocabulary which has been made.

But it is not only vocabulary which characterizes an 'occupational' use of language—a *province*, as it is sometimes called. The grammar is always important too. In scientific English, there are a number of constructions whose usage is different from other kinds of English. The way the scientist tends to make use of passive voice constructions is a case in point. 'The solution was poured ...' is generally found in preference to 'I poured the solution ...'. There are a variety of reasons for this, though probably the most important is the concern to keep the account of the process being described as impersonal as possible. Similarly, legal English, as found in certain documents, displays a highly distinctive and much more complex syntax than can be found elsewhere —unpunctuated sentences that continue for pages are by no means exceptional. And in addition to grammar, the way in which the language is written down or spoken may be further indications of a specific brand of occupational activity. Probably the most immediately distinctive feature of written advertising language is the way in which different sizes and colours of type are made use of, a flexibility not normally seen in other written forms of the language. And a distinctive method of 'speaking an occupation', so to say, can be seen in the 'tone of voice' which may be adopted: those of the lawyer and clergyman (while speaking in court and preaching respectively) are frequently-quoted examples, and in addition the pronunciations adopted by radio news-readers, political speech-makers, and railway-station announcers could be cited—or indeed that of most people who find themselves speaking in public as part of their professional life. There are criteria for successful and unsuccessful uses of English in all these cases; and if we take the successful uses as a norm, then it can be shown that there are certain linguistic features which have a high probability of occurrence on any occasion when a particular province is used. In this way, it makes sense to talk about the 'style' of a legal document, or a political speech, as we can readily refer to the distinctive features in the pronunciation, spelling, grammar, and vocabulary which we would associate with these kinds of English, and which would not appear in the same combination elsewhere.

A second situational variable which conditions particular uses of English is the relationship between the participants in any dialogue: this will be an important factor governing the kind of language we choose to use. If two people are, broadly speaking, separated socially (as in the relationships existing between employer and employee, student and teacher, civic leader and man in the street, or old and young member of a family), then it is generally the case that different language structures will be used by the two parties, which will reflect this distinction. The socially 'inferior' person will show deference to the 'superior' in various ways, for example by the form of address, or by avoiding the more slangy words and constructions he might make use of in informally talking to his social equals; and other linguistic correlates can be found to indicate the dominance of the superior. Children are drilled in these conventions from an early age: 'Don't talk like that to the vicar/Mr. Jones/your grandfather ...' is a common exhortation; and the emergence of social linguistic norms of this kind can be seen in the role-playing which all normal children enter into—'being' daddy, or the grocer, carries with it the linguistic forms of daddyness, or grocerdom, and children show remarkable powers of mimicry and memory in these matters.

There has been relatively little research into this field of interpersonal relationships—where social psychology and linguistics overlap—but certain types of reasonably predictable variation have been shown to exist, e.g. the different degrees of *formality* which occur in English. It makes sense to distinguish a 'formal' from an 'informal' style in English (with further sub-divisions within both). The kind of language we speak or write on formal occasions (such as in an interview, making a speech, or applying for a job) is simply not the same as that used on informal occasions (such as in everyday conversations with our family, or writing to an old friend). This is almost a truism. What is often ignored, however, is that the linguistic features which indicate formality and informality are not just idiosyncratic, but are common to all members of the speech community. The evidence suggests that people tend to be formal in more or less the same linguistic way: they choose certain words more carefully, they avoid other words like the plague, they become more self-conscious over what they believe to be the 'correct' pronunciation of words, and so on. This kind of situationally-conditioned language variation, then, is yet another element contributing to the general distinctiveness of a use of language: a convenient way of referring to it is to call these variations of *status*.

There are other situational variables which influence the kind of English we choose to use in a given situation. For example, the *purpose* for which we are using language generally produces a conventional framework or format for our speech or writing, and this can be highly distinctive. The lay-out of a letter, an advertisement, or a legal document, the organization of a lecture or a sports commentary, are all examples of formats which have become to a greater or lesser extent standardized in English. It is not a question of personal choice here: for a commentary or a lecture to be successful, certain principles of 'verbal lay-out' must be followed. Then again, the broad distinction between the spoken and the written medium of the language has its specific linguistic correlates: some words and structures occur solely in speech, others only in writing. Most of the nuances of intonation have to be ignored in the written representation of speech, for example, and most of us are well aware of the social pressures that curtail our freedom to write down 'four-letter words', and the like. And of course the kind of language we use will undoubtedly vary depending on whether we speak with the intention of having our words written down (as in dictation or many kinds of lecturing), or write with the aim of having our words read aloud (as in speech-construction, news-writing for radio or television, drama, and, sometimes, poetry).

It is not the purpose of this chapter to give a complete breakdown of all the categories of situationally-conditioned language which operate in English, even if this were possible in the present state of the art. The cases so far mentioned should suffice to show the heterogeneity and fluidity of the English language. What needs to be emphasized, however, is that this flexibility of usage affects each of us individually, and it is this which provides a crucial perspective for understanding the question of style. In the course of one day, each of us modulates through a wide range of varieties of English: the various levels of domesticity, professionalism, and so on, through which we pass carry with them changes in the nature of the language we use. The level of formality, to take but a single example, will vary considerably every day, ranging from the intimate level of family conversation (linguistically very marked, through the frequent use of such things as 'pet' nonsense words and slang which only the family understands) to perhaps the artificial formality of a chaired business meeting (with all the linguistic conventions made use of there—proposals, secondings, etc.). What must be made clear—and it is this which distinguishes province status, and the like from the dialects discussed earlier—is that these distinctive uses of language are all relatively temporary and manipulable in their use. We do not normally continue at the same level of formality, let us say, for a very long period of time. 'Professional' contexts give way to domestic interchange, which in turn may give way to a receptive appraisal of formality differences, as illustrated on television. And, associated with this, these kinds of variation in English are all matters which we can to a very great extent control: the concept of choice is much more relevant here than it was with the dialects. In a given situation, which has clear extra-linguistic indices of, say, formality, it is possible to exercise some degree of choice as to whether appropriate, formal language is to be used, or inappropriate, informal language. Of course, most normal people choose the former, only lapsing into the latter when they are very sure of their social ground—as, for instance, to make a joke. But the point is that, in principle, we have both awareness and control over a number of linguistic points along the formality scale, and the question of which one to use is primarily up to us. Similarly, we all know the conventions for letter-writing; but we may choose to ignore them if we so wish. Whether we do so will depend almost entirely on our relationship to the person we are addressing: obviously, if we are dependent on someone for advancement, we will restrain ourselves, linguistically, and respect the conventions which we know he expects (e.g. the letter will be neatly laid out, punctuation will be 'correct', formulae—such as 'yours faithfully'—will be appropriately used); on the other hand, a letter to a close friend may carry with it all kinds of differences—loose use of punctuation, use of slang, disregard for regular line-spacing, etc. Such a situation does not apply to the use of dialect features of English, because, as we have seen, apart from on rare occasions, we have little awareness of and control over their use.

We may summarize this discussion by saying that the English language can be seen as a complex of (to a greater or lesser extent) situationally-conditioned, standardized sets of linguistic variations: these can be referred to as *varieties* of the language. A variety is therefore a formally definable, conventionalized group use of language which we can intuitively identify with aspects of some non-linguistic context in which it occurs (and which, as linguists, we try to formalize and explicate). An important qualification here is that we are aware of this relationship 'to a greater or lesser extent'. Some uses of English have a very clear and direct intuitive relationship to a social situation (as when the use of 'thou' and related forms automatically associates with a religious set of contexts); other uses are much less predictable (as when an official-sounding phrase might have come from one of a number of different types of context). The concept of language variety is simply a descriptive hypothesis to account for these intuitions of formal-functional correspondences in language; and in this sense it covers many of what were above referred to as 'styles'. Phrases such as 'formal style', 'the style of radio newsreaders', and so on, are meaningful because it is possible to suggest clear linguistic correlates for these notions.

To say that a particular social situation has a regular association with a particular kind of English is not to say that other kinds of English may not be introduced into that situation. In principle, this is always possible, for after all we can never be *absolutely* certain that people will behave in a maximally predictable way in a given situation. But there are some language-using situations where the possibility of making simultaneous use of a number of varieties of English is relatively normal, in order that a particular linguistic effect be contrived. Literature and humour are the clearest examples of this happening, but cases of 'stylistic juxtaposition' can be found elsewhere too. For example, a political public speaker may introduce quotations from the Bible into his oration to point a particular issue; or a television advertisement may introduce language from a scientific form of English in order to get some of the scientific overtones rubbed off onto the product; or a sermon may introduce television advertising jingles to make an idea strike home more directly. These are reasonably frequently-occurring examples of language from two or more varieties being used in a single situation, and the kinds of juxta-position which occur are to a certain extent predictable, especially when compared with the essentially unpredictable juxtapositions which are introduced into literature and humour. Many kinds of joke are successful because they introduce incongruity of a stylistic kind into the punch line; and in literature, it is a standard procedure for an author to incorporate into his work snatches or even extended extracts from the non-literary varieties of English. It is difficult to see how this could be otherwise, but some authors go in for stylistic borrowing of this kind much more widely than others: the chiaroscuro of overtones and association in much of James Joyce is to a very great extent explicable in terms of other varieties of (particularly religious) English; and T. S. Eliot is another who constantly makes use of this technique in a very definite way. Moreover, many of the so-called 'revolutions' in the use of poetic language in the history of English literature can ultimately be reduced to attempts to replace the methods of expression associated with one variety of the language by those associated with another: an example would be the introduction of scientific language by the Metaphysical poets, or by some twentieth-century authors, into a poetic context where scientific language had been almost completely absent for some time. Whether the 'language of the age' is or is not the language of poetry is not a matter for discussion here; but it should be noted in passing that this argument will never be resolved until an attempt is made to clarify the notion of 'language of the age' as such—and in order to do this, *some* reference to a theory of language variety is going to be necessary.

So far I have been discussing aspects of language variation which are basically group uses of language. The remaining factor accounting for linguistic heterogeneity stands apart from all these, in that it is concerned with the language habits idiosyncratic to a person, those which distin-guish him from the other members of a group, as opposed to integrating him linguistically with them. In one sense, of course, linguistic idio-syncrasy is less important than the dimensions of variety outlined above, as we can only be aware of idiosyncrasy against a background of non-idiosyncrasy: we cannot recognize the individuality of an author until we are first aware of the language habits of his time, i.e. the linguistic features of the various dialects, provinces, and so on, against which background he can display himself. And this means that any study of individuals requires the prior recognition of the more general linguistic usages contemporaneous with him. (This explains the difficulty of try-ing to identify the authorship of texts in languages which are no longer spoken—as in the case of the Pauline epistles. Whether the linguistic idiosyncrasies of the epistles are those of one man [=Paul?] or not depends on whether we can first eliminate from the discussion those features common to other letter-writers of the period, and those common to the language as a whole at that time. And in view of the fact that there is so little comparative material extant, it is doubtful whether the problem is soluble.) In one sense, then, linguistic idiosyncrasy is subordinate to the study of shared uses of English; and this is of course the position taken by those who are engaged in teaching the language, where they are in the first instance trying to teach the language 'as a whole', and disregarding those features which belong to individuals. But from the point of view of the study of style, idiosyncrasy—as some of the viewpoints outlined at the beginning of this chapter suggest—becomes of primary importance.

One thing must be made clear at this point. By 'idiosyncrasy' I am not referring to those uncontrolled, and normally uncontrollable features of our spoken or written utterance which are due entirely to our physical state and which will always be present in everything we speak or write. In everything we say, there will always be an idiosyncratic voice-quality, a background vocal effect which identifies us as an individual, and this we do not normally change (unless we are professional actors or mimics, of course). The analogue to voice quality in the written medium is our personal handwriting. Similarly, if we speak with a particular kind of speech defect, or using some psychopathologically-induced set of recurrent images, these may well be idiosyncratic, but this too is a different sense from that intended by the concept of stylistic idiosyncrasy. In the latter case, I am referring to the linguistic distinctiveness an individual can introduce into his language which is not shared by other members of society (i.e. not a variety) and which is capable of conscious control. The author of the language may choose to put something in or leave something out. The important word here is 'may', as very often, depending on someone's experience of using his language, specific linguistic indices of personality may make their appearance with apparently no conscious effort on the author's part. We are all familiar with the linguistic idiosyncrasies of certain public figures or of favourite authors; we talk about an author's name being 'stamped indelibly on every page', and so forth. But in principle this is something over which the author has a large measure of control: he can change words, alter their order, add and delete at will. His is the decision which ultimately controls what we see or hear, and which ultimately defines his individuality in the use of language. The linguist's job here is to identify and explain the idiosyncratic effects which an author has introduced into his use of language, to see whether these form any kind of pattern, and to try to demonstrate their purpose in relation to the work as a whole.

It is important to emphasize, once again, that the linguist does not have an evaluative role in this matter: his is, basically, a descriptive task.

He is not studying an author's work to decide whether it is good or bad, representative of this quality or literary tradition or that: its 'place' in literature is not of primary importance to him, *as linguist*—though of course this may well have entered into his decision as to which text to analyse in the first place, a decision not made on linguistic grounds. The linguist is primarily concerned with ensuring that all features relevant to the identification of an author's own behaviour are understood. If some features are omitted through ignorance, he would argue, then there is a very real danger of relevant information for the overall qualitative assessment of the author by the critic being overlooked. The reason why *stylistics*, the linguistic study of what is considered to be 'style', has become so popular over recent years, it would seem, is precisely that, using the traditional methods of language analysis and literary criticism, so much of importance for this basic assessment *does* get overlooked. Students of literature, or of any use of English, frequently begin their analysis of a text in a highly impressionistic way, relying on their innate sensitivity to produce the results they seek. But sensitive response alone is—apart from very rare cases—an inadequate basis for reaching a clear understanding of the message which is being communicated. Most people do not have the ability to approach the study of the language of a text in any systematic, objective kind of way. The gifted few, it is true, may be able to sum up the relevance of a poem for them without entering into any systematic procedure of analysis; but for the majority, the initial aesthetic response needs to be supplemented by some technique which will help to clarify the meaning of a text. Stylistics, then, hopes to provide just such a technique of comprehensive analysis, so that, once it has been mastered, students of language may find it easier to appreciate the complexity of language use.

This now brings me to the final aspect of stylistics which I want to discuss here, namely, What *are* the techniques whereby the 'style' of a text can be analysed? The kinds of language variation which may be found in any piece of language, we must remember, reduce to three basic types: there are the features I have called 'dialectal' (regional, class, historical) which partition the English language in terms of one set of dimensions; cutting across these, there is a second set of dimensions, relating to specific factors in social situations, such as occupation, relative status, and purpose; and thirdly, there is the the possibility of idiosyncratic variation, which allows for the modification of the group norms by individual users. It needs a fairly sophisticated stylistic theory to be able to account for every factor; but from the point of view of specifying a procedure for analysis, *all* these dimensions of language variation can be studied in precisely the same way, using any of a number of possible techniques suggested by General Linguistics.

Exactly which technique we use will of course be the outcome of our particular training and predilections, and of the specific theory of language structure we may adhere to. These days, there is a great deal of controversy as to which of the many linguistic theories available provides the best basis for the analysis of any given piece of language, but the existence of certain features, or 'levels' of language structure, seems to be generally recognized; consequently it is probably easiest to illustrate the kind of preconception a linguist might bring to bear in studying a text from the stylistic point of view by outlining what is involved in these levels. The most useful levels of structure to recognize for stylistic purposes have already been discussed in the earlier part of this book: phonetics, phonology, grammar, vocabulary, and semantics. (The concepts of phonetics and phonology are primarily reserved for the study of speech: for the study of a written text, the analogous levels could be referred to as 'graphetics' and 'graphology' respectively.) I would argue that the distinctiveness of *any* text can be broken down in terms of these levels: whatever distinctive stylistic feature we may encounter in English, it can be described as operating at one or some combination of these levels.

To obtain a clearer picture of what is involved, I shall illustrate the kind of distinctiveness which might occur at each level, taking my examples primarily from literary texts. At the phonetic level would be studied any general features of sound which help to characterize a text, such as when a particular voice quality (or set of qualities) is associated with a particular use of language (as in much religious and legal professional speech). The 'clerical' voice is a well-recognized phenomenon, and this principally refers to a quite different 'set' of the vocal organs from that normally used by the clergyman in everyday conversation. Also under phonetics, one would consider those aspects of speech which would normally be referred to under the heading of 'sound symbolism'—a hypothesized capacity of sounds to reflect intrinsically objects, events, and so on, in real life. This view may be illustrated by people who claim that there is something in the nature of an [i:] sound, for instance, which makes it necessarily relate to smallness in size, or whiteness, or something else; or that onomatopoeic words—such as 'splash', or 'cuckoo'—could have no other shape because they contain the sounds of real life ('biscuits are so called because of the sound they make when you break them'). These arguments have been generally shown to be unfounded. Even such clearly onomatopoeic words as 'splash' vary in their form from one language to the next, showing evidence of non-naturalistic influence; and there are always counter-examples to any generalization we might care to make about the 'inherent meaning' of sounds such as [i:]. But it is nonetheless the case that various uses of language (poetry being the clearest example) do

261

try to make use of speech sounds in as evocative a way as possible. If a poet considers a particular sound to have a powerful atmosphere-creating potential, then he may well make use of it (i.e. words containing it) more frequently than usual. Of course we have to remember that in general we can only interpret sounds in a given way once we know the theme being expressed by the words: [s] sounds in a poem about a swan may well reflect the noise of the water, but in a poem about evil might equally appropriately be intended to conjure up the noise of serpents, and the like—in other words, there is no 'general meaning' for the [s] sound in language, or even in English. But having said this, we may still plot the way the poet manipulates specific sounds, seen as individual, atmosphere-setting sonic effects, to reinforce a particular theme, and this would be studied at the phonetic level of analysis. In the written medium, we would be referring on similar grounds to such matters as the general size and shape of the type being used (such as in the distinctiveness of posters, newspapers), and the lay-out of a text on a page (as when Herbert writes a poem about an altar in the shape of an altar). The phonetic and graphetic levels of analysis, then, to a certain extent overlap with non-linguistic considerations (e.g. matters of colouring), but the point is that from the stylistic point of view, even such non-linguistic matters as choice of colour might have a contribution to make to the definition of the distinctiveness of a particular use of language—and thus by definition would have to be allowed for in any stylistic theory.

The phonological and graphological levels are easier to illustrate as they relate to more familiar matters. There are, broadly speaking, two areas of potential distinctiveness: what I would refer to for speech as the *segmental* and the *non-segmental* areas. Segmental characteristics of style would cover the use of specific vowels and consonants within a particular language's sound system in combination in a distinctive way, as when we make use of reduplicative effects such as alliteration, assonance, and rhyme in English. It is important to note that these devices have a major structural, as well as an aesthetic, function—that is, they are the province of phonology, as opposed to phonetics. Alliteration, for example, may well have an important aesthetic appeal; but from the point of view of its overall function in a poem, it has an equally important—and sometimes a more important—role as an organizing process, linking words more closely than would otherwise be the case. For example, when we read such a line as 'Thron'd in the centre of his thin designs' (from Pope's *Epistle to Dr. Arbuthnot*), the major function of the alliteration is to force the words 'thron'd' and 'thin' together, and thus produce a juxtaposition of the concepts 'mediated' by the words, which in the present context produces an ironic contrast. This kind of thing is presumably one of the factors underlying phrases such as 'fusion of meaning', or when we talk about a poet's 'intensifying' meaning. And similar illustrations could be found for the other reduplicative segmental processes. In passing, we should note that it is difficult to generalize about phonological distinctiveness for more than one language. Such matters as alliteration and rhyme are essentially deviations from the normal ways of distributing consonant and other phonemes in English. That is why these effects are so noticeable: they are not normally encountered in our contact with English. In a language where initial reduplication of phonemes *was* normal, however—where prefixes were the routine way of indicating cases, for instance—then much less effect would be gained by alliteration, and we could anticipate that other phonological features than this would be used to produce dramatic and other effects. Similarly, in a language like Latin, where—because of the inflectional endings—it is difficult *not* to rhyme to some extent, we do not find rhyme being used as a literary device with anything like the same frequency as in English.

The other aspect of phonology is the non-segmental; that is, the features of intonation, rhythm, speed, loudness of articulation, and other vocal effects we introduce into speech in order to communicate attitudes, emphasis, and so on. Spoken English is highly distinctive from this point of view. Taking intonation patterns alone, there would be good grounds for distinguishing between most varieties of spoken English currently in use. There is the characteristically wide range of pitch movement in the public-speaker as opposed to the narrower range in everyday conversation; the 'chanting' effect of the sermon; the restrained, regular movement of the newsreader; and so on. And when we consider features other than pitch, our classification can become very precise: compare the varying speed and loudness of the sports commentator with the measured speed, loudness and pause of the professional reader; the many vocal effects (such as increasing and decreasing the tension of the muscles of the vocal organs for stretches of utterance, which produces a tense, 'metallic' effect and a lax effect respectively) which are introduced into the use of English for television advertising; or the primary role of rhythmic variations in establishing the linguistic basis of poetry. It should be clear from these examples that a great deal of our awareness of stylistic distinctiveness in speech derives from the perception of 'prosodic features' of this kind. When we vaguely hear speech in the distance and say 'That sounds like . . .', we are generally basing our judgment on the dominant prosodic variations we can hear.

The analogous features to phonology in the writing-system of a language can be roughly summarized as the spelling and punctuation of that language. I say 'roughly', because a great deal more is covered by graphology than is traditionally understood by these labels, e.g. the difference between upper and lower case symbols is of systematic importance in English (and not just a matter of aesthetic appeal): it can be used distinctively, as when we write something out in capitals to achieve extra prominence, or when we introduce a graphological change in order to indicate a change in context (without actually having to say so), as when Eliot writes

> I didn't mince my words, I said to her myself,
> HURRY UP PLEASE ITS TIME
> Now Albert's coming back ... (*The Waste Land*)

In English, variations in spelling for special effects are uncommon, though we do find archaic spellings introduced into poetry, or notices printed in an old-fashioned way. An example of this, again from Eliot (*East Coker*), is a good example of the impact of the visual medium which could not possibly be translated into spoken form:

> And see them dancing around the bonfire
> The association of man and woman
> In daunsinge, signifying matrimonie—
> A dignified and commodious sacrament.
> Two and two, necessarye coniunction,
> Holding eche other by the hand or the arm
> Whiche betokeneth concorde.

More commonly in English, we find variations in punctuation, even to the extent of occasionally omitting this altogether (as in the final pages of Joyce's *Ulysses*, for example).

Vocabulary, a language user's 'choice of words', or 'diction', as it is sometimes called, is presumably so familiar an aspect of a person's style that it does not need detailed illustration here. At this level, stylistics tries to determine the extent to which certain words, combinations of words, and types of word are part of the distinctiveness of a use of language. All varieties of English make use of a restricted kind of vocabulary, e.g. the learnéd, technical vocabulary of scientific English, the loosely colloquial vocabulary of informal conversation, the formal, precise vocabulary of legal documents, the archaic vocabulary of much of religious English, and so on. Sometimes a variety can be identified merely on the basis of certain items of vocabulary, as in the use of such words as 'heretofore', which is used only in legal English or attempts to simulate it. More often than this, however, a style is lexically distinctive due to certain words being used more, or less, frequently than in other varieties or individuals—an author may be said to have his 'favourite' words, for instance. Or there may be a particular distribution and proportion of various categories of word in a text, e.g. the highly distinctive mixture of technical, slang, formal and informal vocabulary in sports commentary, or the parallel use of technical terms and non-technical glosses in many kinds of lecturing. Again, an individual may produce stylistic effects by coining new words (e.g. 'theirhisnothis', Joyce) or by putting unexpected words in a standardized context, as in Thomas's 'a grief ago' (where the expectation of a noun of time imbues the notion of grief with temporal associations) and similar examples. The choice of a specific word is one aspect of style; the placing of that word in a specific context is another, quite different aspect.

In studying vocabulary, we are of course studying meaning to a certain extent, but meaning is not restricted to single words or small combinations of words. Of relevance for stylistic study is the way in which the overall meaning of a use of language is organized, and it is this more general study of meaning which takes place at what I call the 'semantic' level. For example, when we talk about the 'theme' of a poem or novel, or discuss the 'progression' of ideas in a play or an income tax form, we are referring to the most general patterns of meaning that we have been able to discern in a text, and there is a great deal of stylistic significance to be said here, if this is done systematically. The semantic organization of a lecture, for example, with its steady development interspersed by passages of recapitulation and anticipatory summary (e.g. 'there are three things I'd like to say about this . . .') is quite different from the regular, alternating flow of descriptive narrative and background comment which characterizes a sports commentary, and this is different again from the near-random progression of ideas in conversation. I take my examples here from the less familiar (spoken) varieties: in the written medium, the concept of the paragraph, which is a semantic unit (cf. the notion of 'topic sentence', and so on), has long been with us, as have such visualist devices as sub-headings, spacing variations, and diagrams, which make the movement of thought relatively unambiguous and easy to perceive.

Finally, there is the grammatical level of analysis, which is probably the most important component of any stylistic description. There is invariably more to be said about the grammar of a text than about any other level, and in order to make a successful study here it is essential to have fairly clear ideas about the general nature of English grammar, as suggested by some grammatical theory. It is impossible even to outline what would be involved in a complete grammatical description of a text here: some further reading on this question is given in the Bibliography at the end of the chapter. But if we consider merely the kind of variations which occur at *one* point in English grammar, it might be possible to get an impression of the overall complexity involved, and so not underestimate the scope of grammatical analysis. The *type of sentence* one may find in a text is often a reasonably unambiguous diagnostic indication of its provenance. There is nothing like the long complex sentences of legal documentation elsewhere in English. The language of instructions has a very restricted range of sentence structures at its disposal (high frequency of imperatives and imperative-like elements, absence of questions). Newspaper reporting generally makes use of relatively short, uncomplicated sentences. Newsreading (and most other forms of radio narrative) never uses anything other than statements. In scientific English, equations and formulae can replace elements of sentence structure and sometimes whole sentences. In commentary, conversation, and advertising, there is a very frequent and varied use of 'minor' sentences (i.e. structures which function as sentences, but which do not have the subject-predicate structure characteristic of the majority of English sentences—as in 'hello', 'sorry', 'Coming!', and so on). The traditional distinction between *simple*, *compound*, *complex* and *mixed* sentence types is relevant for categorizing the kinds of distinctiveness we find in texts, and these categories can be further subdivided—the number and type of subordinate clauses, for example, varies considerably from variety to variety as would be clearly shown by a comparison of political public speaking (where they are very frequent, tending to pile up on each other in rhetorical climaxes) with radio news broadcasting (in the latter, subordinate clauses are common, but their distribution is more sporadic, and they rarely are used in anything approaching a 'cumulative' way). In literature, changes in the direction of the plot, or the theme, can be indicated by altering the kind of sentences generally being used; and this device is of course extremely common as one index (often the most noticeable) of character —Dickens, for example, regularly gives his characters a predictable linguistic basis, and sentence structure usually has an important distinctive role to play in this. Again, the absence of clear sentence boundaries may be a major way of communicating a particular effect, as with certain stream-of-consciousness techniques. And there is a great deal else which can be manipulated to make sentences work in a distinctive way (e.g. the devices that may be introduced in order to *link* sentences to each other, such as cross-referencing, repetitions of words, the use of adverbs like 'however' and conjunctions).

This has been a very brief outline of a possible method of discovering some principle(s) of organization in the mass of linguistic features which constitute the distinctiveness of a use of English. It should be clear that *all* levels of analysis enter into this distinctiveness, though some (the grammatical and lexical in particular) have a more dominant role on most occasions. The concept of 'style' which emerges from this approach, when seen within the perspective of language varieties as presented earlier, is thus very much a cumulative, developing, dynamic one: it is essentially a descriptive convenience which summarizes our awareness at any given moment of the controllable linguistic features that distinguish one use of English from any other. The specification of these uses is in terms of the dimensions of variation outlined in the first half of this chapter: the features are identified and inter-related in terms of the levels of analysis outlined in the second half. It is in such attempts to provide a relatively objective way of talking about and analysing language variation systematically, precisely, and comprehensively, that linguistics hopes to be able to make a permanent contribution to the study of English style.

BIBLIOGRAPHY

For further discussion and illustration of the approach outlined in this chapter, see D. Crystal and D. Davy, *Investigating English Style* (London, 1969). Detailed and systematic discussion of stylistic considerations in the study of poetry can be found in G. N. Leech, *A Linguistic Guide to English Poetry* (London, 1969), and W. Nowottny, *The Language Poets Use* (London, 1962). Further illustration of linguistically-orientated approaches can be seen in R. Quirk, *The Use of English* (London, 1968, 2nd edn.), chapters 10, 14, and 15; N. E. Enkvist, M. Gregory and J. Spencer, *Linguistics and Style* (London, 1964); S. Ullmann, *Language and Style* (Oxford, 1964); T. A. Sebeok (ed.), *Style in Language* (Cambridge, Mass., 1960); and *A Review of English Literature*, Vol. 6, No. 1, for April 1965. A more traditional account of the study of style is J. Middleton Murry, *The Problem of Style* (London, 1st edn. 1922). Detailed study of a specific variety of English is in G. N. Leech, *English in Advertising: a Linguistic Study of Advertising in Great Britain* (Longmans, 1966). An illustration of stylistic detection work is A. Ellegård, *Who was Junius?* (Almqvist and Wiksell, 1962). Useful periodicals on this field are *Style* (University of Arkansas) and *Language and Style* (Southern Illinois University). A good bibliography of stylistics in relation to English is R. W. Bailey and D. M. Burton, *English Stylistics: A Bibliography* (Cambridge, Mass., 1968). Two valuable authologies of articles are S. Chatman and S. R. Levin (eds.), *Essay on the Language of Literature* (Boston, 1967), and D. C. Freedman (ed.) *Linguistics and Literary Style* (New York, 1970).

7

THE EARLY HISTORY OF ENGLISH

Professor W. F. Bolton, Douglass College, Rutgers University

I

We do not know when, how, or where language began. It was in any case immeasurably long before written documents, and beyond the earliest recollections of surviving folk-memory. Some students have argued that this or that kind of datable edifice or tool could not have been made or used except by human creatures capable of speech. The argument is subjective. Nor can we say that the progress of language in mankind was like the progress of language-learning in an infant; almost surely it was not. And we do not know whether language began in a single place on the globe and spread through the world, diversifying from region to region until its common origin became completely disguised, or whether it grew up as an independent development at various times and places when different societies reached the stage that would initiate and support it. The latter is more probable. All of our knowledge is based on written records, a comparatively recent development, and on what the written records enable us to infer: half a dozen surviving words in related languages may suggest a hypothetical formula for the lost original from which all derive.

This comparative method, however, enables us to push back only a little further than the earliest written records to their immediate antecedents. Now the earliest documents in some western language families are about 4,000 years old, but those in others little more than 1,000 years. It is plain that we cannot get uniform results with uneven evidence like this. And of course the results are most uncertain just when they are most interesting, that is, when they are pushed back the furthest beyond written evidence. But one feature of language as it passes from one time and place to another is of great help: we know that the alterations of linguistic sounds are regular, that is, the same sound in language A will not become two or three different sounds as it passes into language B, so long as other conditions remain the same. We are thus enabled to study the history of sounds rather than the history of words, and we are not obliged to find the same word in all the languages under study before we can make a start. Sound, for the historian of language, is the basic material just as it is for the analyst of our contemporary language, although for somewhat different reasons. The historian is also like the modern analyst in that he goes on to classify the further categories of language as morphology (shapes of words) syntax (shapes of sentences), and vocabulary. He differs from his colleague in depending wholly on what he can learn from surviving written records—and the ones that survive are not always the ones he would have chosen for his purpose.

In fact, the written records are at once essential and inadequate for the historian of any language, and it is best to take a page or two at this point to say what the inadequacies are: these general considerations must be applied to almost everything that follows, for they have much the same force in every age of the English language before the invention of printing. Incompleteness of survival is the first difficulty. We may take it as an axiom that no historian of language ever has sufficient documents old enough to satisfy him. Of course the employment of writing goes back much further than the beginnings of English, but as it happens the first speakers in England of what was to become our language were almost certainly unlettered when they arrived in the middle of the fifth century. Literacy arrived about 150 years after, but it was Latin literacy, and the earliest surviving records in English—which used and adapted the Latin alphabet—are another 150 years later, that is mid-eighth century. And the late date of these papers is only one feature of their unrepresentativeness; language exists in time *and* space, and the distribution of the evidence in space is as poor as that in time. We find a feature or form in the south-west of England, for example, but we are very fortunate indeed if we find anything to compare it with in the north-east, so we are unable to say that 'X is distinctive and restricted to the south-west' but usually only that 'X is found in the south-west'. For a linguistic level like sound it is not perhaps so disastrous, because the stock of sounds in any one dialect is small and therefore most sounds will be represented in even a restricted body of evidence. But it becomes a different matter for morphemes and even more so for words.

The second difficulty is that of the relation of spelling to sound. If a thousand years from now a linguistic historian found English *confection*, French *confection*, and German *Konfektion* in several documents, he would rightly conclude that they were connected, especially as the only difference was constant, that is, the German represents English and French *c* with *k* on both occasions. But he would not know that this regularity corresponded to a spelling habit rather than a speech habit, and that in fact the *c* or *k* in the three forms of the word represents the sound which is most alike in the different languages, and that the word is otherwise almost unrecognizably varied in the way Englishmen, Frenchmen and Germans pronounce it. The only way he might arrive at this important differentiation would be by hearing tapes or records made a thousand years before, or by reading what writers said the words sounded like—especially if those writers described the sounds in terms of their articulation (unvoiced velar stop, etc.) instead of using subjective or relative terms ('the hard *c*' uses both). The historian in the far future will have these two kinds of evidence to work with, for they are being produced in profusion today; but the historians today have nothing of the sort with which to investigate the English of a thousand years ago. They must depend on inferences drawn from the previous and later history of the language insofar as they know it, and they always run the risk of circular reasoning.

The third difficulty relates to the first, the matter of adequate records from every point in time and space, but we can illustrate it with our hypothetical future historian. We must presume that he recognizes that his documents are written in three different languages, but he cannot write linguistic history with only that information. It would be very difficult for him to make much historical use of his documents unless he also knows whether they represented American or British English, Parisian or Marseilles French, Hamburg or Munich German, and so forth; and if British, whether that of London or Liverpool, and if London whether that of Belgravia or Battersea. Nor—unless a title page, or the dateline on a letter, or the like survived—would he know within several hundred years when the documents were written, and whether his copy was perhaps made at a place and time far removed from the original; if so, the writer of the late copy would very likely have mixed a large number of his own speech forms and spelling conventions with those of his source. Once again there is evidence ... handwriting, binding, references to historical events, etc. .... that will help when explicit statements about time and place are missing, but it is relatively uncertain. During much of the time we are studying, the kind of documents that often begin with a date and a place, like deeds, were usually written in Latin.

Our history of the early stages of the English language, then, can be realistically written—and realistically read—only if writer and reader make the following admission: that a term like 'early West Saxon' does *not* refer to the language spoken in Wessex up to the year about 900, but rather to the linguistic agreements among the sounds, forms and words as they are reflected in the few surviving documents which, although of uncertain date and origin, appear to represent that time and area. Of course this is putting the case at its worst, and in fact careful work over the last century and more has produced and is still producing results of remarkable solidity on which the following pages are based. But almost none of these results is so solid that it might not be changed by the addition of new evidence, in some cases the discovery of only one more document, or by the application of new methods, especially the mechanical or computer analysis of existing material.

2

With so much at our disposal, we can say a few things about the pre-history of English, the story of what it was before it appears in the oldest surviving documents. We know that the natural history of any language or language family is that of continual differentiation: that is, in the course of time one language becomes two or more, and they in turn divide again. Some aspects of modern communications have a superficial levelling effect, so that features of different dialects sometimes appear to coalesce; but such changes are few, and the causes that bring them about are very recent. In the main, language tends the other way, and the migrations of people make such change more rapid and extreme, both because it isolates them from other speakers of the same mother-tongue, and because it exposes them to the influences of other linguistic communities.

The very existence of variety in any one language proves this view. If we take several of the many present-day varieties of English, we may account for the differences among them in one of three ways:

(1) The differences go back to the very beginning of language, that is, several varieties of English existed from the first moment man began to speak, and continue to exist today. OR

(2) English is the point of convergence of many different languages, and the varieties of modern English are merely the descendants of even more different tongues all on their way to becoming English. OR

(3) English is merely the general name for a variety of linguistic practices, the differences among which are the result of the natural tendency of languages to diverge from common originals over the course of time.

The first explanation sees the varieties as parallel in their development: ↓ ↓ ↓

The second sees them as convergent: ↘ ↓ ↙

The third sees them as divergent: ↙ ↓ ↘

No other explanation fully accounts for the situation of variety which we confront today, and of the three, the first two are obviously impossible. The third therefore stands demonstrated, proving that languages change over time in the direction of greater differentiation.

On this principle, what we should expect—and what we find—is that the various forms of English now spoken go back to a relatively few originals of which we have record, and that they in turn go back to a single original of which we have no record. This original likewise is one of several branches from a single stock, some others of which still survive or leave descendants. The image of a tree implied in words like 'stock' and 'branch' will serve well enough for a visual model of this development (so long as we do not think that the process involved in linguistic change is anything like that which makes a tree grow as it does). As far back as we can go by hypothetical reconstruction ... 'ground level' ... is the common language spoken about five or six thousand years ago, perhaps somewhere in central Europe. Because the speakers of this tongue who went eastward gave rise to some of the languages of modern India, and those who went westward brought the parent of the most of the languages of modern Europe, the language of the stock is usually called Indo-European. It had nine main branches: Indian (which gave, among others, Sankskrit and Hindi); Iranian; Armenian; Albanian; Baltic-Slavonic; Celtic; Greek; Latin; Germanic. Not all of these branches sprang from the parent stock at the same point so that some branches are more distantly related than others. English is a member of the Germanic branch, and its closest external affinities are with the Greek and Latin branches. By the time the earliest surviving documents in English were written, classical Greek and even more classical Latin had altered and vanished. We are consequently unable to make direct comparisons between these related languages in the same state of their development. Even so, some Old English words can, when compared with Latin words, suggest a great deal about the relationship between them. Old English *hwæt*: Latin *quod*, *fæder*: *pater*, *heaford*: *caput*, *fotes*: *pedis*.

Not much here strikes us at first, but after a bit we notice that Old English *t* regularly appears as Latin *d*, Old English *f* as Latin *p*, and—if we recall that Latin *quod* begins with a *kw-* sound—Old English *h* as Latin *k*, spelled with a *c* or *q*. These generalizations can be extended in our description of Old English and Latin, and other different ones could be formulated for Old English and other languages. But the point to remember is this: it is not the similarity of individual words which shows the relation of two languages. Modern Arabic is unrelated to English, but has borrowed a number of English words. It is rather the pattern of the sounds in corresponding words that shows the relationship. Grammar too—another kind of pattern—tells us a great deal about related languages, and we shall see that Old English retains many similarities with Latin that Modern English has long lost. Our word *consolation*, on the other hand, although it is closely akin to a Latin word, tells us nothing about the relation of English and Latin to their common stock, because it is borrowed directly from Latin, not a collateral descendant of it.

273

Just as a number of branches radiate from the common stock of Indo-European, so a further number spring from the branch we have called Germanic. They are three: East Germanic, which has no survivors and was represented chiefly by Gothic; North Germanic, of which the modern Scandinavian languages are the survivors; and West Germanic, including modern Dutch, German, and English. (A sub-branch of West Germanic, 'Ingvaeonic', included all the languages but Old High German.) These groupings can all be traced in each category of language: sound, vocabulary, morphology, and syntax. We have seen how a certain sound-change sets the Germanic languages apart from the others in the Indo-European family. Sound changes give the clearest evidence, but the distribution of vocabulary is significant too. Some words, in one form or another, are common to all members of the Indo-European family, and some to only one branch or sub-branch or language, thus:

English: Old English *acan* ('ache')

Common Ingvaeonic: Old English *bysig*, Old Dutch *bezich* ('busy')

Common West Germanic: Old English *gast*, Old Low German *gêst*, Old High German *geist* ('ghost', 'spirit')

Common Germanic: Old English *sæ*, Old Icelandic *sær*, Gothic *saiws*, etc. ('sea')

Common Indo-European: Latin *pater*, Old English *fæder*, Sanskrit *pitar*, etc. ('father')

Hence we may talk of common 'levels' of vocabulary which, along with the other features of sound, morphology, and syntax, enable us to distinguish the branches and sub-branches of the Indo-European language stock. We can observe that Old English has a pre-history, a period of development which is older than our oldest records. We have no written records of Common Indo-European, Germanic, West Germanic, Ingvaeonic, or early Old English (although Greek, Sanskrit and Latin records give us evidence of languages contemporary with and related to Germanic and its descendants). We can judge, from the late surviving records in related languages, something of what this pre-history was, and we shall need to do so in order to understand the surviving records properly; but we can never reconstruct the earliest days of the English language fully.

3

The Germanic tribesmen from northern Europe who settled in Britain in the mid-fifth century were not the first invaders of the island: the Romans in 55 B.C. and, long before them, the Celts had come, the

Romans for an occupation that lasted five hundred years and the Celts as permanent inhabitants who survived both the Roman and the Saxon invasions. The departed Romans left little linguistic heritage except in some place-names and in a few words taken over from Latin by the Celts. The Saxon invaders, when they came, likewise brought a few words of Latin taken over from the Romans who occupied territory near the Saxon homeland on the Continent. And of course when the Saxons subjugated the Celts in Britain, the resulting mixture of races left a Celtic imprint on the Saxon vocabulary, but again it was a very slight one, largely restricted to place-names. All in all there was little language mixture in England between the coming of the Saxons around 450 and the coming of the Roman missionaries 150 years later.

As Bede tells us, the Germanic tribesmen whom we have been calling 'Saxons' for convenience were in fact from three tribes, the Saxons, Angles and Jutes, and they settled in different parts of the country: the Jutes in Kent and the Isle of Wight, the Saxons in the southwest, and the Angles in the Midlands and north. Doubtless, for the reasons already mentioned, the tribes spoke different dialects of the Ingvaeonic branch of West Germanic, and these differences became accentuated in England. As a result there are four chief dialects of Old English, two of which correspond to tribal origins: Kentish in the Jutish area and West Saxon in the Saxon; the Anglian area divided linguistically into Mercian between the Thames and the Humber, and Northumbrian northwards.

Among the varieties of speech, we can sometimes mark a difference in rate of change: many features of American English, for example, are more conservative than British English. But all languages change, and no tongue represents fully and faithfully the features of its antecedents. Those derivatives of a common original which are relatively more conservative than others have, in any case, no claim to be 'better' because of their conservatism: conservatism in language neither results from nor imparts linguistic superiority, and in fact 'superiority' is not a notion that relates to any demonstrable feature of language.

We have no way of knowing which of the three Germanic dialects brought by the invaders was most like Ingvaeonic, and in any case the isolation of the settlers in various parts of England prevented any one from gaining the ascendancy over the others. It was only much later, probably during the ninth century, that the increasing political unity of the country brought the dialects into contact and hence, in a manner of speaking, into competition: and then the event was not decided on the basis of the comparative adequacy of Kentish, West Saxon, Mercian or Northumbrian, but on the dialect origins of the men who had brought about the unification, who were in the main West Saxons. Hence it was for entirely non-linguistic reasons that West Saxon became the premier dialect of Old English. But because our written records for the most part do not go back further than the century of this linguistic domination, they reflect it. We have scant evidence for any Old English dialect but West Saxon, and the study of Old English must concentrate on the forms of that variety, much as the study of Old Norse comes down to the study of Old Icelandic because the literary survivals in that language dominate the documents in early Scandinavian. Some of the features we are going to describe are therefore common features of Old English over the six hundred years it was spoken in England, but some may be only West Saxon, especially West Saxon of the last century and a half before the Conquest when our documents are most plentiful.

Let us have a look at some literary Late West Saxon. This passage comes from the opening lines of Blickling Homily IX:

> We gehyrdon oft secggan be þam æþelan tocyme ures Drihtnes, hu He Him on þas world þingian ongan, þæt heahfæderas sægdon and cyþdon, þæt witigan witigodan and heredon, þæt sealmsceopas sungon and sægdon, þæt se wolde cuman of þam cynestole and of þæm þrymrice hider on þas world . . . 'We have often heard say regarding the noble advent of Our Lord, how He commenced to reconcile Himself with this world, which the patriarchs said and made-known, which the prophets prophesied and praised, which the psalmists sang and said, that He would come from the royal throne and from the realm of glory hither into this world . . .'

A number of the words are still perfectly familiar, with the same form and meaning: *We*, *oft*, *he*, *him*, *on*, *world*, *and*, *of*. A further number have changed in spelling but not very much in form and meaning: *þæt*, 'that'; *hider* 'hither', *wolde*, 'would', *ures*, 'our, ours', *hu*, 'how', *cuman*, 'come', *be*, 'by, regarding'.

But some words from this passage which still survive have changed much more radically in form: *gehyrdon*, 'heard', *seccgan*, 'say', *sægdon*, 'said', *sungon*, 'sang', *þas*, 'this', *þam* or *þæm* (pronounced 'tham'), 'the'. Finally, there are a number of words which have disappeared from the language entirely, or which survive only in distantly related forms or in dialect words: *æþelan*, 'noble' (cf. the name Ethel); *Drihtnes*, 'Lord's'; *þingian*, 'reconcile'; *ongan*, 'commenced' (cf. 'began'); *cyþdon*, 'made known' (cf. 'uncouth', 'not familiar'); *witigan*, *witigodan*, 'prophets', 'prophesied' (cf. 'wit', 'witty'); *heredon*, 'praised'; *se*, 'he'. A special group of these lost words includes the compounds *tocyme*, 'advent', *heahfæderas*, 'patriarchs', *sealmsceopas*, 'psalmists', *cynestole*, 'royal throne', *þrymrice*, 'realm of glory.' It is noteworthy that in translating the words and compounds that have disappeared from the language, I have almost always used modern words which are of Latin or Greek origin: 'noble', 'reconcile', 'commenced', 'prophets' and 'prophesied', 'praised', 'advent', 'patriarch', 'psalmists', 'royal throne', 'realm of glory'. When the native Old English words passed out of use after the Norman Conquest, their place was taken by words the Normans brought with them, Latin words or French words taken from the Latin, and many of these are the words we use today.

Now if we look at these four groups of words more carefully, we shall see that they have something more in common than their resemblance to or difference from their modern equivalents. The words that changed least include three pronouns, two prepositions, and one conjunction, as well as one adverb and one noun. Most of these words, that is, are 'grammatical' words, words which help form the backbone of the sentence but are not full of referential meaning in their own right. They are called closed-class words, because they are relatively few in number, and because they change in membership and form very slowly. The next group, the words which have changed only a little, is mostly other closed-class words: two conjunctions, a preposition, a modal auxiliary verb, as well as another adverb and a verb. When we move on to the third class, the words that have survived but only in a deeply changed form, we find there are only two closed-class words, the definite and demonstrative articles, but there are three verbs (including two tenses of one of them). The verbs are common ones in every-day use: 'hear', 'say', 'sing'. When finally we come to the group in which the changes have replaced the Old English words entirely, we find only one closed-class word, *se*; but five verbs, seven nouns, and one adjective. Many of these words are of less common use than 'world', 'come', 'say', 'hear', and 'sing', and some of them are very specialized.

These observations on the survival of words from Old English into Modern English hold pretty well for all the vocabulary of Old English. Of course we must not jump to conclusions about the familiarity of Old English words. Some of them changed a great deal in form, like *pæt* which we now spell 'that', but not much in sound; others changed more in sound than spelling: *we* was pronounced 'way', *he* 'hay', *world* rather like 'whorled'. Even when we are dealing with such old texts, the spelling is more stable over the years than the sound, and our passage would sound very unfamiliar if we heard it spoken aloud as the Anglo-Saxons heard it. A number of the sounds in Old English, like a number of the words, do not survive into our modern speech: one in particular is represented in the spelling of 'eight', 'high' and other words with 'gh', and sounded much like the 'ch' in German *ach*, but here the modern spelling commemorates a sound lost soon after the spelling became fixed. The Anglo-Saxons, indeed, pronounced all the letters in the words they spelled, so *ward* kept the 'r' it has lost in many modern forms of English, and even trilled it; *hwær* (modern 'where') sounded the *h* clearly, as did *hring* ('ring'), *hnecca* ('neck') and *hlinca* ('link'). On the other hand, some sounds of Modern English were absent from Old English: they are the ones that English took over from other languages after the Norman Conquest, or that came about as the result of sound-changes since then. They include the vowel sounds in 'house', 'proud'; 'joy', 'join'; 'my', 'might'.

But many of the changes that influenced the sound so greatly did not come about until five hundred years after the passage was written, and they are a later part of our story. We should not go on, however, without remarking on some common features in the sound and spelling changes that have taken place. You will have noticed how the symbol *þ* is replaced by our 'th'. Other changes are regular as well. The *d* in *hider* and *heahfæder*, for example, have both become 'th' in 'hither' and 'father'. And just as the symbol *æ* in *fæder* has been replaced by *a*, so it has too in *þæt*. The *u* in *ures* and *hu* has been replaced by 'ou' where it does not end the word ('our') and 'ow' where it does ('how'). So even though modern spelling is not entirely systematic, it has some regularities in its relation to the sound and spelling of Old English.

The words which have vanished from standard Modern English include five compounds. Old English was very fond of compounds, and often used them where we would use two words ('royal throne') or a phrase ('realm of glory'). Those two examples are made up entirely of native, that is Germanic, elements in the Old English vocabulary. Sometimes Old English writers would use native elements to render a Latin or other foreign word part by part, much as Modern German still often does when, for example, it writes *Fernsehe* 'far see' for *television*, a word whose Greek and Latin elements mean just what the German word does. Such renderings—element-for-element translations, if you like—are called *calques*. Both *tocyme* and *heahfæderas* are calques on *adventus* and *patriarchos* respectively: *to = ad*, *cyme, = -ventus*, *heah = archos*, *fæder = patri-*. (Actually, as we have already seen, *fæder* and *patri-* come from the same Indo-European source, as so, for that matter, do *cyme* and *-ventus*.) Yet another kind of compound which is characteristic of Old English word-formation is *sealm–sceopas*. The first element is Greek (by way of Latin) *psalm*; the *ps-* sound simplified in Old English pronunciation, as it is in Modern English, but they were more honest about the spelling. The *-a-* has become *-ea-* by the influence of the following *-lm*, a sound-change which—though perhaps not of great importance itself—shows how early the word came into Old English, for the intermediate change of *-a-* to *-æ-* took place at a very early date indeed, when English was only just becoming English. To this now well-naturalized word the Old English writer has added *sceop*, 'poet or singer', and created a compound of foreign plus English word. Such compounds were not so common in Old English as those in which both elements were native, and were largely restricted to foreign words which, like *sealm*, had become familiar and naturalized. The great period of combining foreign and native elements was the Middle English.

So far we have been looking at some aspects of Old English vocabulary that entered into the alteration or extinction of different sorts of word. Even after this discussion and the aid it brings in recognizing what are at first unfamiliar-looking words, you might not be able to read the sample passage by yourself. That is because Old English differs from Modern English not only in the membership of its vocabulary, and in the sounds and spellings of its words: it differs also in the way it relates words one to another in a sentence. There are three main ways of doing this in Modern English; we can alter the shape of a word, usually by adding an '-s' to denote the plural or the possessive ('father', 'fathers', 'father's'); we can alter the order of the words ('Father sees Jim', 'Jim sees father'); or we can introduce prepositions ('The father of Jim', 'The book of Albert'). Clearly all three ways work together to form a system, and if one of them changes, the others will too.

Now in Old English the first way was easier and more flexible to employ, because there were many meaningful endings to words in addition to the '-s' of plurality or possession. They had the '-s' as well, of course: you see it in the plural *heahfæderas* (singular *heahfæder*) and *sealmsceopas*, the possessive *Drihtnes* (nominative *Drihten*). There are also plurals in *-an*, like *witigan* (cf. modern 'oxen', 'children', 'brethren'), and a number of others; but a variety of ways to signal 'plural' does not really add to the number of things you can signal, merely to the ways you can do it. Old English gained its flexibility in being able to signal, in addition to the nominative and possessive, the direct and indirect object, singular and plural, masculine, feminine and neuter, all with word endings; and these word-endings applied not only to nouns, as the plural and possessive do today, but to adjectives as well, with a few changes, and to the definite articles. When, a few lines after the passage quoted, the writer says

> þa ealra fæmnena cwen cende þone soþan Scyppend and
> ealles folces Frefrend,
> 'the queen of all women gave birth to the true
> Maker and Comforter of all people',

we can follow him only if we know that *ealra fæmnena* is possessive plural, *ealles folces* possessive singular, and *þone soþan Scyppend* accusative singular; and we can make the distinction in the case of *Scyppend* only because the definite article is present, for as it happens *Scyppend* has no distinctive accusative ending, and the *-an* ending of *soþan* is shared with a number of other signals, of which the plural in *witigan* noted above is only one (the dative *æpelan* is another). A literal translation of the short example would be

> The of-all of-women queen gave-birth-to the
> true Maker and of-all of-people Comforter ...

We do not need to spell out all of the many variations in Old English word-ending to see how they signal the relation of one word to another in a way that word-order or the use of prepositions might otherwise be called on to do.

Of course prepositions and word-order do enter into the signalling system of Old English: the writer of the Blickling Homily used them extensively, more so than some other writers whose style was mainly dependent on word-endings. The Blickling writer has *be* ('by', 'regarding'), *on*, and *of* in important places, and his word-order is not altogether strange; but a measure of its variety is the placing of *pingian ongan* ('to reconcile commenced') at the end of its clause but of *wolde cuman* ('would come') near the beginning of its clause, and the reversal of the relative position of the finite and infinite verbs in the two phrases.

So the supply of word-endings for nouns was greater by far in Old English than in Modern English, and adjectives and articles—which are today completely without even the reduced word-endings of our nouns —had a full range too. What is more, verbs were capable of equally wide variation. In our example *seccgan*, *pingian* and *cuman* are all infinitives, marked with the termination *-an*. Sometimes today we mark infinitives with a signal borrowed from the prepositions, 'to': 'he commenced to reconcile . . .,' but often we do not: 'we have heard say', 'would come'. The forms of the Old English infinitives are thus more regular and more distinctive. The passage includes a number of finite verbs, two past singular (*ongan*, *wolde*) and many past plural (*gehyrdon*, *sægdon*, *cypdon*, *witigodon*, *heredon*, *sungon*). We may take note of two features of these finite verbs. One is that the plural verbs all have a distinctive ending *-on*, which the singular verbs lack. In Modern English, only the verb 'to be' distinguishes in the past between singular and plural; in the rest, one form caters for the past of all numbers and persons. Here again Old English has a greater range of signals built into the grammar of the language. We should also note that many of the verbs in the past tense have a *-d-* in them, but *ongan* and *sungon* have not. Here the situation is unchanged in Modern English: we still observe a difference between verbs which take a *-d* in the past, like 'heard', 'said', 'made', 'praised', and those that do not, like 'began' and 'sang'. The only difference is that Old English had many more verbs of the kind that do not take *-d* in the past, and a somewhat more elaborate system of signalling the past tense in the absence of -*d*. As in so many things, the variety of the Old English system has been lost. Old English had many forms of the noun: we have only the possessive and plural. Old English could signal possessive and plural in a number of ways: we rely almost entirely on the ending '-s'. Old English could make distinctions between several persons and both numbers in the past: we cannot. Old English had many verbs that could show, in a variety of ways, the past tense without recourse to -*d*: many of these, including 'help', 'climb', and other ones in frequent use, we have lumped together with the ordinary conjugation in -*d*.

So two things stand out about the vocabulary and grammar of Old English. One is that its stock of words was a rich one, and capable of increase from its own resources in the face of new needs; and that this stock underwent change and replacement over time, with some kinds of words more vulnerable than others. The other is that the grammar provided a wealth of inflectional capabilities that have since declined, and the decline has resulted in an increasingly rigid word-order and dependence on lexically-empty words like prepositions.

4

Old English did not become Middle English the moment William the Conquerer set foot on the beach at Hastings in 1066. In some ways, in fact, the classification of Old English as 'English before the Norman Conquest', and of Middle English as 'English from the Norman Conquest to the beginning of the renaissance in England', is inconvenient and misleading. For one thing, it is entirely the result of hindsight. Although we have relatively few statements of the ideas that medieval Englishmen held about their language, we can be sure that our present ways of looking at medieval English would be utterly strange to them. It is unlikely that an Englishman in the year 1100 would have seen such a difference between his own language and that of his grandfather that he would have called it by a different name.

For another thing, the divisions 'the Norman Conquest' and 'the renaissance' are not very helpful. They are quite unlike each other: anyone near the scene would have recognized the Norman Conquest, an identifiable event that took place at a fixed point in time. But not so the renaissance, which is another relatively modern way of describing a gradual change that altered a number of human activities, political, cultural, and—least of all—linguistic. Indeed neither the Conquest nor the renaissance were linguistic events, and so they are even more inconvenient for classifying language.

How then can the classification proceed? It must follow the categories of language, obviously, and not those of politics, warfare or culture.

As we have remarked, it is often helpful, at least in the case of English, to analyse language in terms of its sounds, its word-shapes, its sentence-shapes, and its vocabulary. We have reviewed Old English with special reference to these categories. Now, if we turn to Middle English, we shall notice several things about the categories as they appear in the later form of the language:

1. There are marked changes in all of them.
2. Such changes are all in evidence during the late Old English period, but they accelerate rapidly in the centuries following the Norman Conquest.
3. Some of the changes (notably vocabulary) begin earlier and go further than some others (notably sound).
4. The changes are continuous, and although they can be traced in early documents, they are most obvious in late ones.

Let us look again at a sermon for our evidence. Of course no one document is going to give us testimony to everything we need to know about, but sermons are a particularly satisfactory source of information. They are abundant in every age; they are not so conservative as translations of the Bible, nor so influenced by considerations of style as poetry; but they have a stylistic unity all the same which helps us to compare them.

Here is part of a twelfth-century sermon on the parable of the bad servant:

> Ða yrsode ðe laford, ant læt hine bitæcen
> þam stiðum witnerum, þe hine witniæn
> sceolden, oð ðet he forgylde al ðæt feoh
> him seolfum. .... Her is mucel andgit eow
> monnum to witenne; and we nimæð her to
> ðissere trahtnunge Augustinum ðone wisæ.
> 'Then became-angry the lord, and caused
> him to-be-committed to-the cruel torturers,
> who him torture should, until that he
> repaid all that money unto-him self. ...
> Here is (a) great significance for-you
> men to understand; and we take for this
> exposition Augustine the wise.'

A few changes from Old English have taken place in the century since the Conquest: *þe laford* would have been *se hlaford* before, but the definite article *se* has altered to resemble the other definite articles that finally all became modern 'the', while the initial cluster *hl-* has simplified to *l*. On the other hand, the verbs still show their full complement of endings: plural present (*nimæð*) in -*æð*, past (*sceolden*) in -*en* (Old English -*að*, -*on*); infinitive (*betæcen, witniæn, witenne*) -*en* or -*æn* without the marker *to* and in -*enne* with it (Old English -*an*, -*anne*); past singular (*yrsode, forgylde*) in -*de*. The pronouns still observe a difference between the direct and indirect object (*hine, him*), later levelled to 'him' for both. The definite articles are inflected likewise (*ðone, þam*), as are the demonstratives (*ðissere*, feminine dative singular), the adjectives (*stið-um*, dative plural) and nouns (*witner-um, monn-um*, even—with a Latin ending but following the English syntax—*Augustin-um*). This full inflectional system is reflected in the relatively light use of prepositions; the translation into Modern English has to insert them in a number of places where the passage under study can omit them without ambiguity. And (aside from the name Augustinus) there is not a single word of non-Germanic origin.

We have already noticed that a number of Old English words did not survive into Modern English, and some of these are still in use in this passage: *yrsode* (as a verb, but cf. modern 'ire'); *stiðum*; *witnerum*, and its associated *witniæn*; *forgylde*; *andgit*; *nimæð*; *trahtnunge*. But there was another kind of change that went with this loss, and that is the way vocalic verbs and nouns often crossed over into the consonantal class. The example *læt* in this passage is a bit untrustworthy, because the scribe obviously uses *æ* in a number of different ways: but in Old English the present was *læt*- and the past was *let*. Here the difference between the two vowels seems to be ironed out. 'Let' never got beyond this point, because it ends with 't', and English usually doesn't add a '-ed' suffix to verbs ending with 't' or 'd'; but the reduction of the Old English vowel contrast has left us with an ambiguity in phrases like 'I let him out', which does not appear to be obviously either past or present. In a word like 'help', the Old English contrast between the present *help*- and past singular *healp* (the past plural was *hulpon* and the past participle *geholpen*) was similarly neutralized, and the modern form 'helped' emerged, although for a time both the vocalic and the consonantal systems operated side-by-side in this word, as they continue to do today with 'hang' (past 'hung' or 'hanged'), 'shine' (past 'shone' or 'shined'), and 'dive' (past 'dived' or 'dove', although in fact this was a consonantal verb in Old English and the past 'dove' is a relatively modern creation in imitation of 'drove').

A similar situation obtained with nouns and, to a lesser extent, adjectives. We still say 'man', 'men' and 'goose', 'geese', but a host of other nouns of the same sort have changed over to the 'boy', 'boys' class: otherwise we should now say 'book', 'beek'; 'goat', 'geat', and so forth. Similarly we can still say 'old', 'elder', but not 'long', 'lenger', as we should if the Old English forms still persisted. In none of these cases did the Middle English period begin with the change to the modern form, but rather the change took place during the centuries following the Norman Conquest and was frequently incomplete by 1500 or even later.

At least the written language, then, kept much of the characteristic features of Old English for several lifetimes after the Norman Conquest, and we should not go far wrong to describe this passage as late Old English of the twelfth century, basing our terminology on the linguistic facts rather than the date of the text. Conversely, some of the characteristics that do distinguish Middle English can be traced sporadically in texts from before the Conquest.

Even in this early example of post-Conquest English, for example, we have seen that Old English word-endings like *-an* for the infinitive and *-on* for the past are both being spelled *-en*. That is a loss of one kind of distinction, and if it continues, another kind of distinction—with prepositions, word-order, or both—will have to take its place. We have also seen that a distinction was lost when *let-* and *læt* became the same. And we have noticed that Old English differs from later forms of the language in its all but exclusively Germanic vocabulary, which is inclined to form calques on foreign words rather than to borrow them. If we then go on to list these points, we would have a catalogue of the chief ways in which Middle English differed from Old English:

1. Old English is the period of full inflections in final syllables, Middle English the period of levelled inflections (in most cases, Modern English is the period of lost inflections).

2. Old English also preserves more vowel distinctions *within* the word than does Middle English, as well as those distinctions in the word-ending mentioned under (1).

3. As a result of (1) and (2), Old English depends less on prepositions and word-order than Middle English.

4. Old English has a vocabulary almost entirely Germanic; Middle English, especially among the open-class words, makes much use of words borrowed from non-Germanic languages.

We have already had a great deal to say about (3) and (4), and their consequences in any given text are relatively easy to identify. We have also seen how, in the twelfth-century text under discussion, (1) and (2) make an appearance, but not to a dramatic degree. Looking backward, we must ask whether even those hints of levelling are new in a text of the twelfth century. We shall find that they are not. Not only do tenth-century texts, written at least a full hundred years before the Conquest, reveal many cases of the weakening of *-an* to *-en* (e.g., *nesen* for *nesan*) and similar levelling of other inflections (e.g., *þances* for *þancas*); they also reveal a loss of the *-n* or *-m* altogether (*cyðe* for *cyðan*, *gode* for *godum*), and—even more significantly—mistaken cases of the fuller form where the weaker was required (*sceawedon* for *sceawede*, *pendan* for *penden*), sure evidence that these endings are no longer playing a fully meaningful role. If we bear in mind that at every stage of the medieval language the scribes were prone to employ archaic forms that were decades behind the real speech-habits of the time, we shall realize how important these occasional 'mistakes' in tenth-century manuscripts really are.

The same can be said for (2). One of the distinctions lost in Middle English was the one Old English made between the vowel of the past singular and that of the past plural in some verbs. 'Bite', for example, had *bāt* in the past singular and *biton* in the past plural; similarly, 'ride' had *rād* and *ridon*. In Middle English, the ending of the plural, as we have seen, weakened to *-en* and finally vanished. But another change took place even earlier: the distinction between the two vowels of the past was levelled, and while the past of 'bite' became *bit* (the vowel of plural), that of 'ride' became *rād* (the vowel of the singular). There is no way of telling which vowel will predominate, but the levelling was universal. Thus 'find' had *fand* (past singular), *fundon* (past plural), and we can tell by our modern 'found' that the plural vowel persisted. Yet even before the Conquest the levelling in this verb has begun: there is late Old English *fund* alongside *fand*. Here, too, then, a Middle English characteristic is anticipated in Old English. If we turn to a text of the early thirteenth century, however, what were mere stirrings in the tenth, eleventh or twelfth centuries now begin to appear as profound changes.

> Hise deciples hedde gret drede of pise tempeste, so hi awakede hine and seiden to him, 'Lord, save us, for we perisset'... po aros up ure lord and tok pane wynd... pis is si vaire miracle pet pet godspel of te day us telp.
> 'His disciples had great dread of this tempest so they woke him and said to him, "Lord, save us, for we perish." Then our Lord rose up and rebuked the wind. ... This is the fair miracle that the Gospel of the day tells us.'

Words like 'disciple' and 'miracle' are the kind that Old English was most likely to borrow when its own vocabulary did not provide an adequate term: recall 'psalm' in *sealm-sceop*. So we need not take such words by themselves as evidence for the wholesale penetration of foreign vocabulary into English writing. But 'tempest' and *perisset* (i.e., *perisheth*; the *ss* represents 'sh', and *th* often appears as *t* in this text, for example in *te*, 'the') are another matter, and 'save' clinches the question. The vocabulary of the piece is in a different linguistic world from that of our twelfth-century example.

The form of words differs too. Old English *hlaford*, itself already a simplification from unrecorded Old English *hlaf-ward, 'guardian of the loaf', became *laford* in our last text and now 'lord' in this one. Old English *godspel*, 'good story', a calque on *evangelium*, a Latin form of the Greek word meaning 'good story', was soon to follow the way of *hlaford* and simplify to 'gospel'.

The Old English practice of compounding that we see in *hlaf-ward and *god-spel* took a new turn in the Middle English period, when the stock of French and Latin words became available for compounding with native English forms. Our examples show that whereas *Augustinus* was felt as a foreign word in Old English and accordingly inflected with a Latin accusative ending, *Augustinum*, the present passage gives *deciples* and *perisset*, among others, as instances of foreign words whose terminations are English. It is as though we first said *musea* and *rhinocerotes* as plurals of *museum* and *rhinoceros* until we became accustomed to them and began to treat them as fully English words. From there it is but a step to taking other kinds of suffix beside plural and adding those to foreign words, giving *martyrdom*; or adding a full foreign word to an English one, to get *gentleman*. This kind of combination appears quite early in Middle English, as the Old English example *sealm-sceop* would lead us to expect; but naturally enough, its fullest effect is delayed until the period of greatest borrowing from French and Latin, the thirteenth and later centuries.

The inflections are simpler than in the twelfth-century example, but not so simple as they were to become. There is no longer a distinctive past plural (*hedde, awakede*) except in *seiden*; it appears that the *-on*, now weakened to *-en*, is optional. But there is at least the possibility of a distinctive present plural in *-eth*, represented here as *-et*, and the third person in *-(e)þ* remains (*telþ*) as it did at least in some writing on into the eighteenth century. The definite article *se* is preserved (as *si*), and *þæt* (as *þet*), and so is the accusative form in *þane*; but against these survivals we must note *þise* (a greatly simplified form of *ðissere*, as in the former passage) 'this', and *te* 'the'. The nouns show no inflection at all, nor do the adjectives *gret, vaire*; but *hise* has the plural *-e*.

The pronouns, indeed, retain fairly full inflection, as they do to the present day. The function of the pronoun in the sentence is such that its inflectional simplification will always lag behind that of nouns. Here the nominative plural is still *hi* as it was in Old English, and the distinction between accusative *hine* and dative *him* is still observed. On the other hand, the force of the dative *him* is not sufficient for it to stand alone as it did in the previous example from Middle English; here it is 'helped' by the preposition, *to him*, and similarly *of þise, of te day*, instead of genitive forms like *þissere* and *þæs dæges*. Accusatives like *hine, us*, and datives like *us telþ* do not require prepositional aid even in Modern

English. Word-order, consequently, is much like that of our own language, except in the last sentence where the finite verb in a subordinate clause is, as before, in final position, and in the second sentence where an adverb in initial position displaces the subject to a place after the verb. Both of these differences from Modern English practice can be paralleled in Modern German, and they show the continuing influence on Middle English syntax of the Germanic descent of Old English.

For our last example of Middle English sermon prose we may go ahead to the year of Chaucer's death, 1400, or thereabouts:

> þe hethen philosofres skorned hym, for oure feygthe may not be preved by reson; and þei, þe philosofres, granted no þinge but þat reson enformeþ hem.
> 'The heathen philosophers scorned him, for our faith may not be proved by reason; and they, the philosophers, granted nothing but that (which) reason informs them.'

The translation is hardly needed, so close—save in some details of spelling—is the language of the passage to Modern English; yet it is well over five hundred years old, only a century or two younger than the other Middle English passages we have been looking at. So we can say that Middle English was not the instant and distinctive development in the years that immediately followed the Norman Conquest; its characteristics, on the contrary, developed most rapidly and positively in the centuries beginning two hundred years after the Conquest, that is, from the mid-thirteenth century onwards.

The vocabulary of this example, to begin with, is heavily French, Latin, or Greek through Latin, in origin. Nouns, ordinary verbs, adjectives and adverbs not of Old English stock are *philosofre, skorned, feygthe, preved, reson, granted, enformeþ*; only *hethen* (itself a calque on *paganus*) and *þinge*, of the open-class words, are not imports. On the other hand, the personal and possessive pronouns can almost all be traced back to Old English: *hym*, the objective form now common to accusative and dative; *oure*, the new spelling for *ure* as in the previously examined passage; *þei*, a replacement under Norse influence of the previous *hi*, leading to Modern English 'they'; *hem* still showing the influence of the Old English form that accompanied *hi*, not yet brought into line with *þei*. So also the article *þe*, the special verbs *may* and *be*, particles *not* and *no*, the prepositions *for*, *but*, and *by*, and the relative *þat*. The grammatical framework of the sentence is English, and the 'meaning' words are not—which is, as we have already seen, much the modern distribution of our vocabulary.

Only the plural word-ending marks the nouns, although of course the possessive was available as well. The article and adjective *pe hethen* are unmarked as plurals. The verb inflections too are simplified: no past plural on *skorned* or *granted*, although of course the third person present singular retains its *-ep* ending. The infinitive *be* is unmarked. With the loss of noun, article, adjective and verbal inflections, the word-order has become fixed. Only in one place in the translation, the relative pronoun, is any supplementation needed. It was another century before this construction took its modern form.

5

The conclusions we have reached about the history of the four categories traced in these passages of Middle English give cause for reflection. How is it that the steady change of language seems to have increased so abruptly over a period of two centuries, and how is it that—the superficialities of spelling aside—it has changed so little in the five hundred years since?

The answer is twofold: the kind of evidence we have for making this study at all, and the history of the reputation of English. We have already looked at the first question, and seen how our reliance on the surviving documents influences the kind of study we can make. The second has a great deal to do with the first, for when a language has a high reputation as a literary and official medium, it will be used in many documents, and the documents will stand a good chance of preservation. It is difficult at this distance of time to imagine an England in which English was not the habitual language for literature and official writing, yet for much of the early Middle English period it was in fact eclipsed by French and Latin. The French and Latin vocabulary of English begins to grow rapidly in the mid-thirteenth century when English begins to make its come-back: the vocabulary, it might be said, is the spoils of that victory.

The English that emerges in the greatly increased number of vernacular documents that survive from about 1250 until about 1350 is undergoing the turmoil of this contest. It is purely figurative, but not perhaps altogether misleading, to regard the English that we find in documents of the thirteenth century as something that has been hibernating since the influx of French-speaking conquerors in 1066. Of course the spoken language of England among the middle and lower classes remained English, but the people who mattered—by and about and for whom the documents were made—were French-speaking. The new awakening of official and literary Middle English shows the effects of the hibernation: it is remarkably like the Old English of two centuries before. In the hundred years up to 1350, it undergoes a period of rapid accommodation to its new role, making up for lost time. And

CROWN
HALLMARK SHOP

2 3 DEC 69

6857 $000.90 —

CROWN
HALLMARK SHOP

2 3 DEC 69

$000.03 x
$000.93 TOTL

6857

when, from 1350 or 1400 onwards, it begins to enjoy the rewards of having established itself, it does what any other established person or institution does—it settles down and becomes conservative.

But language itself is not an institution: literature is. It is the literature of England whose history most nearly relates to the figurative account just completed. And it is to the growth of English literature in the second half of the fourteenth century, particularly in the hands of Chaucer, Gower, Lydgate, Wycliff, and their literary successors, that the stabilization of the literary language is largely attributable. Literature is traditional: once it has models, it seeks to follow them. The models for literary English were, until the mid-fourteenth century, few, scattered, and of uncertain reputation. With the coming of a consolidated school of English prose and poetry, the English language gained a literary embodiment that guaranteed its continuity as nothing before could have done.

We speak of the superficialities of spelling as the element of Middle English that has changed the most. Because we are so carefully drilled in spelling, we are supersensitive to anything that goes against what we have learned. In fact, many of our spellings go back to Middle English, even though we—unlike our forefathers then—are allowed only one 'correct' spelling. The 'ea' in 'weather', the 'o' in 'love', the 'gh' in 'night', and very many others, represent various special conditions of Middle English that did not last beyond 1500. Yet they survive in our spelling because the linguistic traditions of 1400 command a large following even today.

Indeed, the superficialities of spelling, as we can even better call them in view of these considerations, did not change anything like so much as did the sound-patterns of English—that is precisely why spelling is so out of step with pronunciation today. The chief change in sound was one that sets Middle English apart from Modern English rather than from Old English, and it is consequently a subject for the next chapter. The point is, however, that the appearance of stability following the great changes of the late Middle Ages is in some ways only an appearance. It relates to conditions of interruption, renewal and conservatism that apply chiefly to the written, literary language. Spoken Middle English would reveal something different. But it is spoken Middle English that we cannot recover, although we can study its modern descendants. We must rely on what was written, but we must avoid taking all it tells us as the whole truth.

6

The changing role of English in the centuries that followed the Norman Conquest had other effects then on the dialects and now on our knowledge of them. Dialects already existed, as we have seen, and do so today; but in a time when literacy and education are not widespread, there is no medium to give currency to any one dialect in preference to others. So much has the situation in this respect changed since the coming of universal literacy, general education and, most recently, radio and television, that we are prone to look upon the preferred dialect of English as the English language itself, and on all other varieties as deviant or substandard. But the 'received' form of English is a dialect like any other, one of the parts that make up the whole, and its reputation is a historical accident that has nothing to do with its linguistic adequacy.

As we have seen, such accidents gave preference to West Saxon among the dialects of Old English, at least for the purposes that brought into being the documents on which our study of Old English is based. The accidents arose from conditions that, generally speaking, went out of being with the Norman Conquest, and so West Saxon lost the basis for its preeminence. So long as French and Latin remained the languages of authority and literary reputation, the dialects of English lacked a national preferred form of the sort of West Saxon had been: all English dialects were out of the kind of fashion that West Saxon had enjoyed. As a result, such documents as were written in English might be in any one of several dialects. All had the same standing and hence the same chance. Naturally enough, there is an early preference for the English of the London region, and the preference becomes more marked as time passes, until London English assumes the role that West Saxon had formerly held. But in the meantime, other kinds of English found record in documents.

The documents tell us a great deal about dialects that already existed but that had left little trace hitherto. For example, the Viking occupation of East Anglia and parts of the North must have resulted in a large number of Old Norse words coming into Old English. We have an early record of some of them, like *call*, and very late in the Old English period, *take*; but most of them, like *window*, *sky*, and many others, appear only in Middle English, by which time the source of the influence was long departed from England and the Vikings themselves almost forgotten. This comes about probably because the 'classical' form of Old English was from an area of minimal Norse influence, and because during the period of the occupation, Norse words were regarded with a measure of hostility. In Middle English the 'underground' vocabulary of Norse finds expression in the absence of the restraints which obtained in Old English, and even the pronouns, as we have seen, are affected, first in the North and then gradually towards the South.

This example of dialect-mixing, the spread of a local—even a foreign

—characteristic to other dialects, brings us to another point. So far as we know, the dialect situation in Old English was relatively stable. Of course the language changed, and as we have seen, change brings an increase in dialect differentiation: the three-fold tribal distinctions were already made four-fold by the division of the Anglian dialect into a northern and a southern variety by the time records begin. But the appearance of a distinctive dialect for the London region is a Middle English phenomenon, as is the splitting of the southern Anglian dialect into two further varieties, West Midlands and East Midlands. Northern Anglian, the Old English Northumbrian dialect, retained something like its old borders, but in Middle English historians call it Northern; West Saxon too underwent little alteration of geography, but its Middle English successor is called South-Western; and Kentish Middle English goes by the name of South-Eastern.

The identification of these areas depends on the discovery of contrasting items in two neighbouring dialects, and the mapping of the frontier between them. The contrasts can be in any of the four linguistic categories we have already discussed: we have seen how the distribution of the various early Germanic dialects can be illustrated by means of vocabulary, for example. But even though vocabulary is convenient for purposes of illustration, and may be the kind of contrast that is most noticeable in our experience of dialect variety today, it has certain important drawbacks for the discovery of dialect frontiers. For one thing, there are very many words in a language: English has perhaps ten thousand times as many words as it has sounds. Thus the likelihood of a given word turning up at the time and place you need it to give you the evidence for a dialect frontier is ten thousand times slighter than the chances of a given sound turning up. For another thing, people can easily use two words for the same thing, particularly if they live near a dialect border, or have biographical reasons for doing so: as an American who lived in England for twelve years, I mix what should be contrasting items of the two forms of English, and no one really knows what part of my car I mean by the 'hood'.

As we have seen, grammatical forms also can be distinctive of dialect, for the replacement of the 'he goeth' by 'he goes' began as a northernism, and the distribution of the various forms of grammatical words like 'she' is an important clue to Middle English dialect borders. To some extent, syntax is also a matter of dialect: even today the use of negatives, for example, differs between 'he won't go' and 'he'll not go', largely according to area. But it is in sound that the most stable contrasts are to be found. Both British and American speakers of English are aware of areas in their parts of the world where historical 'r' after a vowel is pronounced, and other adjacent areas where it is not: some speech communities say 'harder' so you can hear both 'r's, and some so you can hear neither. And so forth. Whatever the local practice, it is almost certain to be consistent in *all* cases involving the sound in question. Now of course modern English spelling gives us very little to go on in such cases, because, as we have seen, it is more uniform than the varieties of speech are . . . in fact, with very few exceptions, it is entirely uniform throughout the English-speaking world, masking a wide range of differences in the spoken language. In Middle English, however, spelling had only begun to become uniform toward the very end of the period, and the surviving spellings give us a far better guide to the actual sounds than do their modern equivalents. Of course the problems that were mentioned at the outset of this chapter, regarding the localization and dating of documents, still hinder the investigator, but he can come to some important conclusions, and these are being perfected continuously.

We are able to say, for example, that the Old English long *a* as in *rād* became long *o* everywhere outside the Northern region. Now *rād* is only one example; all instances of the vowel underwent the same change except in the North. Sometimes we get a result that survives in dialects, such as non-northern 'home' against Scots 'haim' (Old English *hām*). Sometimes it survives in place-names, such as non-northern Stonton (Leicestershire) against northern Stanton (Northumberland), or Stonebury (Hertfordshire) against Stanbury (Yorkshire), from Old English *stān*. In the case of *rād*, the result is more complex but still consistent. The Old English word was both a verb, the past of 'ride', and a noun, 'a riding'. In the South the long *o* duly appeared, but two different solutions were found for the problem of how to spell it: the verb became 'rode', although the final '-e' has nothing to do with the history of the word and only serves to mark the sound of the 'o'; and the noun became 'road', although the 'a' once again is just a notation to mark the sound of the 'o' and doesn't reflect the long *a* that was its ancestor. In the North, the long *a* remained, and the marker that was chosen to indicate its length was *i*, giving 'raid' (like 'haim'). In due course of time this vowel, which sounded like that of 'father', changed to that of—well, 'change'. But unlike 'haim', the new 'raid' did not remain a dialect word. It came into use in Scotland and elsewhere to mean 'the object of a riding, an attack', just as 'road' came to mean 'that on which a riding takes place'.

The border between the *a* that became *o* and the *a* that remained *a* provides us with a dialect frontier, called an isogloss. Other contrasts provide still others: the *y* sound in Old English *hyll*, 'hill', '*byrig*', 'bury', and so forth, became variously 'e' (mostly in Kent), 'u' (in the South West and South West Midlands), and 'i' elsewhere. Such an outcome enables us to divide up the area south of the Humber in a way that the *a/o* test does not; on the other hand, the *a/o* test helps us divide the area in which Old English *y* becomes 'i'. And so it goes. Not all the iso-glosses coincide, and that is a good thing, for between wide-spread isoglosses we can identify usefully confined dialect areas. But where there is an overlap of several isoglosses, we have a major dialect frontier.

Like the continuity of language in time that we remarked on when talking about the change from Old English to Middle English, the continuity of language in space—for language exists in both—means that our dialect frontiers are to some extent falsifications: dialects alter gradually, not at borders. But the schematic results obtained by the discovery and comparison of isoglosses do provide a useful way of analysing the past and present varieties of English.

The area that was the source of the London dialect differs from some of the others in its eclecticism. Linguistically as well as geographically it is an extreme south-eastern corner of East Midlands, but Kent is on its southern border and the easternmost tip of South Western—the old West Saxon—approaches to within a few miles. Thus the rule, that one or another but not more than one development of a given sound will be characteristic of a dialect, breaks down in the London dialect as we observe its outgrowth in modern English. For example, the develop-ment of Old English *y* which we spoke of above gives us modern Eng-lish 'hill', the Midlands and Northern form, but alongside it modern English 'bury', spelled in the South Western form and pronounced in the South Eastern: all three possibilities are illustrated in these two words alone. Or notice the early Middle English *vaire* in the thirteenth-century Kentish text above on p. 285. It illustrates the rule that says Old English initial *f*- became *v*- in Southern, and particularly South Eastern, texts. If we look at modern 'fox', 'vixen', we can see that 'vixen' (Old English *fyxen*) has this Kentish characteristic but 'fox' hasn't. And to conclude, while 'vixen' has a Kentish initial consonant, it has a Midland *i* following it. Such cases show clearly the mixed or eclectic nature of the London dialect.

Thus in place of the four Old English dialects, we have five in Middle English, with an emergent sixth in the London region, an amalgam of the characteristics of East Midlands with some of those of South Eastern and a few of South Western, as well as such northernisms as became general throughout the country by 1450 or 1500: the plural pronoun 'they', and the third person present singular verb ending in '-s' ('loves' displacing 'loveth') chief among them. So it is not only in the evidence for the Middle English dialects that the change in the role of English had its effects: it is in the dialects themselves. The descendant of West Saxon, South Western, is not the premier dialect of Middle English. It is only a minor component in that dialect. Vocabulary and grammar too show the influence of the Norsemen, who came and went during the Old English period but whose linguistic heritage becomes disseminated only in the Middle English. The way that the survivals of Old English were handed on by Middle English to our modern language is fundamentally affected by the changes in status that English underwent after the Norman Conquest.

BIBLIOGRAPHY

Texts Quoted
The Blickling Homilies, ed. R. Morris, Early English Text Society, vol. 73, 1880.
Twelfth Century Homilies, ed. A. O. Belfour, EETS, vol. 137, 1909.
An Old English Miscellany, ed. R. Morris, EETS, vol. 49, 1872.
Middle English Sermons, ed. W. O. Ross, EETS, vol. 209, 1940.

Further Reading
C. Barber, *The Story of Language*, 1964.
J. W. Clark, *Early English*, 1957.

8

THE LATER HISTORY OF ENGLISH

Dr. C. Barber, University of Leeds

The English language since about 1500 is called Modern English, or New English. I shall call it Modern English, and use the abbreviation ModE. The abbreviation ME will stand for Middle English (c. 1100–1500), and OE for Old English (before 1100). There is of course no sudden change in the language at 1500, but if a text from 1400 is compared with one from 1600, the differences between ModE and ME can be seen clearly enough. These differences are numerous, but we can well begin by noting just a few of the major ones. In phonology, the most striking difference is in the pronunciation of the long vowels, a difference produced by the change known as the Great Vowel Shift. In grammar, the loss of inflections begun in the ME period has continued in ModE, and a relatively small number of inflectional endings have been standardized; the personal pronouns have been reduced in number; and there has been extensive development of the use of auxiliaries (words like *will*, *must*, *should*), a development facilitated by the rise of the 'dummy' auxiliary *do*. In vocabulary, the ModE period has been one of great expansion; in the earlier part of the period, the favoured method of word-formation was the borrowing or adaptation of words from Latin, but throughout the Modern period great use has also been made of affixation, conversion, and compounding.

During the ModE period, too, the language has spread widely over the world; in 1500 it was spoken by perhaps five million people in England and southern Scotland; today (1971) it is the language of more than 280 million people, and the largest English-speaking communities are of course in North America. This spread of the language has encouraged divergent development, and there are now distinctive varieties of English in different parts of the world. However, the improvement in communications may now be putting a brake on this divergence; the different forms of English are influencing one another, and the influence of American English is particularly potent.

In enlarging on these topics, it will be convenient to deal separately with Early Modern English (eModE), from 1500 to 1700, and Later Modern English (lModE), since 1700. Within each sub-period, we shall consider in turn vocabulary, grammar, and phonology.

EARLY MODERN ENGLISH, 1500–1700

The Expansion of the Vocabulary

In the late medieval period, English had been re-established as the language of administration, government, and literature in England, and a standard literary language had arisen, based on London usage. But, even after the disappearance of French as a living language in England, the English language was not entirely without a rival: Latin was still the language of international scholarship, and it was only in the course of the eModE period that it finally fell out of use in England. As late as 1689 a major scientific work, Newton's *Principia*, could be published in Latin; though it is interesting to notice that his *Opticks*, fifteen years later, was published in English. In the 16th century many people believed that learning was not learning at all unless it was written in Latin, and this attitude was often reinforced by the vested interests of those who wished to preserve their position as an élite: physicians for example were bitterly hostile to the publication of medical works in English, which might undermine their monopoly. But there were also strong forces making for the use of English: patriotic feeling, typical of the new nation-states of Europe; the religious disputes during and after the Reformation, in which controversialists wished to be read by a wide audience; the importance attached by Protestants to the reading of the Bible in the vernacular; the increasing importance of social groups which lacked the classical education of the gentry, but which were eager for instruction; and, behind all these, the introduction of printing, which had expanded the reading-public.

But when translators or popularizers produced works in English for this new reading-public, they often found the language deficient in technical terms for the subjects they wished to handle (geometry, rhetoric, medicine, and so on), and were obliged to invent new English words or expressions. The following passage illustrates both the concern with a new technical vocabulary and the necessity that the popularizers felt to defend their English writings against the traditional academics; it is taken from the preface to the first English translation of the *Logic* of Ramus, made by a Scot but published in London in 1574:

Heare I will speake nothing of the enuious, that thinkethe it not decent to wryte any liberall arte in the vulgar tongue, but woulde haue all thinges kept close eyther in the Hebrewe, Greke, or Latyn

tongues. I knowe what greate hurte hathe come to the Churche of God
by the defence of this mischeuous opinion: yet I woulde aske them one
thing that thou mayest knowe their deceiptfull policie, and that their
saying hathe no grounde of veritie. Whether wrote Moyses (the
Hebrewe and deuyne) and after him Esdras in the Hebrewe and
vulgar tongue or in some other straunge tongue? Did Aristotle and
Plato Greke Philosophers, Hipocrates and Galen Greke Phisitions,
leaue the Greke tongue, because it was their natiue language, to seke
some Hebrewe or Latin? Did Cicero who was a Latinist borne write
his Philosophie and Rethoricke in the Greke tongue, or was he content with his mother tongue? and suerly as he testifiethe hym self he
had the perfecte knowledge of the Greke tongue, yet he wrothe
nothing therin which we haue extant at this daye. Shall we then
thinke the Scottyshe or Englishe tongue, is not fitt to wrote any
arte into? no in dede. But peraduenture thou wylt saye that there is
not Scottyshe wordes for to declare and expresse all thinges contayned
into liberall artes, truth it is: neither was there Latin wordes to
expresse all thinges writen in the Hebrewe and Greke tongues: But
did Cicero for this cause write no philosophie in Latin? thou wilt not
saye so, lest I take the with a manifest lye. What then did Cicero? he
laborethe in the Latin tongue, as Aristotle before hym did in the
Greke, and thou enuious felowe ought to do in thy mother tongue
what so euer it be, to witte he amplified his natiue tongue, thinking
no shame to borrowe from the Hebrucians and Grecians suche wordes
as his mother tongue was indigent of. What, shall we thinke shame
to borrowe eyther of the Latin or Greke, more then the learned
Cicero did? or finde some fitt wordes in our owne tongue able to
expresse our meaning as Aristotle did? shall we I saye be more
vnkynde to our natiue tongue and countrey then was thiese men to
theirs? But thou wilt saye, our tongue is barbarous, and theirs is
eloquent? I aunswere thee as Anacharsis did to the Athenienses, who
called his Scithian tongue barbarous, yea sayethe he, Anacharsis is
barbarous amongest the Athenienses, and so are the Athenienses
amongest the Scythyans, by the which aunswere he signified that
euery mans tongue is eloquent ynoughe for hym self, and that others
in respect of it is had as barbarous.

The translator here advocates the method of borrowing words from
Latin and Greek to remedy the deficiencies of the English vocabulary,
and also mentions the possibility of finding 'fitt wordes in our owne
tongue', i.e. adapting existing words to new uses. In fact there were in
the 16th century opposing schools of thought about vocabulary-
expansion, and three main methods were advocated: (1) The borrowing
of words from other languages, especially the classical languages; (2)

The coining of words from native elements (by affixation, compounding); (3) The revival of obsolete words, and the adoption of dialect-words into the standard language. The whole process was highly conscious; Spenser, for example, was not just acting on individual whim when he used archaisms and dialect-words in his poetry: he was part of a whole movement. The preface to *The Shepherd's Calendar* (1579), in which one of Spenser's friends ('E.K.') attacks the borrowing of words from foreign languages and justifies the use of archaisms, is just one document in a controversy that raged for decades.

The disadvantage of words borrowed from Latin or Greek was that they were likely to be opaque to the reader lacking a classical education —precisely the reader aimed at by the translators and popularizers. The coiners and early users of new learned words are therefore often careful to paraphrase them. There is a well-known passage in Sir Thomas Elyot's *The Governour* (1531) in which he speaks of 'an excellent vertue where vnto we lacke a name in englisshe', and thereupon coins a name for it:

> Wherfore I am constrained to vsurpe a latine worde, callyng it *Maturitie*: which worde, though it be strange and darke, yet by declaring the vertue in a fewe mo wordes, the name ones brought in custome, shall be as facile to vnderstande as other wordes late commen out of Italy and Fraunce, and made denizins amonge vs.

He then explains at length what he means by the word, and concludes: 'And this do I nowe remembre [i.e. record, mention] for the necessary augmentation of our language'.

The defenders of native coinages could argue that their new words were more easily comprehensible to the ordinary reader. This argument was used by Ralph Lever in his book on logic, *The Arte of Reason, rightly termed, Witcraft* (1573). Lever puts his principles into practice by coining new compound words to translate the technical terms of logic found in Latin. Examples of his coinages are *endsay* ('conclusio'), *foresays* ('premissae'), *ifsay* ('propositio conditionalis'), *naysay* ('negatio'), *saywhat* ('definitio'), *shewsay* ('propositio'), and *yeasay* ('affirmatio'). None of these has survived, and today we in fact use anglicized forms of the Latin words that Lever was translating—*conclusion, premises, negation, conditional proposition*, etc.; some of these indeed already existed in Lever's time, though not all of them were yet used as technical terms of logic. And in general it is true that, in the eModE period, the usual way of coining technical and scientific terms was by borrowing words from Latin or Greek, or inventing words from Latin or Greek elements. In form, such coinages are often influenced by earlier English borrowings from French; for example, Elyot says that his new word *maturity* is borrowed from the Latin, presumably meaning *maturitas* (though the only Latin word he actually quotes in his discussion is *maturum*); but *maturity* has the ending *-ity* typical of words borrowed from French, and could well be from the French *maturité* (itself of course derived from Latin). Indeed, it is often difficult to say whether a word has been borrowed from Latin direct, or whether it has come from French. In the Ramus passage quoted earlier, there are four words which the Oxford English Dictionary does not record as being in use before the 16th century. Three of them are coined from Latin elements: *barbarous* (1526), *Latinist* (1538), and *extant* (1545), though the ending *-ous* of *barbarous* shows the influence of French. The fourth, *decent* (1539), while ultimately deriving from Latin, has probably come via French. However, it also happened that words which had been borrowed from French in the ME period were reshaped in the eModE period under the influence of Latin. Two examples in the Ramus passage are *perfecte* and *peraduenture*; the ME forms are *parfit* and *perauenture*, derived from the French; the modern forms are renaissance remodellings under the influence of Latin *perfectum* and *aduenire*.

Of course, not all the new words derived from Latin were the coinages of translators and popularizers. The expansion of knowledge and the rise of the natural sciences inevitably led to word-formation; there are many new scientific words, like *pollen* (1523), *vacuum* (1550), *equilibrium* (1608), and *momentum* (1699), and mathematical terms like *area* (1538), *radius* (1597), *series* (1611), and *calculus* (1672); though the earliest uses of such terms are not always the technical ones. There are also Latin loans in other spheres, for example legal terms like *alias* (1535), *caveat* (1557), and *affidavit* (1622), and even relatively ordinary words like *miser* (1542), *circus* (1546), and *album* (1651). Moreover, many Latin loans, far from being utilitarian, were an expression of linguistic exuberance, a love of the high-sounding or pompous word. Richard Mulcaster, writing in 1582, speaks of the words which the English language 'boroweth daielie from foren tungs, either of pure necessitie in new matters, or of mere brauerie, to garnish itself withall', where *mere brauerie* means something like 'sheer ostentation'. Even writers who approve of Latin loans often attack the extravagances of such coinages, which are condemned as 'ink-horn terms'; and dramatists ridicule the pompous affecters of Latinisms, like Holofernes in Shakespeare's *Love's Labour's Lost*. But ridicule of excesses did not of course stop the great influx of Latin loans, which was at its peak round about 1600.

While Latin was the main source of new words in the eModE period, other languages were also drawn on. From classical Greek came especially technical terms of rhetoric, literary criticism, and the natural sciences; examples are *phrase* (1530), *rhapsody* (1542), *larynx* (1578), *pathos* (1591), and *cosmos* (1650). Of the living languages, the most influential was French, followed by Italian, Spanish, and Dutch. Many of the French loans were military or naval, but there were also many words connected with the arts, fashion, and social life, especially in the late 17th century; examples are *pioneer* (1523), *sally* (1542), *bourgeois* (1564), *volley* (1573), *stockade* (1614), *parterre* (1639), *crayon* (1644), *ballet* (1667), *commandant* (1687), and *denim* (1695). The Italian loans too were often military, like *squadron* (1562), *parapet* (1590), and *barrack* (1686); there were also words from commerce, like *traffic* (1506) and *mercantile* (1642), and from the arts and architecture, like *cupola* (1549), *stucco* (1598), and *opera* (1644). Fewer words were borrowed from Spanish, but here too warfare and commerce were prominent, as in *cask* (1557), *comrade* (1591), *parade* (1656), and *cargo* (1657). Of the Dutch words, many are to do with seafaring, like *dock* (1513), *sloop* (1629), and *cruise* (1651); there are also words to do with the visual arts, especially in the 17th century, e.g. *easel* (1654), *stipple* (1669).

All in all, the influx of words during the eModE period was enormous. Some years ago, Mr. F. W. Bateson took forty pages of the *Shorter Oxford Dictionary* and examined all the words that were in use in 1600; he found that no less than 39 per cent of them had entered the language after 1500. This enormous expansion of the vocabulary sets a problem for the reader of eModE literature. When we meet a word in the literature, it is often difficult to judge how it struck the original readers: a word that to us seems quite ordinary or neutral may then have sounded affected, or startling, or delightfully new. Some of the words that were condemned by contemporary critics as pompous or affected now sound quite unobjectionable; for example, words ridiculed by Ben Jonson in *Poetaster* include *strenuous* and *spurious*, which to us are not self-evidently absurd.

Another difficulty for the reader of Renaissance literature, of course, is the fact that many words have changed their meanings since that time. Examples can be seen in the Ramus passage already quoted. The word *decent* there means 'suitable, decorous'; *close*, as often in this period, means 'secret, hidden'; *straunge* means 'foreign'; and so on. Particularly difficult are the words that have behind them a whole way of looking at the world which has now passed away; such is the word *vnkynde*, which means 'unnatural', and implies a whole view of what constitutes naturalness in human behaviour.

The Grammar of Early Modern English

With vocabulary, we are concerned with what are sometimes called 'open-ended' word-classes (nouns, verbs, adjectives and adverbs) whose members cannot be listed exhaustively—since, after all, any speaker of the language can invent a new one at any time. In grammar, by contrast, we are dealing with closed systems containing relatively few members, which can be listed exhaustively: word-classes like pronouns, determiners, conjunctions, auxiliaries; sets of inflections; permissible phrase- and sentence-patterns; and so on.

In eModE the system of determiners had reached very much its present-day form. Determiners are the grammatical words used to mark nouns, like *the, a, each, any, my*. One important group of determiners in English is formed by the demonstratives. Modern English has a three-term system of demonstratives, *the/this/that*; Old English on the other hand had a two-term system, *se/þes*. The two OE demonstratives had a large number of different forms, which were selected according to the gender, number, and case of the following noun. The three ModE demonstratives, on the other hand, have few forms: *this* and *that* have plural forms *these* and *those*, and *the* has a single invariable form. The modern situation was reached in about 1500. In Early Middle English, there were still numerous forms of *se*, like *þane* (accusative singular masculine) in the passage quoted by Professor Bolton, on p. 287; but in the course of the ME period *the* established itself as the normal form, though even at the end of the ME period we sometimes find a plural form *tho*. But in the early 16th century even *tho* disappears from the standard language, and *the* becomes the sole form. The demonstrative *that* (OE *þæt*) was originally the neuter of *se*, but in Early Middle English it broke away and became a contrasting demonstrative; in Late Middle English it appropriated to itself the plural *those*, which originally had been the plural of OE *þes*. From other forms of *þes* comes the ModE plural *these*, which spread from the Midland dialects and was in general use by about 1500.

We perhaps ought to say that in eModE there was in fact a four-term system of demonstratives, for in addition to *the/this/that* it had *yon*, as in Shakespeare's 'see how yon Iustice railes vpon yon simple theefe' (*King Lear* IV.vi). There is an OE form *geon*, but it is rare, and its grammatical status is uncertain. Its descendant *yon* (with a ME variant *yonder*) occurs as a determiner in ME and eModE; like *that*, it means 'the one over there' or 'the one further away', but it carries the additional implication 'and in sight'. Outside Scots, it does not survive in lModE except as an archaism.

The remaining determiners were also in much their present-day form by the 16th century. One difference, however, is that the form *its* is not found in the 16th century, *his* being used instead, as in Old and Middle English; *its* is not found before the 17th century, is very rare in Shakespeare, and does not occur in the A.V.; so in the A.V. we find 'But if the salt haue lost *his* sauour, wherewith shall *it* be salted?' (*Matthew* V.xiii). Throughout the eModE period, the determiners *my* and *thy* have alternative forms *mine* and *thine*, which occur only before vowels; so we find *my father* but *mine uncle*. But *my* and *thy*, originally used only before consonants, tend more and more to occur also before vowels, and to displace *mine* and *thine*. In Shakespeare, both types are found before vowels, as in *mine eye, my eye*.

Although the system of determiners was in very much its present-day form by the 16th century, the phrase-structures in which the determiners occurred sometimes differed from ours. Shakespeare for example has 'At each his needlesse heauings' (*Winter's Tale* II.iii), 'of euery/These happend accidents' (*Tempest* V.i); the A.V. has 'Art thou that my lord Eliiah?' (*I Kings* XVIII.vii); these all have sequences of determiners not now possible. And in vocatives we find phrases like 'Dear my lord', 'O poor our sex', where the determiner comes between the adjective and the noun.

In the Ramus passage, the word *who* occurs as a relative pronoun ('the Athenienses, *who* called . . .'); this usage is not found before Modern English times. Earlier, *who* (OE *hwā*) was interrogative or indefinite, never relative. In the course of Middle English, the inflected forms *whom* and *whose* came to be used as relatives, but the nominative *who* was not used in this way until the 16th century. The common relatives in Middle English were *that*, *which*, and *the which*; these continued to be used in eModE alongside *who*, as can be seen from the Ramus passage, where all three occur. In eModE, *which* could be used to refer to persons, a use which is not now possible; Shakespeare writes 'The Mistris which I serue' (*Tempest* III.i), and in the A.V. the Lord's Prayer begins 'Our father which art in heauen' (*Matthew* VI.ix). The present-day regulation of *who*, *which*, and *that* is not reached until the lModE period.

In the Ramus passage, nouns regularly form their plural by adding *-s* or *-es* (*thinges, tongues, Phisitions*, etc.). In ME, the plural ending *-n* or *-en* had been general in the south, but it was gradually displaced by the northern *-(e)s*. In Chaucer, *-(e)s* is the most frequent plural ending, though the *-(e)n* plural occurs sometimes, as in *eyen* 'eyes', *foon* 'foes', *eldren* 'ancestors', *doghtren* 'daughters'. In eModE, the *-(e)s* plural has become the normal form (in the early 16th century often spelt *-ys*). There are indeed a few *-(e)n* plurals in eModE, like *shoon, peasen, hosen, housen*, though they occur only sporadically; and a few vestiges remain today, like *oxen* and *children*; but the regular Modern English plural is *-(e)s*, pronounced /s/ or /z/ or /ɪz/ according to the preceding phoneme, and this pattern is established in the standard language in Early Modern times. There are indeed some deviations from the pattern. There are some uninflected plurals descended from OE neuter nouns, like *sheep, deer, swine*; eModE retains rather more of these uninflected plurals, and we sometimes meet plural forms like *horse, thing, winter, lamb*. And throughout the Modern English period we have complicated things by introducing Latin and Greek loan-words complete with their plurals, like *formula/formulæ, phenomenon/phenomena, stratum/strata, nucleus/nuclei*.

However, if such words are used frequently, they tend to go over to the regular -(e)s plural; an example is *formula*, which has a plural *formulas* beside *formulae*. If a loan-word of this type is used in the plural more often than in the singular, its plural form may come to be used as a singular, since it does not bear the expected mark of the English plural. This seems to be happening to the word *datum*, for *data* is now often treated as a singular ('this data'), and given an -(e)s plural ('these datas'). In the 18th century the same thing happened to *strata*, which was given a plural *stratas*, but this has died out.

By early Modern times, the old dative inflections of the noun had disappeared, and the ending -(e)s had been standardized for the genitive, both singular and plural. Since this genitive ending is identical with the plural ending, most ModE nouns have only two forms: *boy* has the baseform /bɔɪ/, and a form /bɔɪz/ which serves for genitive singular and plural and for non-genitive plural. In lModE, of course, we distinguish the three functions of the second form by having three different spellings (*boy's*, *boys'*, *boys*); and there are in fact a few nouns that have four separate forms, e.g. *man*, *child*. In the 16th century, there are occasional examples of nouns being uninflected in the genitive: *my ffather and mother soules*; *our Lady Day last*. Indeed, *Lady Day* has survived as a set phrase in lModE (cf. *the Lord's Day*), as has another example of the uninflected genitive, which occurs in the Ramus passage, namely *mother tongue* ('mother's language'). In the 16th century there are also numerous examples of the use of *his* after the noun instead of a genitive inflection: 'in a sea-fight 'gainst the Count his gallies' (*Twelfth Night* III.iii). Broadly speaking, however, the inflection of nouns had reached its present state by the 16th century.

Adjectives, which in Old English had been inflected for number, case, and gender, had reached their present state, in which there is a single invariable form, well before the Modern period opened. Changes have continued, however, in the comparison of adjectives. In Old and Middle English, a number of adjectives change the stem-vowel in the comparative and superlative, and occasional examples of these 'mutated' forms are still found in the 16th century, like *long/lenger/lengest* and *strong/strenger/strengest*. However, these die out in the course of the eModE period, and the only relics today are the forms *elder*, *eldest*. In eModE, comparatives and superlatives often have -er/-est where today we use *more/most*: we invariably use *more/most* with polysyllabic words, but in the 16th and 17th centuries we meet forms like *delicatest*, *notoriousest*; we also select *more/most* with certain disyllabic adjectives, for example those ending in -ous or -ect, but in eModE there are forms like *perfecter*, *famousest*. The Modern English tendency for *more/most* to supplant -er/-est is still going on. Moreover, in eModE it was possible to use double comparatives and superlatives, and we meet expressions like *more swifter*, and Shakespeare's 'This was the most unkindest cut of all' (*Julius Caesar* III.ii).

As for verb-inflections, many Middle English endings have disappeared by eModE times: whereas Chaucer had infinitives like *to expressen*, the Ramus passage has *to expresse*; Chaucer has imperatives like *Gooth!*, where Shakespeare uses forms like *Go!*; and Chaucer has plural forms like *they diden*, where eModE has *they did*. However, the old northern present-plural in -(*e*)*s* is still found in the 16th century, and Shakespeare uses it not infrequently, as in 'His teares runs downe his beard' (*Tempest* V.i). It will also be noticed that the Ramus passage has some verb-inflections that are no longer used: it has special forms for concord with *thou*, like *mayest* and *wylt*; and in the third-person singular it does not use -(*e*)*s*, but -(*e*)*the* as in *thinkethe, hathe, laborethe*. (The final -*e* was not of course pronounced in eModE, and -*ethe* is merely a spelling-variant of -*eth*.) However, -(*e*)*th* was not the universal third-person singular inflection in the 16th century, as is illustrated by the following extract from Shakespeare:

Ol. What thinke you of this foole *Maluolio*, doth he not mend?

Mal. Yes, and shall do, till the pangs of death shake him: Infirmity that decaies the wise, doth euer make the better foole.

Clow. God send you sir, a speedie Infirmity, for the better increasing your folly: Sir *Toby* will be sworn that I am no Fox, but he wil not passe his word for two pence that you are no Foole.

Ol. How say you to that *Maluolio*?

Mal. I maruell your Ladyship takes delight in such a barren rascall: I saw him put down the other day, with an ordinary foole, that has no more braine then a stone. Looke you now, he's out of his gard already: vnles you laugh and minister occasion to him, he is gag'd. I protest I take these Wisemen, that crow so at these set kinde of fooles, no better then the fooles Zanies.

Ol. O you are sicke of selfe-loue *Maluolio*, and taste with a distemper'd appetite. To be generous, guiltlesse, and of free disposition, is to take those things for Bird-bolts, that you deeme Cannon-bullets: There is no slander in an allow'd foole, though he do nothing but rayle; nor no rayling, in a knowne discreet man, though hee do nothing but reproue.

Clo. Now Mercury indue thee with leasing, for thou speak'st well of fooles.

Enter Maria

Mar. Madam, there is at the gate, a young Gentleman, much desires to speake with you.

Ol. From the Count *Orsino*, is it?

Mar. I know not (Madam) 'tis a faire young man, and well attended.

305

Ol. Who of my people hold him in delay?

Mar. Sir *Toby* Madam, your kinsman.

Ol. Fetch him off I pray you, he speakes nothing but madman: Fie on him. Go you *Maluolio*; If it be a suit from the Count, I am sicke, or not at home. What you will, to dismisse it.

Exit Maluo. Now you see sir, how your fooling growes old, & people dislike it. *(Twelfth Night, I.v)*

In that passage, the normal third-singular ending is -*(e)s*, as in *decaies, takes, has, desires, speakes, growes*; there are only two occurrences of -*(e)th*, both in the word *doth*. In Chaucer, by contrast, the normal ending is -*(e)th*. The -*(e)s* ending spread from the north, and it was only in the course of the 16th century that it became the predominant form in the standard language. In the A.V. of 1611, it is true, the -*(e)th* forms are still normal; but the A.V. is archaic in style, and closely follows earlier translations. In Shakespeare, -*(e)s* is decidedly more frequent than -*(e)th*, and the latter is especially found in a few favoured forms, notably *doth* and *hath*. There is indeed evidence to suggest that, in the later 16th century, -*(e)s* was often pronounced even when -*(e)th* was written. For example, William Camden, in 1605, gives an account of Sir Thomas Smith's proposals for spelling-reform, including the use of *z* instead of *s* to represent the pronunciation /z/:

Z; he would haue vsed for the softer S, or eth, and es, as *dîz* for dieth, *lîz* for lies.

This clearly implies that the spelling -*eth* represents the pronunciation /z/. In any case, the ending -*(e)th* was obviously on its way out in the 16th century, and had disappeared from the normal standard language by the end of the eModE period.

Some third-singular verbs in the passage, however, have no inflection at all: *though he do, if it be*. These are subjunctive forms, which are merely vestigial in lModE but still quite common in eModE. They are found especially in subordinate clauses of condition and concession, and in noun clauses after verbs of requesting and commanding, as in the following sentence from *The Taming of the Shrew*: 'Tell him from me (as he will win my loue)/He *beare* himselfe with honourable action' (I.i.).

In both the Ramus and the *Twelfth Night* passages, all past tenses and past participles of verbs are in their present-day form (disregarding minor differences of spelling): past participles like *kept, come, sworn, gag'd*, past tenses like *wrote, called, saw*. Historically, English verbs can be divided into two main clauses: strong verbs, that form their past tense by changing the vowel of the stem (*give, gave*); and weak verbs, that form their past tense by adding a dental suffix to the stem (*walk,*

306

walked). In Old and Middle English, strong verbs had different stem-vowels for the past singular and the past plural: Chaucer writes *he rood* ('he rode'), but *they ryden* ('they rode'). In Modern English, this distinction between past singular and past plural has disappeared, with the sole exception of *was/were*. Sometimes the modern form has the vowel of the old singular, as in *rode*; sometimes it has the vowel of the old past participle, as in *bore*; sometimes it has a vowel that could come either from the past participle or from the old plural, as in *found*. In general, the strong verbs had reached their present form by the 16th century, but eModE does show some divergences from present usage, and in such cases there are usually alternative forms: *he wrote, he writ*; *he smote, he smot; he flung, he flang; he spoke, he spake*; and so on. In the piece of Sir Thomas Elyot quoted on p. 299 above there occurs the past participle *commen* 'come'; this preserves the Old English ending *-en* which was once standard for the past participles of strong verbs but now survives in only a few, like *given*. However, in some cases where lModE preserves the *-en* ending, it is not uncommon in eModE to find an alternative past participle modelled on the past tense, as in *I have wrote*. The prefix *y-* found on past participles in Middle English disappears in eModE; when Spenser, in the late 16th century, uses forms like *ygoe* ('gone') and *ybound* ('bound'), these are intentional archaisms for literary effect.

In general, there has been a tendency in all periods of English for strong verbs to become weak, and for newly formed or borrowed verbs to be declined weak, so that today there are fewer strong verbs than there were in Old English. An example of a strong verb that became weak in the Early Modern period is *climb*; the old strong past tense *clomb* is still found in the 16th century, alongside various other forms like *clam*; but weak forms *climmed* and *climbed* also occur in the 16th century, and *climbed* is the predominant form by about 1600.

The eModE system of personal pronouns shows some changes from Middle English, but is not yet that of lModE. In Middle English, the pronoun of the second person plural was *ye*, of which the accusative form was *you* (originally, like the other accusatives of personal pronouns, a dative form). This distinction between *ye* and *you* is still found in the early 16th century, and is usually maintained in the A.V. of 1611, as in the following passage:

> Ye cannot serue God and Mammon. Therfore I say vnto you, Take no thought for your life, what yee shall eate, or what ye shall drinke, nor yet for your body, what yee shall put on. . . . Which of you by taking thought, can adde one cubite vnto his stature? And why take ye thought for raiment?
>
> (*Matthew* VI.xxiv)

There, *ye* and *you* are regularly distinguished in a way exactly parallel to *he* and *him* or *we* and *us*: the form *ye* or *yee* is used for the nominative, and *you* for the accusative (*vnto you*, *of you*). But, as we have seen, the A.V. is archaic in style, and in fact in ordinary usage the distinction between *ye* and *you* had broken down by the middle of the 16th century, and both forms were used in free variation for either nominative or accusative. For example, the distinction is still preserved in Sir Thomas Elyot's *Governour* (1531), but in Roger Ascham's *Toxophilus* (1545) the two forms are used indiscriminately for the nominative, though *you* is the preferred form for the accusative. In the second half of the 16th century, *ye* tends to be replaced by *you*: it will be noticed that, in the passage quoted from *Twelfth Night* (c. 1600), Shakespeare regularly uses *you* both for nominative and for accusative. However, *ye* continued to occur as a variant until the second half of the 17th century, when it disappeared from the standard language.

Beside *ye/you*, eModE had the pronoun *thou/thee*, as can be seen in the Ramus and Shakespeare passages. Originally, *thou* was singular and *ye* plural, but in the 13th century *ye* came to be used as a respectful singular form for addressing a superior. In Early Modern English, *ye/you* is of course used if more than one person is addressed. If only one person is addressed, *thou/thee* is used to intimates, to children, and to inferiors; *ye/you* is the polite form used to superiors or to non-intimate equals. To use *thou/thee* to a superior or to a non-intimate equal is insulting; in *Twelfth Night*, Sir Toby advises Sir Andrew to insult Cesario when he writes him a challenge:

> taunt him with the license of Inke: if thou thou'st him some thrice, it shall not be amisse. (III.ii).

However, even in Shakespeare it can be seen that the *thou/you* distinction was beginning to break down, and speakers sometimes switch from one form to the other for no obvious reason. In fact, *thou/thee* was beginning to give way to *you* as the sole second-person pronoun, though *thou/thee* continued in common use to the end of the 17th century. Indeed, the distinction between *thou* and *you* must still have been felt quite strongly in the mid-17th century, or there would have been no point in the Quaker habit of using *thou/thee* to everybody indiscriminately. Originally, it is plain, this was a subversive gesture, a refusal to pay due respect to those in secular authority over you, rather like refusing to remove your hat in the presence of a social superior; indeed, George Fox himself links the two pieces of behaviour when he describes in his *Journal* how in 1652 a Justice was scandalized 'because I did not putt off my hatt and saide thou to him'. However, *thou* fell out of use in the standard language in the 18th century, though it has persisted in regional dialects, and also in the special register of prayer.

The third-person plural pronouns *they*, *them*, *their* are Scandinavain loan-words which spread from the north in the course of the ME period. The nominative *they* spread faster than the other two, and we find that Chaucer uses *they*, but not *them* and *their*, in place of which he has *hem* and *hire*, from Old English. But in eModE the spreading process is complete, and *they/them/their* are the normal forms in the standard language. However, *hem* has survived as an unstressed form down to the present day, now written *'em* and pronounced /əm/.

A final point about eModE grammar is more important than it appears at first sight. This is the development of the auxiliary *do*. In the *Twelfth Night* passage there are two different ways of asking questions: Olivia says 'What thinke you?', simply inverting the order of subject and verb, whereas today we say 'What do you think?'; but in the same speech she says 'Doth he not mend?', where the question is formed by putting some part of *do* in front of the subject, in the present-day manner. There is a similar variation in affirmative statements: beside 'the pangs of death shake him' we find 'Infirmity ... doth euer make the better foole'. In that last sentence, the *doth* is not emphatic: 'Infirmity doth make' is simply a stylistic variant of 'Infirmity maketh'. We find a similar free variation in negative sentences: Maria says 'I know not (Madam)'; but it will be remembered that Hamlet says 'I doe not know/ Why yet I liue to say this thing's to doe'. So we see that in eModE there is an auxiliary *do*, but its regulation is not as it is today: whereas today we use *do* in questions and negations, but not in unemphatic affirmations, in eModE it could be inserted or omitted at will in all three types of sentence.

To see the importance of this situation, let us digress for a moment and consider the auxiliaries in Present-day English (PresE). In PresE the auxiliaries are a class of grammatical words, i.e. they form a closed system. There are two types of auxiliary, the non-modals (*be, have, do*), and the modals (*can, could, may, might, shall, should, will, would, dare, must, need, ought to, used to*). The modals are distinguished by not having the *-(e)s* inflection of the third-person singular: we say *he does* but *he can*. They are also distinguished by position: when modals and non-modals occur together in a verb-phrase, the modal always comes first (*he might have gone*; *you ought to be going*). Both kinds of auxiliary are of great importance in PresE grammar.

One function of the auxiliaries is in the forming of negative statements. The normal way of negating a sentence in PresE is to put *not* (or its weak form /nt/) after the auxiliary: *She may not come*; *It isn't raining*. In some cases the auxiliary has a special form when it precedes /nt/: *will* becomes *won't*, *shall* becomes *shan't*, and so on. Another function of the auxiliaries is in the forming of questions. The normal way of asking a question in PresE is to put the subject of the sentence after the auxiliary: *Can she come?*; *Is it raining?* It will be noticed that this has the effect of preserving the word-order subject-verb (*she come*) which is an important feature of PresE.

The auxiliaries are also used for sentence-emphasis. This is achieved when the auxiliary is given the main stress in the sentence and ordinary falling intonation is used ('John *can* come', 'They *won't* know'). This gives a different effect from stressing any other word in the sentence. If I say '*John* can come' I mean 'John and not somebody else'. If I say 'John can *come*' I mean 'come but not do something else'. In both cases the emphasis singles out just one part of the sentence for contrast. But if I say 'John *can* come' I am not contrasting *can* with some other possible auxiliary, but am underlining my belief in the truth of the whole sentence, rebutting an assertion to the contrary. (Though a contrast with the auxiliary alone can be achieved by using a rise-fall-rise intonation, giving the meaning 'can but won't'.)

The importance of auxiliary *do* in PresE grammar is that it is the dummy auxiliary: it performs the various functions of an auxiliary, but is empty of meaning. So we use it when no other auxiliary has an appropriate meaning. If we want to negate a sentence, or to ask a question, or to achieve sentence-emphasis, and none of the other auxiliaries is required in our sentence, we use auxiliary *do*: 'We didn't go'; 'Do you know him?'; 'But John *does* live there'. These uses of *do* are often found queer and puzzling by foreign learners of English, but in fact they are not queer at all, but entirely in accord with PresE sentence-patterns.

The establishment of the dummy auxiliary *do* was essential for the existence of the system of auxiliaries as we know it. In the absence of a dummy auxiliary, Chaucer has sentences like the following: *I pray yow that ye take it nat agrief* ('I pray you that you do not take it amiss'); *Seyde he nat thus?* ('Did he not say thus?'); *Ware the sonne in his ascencioun/Ne fynde yow nat repleet of humours hoote* ('Beware that the sun in its rising does not find you full of hot humours'). There we have sentences negated and questions asked without an auxiliary being used. Auxiliaries, therefore, lacked the central function that they have today, for they were not the normal means for forming questions and negatives. Indeed, it is not entirely clear that there was a system of auxiliaries in English before the invention of the dummy auxiliary; for, until that event, the items that later became auxiliaries behaved very much like ordinary lexical verbs, and perhaps just were ordinary lexical verbs.

The full establishment of *do* as a dummy auxiliary took place in eModE, but the present-day regulation of its use was not reached until about 1700. The use of *do* followed by the infinitive of a verb is not uncommon in Middle English, but there it is not usually a dummy auxiliary, but has a causative sense. The ME sentence *Wrightes he did make haules & chambres riche* means 'He caused carpenters to make rich halls and chambers'. In the south-western dialects there was a variant of this construction, in which *Wrightes* or the corresponding word is omitted. An example is *a kastelle he did reyse*, which means 'he caused a castle to be built' (it is in fact a translation of the French *Chastel fet lever*). But sentences of this last type are potentially equivocal. If we say *He built a castle*, there is already a causative element in the meaning of *built*, since we do not necessarily mean that he built it with his own hands. So ME sentences like *He did build a castle* would be identical in meaning with sentences like *He built a castle*. So speakers would equate *did build* with *built*. At first the equation would only take place in causative contexts, but before long it would be transferred to non-causative contexts. And at that point *did* had become a semantically empty word, a dummy auxiliary, and *He did build* was merely a stylistic variant of *He built*.

The development of this non-causative use of *do* took place in the south-western dialects round about 1300, and spread from there. At first it was used mainly in poetry, because it was a convenient device for putting a verb into rhyme-position at the end of the line. Then it spread to prose, where it is first found about 1400. It spread slowly in the 15th century, and rapidly in the 16th century, and at the same time the old causative use of *do* died out, its place being taken by *make* and *cause*. In Shakespeare's time, as we have seen, *do* is commonly used as a dummy auxiliary, but its use is not regulated as it is today. This regulation takes place during the 17th century: *do* gradually drops out of affirmative sentences (except for the emphatic use), and comes to be used more and more regularly in negative and interrogative ones, until the present-day situation is reached in about 1700.

The Phonology of Early Modern English

In eModE, just as today, there was great variety of pronunciation. There were regional variations, and even though the educated pronunciation of the London area had great prestige, and was on the way to being recognized as a standard, it was not at all uncommon or disgraceful for gentlemen or noblemen to speak with a regional accent: Sir Walter Raleigh, that eminent courtier, retained a Devon accent to the end of his days. And even within the speech of a regional or social group there were variations of pronunciation, just as there are today. I shall have to confine myself to the pronunciation of the educated classes of the Court and of the south-east of England (which I shall call *standard* pronunciation). When I refer to ME phonology, I shall mean that form of ME from which the standard form of eModE descended. When I make comparisons with PresE pronunciation, I refer to the

British accent known as Received Pronunciation (RP), and in particular to RP in the first half of the 20th century, as described by Daniel Jones.

The long vowels: the Great Vowel Shift

One of the striking changes between Middle English and eModE is in the pronunciation of the long vowels, a change often called the Great Vowel Shift. In Late Middle English there were seven long-vowel phonemes, which we can denote by the symbols /iː/, /eː/, /ɛː/, /ɑː/, /ɔː/, /oː/, and /uː/. (The dots after each symbol indicate that the vowel is long.) In the Great Vowel Shift these seven long vowels underwent a systematic transformation, which can be illustrated diagrammatically as follows, the arrows showing the direction of change:

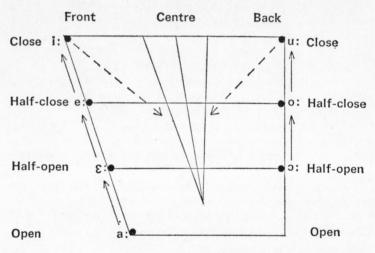

The diagram is a conventionalized cross-section of the mouth-cavity seen from the left-hand side. Vowels are marked on the diagram as dots, which represent the position of the highest point of the tongue when the vowel is uttered. It will be seen from the arrows that all vowels became progressively closer in quality, i.e. made with the tongue higher. However, this could not happen to /iː/ and /uː/, which were already as close as they could be, and these two vowels became diphthongized; the progressive change in position of the starting-point of these diphthongs is suggested by the dotted arrow. The changes involved will perhaps become clearer if we consider each vowel in turn.

Late ME /uː/ was a close back vowel, resembling that of Modern French *vous*, or of PresE *who*. It was usually written *ou* or *ow* (*found, hous, now*). By about 1500 it had become diphthongized to /ʊu/, and in the 17th century it became the /aʊ/ diphthong which it is in PresE.

In Shakespeare's time it had not developed quite so far as this, and was probably /əu/, not unlike the vowel in PresE *home*. (The symbol ə represents a central vowel, like that in the *er* of PresE *father*).

Late ME /oː/ was a half-close back vowel, resembling that of Modern French *beau* or Modern German *wo*. It was written *oo* or *o* (*food*, *who*). In the 15th century it became closer in quality, and by 1500 it had become /uː/, which it remained.

Late ME /ɔː/ was a half-open back vowel, resembling that of PresE *law*. In ME it was spelt *oo* or *o* (*goot*, *hope*), but in Modern English the words that had ME /ɔː/ are usually spelt with *oa* or *o* (*goat*, *hope*). In the early 16th century the vowel became closer in quality, until it reached the half-close position /oː/, where it remained until the 18th century.

Similarly with the front vowels, except that here we have to deal with four long vowels where PresE has only three.

Late ME /iː/ was a close front vowel, resembling that of PresE *machine* or Modern French *si*. It was usually spelt *i* or *y* (*tide*, *tyde*, *why*). By 1500 it had become diphthongized to /ɪi/, and in the 17th century it became the /aɪ/ diphthong which it is in PresE. In Shakespeare's time it had not developed so far as this, and was probably /əi/, starting from a central position.

Late ME /eː/ was a half-close front vowel, resembling that of Modern French *thé* or Modern German *zehn*. It was spelt *ee*, *e* or *ie* (*green*, *grene*, *field*). In the 15th century it became closer in quality, and by about 1500 it became /iː/, where it remained.

Late ME /ɛː/ was a half-open front vowel, resembling that of Modern French *même*, or the first element of PresE *air*. In ME it was spelt *e* or *ee*, but in Modern English the words that had ME /ɛː/ are most often spelt with *ea* (*clean*, *meal*). In the 15th century it became closer in quality, and round about 1500 it had become /eː/, where it remained throughout the Early Modern period. In PresE, ME /ɛː/ has of course fallen together with ME /eː/, and we have the same vowel in *clean* as in *green*; but in eModE this was not so, and Shakespeare distinguished between *see* /siː/ and *sea* /seː/, between *meet* /miːt/ and *meat* /meːt/. For the modern reader, a good guide (though not an infallible one) is the spelling: the spelling *ea* is characteristic of words which in eModE had the opener vowel, while the spellings *ee* and *ie* are characteristic of words that had the closer vowel.

Finally, Late ME /aː/ was an open front vowel, with a quality like that of the vowel of Modern French *la* or Modern German *Vater*. It was usually written *a* (*bake*, *dame*). In the 15th century it became closer in quality, and by about 1500 had become /æː/ (like the vowel in PresE *bad*.) It continued to become closer during the 16th century, and in Shakespeare's time was probably /ɛː/. However, unlike the other long vowels it did not then remain stable, but continued to become closer, and there is considerable evidence to suggest that, in the second half of the 17th century, it became /eː/, and therefore fell together with ME /ɛː/, so that the same vowel was used in *bake, dame, clean, meat*. This obviously raises problems, since the two phonemes have *not* fallen together in PresE, and we shall return to the point when we deal with Later Modern English phonology.

The following table will serve as a summary of the Great Vowel Change. It gives the probable pronunciation of seven words for Chaucer, for Shakespeare, and for PresE (RP).

ME Phoneme	Chaucer	Shakespeare	20th Century	Modern Spelling
iː	tiːd	təɪd	taɪd	tide
eː	greːn	griːn	griːn	green
ɛː	mɛːt	meːt	miːt	meat
ɑː	mɑːk	mɛːk	meɪk	make
ɔː	gɔːt	goːt	gəʊt	goat
oː	foːd	fuːd	fuːd	food
uː	huːs	həus	haʊs	house

The Short Vowels

In contrast to the long vowels, the short vowels have been relatively stable. However, one change occurred in the system of short vowels in eModE: a new short-vowel phoneme arose, giving seven short vowels as compared with the six of Late Middle English.

The six short vowels of Late ME can be denoted by the symbols /ɪ/, /e/, /a/, /ə/, /ɔ/, and /ʊ/. The first of these, /ɪ/, has remained unchanged to the present day; it is the vowel of *bid* /bɪd/, *chin* /tʃɪn/. The second, /e/, is also practically unchanged, though perhaps it has become a little closer in quality since ME times; it is the vowel of *bed* /bed/, *fresh* /freʃ/.

The third, /a/, was a front open vowel, resembling that of Modern French *la*; it occurred in words like *hat* /hat/, *black* /blak/. In the course of the 16th century it became closer in quality, and by 1600 it was /æ/, and there it has remained, giving the PresE pronunciations /hæt/, /blæk/. However, the older quality of the vowel has been retained in Northern England and in much of the Midlands, and there the pronunciations [hat] and [blak] are still normal.

The fourth, /ə/, was a central vowel, like the *er* of PresE *father*. In Late Middle English it occurred only in unstressed syllables, where it arose as the weakened form of various ME short vowels (which explains why we have no regular representation for it in ModE spelling). Throughout the ModE period there has been a tendency for unstressed vowels to become either /ə/ or /ɪ/, but the process had already begun in Late ME, and the /ə/ phoneme was probably well established by the opening of the eModE period. In the course of eModE, /ə/ also came to be used in stressed syllables; in about 1600, the groups /er/ and /ɪr/ both became /ər/ when they preceded a consonant, and later in the 17th century the group /ʊr/ also became /ər/. This situation has not of course persisted in Later Modern English, since the /ə/ has been lengthened in such positions, and today we once again have /ə/ only in unstressed positions. So at the beginning of the eModE period, *herb* was /herb/, and *bird* was /bɪrd/; in the early 17th century the pronunciations were /hərb/ and /bərd/; but today they are /hɜːd/, bəd/; and we have /ə/ only in words like *about* /ə'baʊt/, *father* /'fɑːðə/.

The fifth, /ɔ/, was about half-open in quality, like the *o* of Modern German *Sonne*, or like a shortened version of the vowel of PresE *law*. It occurred in words like *dog* /dɔg/, *fox* /fɔks/. Today, however, it is /ɒ/, a vowel of much opener quality, very nearly fully open, as in *dog* /dɒg/, *fox* /fɒks/. The change to an opener quality took place in the course of eModE, and the very open vowel was fully accepted in standard speech by the middle of the 17th century. In some forms of American speech, /ɒ/ is unrounded to [a], giving pronunciations [dag], [faks], in which the vowel is rather like the *a* in RP *father*.

The sixth and last short-vowel phoneme of Middle English, /ʊ/, had a quality like the vowel of PresE *put, full*. In Later Modern English it has split into two phonemes, /ʊ/ and /ʌ/. The phoneme /ʌ/ is the one that occurs in PresE *cut* /kʌt/ and *luck* /lʌk/; in the 16th century these were /kʊt/ and /lʊk/. To understand the process by which this split probably took place, we must pause a moment to distinguish between *phonemes* and *allophones*.

A phoneme is one of the basic units in the sound-system of a language, like /p/ in PresE. It is contrasted with the other phonemes of the language, and it is by these contrasts that different words, different meanings, are distinguished. So, in PresE, /p/ contrasts with /b/ (*pin, bin*), with /f/ (*pin, fin*), and so on. But /p/ is not always pronounced in the same way in PresE, even by a single speaker. For example, it is usually followed by an aspiration, a kind of [h] sound, giving the pronunciation [pʰ]: and *pin* (if you listen carefully) is in fact pronounced [pʰɪn]. But when the /p/ is preceded by an /s/ belonging to the same syllable, this aspiration is absent, and the pronunciation is [p]; so *spin* is pronounced [spɪn]. These two variants, [pʰ] and [p] are called *allophones* of the phoneme /p/. Allophones are contextual variants of a phoneme; they can never contrast with one another, and hence are never used to distinguish different words or meanings, which is why the native speaker is usually unconscious of them.

To return to /ʊ/ and /ʌ/: it is probable that the bifurcation of /ʊ/ into two phonemes began by its developing two allophones, and that later these achieved the status of phonemes. In the early part of the 17th century, the /ʊ/ phoneme developed an allophone [ʌ], which was used in a large number of words like *cut* [kʌt] and *luck* [lʌk]; but in other words, especially in the neighbourhood of certain consonants like /p/ and /l/, the allophone [ʊ] continued to be used, as in *put* [pʊt], *full* [fʊl]. At this stage [ʊ] and [ʌ] were merely contextual variants, but in the mid-17th century other changes occurred which brought them into positions where they contrasted with one another, so that they now constituted two separate phonemes. As an example we can take the words *luck* and *look*. In the 16th century, *luck* was /lʊk/, but it was one of the words where the [ʌ] allophone came to be used, so in the early 17th century it was pronounced [lʌk]. In the 16th century the verb *look* (from OE *lōcian*) quite regularly had a long vowel, and was pronounced /luːk/ (as it still often is in the north of England). But in the 17th century the vowel of *look* underwent shortening, as happened with many monosyllabic words in eModE, and it became /lʊk/. But the shortening of /uː/ produced [ʊ], not [ʌ]; so at this stage there were in English the words *look*, pronounced /lʊk/, and *luck*, pronounced /lʌk/; and so /ʊ/ and /ʌ/ were now separate phonemes, since they served to distinguish these two words.

This may seem a little complicated, but it is worth making an effort with it, because it illustrates an extremely common way in which change takes place in the sound-system of a language: a phoneme develops two or more allophones, contextual variants; then other changes in the language bring these allophones into positions where they contrast with one another, and they have become separate phonemes.

Diphthongs

Late ME also had a number of diphthong-phonemes. A diphthong is a glide-vowel, in which the speech-organs change their positions while the vowel is produced. It can be represented by a digraph, of which the first symbol shows the starting-position of the diphthong, and the second symbol the position towards which the speech-organs move. So the diphthong /aɪ/ begins with the speech-organs in the position for [a], but almost immediately they glide away in the direction of [ɪ] (though they may not go the whole way).

There were seven diphthongs in Late Middle English: /aɪ/, /aʊ/, /ɛʊ/, /ɪʊ/, /ɔɪ/, /ʊɪ/, and /ɔʊ/. They underwent various changes in eModE, but there was a general tendency for them to be monophthongized, i.e. to change from diphthongs to pure vowels.

Late ME /aɪ/, which resembled the vowel of PresE *die*, was found in words like *day*, *nail*, *rain*. In the 16th century it became /ɛɪ/, and in the first half of the 17th century was monophthongized to /ɛː/; it therefore fell in with the /ɛː/ from ME /aː/, so that we now have the same vowel in *day* and *rain* as in *bake* and *dame*.

Late ME /au/, which resembled the vowel of PresE *how*, was found in words like *claw*, *hawk*, *cause*. It had a similar history to ME /ai/. In the 16th century it was retracted to /ɒu/, and in the first half of the 17th century was monophthongized to /ɒː/. In Later Modern English its quality became closer, and it is now the half-open vowel /ɔː/.

Late ME /ɛu/ and /ɪu/ were still kept distinct in the 16th century; /ɛu/ occurred in words like *few*, *dew*, *ewe*, *beauty*, and /ɪu/ in words like *new*, *true*, *blew*, *view*, and the two pronunciations were still distinct in Shakespeare's time. However, in the first half of the 17th century /ɛu/ became /ɪu/, and the two diphthongs fell together. In the second half of the 17th century /ɪu/ became /juː/, i.e. with a pronunciation like PresE *you*, and in many positions this still remains, as in *new* /njuː/, *view* /vjuː/, *few* /fjuː/. However, in some positions /juː/ has been simplified to /uː/ in Later Modern English. In PresE we invariably find /uː/ after /r/, as in *rule* /ruːl/; after dʒ/, as in *June* /dʒuːn/; after /tʃ/, as in *chew* /tʃuː/; and after Consonant + /l/, as in *blue* /bluː/. But in some positions we find alternative forms with either /juː/ or /uː/: so *suit* can be /sjuːt/ or /suːt/, *lute* can be /ljuːt/ or /luːt/; and similarly with *enthusiasm*, *absolute*, *resume*. It seems likely that in such positions /uː/ is now in process of displacing /juː/; the younger generation certainly seem to favour /uː/.

The Late ME diphthong /ɔi/, found in words like *choice*, *joy*, *noise*, has remained unchanged in the Modern English period. However, some words now pronounced with /ɔi/, like *boil*, *destroy*, *poison*, had alternative pronunciations with Early Modern English /ʊi/. In the later 17th century, /ʊi/ developed into /ai/, and so fell together with the /ai/ from ME /iː/, This accounts for early 18th century rhymes like Pope's *join*/*divine*. However, in the course of the 18th century the /ɔi/ pronunciation displaced the /ʊi/ pronunciation in such words, the process no doubt being aided by the influence of the spelling.

And finally the Late ME diphthong /ɔu/, found in words like *know*, *own*, *low*, remained in the early part of the eModE period, but in the 17th century was monophthongized to /ɔː/; this was raised to /oː/, and so fell together with /oː/ from ME /ɔː/; so that today we have the same pronunciation in *know*, *own*, *low* as in *goat*, *hope*.

The Shortening of Long Vowels

As we have already seen in the case of the word *look*, long vowels were frequently shortened in the Early Modern period. The shortening is sporadic, so that it is difficult to lay down rules for it, but it is particularly common in monosyllabic words ending with a single consonant, like *sieve*, *grit*, *dead*, *sweat*, *blood*, *cook*, *hot*. As can be seen, it is often (but not always) possible to detect these shortenings from the spelling: as the spellings suggest, *sieve* had ME /e:/, *dead* and *sweat* ME /ɛ:/, *blood* and *cook* ME /o:/. But we could not have guessed from the spellings that *grit* had ME /e:/ and *hot* ME /ɔ:/.

The vowel that results from the shortening may depend on the date at which the shortening took place. If ME /e:/ was shortened during the Early ME period, it resulted in /e/: the words *friend*, *depth*, *fellow*, *kept* all had /e:/ in Early Middle English, but Early ME shortening produced /e/. But at the beginning of the eModE period, ME /e:/ became /i:/, and the shortening of this is ModE /ɪ/; examples are the words *riddle*, *nickname*, *sieve*, and *grit*, all of which had ME /e:/, and which underwent shortening in late ME or Early Modern English. Again, the words *blood* and *cook* both had ME /o:/ (= eModE /u:/), but one has PresE /ʌ/, the other /ʊ/. The earlier shortening is *blood*; it changed from /blu:d/ to /blʊd/ before the allophone [ʌ] had developed, and so shared in this development; but *cook* was shortened from /ku:k/ to /kʊk/ after the distinction between [ʊ] and [ʌ] had already been established, and therefore remained /kʊk/.

Many words fluctuated in eModE, some people using a long vowel, others a short. The spelling is a good guide to the most frequent eModE pronunciation.

The Consonants of Early Modern English

A new consonant-phoneme arose in eModE, namely /ŋ/, the phoneme that occurs in PresE *sing* /sɪŋ/ and *sink* /sɪŋk/. The pronunciation [ŋ] did indeed exist in Middle English, but it was not an independent phoneme: it was simply an allophone of the phoneme /n/, the variant of /n/ that occurred before /k/ and /g/. In ME, the pronunciation of *sing* was [sɪŋg], and similarly with *singing* ['sɪŋgɪŋg], *strongly* ['strɔŋglɪ], and so on. But in the 16th century the /g/ was lost in such positions, giving the PresE pronunciation /sɪŋ/, /'sɪŋɪŋ/, /'strɔŋlɪ/. When this happened, /ŋ/ became an independent phoneme, for there were now contrasting words like *sing* /sɪŋ/ and *sin* /sɪn/, where the contrast depends wholly on the distinction between /n/ and /ŋ/.

Otherwise, the consonant-system of eModE differs from that of ME mainly in the distribution of the consonant-phonemes; in particular, the positions which some consonants could occupy became more restricted in eModE. An example is the phoneme /h/. In late ME this had an allophone [h] which occurred in syllable-initial position, as in *habit*, *behind*, just as in PresE. But /h/ (written ȝ or *gh*) could also occur in syllable-final position (*plough*, plo̬ȝ 'plough', *laughen*, lauȝen 'to laugh'), and before /t/ (*light*, liȝt 'light', *doughter*, do̬ȝter 'daughter'). In these positions it had allophones [ç] and [χ] (as in Modern German *ich* and *ach*), which occurred after front vowels and after back vowels respectively.

But at the beginning of the eModE period the /h/ phoneme disappeared in all positions except the syllable-initial one (though before it did so it often lengthened or diphthongized the preceding vowel). In most cases, PresE has no consonant at all in these positions (*light, daughter, plough, high*), but in some words we have /f/ (*enough, draught, dwarf*), which stems from a dialectal variant.

Another example of restrictions on consonant position is provided by /g/ and /k/. In Middle English these could occur initially before /n/, as in *gnawen* /ˈgnɑʊan/ 'to gnaw' and *knelen* /ˈkneːlən/ 'to kneel', but in the course of the Early Modern period the initial plosive disappeared, leading to the PresE pronunciations /nɔː/ and /niːl/. It was also common for clusters of three consonants to be simplified by the loss of the middle one; an example of this is /t/, which disappeared when the preceding consonant was /s/ or /f/ and the following consonant was /l/ or /m/ or /n/, as in *bristle, chestnut, Christmas, soften*. The semivowel /w/ also disappeared from certain positions in eModE: in the initial cluster /wr/, as in *write, wrap*; between a consonant and a back rounded vowel, as in *sword* and *two*; and in the first syllable of the second element of compound words, as in *boatswain, Greenwich*. It will be noticed that when consonants are lost in eModE our present-day spelling tends to preserve the evidence of the earlier pronunciation. In some cases the influence of the spelling has led to the restoration of the lost consonant in Later Modern English pronunciation, as in *awkward, forward, housewife*, in which a lost /w/ has been restored in the standard language (though *hussy* and *hussif* still exist alongside *housewife*).

Stress, Rhythm, Intonation

It is difficult to be certain about features like stress, rhythm, and intonation, when we are dealing with a stage of the language before the invention of the gramophone and the tape-recorder; but on the whole it seems likely that in these respects the system of eModE was not markedly different from that of PresE. But there are of course differences of detail. It is clear, for example, that in eModE many individual words had stress-patterns different from their present ones. When Hamlet refers to the Ghost as clad 'in compleat steele', we can be pretty sure that the adjective was stressed on the first syllable. And the attentive reader of Renaissance poetry will soon be familiar with words like *re'venue, en'vy,* (verb), *ad'vertising, auth'orize, char'acter* (verb), *'commendable, 'confine* (noun), *con'jure, 'construe*—words where, either regularly or sporadically, the stress-pattern is different from ours.

By the 18th century, English had reached very much its present form, as the following passage illustrates; it is an extract from a letter from Swift to Pope, written in 1736:

Pray do not use me so ill any more . . . I have nobody now left but you. Pray be so kind as to outlive me, and then die as soon as you please, but without pain; and let us meet in a better place, if my religion will permit, but rather my virtue, although much unequal to yours. Pray let my Lord Bathurst know how much I love him. I still insist on his remembering me, although he is too much in the world to honour an absent friend with his letters. My state of health is not to boast of; my giddiness is more or less too constant; I have not an ounce of flesh between skin and bone; I sleep ill, and have a poor appetite. I can as easily write a poem in the Chinese language as my own. I am as fit for matrimony as invention; and yet I have daily schemes for innumerable essays in prose, and proceed sometimes to no less than half a dozen lines, which the next morning become waste paper. What vexes me most is, that my female friends, who could bear me very well a dozen years ago, have now forsaken me, although I am not so old in proportion to them, as I formerly was, which I can prove by arithmetic, for then I was double their age, which now I am not. Pray put me out of fear as soon as you can, about that ugly report of your illness; and let me know who this Cheselden is, that has so lately sprung up in your favour. Give me also some account of your neighbour who writ to me from Bath . . . Farewell, my dearest friend, ever, and upon every account that can create friend- ship and esteem.

In vocabulary, that seems thoroughly familiar to the present-day reader. In grammar it differs little from PresE: the sole second-person pronoun is *you*; the third-singular inflection is invariably -(e)s (*vexes, has*); and auxiliary *do* is regulated in the present-day manner (*do not use me*). There is indeed one past tense of a strong verb which is archaic (*writ* for *wrote*); and a present-day writer would probably put *badly* instead of *ill*, and would probably not use the construction *is not to boast of*. But such differences are minor.

Swift's spelling, too, is standardized in accordance with present-day conventions. In the 16th century, spelling varied a good deal from writer to writer, and even within the work of a single writer. But there were forces making for standardization (like printing), and there were a good many generally accepted spelling-conventions. These conventions, however, often differed from our own. For example, *u* and *v* could both be used either for the consonant or for the vowel, and it was normal to use *v* at the beginning of a word (*voice, vnto*) and *u* elsewhere (*cause, giue*). Standardization did not take place until the second half of the 17th century, and the spellings then established were on the whole the ones we still use.

In 'polite' circles in the 18th century there were also ambitions to 'correct' and 'fix' the language in other ways—to remove what were considered corruptions and deficiencies, and then to establish its vocabulary, grammar, and pronunciation once and for all, possibly by means of an Academy. Such ambitions are delusive: no language which is being used can be prevented from changing. But it is from this period that we inherit the prescriptive attitudes towards the language which have been so influential in the last couple of centuries.

Although the Swift passage looks extremely modern, change has of course continued to take place during the lModE period, in vocabulary, in grammar, in pronunciation.

The Vocabulary of Later Modern English

During the Later Modern period, the vocabulary of English has continued to expand, and indeed at the present time the expansion seems to be going on at a prodigious rate. As in the Early Modern period, we have continued to form numerous words from Latin and Greek elements; this method is used especially for learned words, and in particular for the vocabulary of science, which has expanded at an ever-increasing rate. Much of the vocabulary of the sciences, of course, never moves outside the narrow specialist sphere, but some scientific words gain a more general currency, like *gene, oxygen, molecule, hibernate, conifer, metabolism, isotope*. Words will move into general use if they bear closely on everyday problems of health and the treatment of disease (*vitamin, penicillin, antibiotic*), or if they are connected with widely used products of technology (*nylon, transistor, television*). When they do move into general currency, they are quite likely to change their meanings: to the man in the street, a *transistor* is a kind of wireless-set; *atomic* often means 'powerful, shattering'; *allergic* is commonly used to indicate a disinclination or dislike; a man who tells you that he has a *complex* may have no psychological theories about repression; and *syndrome* is now going the same way.

In contrast to ME and eModE, borrowing from living languages has played only a small part in the expansion of the lModE vocabulary. French has remained the most popular source for borrowings, especially for words connected with the arts (*critique, connoisseur, montage*), with clothes and fashion (*rouge, blouse, suede*), with social life (*etiquette, parvenu, élite*), and more recently with motoring and aviation (*garage, hangar, chauffeur, fuselage*). We have borrowed a few more nautical terms from the Dutch (*schooner, caboose*), and from Italian a few more words to do with the arts (*studio, replica, scenario, fiasco*). From German come scientific words, especially in chemistry and mineralogy, like *paraffin, cobalt,* and *quartz,* and a few wartime words like *strafe, blitz, ersatz.* Because of Britain's active part in world trade, we have also borrowed odd words from distant and exotic countries, like *pyjamas* from India, *budgerigar* from Australia, and *raffia* from Indonesia. And we continue to borrow words from abroad when there is some special reason, like *sputnik* from Russian (though *lunik,* surprisingly enough, was not borrowed from Russian, but coined in the United States on the analogy of *sputnik,* and then borrowed back by the Russians).

More important for word-formation in lModE has been affixation—the making of words by the use of prefixes and suffixes. This has been important throughout the history of English, and continues to be so. For example, the prefixes *un-* and *de-* are freely used to create words like *unsympathetic, unfunny, deration, decontrol.* Other prefixes very much alive in the lModE period are *dis-, pre-, anti-, pro-, mis-*; and recent additions to the list include *neo-, pseudo-, crypto-,* and *mini-.* An example of a living suffix is *-ize,* which can be added to adjectives (*national, miniature, tender*) or to nouns (*carbon, vitamin, vapour*) to form new verbs; and from these in turn can be formed abstract nouns in *-ization,* like *nationalization.* Other active suffixes include *-er* (*bumper*), *-ee* (*trainee*), *-ist* (*stockist*), and *-y* or *-ie* (*civvy, goalie*); a recent addition is *-wise,* used for forming adverbs (*computerwise, examinationwise*).

We have also continued to form words by compounding, conversion, and shortening. In compounding, two words are put together and given a single main stress, as in *oilcloth, nosedive, airscrew, postman, paperback*; later, it often happens that changes take place in the pronunciation of the word, and one element ceases to be a free morpheme; this has happened with *postman* (a 16th century formation), which in RP is /ˈpəʊstmən/, not /ˈpəʊstmæn/. Conversion is the process of transferring a word from one grammatical category to another, for example from noun to verb, or from adjective to noun; it has gone on all through the Modern English period, and is particularly active in the present century, producing new verbs like *to feature, to film, to process, to service, to audition, to garage,* and new nouns like *a highup, a must, a handout, knowhow* (the last two being formed from the phrasal verbs *to hand out* and *to know how*). Shortening in Modern English usually consists in dropping the end part of a word, giving forms like *photo, cab,* and *telly,* but sometimes it is the first part of the word that is lost, as in *bus* and *plane.* Sometimes it is not a single word that is shortened, but a phrase, as in *prefab* ('prefabricated house') and *nylons* ('nylon stockings'). The shortened forms sometimes have a spelling-pronunciation, as with *photo* /ˈfəʊtəʊ/ (from *photograph* /ˈfəʊtəgrɑːf/) and *bra* /brɑː/ (from *brassière* /ˈbræsɪɜ/).

There are other ways in which lModE has acquired new words: by

322

blends (*brunch*, *motel*); by taking over proper names (*cardigan*, *mackintosh*, *bikini*); by taking over proprietary trade-names (*thermos*, *primus*); by means of acronyms (*radar*, *Nato*); but these are minor sources. Words also move into general currency from regional dialects or from the language of specialized groups within the speech-community; such borrowings are called 'internal loans'. The Industrial Revolution brought a few words from regional dialect into wider circulation, like *bogie* (on railway rolling-stock), *bank* ('hill, gradient'), and *trolley* (originally a Suffolk word). There are also words from lower-class speech and from the language of occupational groups: *gadget* is first known as sailors' slang in the 19th century; *wangle* began as printers' slang; *spiv* has come from the language of race-gangs; and recently the word *square* ('un-aesthetic') has come in from jazzmen's slang. These particular words, perhaps, are not yet fully respectable, but they may become so; we have many words which were once considered low or vulgar, including respectable words like *coax*, *flimsy*, *flippant*, *fun*, *sham*, and *snob*, all of which were frowned on as vulgarisms in the 18th century.

The Grammar of Late Modern English

There have been no major changes in the grammar of English since the 18th century, but a few minor developments. We saw in the Swift passage the use of a past tense *writ*, where we use *wrote*, and there are other examples in the 18th century of past tenses differing from PresE ones—forms like *choosed*, *creeped*, *swum*, *sung*, *grinded*. Past participles, too, sometimes have different forms in the 18th century, and we meet expressions like *he had spoke*; other examples include past participles like *arose*, *drove*, *rode*, *ran*, and *shook*. Some of these forms persisted into the 19th century.

In the system of auxiliaries, some changes in usage have been going on. The modal auxiliary *can* has been encroaching on the territory of *may*, and it is now common to use *can* in asking or giving permission ('Can I go now?'). In its turn, *may* is encroaching on the territory of *might*; for many of the younger generation in England, the auxiliary *might* hardly exists at all, its place being taken by *may*; and recently I read in a national newspaper an account of a football-match which had ended in a goalless draw, in which occurred the surprising sentence 'Just before half-time, Leeds United may have scored a goal' (meaning 'they might have scored a goal, they had a chance of scoring a goal'). Similarly, *will* and *would* are encroaching on *shall* and *should*, and the old school-book rule that *I/we shall* denotes futurity while *I/we will* denotes volition is certainly not true; it is common to use *will* with the first person pronouns to denote simple futurity, as in *We will all die some day*.

It seems likely that some of the modal auxiliaries are ceasing to be auxiliaries, and turning into ordinary lexical verbs. The clearest cases are *need* and *dare*; sometimes these are used as auxiliaries (*Need he go? He dare not go*), and sometimes as lexical verbs (*Does he need to go? He doesn't dare to go*); and it seems likely that they are moving into the latter class. The same process is seen in *ought to* and *used to*; these are normally auxiliaries (*Oughtn't he to go? He usedn't to go*), but nowadays they are sometimes used as lexical verbs (*Didn't he ought to go? He didn't used to go*), though these are perhaps still substandard. As lexical verbs, of course, *ought to* and *used to* are odd: their lack of the third-singular inflection -*(e)s* can be explained by saying that they have the past-tense inflection -*(e)d*, but then this inflection ought to be dropped after auxiliary *did* (cf. *he walked*, but *he didn't walk*.)

Changes continue in the comparison of adjectives. In the lModE period it has been normal for monosyllabic adjectives to be compared with -*er/-est* (*ruder, rudest*), and for polysyllabic adjectives to be compared with *more/most* (*more beautiful, most beautiful*). Dissyllabic adjectives have been variable, some taking -*er/-est* (*clever, narrow, profound, cloudy, common, pleasant*, etc.), and the others *more/most* (*thoughtful, pleasing, famous, sheepish*, etc.). The tendency during the lModE period has been for *more/most* to encroach on -*er/-est*, and it is now normal to say *It's more common than I thought*, and *He is the most clever of the three*. Among the younger generation, it is even becoming normal to use *more/most* with monosyllables, and you hear things like *He was more rude than I expected*. The trend from -*er/-est* to *more/most* is in line with the broad development of English over the last thousand years: it is a change from the synthetic to the analytic, from the use of inflections to the use of grammatical words and word-order.

Another development of Modern English which is in the same direction is the proliferation of phrasal verbs, formed from a lexical verb followed by an adverbial particle, like *try out, let on*. They are of course found before Modern English times, but there has been a great expansion of them in the ModE period, and new ones are still being formed. They may be transitive, like *shrug off* or *fall for*, or intransitive, like *lose out* or *butt in*. Sometimes the phrasal verb can be followed by a preposition, giving forms like *walk out on, gang up against, face up to, fix up with, get away with, meet up with*.

However, one change going on in recent times is in the opposite direction: it is becoming more normal to use the '*s* genitive inflection of nouns instead of constructions with the preposition *of*. Earlier in the lModE period, people said *the man's face*, but *the face of the clock*. Broadly speaking, the '*s* genitive was confined to nouns referring to animate creatures, though there were also other types (*a week's holiday, the water's edge*.) However, the recent tendency, at any rate in the written language, has been for the '*s* genitive to be used with all types of nouns, and we meet expressions like *the clock's face, the pound's devaluation, evil's power, the game's rules, London's East End.*

The system of determiners has remained stable in the lModE period, but there has been a tendency recently for the definite article to be omitted in a number of positions where formerly it was inserted. In the 19th century, children caught *the mumps* or *the measles*, but nowadays they are more likely just to catch *mumps* or *measles*. People now talk about being *at university*, or of going *to grammar school*. They discuss the *art of theatre* (though they still go *to the theatre*); and similarly with *cinema*. And they enquire whether there has been any change *in Bank Rate*. The similar tendency to say *Government* instead of *the Government* is probably an Anglo-Indianism.

The Phonology of Later Modern English

In Later Modern English, there has perhaps been some reduction in the amount by which pronunciation varies. Inside England, for example, the old rural dialects have been dying out, as a consequence of improved communications, greater mobility of population, the establishment of universal education, and more recently the rise of the mass media. Of course there are still class and regional accents in England, but the range of variation is perhaps less than it used to be. One of these accents has continued to be considered standard inside England; in the 18th century, indeed, it was still possible for a self-respecting country gentleman to speak with a regional accent, but this has become rarer. One of the forces making for the propagation of a standard pronunciation has been the public school, the boarding school for the sons of the rich, which has been the favoured means of education for the English gentry at least since the time of Arnold of Rugby in the early Victorian age. The public schools have propagated a pronunciation which, inside England, is non-regional, and is used by upper-class speakers from all parts of the country. This is the pronunciation which, earlier this century, was described by Daniel Jones in his *Pronouncing Dictionary*, and called by him Received Pronunciation (RP). There are signs, however, that nowadays the educated speech of south-eastern England is regarded as a standard, rather than the speech of the public schools. Moreover, as a result of the social changes of the last half-century, educated regional speech has risen in prestige in England, and is quite common among the professional classes. So RP in the old sense seems to be losing its monopoly.

Outside England, of course, RP has no special status. The Scots, the Irish, the Americans, the Australians, and all the other national groups in the English-speaking community, have their own accents, and see no particular virtue in the pronunciation of the English upper classes. During the colonial period, indeed, the language of England had prestige and influence throughout the English-speaking world; but that age is past, and RP is now merely one accent among many. However, it is one of the accents that has been fully described, and whose history has been examined in detail; and in my brief account of lModE phonology I shall concentrate on the standard language of England.

The Long Vowels

It will be remembered that we were left with a problem about the long vowels at the end of the eModE period. In the late 17th century, ME /ɑː/ and ME /ɛː/ had fallen together as /eː/, so that *bake* and *mate* had the same vowel as *clean* and *meat*, and were in contrast to ME /eː/, which had become /iː/, as in *green* and *meet*. Whereas of course in PresE it is not so: on the contrary, it is ME /ɛː/ and ME /eː/ that have fallen together (*clean, meat, green, meet*), and are in contrast to ME /ɑː/ (*bake, mate*). But if two phonemes have once fallen together, there is no means of unscrambling them again: ordinary speakers do not know the histories of the pronunciations that they use, and are unable to restore distinctions that have vanished in their own speech. So what are we to think? One possible view is that after all ME /ɑː/ and ME /ɛː/ did not fall together in the late 17th century, that *bake* and *mate* never did have the same vowel as *clean* and *meat*; and that, on the contrary, at that date ME /ɛː/ became /iː/, thus falling together with the /iː/ from ME /eː/. This may be right, but it must be said that the evidence for the falling-together of ME /ɑː/ and ME /ɛː/ is quite considerable, and is not too easily disposed of. An alternative view, which accommodates this evidence, is that there were two variant styles of pronunciation in eModE; in the style which was standard at that period, ME /ɑː/ and ME /ɛː/ fell together in the late 17th century; but there was also a substandard style of speech in which ME /ɛː/ had fallen together with ME /eː/, perhaps even before the Modern Period had begun, and in which the resulting phoneme was kept distinct from ME /ɑː/. The modern pronunciation would then result from a change of fashion: in the 18th century, the style which had formerly been substandard became standard, and the old standard style fell out of use. Such a change of style might be explained by regional movements of population, or, more probably, by social changes: the modern style of pronunciation may have been characteristic of the middle classes, who carried it into the standard language when they rose to positions of power and prominence in English society. If this view is accepted, certain aberrant pronunciations in PresE (*great, steak, break, yea*) can be explained as vestiges of the older style.

In the later 18th century, then, there was a phoneme /iː/ (from ME /eː/ and ME /ɛː/), and a phoneme /eː/ (from ME /ɑː/, and also ME /aɪ/). At the end of the 18th century, the /eː/ was diphthongized to

/eɪ/, which remains in PresE, as in *bake* /beɪk/, *mate* /meɪt/; but in some styles of speech, like Scots, the pure vowel has remained.

The long back vowels in the 18th century were /uː/, /oː/, and /ɒː/. At the end of the 18th century the /oː/ was diphthongized to /oʊ/, and in the 20th century this became /əʊ/, as in *goat* /ɡəʊt/, *home* /həʊm/. The /ɒ/ phoneme, which was an open rounded back vowel, has become progressively closer during the lModE period, and is now /ɔː/, a half-open vowel; it is the vowel heard in PresE *law* /lɔː/, *cause* /kɔːz/.

During the present century, the close long vowels /iː/ and /uː/ have become diphthongized; Daniel Jones, earlier in the century, described them as long pure vowels, but in educated speech today they are usually pronounced [ɪi] and [ʊu], especially when the vowel is in final position, as in *see* and *who*. In substandard speech the diphthongization has proceeded further, and one hears pronunciations like [əi] and [əu].

Later Modern English, as we shall see, also has two new long-vowel phonemes that did not exist in eModE. They are /ɜː/, the vowel that occurs in PresE *bird* /bɜːd/ and *turn* /tɜːn/; and /ɑː/, the vowel of PresE *pass* /pɑːs/ and *father* /ˈfɑːðə/.

The Short Vowels

The short vowels have remained reasonably stable. The new short vowel /ʌ/ (as in *cut* and *luck*), which probably began as a moderately close back unrounded vowel, has become opener and moved further forward during the lModE period. Early this century it was still in the back half of the vowel-diagram, but was fairly open; and in recent years it has been moving forward, so that in the speech of the younger generation it is now a central or even front vowel, moving towards the quality of the vowel of Modern French *la*.

There has been a tendency for /æ/ to be lengthened; the lengthening is sporadic, occurring in some speakers but not others, in some words but not others; but it is particularly common in monosyllables ending in a voiced consonant, and some speakers regularly use a fully long [æː] in words like *bag*, *bad*, and *man*.

In unstressed syllables, there has been a recent tendency for /ə/ to spread at the expense of other vowels, especially /ɪ/. Typical PresE pronunciations are *system* /ˈsɪstəm/, *ability* /əˈbɪlətɪ/, *kitchen* /ˈkɪtʃən/, where formerly the pronunciations were /ˈsɪstɪm/, /əˈbɪlɪtɪ/, /ˈkɪtʃɪn/. This development is bringing RP more into line with other forms of English speech, like American and Australian, where such /ə/ pronunciations are common.

Lengthening Before Voiceless Fricatives

At the end of the 17th century, the short vowels /æ/ and /ɒ/ were lengthened, in one style of speech, when they occurred before the voiceless fricatives /s/, /f/, and /θ/. The lengthened forms were accepted as standard in the 18th century, but the short vowels have continued to exist alongside them in some varieties of English.

The lengthening of /æ/ was /æː/, which was later retracted to /ɑː/. So *ask* was 17th century /æsk/, 18th century /æːsk/, and 19th century /ɑːsk/, which it has remained. And similarly *staff* and *bath*, which had 17th century /æ/, have become PresE /stɑːf/ and /bɑːθ/. The lengthening did not take place before /s/ if another vowel followed, so we have *class* /klɑːs/, but *classic* /ˈklæsɪk/. The development of 17th century /æ/ to 18th century /æː/, and later to /ɑː/, also took place in some other cases, as in the words *father* and *answer*. As a consequence of the process, we have in lModE a new phoneme, /ɑː/. (Middle English /aː/, it will be remembered, had become /eː/ by the late 17th century, and is now /eɪ/.) However, some forms of English have retained a short vowel before the voiceless fricatives; in northern England you often hear pronunciations like [ask] and [baθ] (where [a] corresponds to RP /æ/). And some forms of English have retained the 18th century lengthened [æː], giving pronunciations like [æːsk] and [bæːθ], often heard in American English.

The lengthening of /ɒ/ was /ɒː/, which fell together with the /ɒː/ from ME /au/, and with it developed into PresE /ɔː/. The pronunciation with the long vowel was accepted as standard in the 18th century, but the forms with a short vowel have always continued to exist alongside those with a long, and both pronunciations exist in PresE, as in *cross* /krɔːs, krɒs/, *off* /ɔːf, ɒf/, *broth* /brɔːθ, brɒθ/. At the present time, the pronunciations with the long vowel seem to be dying out, and sound rather old-fashioned.

The Loss of /r/

The biggest change in the consonant-system of lModE has been the loss of /r/ when it occurs before a consonant or a pause. In eModE, /r/ was still pronounced in such positions, as in arm /ærm/, *dare* /dɛːr/. But during the 17th century the /r/ was weakened in such positions, and in the mid-18th century it disappeared. At the end of a word, the /r/ was lost only if a pause or a consonant followed; if a vowel followed, the /r/ was retained. So in PresE the word *father*, pronounced in isolation, is /ˈfɑːðə/; *father could* is /ˈfɑːðəkʊd/; but *father and mother* is /ˈfɑːðərənˈmʌðə/.

However, although this change is characteristic of RP, it has not taken place in all forms of English, and indeed the majority of the English-speaking community retain pre-consonantal and final /r/. It is retained, for example, by most American speakers, though there are a few areas where it is lost (the coastal South, eastern New England, New York City).

The consonant /r/ has exercised considerable influence on preceding vowels during the ModE period. Many of these changes began in the eModE period, and some even in ME; but their full consequences for the phonemic system of English were not apparent until the loss of final and pre-consonantal /r/ in the 18th century, so it has been convenient to defer their consideration until this point. The changes were far-reaching and of many kinds. We can consider briefly three of them: changes of quality, lengthening, and diphthongization.

One of the changes of quality, that of /er/ to /ar/ goes back to Late Middle English. It occurred especially before consonants, and accounts for PresE forms like *farm* and *star* from ME *ferme* and *sterre*. But it occurred somewhat sporadically, and in eModE there are many words which retain /er/. There are also words in which both pronunciations are recorded in eModE; and a few doublets have survived to the present day, like *person/parson*, *perilous/parlous*, *university/varsity*.

In the words in which /er/ was retained in eModE, this developed in about 1600 into /ər/; so *herb*, which had been pronounced /herb/, became /hərb/. At about the same date, the group /ɪr/ before a conso-nant also became /ər/; so *bird*, which had been pronounced /bɪrd/, became /bərd/. In the course of the 17th century, /ʊr/ also became /ər/; *curse* was first /kʊrs/, and then /kʌrs/, and finally /kərs/. In the early 18th century /ə/ was lengthened before /r/ in stressed syllables, and then the /r/ was lost; this gave us the new long-vowel phoneme /ɜ:/ of lModE, as in PresE *herb* /hɜ:b/, *bird* /bɜ:d/, *curse* /kɜ:s/.

In the 17th century, /æ/ and /ɒ/ were lengthened before /r/ when another consonant followed, so *arm* developed from [ærm] to [æ:rm], and *corn* from /kɒrn/ to /kɒ:rn/. In the case of /æ/, the lengthened vowel must in the first place have been a mere allophone, the variant of /æ/ which appeared before /r/; but when the /r/ disappeared in the 18th century, the long /æ:/ became an independent phoneme, since for ex-ample the distinction between *am* and *arm* no longer depended on the /r/, but on the length of the vowel, /æm/ as compared with /æ:m/. The long /æ:/ fell in with the one which had arisen before voiceless fricatives (and which until this time was presumably also only an allophone), and with it developed at the end of the 18th century to /ɑ:/, giving the PresE pronunciation /ɑ:m/. In the case of /ɒ/, the lengthened vowel fell in with /ɒ:/ from ME /au/, and with it developed into PresE /ɔ:/, so that we now have the same vowel in *corn* /kɔ:n/ as in *cause* /kɔ:z/.

And finally diphthongization. In the eModE period, the long vowels had special allophones which occurred before /r/. These allophones were opener in quality that the normal allophone of the phoneme in question. In the 17th century, we can postulate that *here* /hi:r/ was actually pro-nounced [hɪ:r]; *dare* /dɛ:r/ was [dɛ:r]; *roar* /ro:r/ was [rɔ:r]; and *poor* /pu:r/ was [pʊ:r]. However, in the course of eModE, an [ə] glide developed between the long vowels and the following /r/, giving the pronunciations [hɪər], [dɛər], [rɔər], and [puər]. At this stage, the diphthongs were still only allophones: [ɪə] for example was merely the variant form of /iː/ which happened to occur before /r/. But when the /r/ vanished, in the 18th century, these diphthongs became phonemes in their own right, and are the centering diphthongs of PresE, /ɪə/, /ɛə/, /ɔə/, and /uə/. The PresE pronunciations of the four words are /hɪə/, /dɛə/, /rɔə/, /puə/.

A similar [ə] glide developed between diphthongs and /r/, so that *fire* and *flour*, which were eModE /fəir/ and /fləur/, have become PresE /faɪə/ and /flɑuə/.

English as a World Language

The expansion of the English language over the world began in the 17th century, with the first American settlements, but it is in the Later Modern English period that this expansion has been really spectacular, and that English has become the principal international language. Until about a century ago, the major speech-area of the language was still Britain, but in about 1850 the population of the United States overtook that of England, and then shot far ahead, so that North America is now (1971) the main centre of the English-speaking community, with some 20 million native speakers in Canada and over 200 million in the United States. The British Isles remain the second most important area (nearly 58 million), followed by Australia (11½ million), New Zealand (2½ million) and South Africa (over 1 million). English is also important as a second language in many parts of the world, especially in former British colonial possessions like Nigeria and India.

With this expansion, divergent development has taken place, so that there are now distinctively American forms of English, Australian forms, and so on. The most striking differences are in pronunciation, but there are also differences in vocabulary, and small differences in grammar. When a speech-community expands geographically, there is a tendency for the peripheral areas to be the most conservative linguistically, while the original homeland of the language tends to be the most innovating area. And in fact we have already noticed cases where standard British English has innovations not shared by most peripheral areas: most American forms of English retain preconsonantal and final /r/, which is lost in RP; and American English retains the 18th century pronunciation [æː] for the phoneme /ɑː/ (though in this case the speech of northern England is even more conservative, preserving the even earlier unlengthened [a]). In grammar, American English preserves a past participle *gotten* which is more archaic than *got*, the only form found in standard British English. Even in vocabulary, where the peripheral areas are most likely to innovate, some items are retained which have been lost in England; in Australian English, for example, we find old dialect words which no longer survive in England, like *dinkum* 'genuine', *larrikin* 'hooligan', and *fossick* 'seek'.

On the whole, however, the peripheral areas tend to innovate in vocabulary, because they encounter new objects, new flora and fauna, new situations. Australian *outback*, *stockman*, *swagman*, and American *rapids*, *cowboy*, *groundhog* are the products of a new geographical setting and a new way of life. Speakers in the peripheral areas may also encounter speakers of other languages, from whom words are borrowed. The Australians borrowed words from the local aboriginal languages, like *dingo*, *gunyah*, *billabong*. North American English has borrowed from Amerindian languages (e.g. *chipmunk*, *totem*, *pow-wow*); from Spanish (e.g. *canyon*, *ranch*, *stampede*, *desperado*); and from French (e.g. *prairie*, *rapids*, *pumpkin*). And of course similar processes of word-formation—using affixation, shortening, conversion and so on—go on independently all the time all over the English-speaking area. Sometimes, as a consequence, different areas have different words for the same object: American *railroad*, *auto*, *sidewalk*, *subway*, beside British *railway*, *car*, *pavement*, *underground*. But, with the improvement in international communications, there has come a tendency for such vocabulary items to become common property; a speaker will know both forms, even if he uses only one himself; and in some cases the local form will ultimately be displaced by a more distant one which is conquering the whole speech-area. American influence, as could be expected, is particularly powerful, and the English language all over the world now has an enormous number of words and phrases of American origin, many of which are no longer thought of as specifically American at all.

If we consider the formal literary language, differences in grammar between the regional varieties of English are very small. We have already noticed that American English has a past participle *gotten* beside *got*; it also has a past participle *strived* beside *striven*. In the Northern dialects of the United States, the verb *dive* has a past tense *dove*, but in the Midland and Southern dialects it is *dived*, as in Britain. An American can use impersonal *one*, and then continue with *he* and *his*, as in *If one loses his temper, he should apologize*, where an Englishman would replace *his* and *he* by *one's* and *one*. An Englishman can use a plural verb and plural intensive or reflexive pronoun after a collective noun, as in *The government are considering the matter themselves*, whereas an American prefers singular forms. There are also differences in the use of prepositions. For example, an Englishman would live *in* King Street, but most Americans would live *on* it (though *in* is heard in New York City, and also in Canada); and an Englishman caters *for* somebody, while an American caters *to* him. But, while points of this kind could be multiplied, they are all very minor.

If one turns from the literary language to familiar speech, and especially to less educated speech, the differences in grammar become greater. Even so, one can say that the different regional varieties of English have essentially the same grammatical system.

Differences in pronunciation are greater still. Some varieties of English have the same system of phonemes as RP, but the actual realizations of some phonemes are different. Educated Australian has the same phoneme system as RP, but has rather different qualities for the vowels: for example, the Australian /ɑ:/ is pronounced [a:], much further forward than in RP, somewhat like the vowel of German *Vater*; while the Australian /ɪ/ phoneme is pronounced [i], closer than that of RP, so that to an Englishman it often sounds like /i:/. In some varieties of English, the actual system of phonemes differs in some ways from that of RP; for example, where RP has two phonemes, /ʊ/ and /ʌ/, the speech of northern England has only one, usually realized as some kind of unrounded [u]. In yet other cases, the system of phonemes is the same, but their distribution in actual linguistic forms is different. For example, RP and educated Australian both have an /ə/ phoneme and an /ɪ/ phoneme, but Australian frequently uses /ə/ where RP has /ɪ/: RP *waited* and *loaded* are /'weɪtɪd/ and /'ləʊdɪd/, but in Australian are /'weɪtəd/ and /'ləʊdəd/; and similarly *boxes* is RP /'bɒksɪz/ but Australian /'bɒksəz/ (which in RP could only be *boxers*). Differences of all three kinds—of realization, of system, of distribution—are found between RP and American English, and also between the different regional varieties of American English. The vast majority of the differences are concerned with the vowels; the consonant-system of English is pretty much the same in all present-day varieties of the language.

During the lModE period, then, English has become a multi-centred language, whereas in eModE (despite the Scots) it was to all intents and purposes single-centred, with London as its focus. It has taken the English a long time to recognize this situation; through most of the lModE period they have tended to assume that their own form of the language is the only 'correct' one, and that other varieties, like the American, are in some way inferior and corrupt; and it is not surprising that the arrogance and provinciality of this attitude have provoked violent nationalist counterblasts, especially from Americans. Things are changing, however, and even the English are at last realizing that the Queen's English has no special divine right. A tolerant acceptance of all regional varieties of English, an accordance of parity of esteem, may not quite have come yet, but at any rate it looks as though it may be on the way.

FURTHER READING

Good general histories of English are A. C. Baugh, *A History of the English Language* (2nd ed., London, 1959) and (more advanced) B. M. H. Strang, *A History of English* (London, 1970). General works on the history of the English vocabulary are J. A. Sheard, *The Words We Use* (London, 1954), and M. S. Serjeantson, *A History of Foreign Words in English* (London, 1935).

The fullest historical treatment of Modern English is Otto Jespersen's massive work, *A Modern English Grammar on Historical Principles* (7 vols, Heidelberg I–IV, London V–VI, Copenhagen VII, 1909–49). More manageable, but still very detailed, is H. C. Wyld, *A History of Modern Colloquial English* (3rd ed., Oxford, 1936), which deals with the 15th to 18th centuries, and devotes most attention to phonology.

For 16th century attitudes to English, an indispensable work is R. F. Jones, *The Triumph of the English Language* (Stanford, California, 1953). E. A. Abbott, *A Shakespearian Grammar* (3rd ed., London, 1870) has an old-fashioned look, but is full of useful material. The phonology of Early Modern English is treated in detail by E. J. Dobson, *English Pronunciation 1500–1700* (2 vols, Oxford, 1968).

For good introductions to non-British varieties of English, see A. H. Marckwardt, *American English* (Oxford, 1958), and G. W. Turner, *The English Language in Australia and New Zealand* (London, 1966). For recent changes in British English, see C. L. Barber, *Linguistic Change in Present-day English* (Edinburgh, 1964).

My account of the development of the dummy auxiliary *do* is based on A. Ellegård, *The Auxiliary Do: the Establishment and Regulation of its Use in English* (Stockholm, 1953); and my formulations on the auxiliaries in PresE owe much to W. F. Twaddell's little booklet *The English Verb Auxiliaries* (Providence, Rhode Island, 1960).

Essays about English are collected in W. F. Bolton, ed. *The English Language* (Cambridge, 1966).

9

THE STUDY OF ENGLISH

Dr. R. C. Alston, *University of Leeds*

A certain licence to depart from the pattern of the rest of this volume, dealing as it does almost exclusively with factual information, will perhaps be permissible in this final chapter. And if mere finality were not enough to excuse what follows then the title of the chapter, with its designedly vague inference of content, should permit what can only be described as a predominantly speculative, if one hopes at times provocative, discussion of some aspects of the 'Study of English.' The chapter falls into two quite distinct parts: a retrospective survey of some aspects of the history of English studies and a review of certain present tendencies. The latter part is a personal statement, and therefore invites disagreement on some rather fundamental suppositions about literature, the literary experience, and the delicate relationship which connects a poet and his audience. I do not expect the majority of readers to agree with everything that is said in this chapter, but it does, I believe, represent a view of English studies which has both logic and appeal, and attempting, as it does, to rationalize linguistic and literary disciplines, its proposition here seems altogether appropriate.

The 'Study of English' as we know it today, in countless universities and colleges throughout the English-speaking world, in common with certain other humanistic disciplines, is a fairly recent development. Compared with, for example, the study of the classics, theology, or grammar (to say nothing of logic and law) it is a newcomer to the academic scene. We tend to forget that the first professorship of English was instituted at Glasgow in 1862[1] and that systematic instruction in English literature at universities in Britain and the United States dates from the last half of the nineteenth century. It is, therefore, a study which has little tradition either to support or encumber it—not altogether a bad thing.

But the non-existence of the formal study of English at universities prior to the last half of the nineteenth century does not mean, of course, that earlier generations did not study literature, and it might be as well to dwell at this point on some aspects of the study of literature during the seventeenth and eighteenth centuries before dealing with some of the more important developments that took place in the nineteenth century.

The study of English ought to have begun during the sixteenth century, when vernacular literatures throughout Europe enjoyed unprecedented esteem and popularity. But criticism, which is one manifestation of a culture confident enough to formulate principles upon which the merits of art can be judged, came late to England. The important critics and scholars belong to the end of the century and it is hard to find in English scholarship rivals to such great scholars and critics as Pietro Bembo (1470–1547), Lodovico Ariosto (1474–1533), Giovanni Trissino (1478–1550), Giraldi Cinthio (1504–1573), Marco Girolamo Vida (1480–1566) in Italy; Johann Reuchlin (1455–1522) in Germany; Guillaume Budé (1467–1540), Mathurin Cordier (1480–1564), Joachim Du Bellay (1522–1560), Pierre de Ronsard (1524–1585) in France; or Desiderius Erasmus (1465–1538) in Holland. Sir Thomas Elyot did, it is true, produce a 'defense' of poetry in Book I of his *Boke of the Governour* (1531), and it is true that Thomas Linacre was a most learned and universally respected scholar (though he produced little), but the brilliant circle that Erasmus eulogized—Grocyn, Latimer, Colet and Linacre—make a slight showing by comparison with the solid achievements of Italian and French scholarship in the sixteenth century. And criticism in England has to wait for Sir Philip Sidney's *Defence of Poesie* (1595) before it has a real point of departure. Furthermore, as is well known, the *Defence* represents a direct importation of ideas current earlier in the century in Italy. And Puttenham's *Arte of English Poesie* (1589)—of which C. S. Lewis has said: 'It cannot even be claimed that Puttenham's taste compensates for his lack of science'— is certainly no match for a work like Claude Fauchet's *Receuil de l'origine de la langue et poésie françoise* (1581).

And so it is that, aside from Sidney's essay, which is a *tour-de-force* rather than a formulation of critical or scholarly principles, it is to the seventeenth century that we must turn for the origins of what we now call 'English Studies': more specifically, to one man who bestowed upon English thought and scholarship benefits which we still enjoy to-day—Francis Bacon.

An intellectual giant and a genius of the highest order judged by any standards, Bacon set himself early in life the task of establishing for learning (which for him included science, philosophy, and the liberal arts) principles which would serve for its 'advancement'. He has been damned and exalted: at one end of the scale there is Pope's celebrated line,

335

The brightest, wisest, meanest of mankind,

and Macaulay's pejorative essay; at the other, there are the lines from Cowley's great ode prefixed to Thomas Sprat's *History of the Royal Society* (1667):

> Bacon like Moses, led us forth at last;
> The barren Wilderness he past;
> Did on the very Border stand ·
> Of the blest promised land;
> And from the Mountain Top of his exalted Wit
> Saw it himself, and shew'd us it.

Comprehending, as he did, human endeavours in such majestic proportions, Bacon provided no minute prescriptions of scholarly or critical method—he was more concerned to invent principles than to propound dogmas. In the first book of the *Novum Organum* (1620) he sought to liberate science from the bondage of dogma and superstition, but students who do not read Latin will find in the manuscript discourse *Filum Labyrinthi* (British Museum MS. Harley 6797, ff. 139–150) an outline in English of Bacon's message. And the text of his dissertation might well be a sentence in that little tract: 'That it is the glory of God to Conceal, but it is the glory of man to invent'. For scholarship, which Bacon regarded as an indispensable concomitant of scientific curiosity, he provides (in the *Advancement of Learning*, 1605) the following terse summary:

> The works touching books are two: first libraries, which are as shrines where all the relics of the ancient saints, full of true virtue and that without delusion or imposture, are preserved and reposed: secondly, new editions of authors, with more correct impressions, more faithful translations, more profitable glosses, more diligent annotations, and the like.

Elsewhere in the same work Bacon becomes more specific, and writing of criticism he says:

> For all knowledge is either delivered by teachers, or attained by men's proper endeavours: and therefore as the principal part of tradition of knowledge concerneth chiefly in writing of books, so the relative part thereof concerneth reading of books. Whereunto appertain incidentally these considerations. The first is concerning the true correction and edition of authors; wherein nevertheless rash diligence hath done great prejudice. For these critics have often presumed that that which they understand not is false set down: as the Priest that where he found it written of St. Paul, *Demissus est per sportam*, mended his book, and made it *Demissus est per portam*; because *sporta* was a hard word, and out of his reading; and surely their

errors, though they be not so palpable and ridiculous, are yet of the same kind. And therefore as it hath been wisely noted, the most corrected copies are commonly the least correct. The second is concerning the exposition and explication of authors, which resteth in annotations and commentaries; wherein it is over usual to blanch the obscure places, and discourse upon the plain. The third is concerning the times, which in many cases give great light to true interpretations. The fourth is concerning some brief censure and judgement of the authors; that men thereby may make some election unto themselves what books to read. And the fifth is concerning the syntax and disposition of studies; that men may know in what order or pursuit to read.

This passage (which Bacon amplified somewhat in the *De Augmentis Scientiarum*) has been quoted in full because it summarizes the course which English scholarship and criticism was to take during the following two hundred years: a tradition complex and rich but which nevertheless was guided by essentially simple principles.

Bacon was not so much a critic himself but rather a rationalizer of criticism. Thus he stands apart from Sidney and Jonson (who owed much of his critical outlook to the *Defence* and paraphrased it in the Prologue to *Every Man in his Humour*), yet his influence can be seen at work in Hobbes, who sought not merely to *identify* the literary experience but to explain the processes of the creative mind and to introduce into criticism an adequate vocabulary for aesthetics. But Hobbes' influence on scholarship was negligible, and for the beginnings of literary scholarship we must turn to a disciple in spirit of Bacon—to Thomas Sprat, historian of the Royal Society and author of what is probably the first literary study of English, the *Account of the Life and Writings of Cowley* prefixed to the collected works published first in 1668 (and reprinted eleven times before the end of the century). Indebted perhaps in some respects to Paul Pellisson-Fontanier's *Discours sur les Oeuvres de M. Sarasin* (1656)[2], Sprat's *Life* incorporated some of the features of Walton's little biographies, and by combining criticism with biographical fact set the pattern for a tradition (best exemplified perhaps in Johnson's *Lives of the Poets*) which continued through the nineteenth century and still operates today. As editor and critic Sprat may be said to have inaugurated two of Bacon's *desiderata*: 'the true correction and edition of authors' and 'some brief censure and judgement of the authors'.

The later seventeenth century had, on the whole, little good to say about Shakespeare and his contemporaries. The prevailing critical theories about the relationship between poetry and morality did not dispose, for example, a critic like Rymer to praise Shakespeare's tragedies, and his condemnation of *Othello*, though excessive, is nevertheless representative:

> What can remain with the Audience to carry home with them from this sort of Poetry for their use and edification? how can it work, unless (instead of settling the mind and purging our passions) to delude our senses, disorder our thoughts, addle our brain, pervert our affections, hair our imaginations, corrupt our appetite, and fill our head with vanity, confusion, *Tintamarre* and Jingle-jangle. . . . There is in this play some burlesk, some humour and ramble of Comical Wit, some shew and some *Mimickry* to divert the Spectators: but the tragical part is plainly none other than a Bloody Farce, without salt or savour (*A Short View of Tragedy*, 1693).

It is no accident that between the 1623 Folio and the six volume edition of Nicholas Rowe in 1709 Shakespeare's *Works* enjoyed little or no benefit of scholarship—the reprints of the Folio in 1632, 1663/64, and 1685 have only occasional significance for the history of the text and have no apparatus. Rowe improved his edition of 1709 by publishing in 1714 a nine-volume edition which included, for the first time, a glossary 'explaining the Antiquated words made use of throughout his Works'. However, Rowe, we now realize, did violence to the text by modernizing spelling, punctuation and even grammar. Pope's edition of 1723–25 in six volumes contained no glossary, but a seventh volume with most of the material contained in the seventh supplementary volume of Rowe's edition (1710) appeared in 1725 edited by George Sewell. Succeeding editions, by Theobald (1733), Hanmer (1743–44), Warburton (1747), and Blair (1753) continued to add to the corpus of commentary on the text and its elucidation.

Johnson's *Proposals* for a new edition of Shakespeare were published in 1756 and he was in no doubt about the reasons for undertaking such a great task nor about the principles which would guide him:

> The business of him that republishes an ancient book is, to correct what is corrupt, and to explain what is obscure. . . . No other author ever gave up his work to fortune and time with so little care: no books could be left in hands so likely to injure them, as plays frequently acted, yet continued in manuscript.

We recognize at once two of Bacon's cardinal principles: but Johnson does not ignore Bacon's third and fourth principles, and adds:

> When a writer outlives his contemporaries, and remains almost the only unforgotten name of a distant time, he is necessarily obscure. Every age has its modes of speech, and its cast of thought; which, though easily explained when there are many books to be compared with each other, becomes sometimes unintelligible and always diffi-

cult, when there are no parallel passages that many conduce to their illustration. Shakespeare is the first considerable author of sublime or familiar dialogue in our language. Of the books which he read, and from which he formed his style, some perhaps have perished, and the rest are neglected. His imitations are therefore unnoted, his allusions are undiscovered, and many beauties, both of pleasantry and greatness, are lost with the objects to which they were united, as the figures vanish when the canvas has decayed.

It is significant that the *Proposals*, a landmark in the history of literary scholarship, were published a year after the appearance of the celebrated *Dictionary*, in which Johnson had drawn extensively on the text of Shakespeare and his contemporaries in displaying the history of the English vocabulary: 'I have studiously endeavoured to collect examples and authorities from the writers before the restoration, whose works I regard as *the wells of English undefiled*, as the pure sources of genuine diction'. And, he added, from Tudor English 'a speech might be formed adequate to all the purposes of use and elegance. If the language of theology were extracted from Hooker and the translation of the Bible; the terms of natural knowledge from Bacon; the phrases of policy, war, and navigation from Raleigh; the dialect of poetry and fiction from Spenser and Sidney; and the diction of common life from Shakespeare, few ideas would be lost of mankind, for want of English words, in which they might be expressed'.

Although Johnson paid proper attention to the accuracy of his text, he understood that its elucidation was a more pressing need. Shakespeare's English was, after all, 150 years in the past:

All the former criticks have been so much employed on the correction of the text, that they have not sufficiently attended to the elucidation of passages obscured by accident or time. The editor will endeavour to read the books which the author read, to trace his knowledge to its source, and compare his copies with their originals. ... With regard to obsolete or peculiar diction, the editor may perhaps claim some degree of confidence, having had more motives to consider the whole extent of our language than any other man from its first formation. He hopes that, by comparing the works of Shakespeare with those of writers who lived at the same time, immediately preceded, or immediately followed him, he shall be able to ascertain his ambiguities, disentangle his intricacies, and recover the meaning of words now lost in the darkness of antiquity.

As if mindful of Baconian principles, Johnson concludes his *Proposals* with a passage that exhibits an extraordinarily modern approach to textual criticism:

339

The observation of faults and beauties is one of the duties of an annotator, which some of Shakespeare's editors have attempted, and some have neglected. . . . But I have never observed that mankind was much delighted or improved by their asterisks, commas, or double commas; of which the only effect is, that they preclude the pleasure of judging for ourselves; teach the young and ignorant to decide without principles; defeat curiosity and discernment, by leaving them less to discover; and at last show the opinion of the critick, without the reasons on which it was founded, and without affording any light by which it may be examined.

Not since Bacon had the principles of textual scholarship and criticism been uttered with such clarity, coherence and confidence, and under different disguises, sometimes with different degrees of emphasis, they have formed the nucleus of numerous subsequent redefinitions of the objects of literary scholarship.

The 'Age of Johnson' does not readily admit summary in a sentence: but for our purposes it may certainly be said to inaugurate the study of English in a form approximately as we know it today. It generated a genuine curiosity for our earlier literature on the one hand; and on the other, it stimulated prodigious efforts to excel the Doctor's great *Dictionary* in providing for the study of literature adequate lexicographical tools: efforts which were to culminate a century later in the greatest historical dictionary ever undertaken—the Philological Society's *New English Dictionary*.

It is not our purpose here to outline the history of English lexicography since Johnson (a task that no one has yet undertaken), but the efforts of a few brave spirits deserve mention if only to demonstrate the continuity of development which is one theme in this chapter.

Richard Warner (1713?-1775) is one of those curious and gifted amateur scholars which the eighteenth century seemed to produce in profusion. His published work consists of a flora for the village of Woodford in Essex (*Plantae Woodfordienses*, 1771), a translation of Plautus' *Comedies* (1769), and *A letter to David Garrick, . . . concerning a Glossary to the plays of Shakespeare* (1768). Although he never succeeded in publishing his *Glossary* the manuscript still exists, and occupies (in two versions) seventy quarto volumes (British Museum MSS. Add. 10472-10542). He also compiled a word-index (as preparatory to a glossary no doubt) to the plays of Beaumont and Fletcher (British Museum MS. Add. 10543). Warner's prodigious labours, though unfulfilled in print, nevertheless demonstrated the eighteenth century's determination not only to produce adequate texts but also to elucidate them.

Herbert Croft (1751-1816) might have been known to posterity for more than a translation of King Alfred's will, a handful of satirical epitaphs, and a memoir on Young (contributed to Johnson's *Lives*), had he been able to complete and publish his 'New Dictionary of the English Language'; and the *Unfinished Letter to the Right Honourable William Pitt* (1788) in which he outlined his enterprise might have become as celebrated a document as Johnson's *Plan* of 1747. The growth of Croft's dictionary (which he later re-titled the 'Oxford Dictionary of the English Language') can be traced in the pages of the *Gentleman's Magazine* (Volumes 57, 58, 60, and 63) and finally in the *Proposals for publishing, in May next, Croft's Johnson's Dictionary* (1792). The manuscript, which then comprised over two hundred volumes, has unfortunately never been traced, but if the letter to Pitt does accurately describe his method, perhaps this is no great loss. For the principles on which he proposed to execute his dictionary do not represent any advance on those of Johnson, as the following quotation testifies:

> I am desirous as any lexicographer can be, . . . to fix a final standard of our language; . . . I shall do more to effect so desirable a business than all grammars and dictionaries together have yet been able to do in any one language . . . In the passages which will be almost innumerable, . . . I shall never suffer any one, beautiful or not beautiful, from a writer classical or not classical, living or dead, to appear in my book . . . without correcting it; and I shall correct it always, so as not only to make it right, but to shew the reader why and when it was wrong.

It is perhaps unfair to judge an enterprise by its 'Proposals' alone, and had it appeared principles like these might well have been replaced by others more likely to appeal to a society for whom the words *dictionary* and *Johnson* were virtually synonymous.

Our last eighteenth-century figure shares with Warner and Croft the unusual distinction of having contributed to the history of English lexicography without benefit of publication, though he did succeed in seeing into print a fragment. The Rev. Benjamin Dawson, Rector of Burgh in Suffolk from 1760 until his death in 1814, published in 1797 *Prolepsis Philologiae Anglicanae; or, plan of a philological and synonymical Dictionary of the English Language.* In 1806 appeared the first volume in quarto of the dictionary, with the title *Philologia Anglicana*, published at Ipswich. In the first 500 pages (all that were published) the alphabet extends from A to ADORNMENT only, which gives some idea of the magnitude of Dawson's conception.

The first thirty years of the nineteenth century witnessed a number of new dictionaries, amongst which the following are probably the most important: David Booth's unfinished *Analytical Dictionary of the English Language* (1836—begun in 1822) in which, for the first time, an attempt was made to exhibit 'in one continued narrative, the origin, history, and modern usage of the existing vocabulary of the English Tongue'; John Pytches' unfinished *New Dictionary of the English Language* (1808—only 28 pages appeared); and Noah Webster's *American Dictionary of the English Language* (1828). Though not a 'new' dictionary, H. J. Todd's revision of Johnson's *Dictionary* (published in four volumes in 1818) is nevertheless a landmark in the history of lexicography for he greatly improved Johnson's etymologies and gave more and fuller quotations from sixteenth century texts.

In 1822 Robert Nares, a thoroughly professional scholar (who spent some time as assistant librarian in the British Museum) and a competent self-taught philologist, published his *Glossary*. This is the first 'period' dictionary of English to be published and was intended solely as a lexical aid to the works of Shakespeare and his contemporaries. The Preface to this extraordinarily useful work deserves full quotation for it demonstrates convincingly the pattern which lexicography was beginning to follow:

The common reflection, that our admirable Shakespeare is almost over-whelmed by his commentators, and that the notes, however necessary, too often recall us from the text, first suggested this undertaking; the primary object of which was, to enable every reader to enjoy the unencumbered productions of the poet. The specimen of a glossary subjoined to Richard Warner's Letter to Garrick (1768), still further encouraged the attempt; in the prosecution of which, it soon appeared desirable to extend the illustration to all the best authors of that age. . . . I have carefully abstained from inserting the words and phrases of an earlier period than the reign of Elizabeth, except where the writers of her time at all affected the phraseology of Chaucer; which affectation, in my opinion, is almost the only blemish of the beautiful poems of Spenser. My reason was this: that, to complete the rational view and knowledge of our language, a separate Dictionary must be required, for the works of Chaucer, Gower, Lydgate, Occleve, and all those writers who can properly be called English; that is, who wrote when the language was no longer Saxon. A Saxon dictionary of the same form, with all the examples at length, would complete the historical view of our national speech. . . . It will readily be supposed that, in compiling this Glossary, I have taken advantage of all those indexes, which have lately been subjoined to the editions of our early authors; the assistance of which has rendered this volume much more copious than otherwise it could have been made, in the mode of collection above described. . . . Collections of provincial dialects would often have been extremely useful; many words esteemed peculiar to certain counties, being merely remnants of the language formerly in general use. But these collections are unfortunately few and scanty. . . .

Exactly fifty years later, thirty years after the founding of the Philological Society, James O. Halliwell and Thomas Wright (the former, better known by his later adopted name Halliwell-Phillipps, was one of the great Shakespeare scholars of the nineteenth century, and the latter was a distinguished antiquary and historian of medieval and Elizabethan England) revised Nares' *Glossary*, recommending it with uncommon enthusiasm. It is significant that although, naturally enough, able to supplement Nares' list of words, they found little to correct: 'The errors of his book are comparatively so few, and of so little importance, that it has been thought advisable to interfere as little as possible with his text.'

Before considering the contribution to English Studies made by the Philological Society (1842–) and the Early English Text Society (1864–) mention must be made of a lexicographer whom history has forgotten but who bridges the contribution of Johnson with that of the Philological Society. Charles Richardson (1775–1865) was a great admirer of Horne Tooke, whose revolutionary and influential *Diversions of Purley* appeared in 1786 and 1805, and followed his principles in the *Illustrations of English Philology* in 1815[3]. Like Tooke, Richardson criticized Johnson's dictionary with extraordinary severity. His opportunity to demonstrate the principles on which a dictionary ought to be compiled came when Richardson was invited to contribute the lexical part of the *Encyclopedia Metropolitana* (1819–1845). The full text, with a series of introductory sections on lexicographical method which represent a historic landmark in the development of linguistic theory, appeared in 1836–37 in two volumes with the title *A New Dictionary of the English Language*.

Richardson's dictionary represented a great advance in lexicographical method—his own words (from Section II of the Preface) deserve full quotation:

The great first principle upon which I have proceeded, in the department of the Dictionary which embraces the explanation, is that so clearly evolved, and so incontrovertibly demonstrated in the 'Diversions of Purley;' namely that a word has one meaning, and one only; that from it all usages must spring and be derived, and that in the Etymology of each word must be found this single intrinsic meaning, and the cause of the application in those usages. . . . The lexicographer can never assure himself that he has discovered the thing, the sensible object . . . the sensation caused by that thing or object (for language cannot sever them), of which that word is the name. . . . While investigating, then, the meaning and consequent

343

usage or application of words. I have considered it a duty incumbent upon the lexicographer to direct his view,—1st, To the etymology and literal meaning;—2nd, To the metaphorical application of this meaning—to the mind; 3rd, To the application consequent or inferred from the literal meaning;—and 4th, To the application consequent or inferred from that which is metaphorical.

To these novel, and (Bacon might have added) thoroughly *scientific* principles, Richardson added another of historic importance—a chronological sequence of illustrative quotations. He was aware of the significance of this method:

> By commencing with authorities in the earliest period of English composition, and continuing them successfully through the different stages by which the language has arrived at its present state of copiousness and (I would add) refinement, this Dictionary aspires to the pretension of presenting to the English reader an insight into some very interesting and instructive portions of a history of his native tongue.

The employment of a historical method, coupled with as exact an application of etymological data to sense-history as could be attempted by one man, introduced into lexicography principles which the editors of the Philological Society's *New English Dictionary* were quick to recognize as of fundamental importance.[4]

The history of the first twenty-five years of the Philological Society, founded in 1842, has been admirably told by Hans Aarsleff in *The Study of Language in England, 1780–1860* (Princeton, 1967), and there is no need to duplicate here his illuminating account of how the Society's great dictionary was conceived and planned. What does require our attention here, however, is the realization which dawned upon English scholars in the post-Richardson period that his dictionary represented about the best that could be expected from the labours of a single scholar: a superior dictionary, if it were attempted, would require the energies and skills of a veritable army of scholars and demand a co-operative and systematic programme of unprecedented proportions, to which students of language and literature could contribute with equal effectiveness. In tracing the history of English scholarship during the nineteenth century as it relates to the feasibility of the plan for a new English dictionary as outlined by Richard Chevenix Trench in his celebrated Paper read before the Philological Society in 1857[5], three factors deserve special mention: (1) the comprehensive publication of Anglo-Saxon texts, both in prose and poetry, undertaken by Benjamin Thorpe[6] (1782–1870) and John Mitchell Kemble[7] (1807–1857); (2) the great advances in comparative philology made by the German philologists Bopp and Grimm and in historical lexicography by the German classicist Franz Passow[8]; and (3) the foundation in 1864 of the Early English Text Society to co-ordinate in an orderly fashion the systematic publishing of the earliest literature of English, with all the necessary apparatus (annotative and glossarial) to ensure its intelligibility. By the time that work could begin in earnest on the compiling of the raw material out of which the *New English Dictionary* would eventually grow in 1877 (the year in which J. A. H. Murray's connection with the enterprise begins), a very considerable corpus of essential preliminary scholarship had already emerged.

The story of the evolution of the *New English Dictionary* (to be known later as either *NED* or *OED*) is familiar enough and has been told many times[9], and it only remains to observe here one vitally important fact: that the *NED*, calling (as Trench's plan required) for a massive quantity of research and editing, provided for English philological and literary scholarship a great and imaginative challenge, and the effects of that challenge are still evident in the continuing work of the Early English Text Society which F. J. Furnivall founded in 1864 to serve the needs of the great enterprise.

Several English scholars during the nineteenth century had complained of the fact that German scholarship had succeeded in providing for German literary and linguistic studies tools far excelling those available to Englishmen, and somewhat later Henry Sweet was to bewail the professional way in which German graduate students had begun to monopolize the study of English language. That all this changed during the 1860's, and that the last thirty years of the century witnessed a prodigious increase in the number of early texts edited on the one hand, and in the number of historical treatises in the vernacular on the other, must be credited largely to the enthusiasm for English studies created by the *NED*. Such was the enthusiasm, indeed, that even the University of Oxford was unable to resist requests made in 1893 to consider the founding of an Oxford English School. Congregation approved the idea in 1893 and in the following year the necessary statutes were approved and the English School was inaugurated. English Studies had at last, it seemed, come of age.

But the first ten years of the Oxford School produced only 43 men and 136 women candidates and it was not until the advent of Sir Walter Raleigh as Professor of English Literature that enrolment began to increase significantly. The study of the English language had to wait until 1920 when Henry Cecil Wyld was appointed to the newly named Merton Chair, and in his inaugural lecture, 'English Philology in English Universities', Wyld provided a blue-print for the professional training of English philologists. It is curious, but highly significant, that Wyld, a man whose interests in the history of English were wide and post-medieval, should have proposed a division of English studies into 'literary' and 'linguistic' streams:

> I cannot help feeling that when both Literature and Philology are insisted upon for a University examination, there is a danger that the student may be harassed by being compelled constantly to turn aside from those pursuits in which lies his chief delight, and that his studies in both subjects may suffer—especially that in which he ought most to excel.

Much of the present debate about the relationship between the study of language and literature arises out of curricula directly derived from such an attitude—a matter which now must engage our attention.

In selecting certain isolated movements and individuals from what is obviously a complex history much has necessarily been omitted. Changes and developments during the past twenty or so years in the United States, Canada, Australia, and other parts of the English-speaking world, do not admit synopsis, but it is probably true to say that the spectacular growth of English studies since the last War, with ever increasing enrolments in countless universities and colleges, has resulted in a good deal of fundamental uncertainty about aims and methods. Add to this the number of sub-disciplines now associated with the study of English and it all adds up to a complex and ill-defined subject which urgently needs to have its objects stated with clarity. English has now (as H. M. Chadwick prophetically said it would in 1920 after Cambridge had reformed its Tripos) assumed the role formerly occupied by the Classics. It does not seem, however, to possess that clarity of purpose which the older discipline had had ever since (in modern times at least) Erasmus enunciated it in his *De Ratione Studii* (1511). What follows represents a personal point of view—unusual in that it provides a solution based upon the past, but practical and useful because the results it may be expected to produce are therefore predictable.

The historical study of the English language appears to be a steadily shrinking ingredient in the curricula of most schools of English on both sides of the Atlantic—and in those places where it has all but disappeared one is likely to encounter the familiar apology that the 'old' must give way to the 'new'. Sometimes its disappearance has been honestly credited to the non-existence of anyone competent to teach it—less often is it credited to the non-existence of anyone willing to study it. The disenchantment towards historical linguistics (more frequently referred to as 'philology') which is to be witnessed everywhere to-day is the product of several factors (some of which I shall mention in a moment) but none more significant perhaps than the failure

346

of its proponents to define the purpose of their study. From time to time most academic disciplines find it both necessary and salutary to submit to redefinition, and English studies have undergone several during the last fifty years, but nowhere amongst historians of English do I find a voice speaking with the clarity or conviction of an Eliot, a Crane, a Leavis, or a Frye. Our kindred colleagues the linguists (about whom I shall have something to say later) submit themselves regularly to what must be exhausting revaluations and their disciples speak with that passion and enthusiasm given only to those who have gazed on the beatitude of Truth. Bibliographers, inspired by the formidable doctrine of Professor Fredson Bowers, have commenced a gigantic ransacking of our literature assisted by tools that they are convinced will eventually reveal the Authorized Version. By contrast with such as these it is little wonder that the historical study of English finds itself limping towards obscurity, opposed on all sides by forces it seems unable to resist. The time for revaluation has come, and for various reasons it would seem that the time is a propitious one.

The notion that the study of language and the study of literature are intimately related disciplines has achieved the status of academic cant, glibly professed but seldom practised. It provides, no doubt, a frequent topic of conversation in Senior Common Rooms when professors of 'Lang' and 'Lit' discuss the relevance of their study. Its vestiges are to be seen in the familiar departmental rubric—'Department of English Language and Literature': a label which frequently disguises an uneasy alliance between those whose proper study is literature and those whose proper study is Old and Middle English, with perhaps (in more conservative institutions) some pre-historic philology, Gothic, Old Norse, thrown in for good measure. One constituent, still to be seen in most 'Language' programmes, is the 'History of English' course, for which numerous virtually indistinguishable textbooks have been written, and which is usually taught by the Old English or Middle English specialist. Thus it happens that the entire corpus of vernacular literature up to the fifteenth century comes to be regarded as 'Lang' and everything thereafter as 'Lit'. But the very ambiguity of 'Language', embracing as it does both diachronic and synchronic studies, has forced upon the 'Language' man a further retreat in nomenclature, and he frequently prefers now to be regarded as a 'Medievalist'. The current protest against too much 'Language' in English Studies curricula is possibly a protest against too much Old and Middle English and should be acknowledged as such. I do not propose to enter upon a defence of Old English studies here—that has been undertaken by scholars more competent than myself—but I am deeply concerned over the future of historical linguistics studies which, though inevitably involving Old English and Middle English, seems to me a separate problem and one which, if solved, could have far-reaching consequences beneficial to all.

It is tacitly assumed that linguistic competence is a pre-condition for the meaningful study of the major monuments of Old and Middle English, and few institutions attempt to teach our earliest literature in translation. But at what point does English become 'modern' and therefore presumably wholly intelligible without the assistance of linguistic aids other than those provided in the *Oxford English Dictionary*? Caxton? Skelton? Shakespeare? Donne? Milton? Swift? The question cannot I suspect be answered yet because of our imperfect knowledge of so many aspects of English up to the beginning of the nineteenth century—syntax, pronunciation, semantics, static data on the one hand; and such subjective dynamic aspects as theories of language, diction and style on the other. A truly astonishing variety of other academic disciplines have at one time or another during this century been brought to bear upon the evaluation of literary works, but I am not aware of any significant attempt to re-instate the historical study of English during those centuries which produced the literature that forms, after all, the core of any English Studies programme. A recent pamphlet issued by the Modern Language Association of America, entitled *The Aims and Methods of Scholarship in Modern Languages and Literatures* (New York, 1963) contains four essays by leading authorities in English Studies (W. G. Moulton, F. Bowers, R. E. Spiller, and N. Frye) on 'Linguistics', 'Textual Criticism', 'Literary History', and 'Literary Criticism'. But no essay on historical language studies!

There are several reasons why the study of early modern English has been neglected. One obvious reason is the frankly discouraging amount of basic research which remains to be done before we can begin to construct reliable and accurate analyses of grammatical structures for the varieties of written English during the sixteenth and seventeenth centuries: and before that is done we cannot, I think, hope to establish workable criteria for studying historical stylistics. Again, one indispensable requirement for stylistic analysis is accurate information about what may be loosely termed 'usage', but the student of early Modern English has no period dictionary to guide him other than the *Oxford English Dictionary*. It could, indeed, be argued that the student of Old English literature is better served by the available lexicographical aids than is the student of Shakespeare. Apart from E. J. Dobson's work on early English pronunciation[10]—a great work which nevertheless has grave shortcomings, not the least of which is an obsession with non-existent 'standards' which leads him into frequent erroneous classifications of evidence as vulgar or dialectal—our knowledge of the various phonemic systems used by English speakers during the period 1500–1800 is totally inadequate. I admit that faced with such enormous gaps to fill scholarship may be justified in adopting a cowardly posture, but is not the re-examination of the textual history of our literature necessitated by the prevailing doctrines of bibliography as it applies to textual criticism at least as daunting a challenge?

A second, perhaps more immediately obvious reason for the neglect of historical linguistic studies in recent years, lies in the development of general and structural linguistics—a story too familiar to require comment here. One unhappy product of the newer discipline has been a disposition to discredit the older as founded upon misconceived and untenable assumptions about language described, for the most part, in an unscientific and illogical vocabulary. By comparison with the promise ultimately of producing verifiable theories about language, the historical method, with its promise of little more than probability, has seemed to many a less exciting and less rewarding alternative. Certainly an early phonetician like Bullokar with his awkward and frequently illegible transcriptions is no match for a trained phonetician and a tape-recorder. Yet is not a discipline which might one day enable us better to understand *Hamlet* at least as important in a seat of higher learning as one which will elucidate utterly the structural functions of the indefinite article in an East African dialect? I realize, of course, that I am guilty of an injustice to those institutions which do make an honest attempt to relate the study of language to literature, but I am confident that such institutions constitute an eccentric minority.

The study of English has, for three hundred years at least, been essentially belletristic: this seems undeniably true and is borne out by the brief survey above. However, in keeping with development in other humanistic disciplines it has, of late, shown distinct signs of becoming more and more professional and, as Professor Helen Gardner has observed: 'The notion that anybody with natural taste, some experience of life, a decent grounding in the classics, and the habit of wide reading can talk profitably on English literature is highly unfashionable'. I am not entirely convinced that professionalism in English studies is altogether to be desired, but that it is an inevitable development I have not the slightest doubt, and it seems to be on balance the appropriate procedure for a study which, once the preserve of the few, is being made available to all. And because the professional approach, with its preference for the accumulation of data rather than the cultivation of a refined taste, embodies thoroughness with vigour in dealing with facts of whatever significance, it provides an opportunity for the graduates of countless universities to make a contribution to scholarship: there is, after all, a limit to the amount of interpretive criticism that can be profitable.

Professor Bowers has, perhaps on more occasions than one wishes to remember, preached his gospel that a thorough, uncompromising, and disciplined study of the transmission of the text is an essential part of a critic's duty, and that intelligent editing of early literary texts must form the basis for analytic and evaluate criticism.[11] Such an approach is made possible, of course, by the development of such mechanical aids as microfilm and optical collating machines, and the impact of computer technology is already being felt in certain areas of literary study. A scholar today has little except infirmity of the flesh as an obstacle in examining whatever is relevant to his work. I have already, on another occasion, demonstrated the importance of bibliographical evidence for historical linguists involved with early printed texts:[12] what has yet to be demonstrated, and what may prove even more significant, is the importance of accurate linguistic data for the bibliographer and textual critic.

But important as textual criticism undoubtedly is for the student of literature, can it honestly be supposed that the study of a writer's language—the raw material out of which is fashioned a great poem or play—is of any less consequence? Must not the ascertaining of the text be logically followed by as precise a description of the linguistic medium which it represents as can be achieved before evaluation can begin? When we talk about diction, style, metaphor, imagery, prosody, rhetoric, in a sixteenth-century poem are we not fundamentally talking about sixteenth-century language? Can one, indeed, *criticize* before one has fully understood? Does not an unformulated and predominantly emotive response to a poem—however *valid* its holder regards such a response—run the risk of being false and therefore non-significant? Is it not necessary to *justify* rationally a preference for a poem deemed self-evidently great to one self-evidently bad? Such questions have exercised minds more able than mine, and I would not wish to stand here as an apologist for any particular definition of criticism, but my sense of the direction in which literary scholarship is now moving leads me to suppose that a comprehension of linguistic data may come to be recognized as a precondition of evaluative criticism. The 'significance', 'value', 'appeal', 'capacity to delight' of a piece of writing—any of the many qualities which distinguish an elegy from a laundry-list—exist only in so far as we can relate what we *feel* to what we *perceive* to be significant, valuable, appealing or delightful. Response to literature is necessarily an individual and personal matter, and since a critic is supposed neither to legislate nor to canonize taste, it follows that one of his obligations is to lay before the reader sufficient data to enable him to judge for himself the value a work has. Linguistic data is no less important than textual, bibliographical, biographical, or historical.

The gulf separating linguistic from literary studies today sometimes seems to me all but unbridgeable, but I suspect it is more illusory than real, caused by an unwillingness to meet on common ground, and the dislike which many students of literature feel for the soulless drudgery of a certain kind of philology which seems preoccupied with impenetrably obtuse theories of phonology.

Philologists, too, must share the blame for failing to insist on the relevance of their work for the study of literature, and for publicizing their pretence that the study of language is an end in itself. If we are prepared to invest our energies in studying the English language in its earliest period in order to deepen our comprehension and appreciation of the major literary monuments of Old and Middle English, have we none to spare for later periods? And, unless the current recession of Old and Middle English studies enjoys a dramatic reversal, are we not in danger of becoming members of an esoteric sect, cut off from the main stream of English Studies and dependent for our existence upon a university's benevolence towards disciplines unable to attract students? I realize, of course, that I am doing an injustice to the handful of those scholars who have contributed to our understanding of literary texts— but works like Hilda Hulme's *Explorations in Shakespeare's Language*, and to a lesser extent M. M. Mahood's *Shakespeare's Wordplay*, illuminating as they are, serve only to demonstrate the appalling magnitude of our ignorance about sixteenth-century English. It seems to me that (today and for the foreseeable future) every humanistic discipline must, in the interests of survival, demonstrate convincingly its relevance to the needs of the time. That the study of English literature continues year after year to attract young people in ever increasing numbers is an indisputable fact, and one which, though lamentable to some academic planners who would welcome a greater enrollment in science, I for one find profoundly encouraging, because it provides historical linguistics with an opportunity it may not be given again. If the custodians of our oldest literature (they are usually designated as 'Professors of English Language') feel helpless to oppose the present discontent with and uninterest in Old English, they ought to be seeking for other ways in which to contribute substantially to the English Studies curriculum, and the study of English since Caxton provides clearly a solution of some merit. Does not a discipline which makes a vital and demonstrably relevant contribution to a student's participation in the literary experience deserve a place in the academic sun?

There are several reasons why I believe that the plea which I am making for the study of early Modern English as an integral part of any broadly-conceived English Studies programme should be made now. For one thing, linguistics (whether synchronic or diachronic) because it is a defined, rigorous, and disciplined study, fits in appropriately with the 'professionalism' which I earlier commented on. Again, structural linguists are showing an increasing interest in historical aspects of language insofar as antecedent developments are now seen as positively useful in comprehending current patterns of linguistic structure. In view of the prestige which modern linguistics has earned during recent years such retrospective curiosity ought to be encouraged enthusiastically. Advances in technology now promise the philologist relief from much of the drudgery which has discouraged many a student contemplating a historical linguistic study. Computers can compile accurate word-indexes, produce concordances, and provide the raw material for the student of grammar, syntax, semantics, pronunciation, rhyme, and style, and even the input can frequently be assigned to unskilled labour leaving the scholar free to apply his skills and knowledge to the processed material. Literary bibliography has, of course, revealed a vast number of new texts which still have to be studied. But does the study of literature—granted even the prodigious quantity of unassessed material covered by the revised *Short-title Catalogue*[13] and Wing,[14] to say nothing of what the proposed eighteenth-century *Short-title Catalogue* will yield in undiscovered riches—offer anything to equal the challenge of producing really full dictionaries for the sixteenth and seventeenth centuries? a comprehensive historical grammar and syntax of early Modern English? an historical dictionary of English pronunciation? Would not the prosecution of these gigantic tasks bestow upon students of literature benefits at least as indispensable as those which have been harvested for over sixty years from the Philological Society's *New English Dictionary*?

But all of this is fantasy unless we can secure in the English Studies curriculum a respected place for the historical study of English, for it is therein that the scholars of the future are bred. The day when a department could sustain scholars who carried out major research with minimal teaching duties have all but disappeared and research in English language must, in the future, be carried out by staff whose involvement in undergraduate teaching is indispensable.

I do not wish to be misunderstood in what I have said about Old English Studies—I am not retreating in the face of student protest, nor am I suggesting that they should be allowed to sink into an obscure oblivion along with such once popular studies as Sanskrit or runic epigraphy. I am too much a Saxonist at heart for that—but I am saying that we cannot *much longer* continue to regard Old English as an indispensable ingredient in an English Studies undergraduate programme and therefore as a justification for maintaining in a Department of English a number of so called 'Language' specialists. To those who might be tempted to deplore this fact—even if they do not dispute its logic—I would remind them that the historical study of English in the early Modern period may well do more positively to encourage interest in the earliest period of the language: first, because the historical approach inevitable invites retrospective curiosity; and second, because some knowledge of Old and a good deal of Middle English is a necessary precondition for understanding the English of later periods.

Unless literature is deemed to manifest itself in instant intelligibility it seems obvious that the critical process must involve some sort of reconstruction or reconstitution, and that the critic's function is akin to that of the anatomist. Language, the instrument of a writer's artistry, can smother as well as liberate his yearning to translate sentient and intellectual experiences into verbal structures and patterns, and it has endured both rhapsody and scorn at the hands of its users. For Stevenson it was 'a poor bull's-eye-lantern wherein to show off the vast Cathedral of the world'; for Webster it was 'the immediate gift of God'. But the writer's difficulties with language are compounded for us, interpreters in another time with instinctual responses to a medium deceptively similar but in reality profoundly altered, and we cannot hope to achieve even a partially accurate reconstitution of a poem's intention without first acquainting ourselves with the characteristics of that medium. Comprehension—not merely of *what* the poet says but *how* he says it—ought to precede a disposition to evaluate its significance for us. And, in the end, that is what the study of literature is all about.

Space does not permit further forays into the business of criticism, and I certainly would not wish to add to I. A. Richards' celebrated synopsis: 'A few conjectures, a supply of admonitions, many acute isolated observations, some brilliant guesses, much oratory and applied poetry, inexhaustible confusion, a sufficiency of dogma, no small stock of prejudices, whimsies and crotchets, a profusion of mysticism, a little genuine speculation, sundry stray inspirations, pregnant hints and random aperçus; of such as these, it may be said without exaggeration, is extant critical theory composed'. But it does seem to me extraordinary how writers on the subject of criticism, with some notable exceptions, find it possible to evade linguistic considerations: I. A. Richards himself, for example, in the chapter of his *Principles* specifically labelled 'The two uses of language', comments that: 'Because the theory of language is the most neglected of all studies they are in fact hardly ever distinguished'. But revelation of linguistic usage was not pertinent to Richards' design and the chapter soon dissolves into a discussion of 'fiction' and 'truth'. Indeed, it is possible to find more attention paid to linguistic matters in Ben Jonson's *Timber* than in many a modern manual on criticism, even if the principal object of his strictures was a definition of the properties of style; and his dictum that 'Language most shows the man: speak that I may see thee. It springs out of the most retired and inmost parts of us, and is the image of the parent of it, the mind' recurs, variously disguised, throughout the succeeding centuries. Contemporary interests in stylistics, a study in which the accumulation of statistical data holds preference over purely impressionistic response and individual prejudice, promises to provide an area of research to which the philologist, the linguist, and the critic can all contribute, and from which they can all benefit. But what is style without the context of meaning and purpose? Insofar as most of our sixteenth- and early seventeenth-century literature was written in a rhetorical tradition (whether Ciceronian or Ramist) and much concerned with the problem of style, Jonson's jocular remark has a certain pertinence: 'Would you not laugh to meet a great councelor of state in a flat cap, with his trunk hose, and a hobby-horse cloak, his gloves under his girdle, and yon haberdasher in a velvet gown, furred with sables?'

All simplifications are necessarily misleading, frequently false, but there would, I think, be little dissent from the proposition that all literature has at least meaning and rhetoric: the task that historical linguistics has before it is to provide the literary scholar with the tools required to illuminate these. Among such tools dictionaries, grammars, and systems of stylistic analysis, are probably the most urgently needed.

The Philological Society's *New English Dictionary* has served the needs of English literary and linguistic scholarship for over eighty years, and still remains an indispensable work of reference for English studies throughout the world. That it has limited usefulness for scholars working in the period extending roughly from the invention of printing in England to the middle of the seventeenth century has long been recognized, and was a fact well understood by most of the editors involved in the enterprise. The late Sir William Craigie repeatedly stressed the urgency of completing the lexical record of English by compiling a series of period dictionaries, and he played a significant part in arousing interest in the *Middle English Dictionary*, currently being produced at the University of Michigan. Indeed, through him the whole collection of Middle English quotations for the *Oxford English Dictionary* were transferred from the Clarendon Press to Ann Arbor. Craigie was also largely responsible for starting at Ann Arbor the *Dictionary of Early Modern English* which would, when completed, continue the record of English up to the eighteenth century, and he again arranged for the relevant *NED* material to be deposited there. With substantial assistance from the Rockefeller Foundation, work was begun immediately on the *Dictionary of Early Modern English*, under the general editorship of Albert H. Marckwardt, Warner Rice, and Hereward T. Price. After five years work, however, it became necessary to discontinue the *Dictionary of Early Modern English*, since the University of Michigan decided that it could not adequately support and finance simultaneously two such large enterprises. Consequently, the *Dictionary of Early Modern English* came to a standstill, and there is every reason to believe that it will probably never be completed at the University of Michigan.

As has already been stated, the *Oxford English Dictionary* serves the needs of students of our language and literature covering a period of over seven hundred years, and was intended as a record of the whole history of English since Anglo-Saxon times. As stated in the Preface to the re-issue by the Oxford University Press in 1933:

> The aim of this Dictionary is to present in alphabetical series the words that have formed the English vocabulary from the time of the earliest records down to the present day, with all the relevant facts concerning their form, sense-history, pronunciation, and etymology.

As a very general statement this assertion may be regarded as valid, but is obvious that in endeavouring to cover the *whole* history of English the *NED* necessarily fails to record with completeness the total resources of the language for any given period. Its limitations may be strikingly indicated by pointing out that of the total number of titles listed in the *Short-title Catalogue* for the letters, A, B, and M, two-thirds were not read.

In the preface to her *Explorations in Shakespeare's Language*, Miss Hilda Hulme wrote: 'I hope to show how we may increase our linguistic equipment ... so as to bring ourselves, here and there, a step or two nearer to the language world in which Shakespeare's plays were written, for in feeding our memories more information about Eliza-bethan English we may deepen our sensitivity to the potential meaning of Shakespeare's words and phrases and ... become more alert to those clues within the text by which Shakespeare himself has circumscribed that potentiality, has limited our freedom of response'. Miss Susie Tucker wrote in the preface to her *Protean Shape*: 'The pages that follow are no more than a trial shaft dug into the rich mine of eighteenth-century [English]. The availability of good period dictionaries and grammars would surely make such works, now indispensable, almost superflous. Lexicography does, after all, demand the several contributory skills of the etymologist, the semanticist, the phonologist, and the grammarian —and if, as I hope, a large proportion of the basic text of future period dictionaries is excerpted by computers, the resulting tape-store would provide the student of style and syntax with an invaluable archive.'

I have stressed the need for a redefinition of purpose if we are to succeed in construing a coherent and appealing English Studies pro-gramme. One essential in such a redefinition must, I believe, be an explicit integration between literary and linguistic studies, in which linguistic data is regarded as demonstrably relevant to literary inter-pretation on the one hand and textual criticism on the other. Such an integration, though posing problems of some magnitude, and demanding a huge investment of effort in lexical and grammatical research, can be expected to have far-reaching effects—all the great editors of Shakespeare have testified to the diligence in accumulating linguistic data which his plays demand: Steevens affirmed that 'If Shakespeare is worth reading he is worth explaining; and the researches used for so valuable and elegant a purpose merit the thanks of genius and candour'; Malone declared: 'I scarcely remember ever to have looked in to a book of the age of Queen Elizabeth in which I did not find somewhat that tended to throw light on these plays'. Of the subleties of his language Johnson wrote: 'What can be known will be collected by chance from the recesses of obscure and obsolete papers. Of this knowledge every man has some and none has much'. But Shakespeare's first editors in the 1623 Folio put it best perhaps:

> And there we hope to your divers capacities you will finde enough both to draw and hold you: for his wit can no more lie hid then it could be lost. Reade him, therefore: and againe, and againe; and if then you doe not like him, surely you are in some manifest danger not to understand him.

In attempting what I here urge we might even rediscover the validity of Bacon's tripartite division of criticism into the exact correcting and publishing of authors, the explanation and illustration of authors, and a certain concise judgement or censure of authors: and so reunite, to a common purpose, the several skills of the bibliographer, the editor, linguist and critic.

NOTES

1. Trying to fix a date for the beginning of the academic study of English is not an easy matter. For example, English was studied at Göttingen in the eighteenth century—not surprising perhaps, in view of the part that George II played in its foundation (1736) and the fact that he was its first *Rector Magnificentissimus*; Rhetoric and Belles-Lettres had a chair at Aberdeen in 1762; and Thomas Dale was appointed the first Professor of English Literature and History at University College in London in 1836 (the Chair was instituted in 1828). The point of departure depends, in other words, on what 'English Studies' is held to signify.

2. Sprat's *History of the Royal Society* (1667) may also have been suggested by Pellisson's *Histoire de l'Académie françoise* (1653) which was translated into English by Henry Some in 1657.

3. Richardson also published in 1854 a general work *On the Study of Language* intended as an exposition of Tooke's general principles.

4. Generous credit for Richardson's achievement is given in the 'Historical Introduction' to the Oxford University Press re-issue of the *New English Dictionary*, re-named the *Oxford English Dictionary*, in 1933.

5. 'On some deficiencies in our English Dictionaries', published by the Society in 1857.

6. Thorpe studied under the great Danish philologist Rasmus Rask and translated his grammar of Anglo-Saxon into English in 1830.

7. Kemble studied philology with the 'father' of comparative Germanic philology, Jacob Grimm, whose great *Deutsches Wörterbuch* (1852–1854) was to exert such a powerful influence on the editors of the *NED*.

8. Passow's principles were first embodied in England in Liddell and Scott's *Greek English Lexicon* (1834)—as summarized by the editors: 'to make each Article a History of the usage of the word referred to'.

9. See especially Sir James A. H. Murray's *Evolution of English Lexicography* (Oxford, 1900), and the 'Historical Introduction' to the 1933 edition of the *NED*.

10. *English Pronunciation 1500–1700*, Oxford, 1968, 2 vols.

11. In his essay on 'Textual Criticism' in the M.L.A. pamphlet referred to above he says:

> A definitive edition is dependent for its special status as much upon its material in its introductions and apparatus bearing upon the establishment of the text as it is for the presentation of the established text itself. The two parts can scarcely be separated. No reader should be asked to accept anything in the text on trust. In his introductions and apparatus the editor should place all his textual cards on the table —face up.

12. 'Bibliography and Historical Linguistics', *The Library*, XXI 1966), 181–191.

13. A. W. Pollard & G. R. Redgrave, *A Short-title Catalogue of Books. ... 1475–1640*, Bibliographical Society, 1926.

14. S. Wing, *Short-title Catalogue of Books ... 1641–1700*, Columbia University Press, 1945.

INDEX